CHRISTIAN ETHICS
IN ECUMENICAL CONTEXT

Christian Ethics in Ecumenical Context

THEOLOGY, CULTURE, AND POLITICS IN DIALOGUE

Edited by

Shin Chiba
George R. Hunsberger
Lester Edwin J. Ruiz

WILLIAM B. EERDMANS PUBLISHING COMPANY
GRAND RAPIDS, MICHIGAN

© 1995 Wm. B. Eerdmans Publishing Co.

255 Jefferson Ave. S.E., Grand Rapids, Michigan 49503

Printed in the United States of America

00 99 98 97 96 95   7 6 5 4 3 2 1

Library of Congress Cataloging-in-Publication Data

Christian ethics in ecumenical context: theology, culture, and politics in dialogue /
edited by Shin Chiba, George R. Hunsberger, Lester Edwin J. Ruiz.
p.   cm.
Festschrift for Charles C. West.
Includes bibliographical references and index.
ISBN 0-8028-3787-5 (alk. paper)
1. Christian ethics. I. Chiba, Shin, 1949   . II. Hunsberger, George R.
III. Ruiz, Lester Edwin J. IV. West, Charles C.
BJ1251.C497 1995
241 — dc20   95-9159
                                          CIP

Contents

v

CONTENTS

PART TWO
THEOLOGY, ETHICS, AND SOCIETY

Contents

PART THREE
RELIGION, CULTURE, AND POLITICS

Foreword

DR. CHARLES CONVERSE WEST is the Stephen Colwell Professor of
Christian Ethics Emeritus at Princeton Theological Seminary, an institution he served with distinction both as a member of its faculty (1961
to 1991) and as its academic dean (1979 to 1984) until his retirement
following his seventieth birthday — the occasion of this splendid volume.

The scope of the enclosed essays, prepared and contributed by former
students and colleagues of Professor West, attests to the breadth and the
depth of the man they honor. The term *ecumenical* in the title of the book
may be read ecclesially or culturally or intellectually — or all of the above.
In a time when the vision of the "one holy, catholic, and apostolic church"
is dimmed by denominational tribalism and intrachurch factionalism,
Charles West, a Presbyterian, continues as an advocate and servant of
ecumenical relations and mission. Long before multiculturalism was recognized as a reality to be addressed, Charles West, a missionary to two con-
tinents (Asia and Europe), devoted a decade of his vocational life to the
indwelling of other cultures. Prior to globalization becoming a conscious
concern of theological education, Charles West was engaged in the task of
theology on the frontiers of the church's encounter with the ideologies,
religions, and sciences of the world. This is the context in which he has
pursued his theological ethics.

Similarly, the volume's subtitle, *Theology, Culture, and Politics in Dialogue,* pays tribute to the fact that Dr. West's career contradicts the image
of the missionary as one who establishes religious compounds removed
from the world and its complex realities. His teaching career has consistently
challenged a prevailing cultural mood that trivializes Christian faith by

ix

individualizing, even privatizing, it. When he looks *through* his theological lens, Dr. West looks at human life before God in its social, political, and economic setting. For Charles West, the church is *in* the world *for* the sake of the world, even when it must stand *against* the world. His vision of mission is one of engagement through dialogue in service to the gospel.

Still a welcome presence on the Seminary campus, Charles West remains vitally involved in the issues that have mattered so much to him throughout his adult life, and he continues to represent the institution vigorously at conferences from Southeast Asia to Central and Eastern Europe. Princeton Seminary is pleased by the richly deserved honor this important volume pays to our colleague and friend.

THOMAS W. GILLESPIE
President, Princeton Theological Seminary

Acknowledgments

THE EDITORS thank Daniel L. Migliore of Princeton Theological Seminary, the editor of the *Princeton Seminary Bulletin*, as well as the authors, for permission to reprint several articles that first appeared as follows in the Festschrift volume for Charles C. West, *Princeton Seminary Bulletin*, n.s., 12, no. 2 (1991):

"An Ecumenical Journey: A Conversation between Ruth and Charles West," by Ruth C. West.
"Renascent Religions and Secularism in India," by M. M. Thomas.
"'The Holy Materialism': The Question of Bread in Christian and Marxist Dialogue," by Jan Milič Lochman.
"The Voluntary Principle and the Search for Racial Justice," by Peter J. Paris.
"The Christian Base Communities and the *Ecclesia Reformata Semper Reformanda*," by Richard Shaull.

The editors also thank the Society of Christian Ethics and its editor, Harlan Beckley, for permission to reprint the following article, which first appeared in 1991 in the *Annual of the Society of Christian Ethics:*
"Faith, Ideology, and Power: Toward an Ecumenical, Post-Marxist Method in Christian Ethics," by Charles C. West.

The editors acknowledge and thank the publisher and author for permission to reprint the following article:
"Religious Dimension of Social Change," by Charles Amjad-Ali, which first appeared in *Religion and Asian Politics: National Dialogue — Pakistan,* ed. Charles Amjad-Ali (Hong Kong: Christian Conference of Asia, International Affairs, 1990).

ACKNOWLEDGMENTS

Finally, the editors express their deeply felt gratitude to Eerdmans Publishing Company and to William B. Eerdmans, Jr., for their willingness to publish this volume. The editors acknowledge with great appreciation the generous support of Princeton Theological Seminary and President Thomas W. Gillespie in particular for his constant encouragement and support in every way. Without President Gillespie's warm encouragement this book could not have materialized in its present form. The editors thank all the contributors who joined in this tribute to our friend, teacher, and colleague, Charles C. West.

Toward an Ecumenical Future: The Challenge for Christian Ethics Today

SHIN CHIBA
GEORGE R. HUNSBERGER
LESTER EDWIN J. RUIZ

The Task of Christian Theology and Ethics

Is the question of an ecumenical future an appropriate challenge for Christian ethics today? Such a question expresses both a deep concern and a hope for Christian responsibility in the last decade of the twentieth century. The question raises a number of difficult issues that can be answered only as the questions unfold, not before: What do we mean by "ecumenical"? Which Christian ethics? More important, Who is asking this question? Why? And why ask the question now? Indeed, even as we write, we see the awful images of over one million Rwandans fleeing their homeland, being turned into refugees, and dying by the tens of thousands from starvation and cholera, while the rest of the world looks on either helplessly or apathetically. These miserable events in the world, as they did in the past, raise again profound questions about the task of Christian theology and ethics for which answers are neither simple nor clear-cut.

This volume is the result of a collaborative effort of former students and colleagues of Professor Charles Converse West, who until his retirement in 1991 was the Stephen Colwell Professor of Christian Ethics at Princeton Theological Seminary. This volume is dedicated to our teacher, Charles C. West, who is a compassionate Christian, a vigorous ethicist, and a missionary theologian. What follows is intended to honor him on the occasion of

1

his seventieth birthday and his retirement from the seminary after long and dedicated service to theological education. This collaborative effort, however, has naturally turned out to be a more engaging and fruitful discussion of critical issues in the field to which Dr. West dedicated his life: Christian theology, ethics, and ecumenics. We are certain that Dr. West would endorse this development with a nodding smile and approval. This joyous occasion for honoring our teacher and friend has resulted in a work of serious reflection and common deliberation on pressing, important issues of the world today.

These critical issues, indeed, are wide-ranging: epistemological questions concerning Christian truth and the so-called political correctness; problems related to Christianity and the eclipse of authority and morality in secular society; questions concerning the spiritual resource of Christianity for multiculturalism as well as the possibility of the peaceful coexistence between religions, races, and ethnic groups. They also include problems of a more historical nature in which the authors have attempted to recover theoretical insights from historical examples to the question of ecumenicity or the reformulation of Christian theology today. These reflections address problems of a clearly theological nature such as the restatement of theology and ethics as well as of the gospel of Christ, dealt with in light of our age, which can be characterized in various ways: a post–Cold War epoch, a post-Christendom age, a late modernity, or a postmodernity. They also deal with problems of a more ethical nature, such as biblical, religious, and philosophical resources for a viable environmental ethic and critical questions concerning gender, prostitution, racial justice, social transformation, and peace. The issues raised and treated in our volume clearly suggest that we are indeed witnessing a great turning point in human history. We understand that Christian theology and ethics are called for, that they must engage in a passionate thinking and praxis by partaking of the pains, the sufferings, and the struggles of our age, at the bottom of which we find the suffering Christ, our Redeemer, standing together with the afflicted, the oppressed, and the persecuted.

Charles C. West: Christian Ethicist and Missionary Theologian

In our understanding, Professor Charles C. West is a "missionary" theologian par excellence. The late President James I. McCord of Princeton Theological Seminary often introduced Dr. West as "a missionary on the seminary campus." To be sure, it is important to recognize in this connection that the idea of "Christian mission" and "missionaries" has largely fallen into intellectual, ecclesiastical, and political disrepute as a result of their unfortunate, if unhappy, marriage to the so-called Western project of modernization and its largely imperialist designs. In fact, the history of Western imperialism, colonialism, neocolonialism, and now recolonization, as well as the ideological role that a large segment of Western Christianity has played in them, can today no longer be denied. However, as the personal and professional struggles of Professor West have shown, the title "missionary" theologian need not carry a negative connotation. His example as a missionary theologian, we would like to suggest, recuperates the genuine meanings and responsibilities of Christian "mission." He shows that to be a missionary theologian means one is ready to wrestle with the frontier questions of one's time in a theological manner.

Professor West continues to commit himself to confront, and allow himself to be confronted with, the frontier theological questions of his time. Earlier in his career, those questions included the encounter of Christian theology with Communism, the Christian-Marxist dialogue, the relationship between theology and ideology, and questions concerning science, technology, and ethics. More recently, he has explored themes surrounding the ecological crisis as well as the definition of the "common good" in relation to the plight of the poor in what has been called the world of late modernity. Most recently, he has focused his attention on the question of the church and religion in the former Soviet Union and in Eastern European countries. Moreover, Professor West is now deeply committed, by his involvement in the Gospel and Our Culture Network (GOCN), to the issue of reconceptualization of the gospel message and mission in a "post-Christendom," North American context. Recently he has confessed to us, "Now the GOCN is where my heart is beating." (Concerning the GOCN, see Hunsberger's essay below, and particularly n. 1.)

Certainly his areas of interest have varied from time to time. For this reason we are not surprised when his analyses and assessments of some issues have also changed. However, the theological point of departure for Professor West has always remained the same: the overarching reality of God's presence and grace both in the church and in the world. He has shown an unapologetic commitment to this *fundamentum inconcussum* of theology beyond the vagaries of human caprice and history. This primary theological datum — that is, the dynamic, overflowing reality of God's saving grace — has shaped his Christian ethics and determined his identity as a missionary theologian. In this sense, Professor West resembles in many ways the theologians of the Word, Karl Barth and Dietrich Bonhoeffer, both of whom he has always held in great regard.

Moreover, Professor West's missionary undertakings have always involved an affirmation that theology, ecumenics, and ethics are grounded in, and animated by, a profound sense of *metanoia* and the forgiveness of sins as revealed in the cross of Christ. Not merely in his social and political analyses of power but also in his emphasis on the theology of *metanoia* and reconciliation, Charlie, as his colleagues fondly called him, may be said to be a faithful follower of his two mentors, who happened to be two of the major theologians the United States has produced: Reinhold Niebuhr and H. Richard Niebuhr. For Professor West, Christian ethics operates in the dialectic of revelation, on the one hand, and the historical, communal, and relational context of persons in which it unfolds itself, on the other. This basic approach clearly demonstrates his indebtedness to these two theologians. At the same time, he has sought to forge a distinct way of engaging in the trinitarian task of theology, ecumenics, and ethics in the world of late modernity. The very mission of always engaging in passionate reflection and praxis on the frontier of knowledge in the church and in the world has been the fundamental method by which he has pursued this threefold task. He has always situated this task within the mission of the church in the midst of the world.

Thus it might be justifiable to say that this volume carries forward the very theme to which Professor West as a "missionary" theologian has committed his life, teaching, and research up to now. The fact that our endeavors have resulted in reflections that move in the direction of his own efforts discloses how much we his students and colleagues share in common with Professor West.

The authors in this volume, however, do not necessarily all understand themselves as being adherents of Professor West's particular theological world, as a cursory reading of the essays below will reveal. This volume contains a number of essays whose theological perspectives as well as styles of theorizing are quite different from those of Professor West. Thus, for instance, as we vividly recall from our student days at Princeton, his longtime colleague Richard Shaull is one who, while standing unequivocally within the same Reformed tradition, sometimes expressed his profound disagreements with Professor West, and vice versa. A younger colleague, Mark K. Taylor, seems to have kept self-consciously a creative distance from Professor West's theological proving grounds. Some former students also express their divergence at substantial points from Professor West's theology. Many of these disagreements stem from differences about the impor-

4

tance accorded to history and politics for theology, differences in valuation of the ontological distance between good and evil, and/or differences in the confidence placed in the capacity of human beings to transform their worlds. Other disagreements may stem from differences in the political, ethical, and institutional choices that these individuals have made and differences in experience, especially in terms of one's social and political location.

It is striking, however, that they have all continued an unexhausted dialogue on the basis of a common recognition that theological reflection is always on the way and must be neither absolutized nor fixed *(theologia viatorum)*, just as the Christian community is always an *ecclesia reformata semper reformanda*. In this vein this volume can be aptly characterized as an "ecumenical" undertaking in a broad sense of the term; authors from diverse traditions of Christian faith, from different theological positions, and from various parts of the world have attempted to bear witness to the living presence of our Lord Jesus Christ as the Savior and Liberator of the world. Therefore, readers should see it as a collection of believing voices coming out of the worldwide Christian community.

The Context of Christian Ethics Today:
A World of Profound Transformations and Dilemmas

The depth and breadth of the issues covered by the essays in this volume, and the differences that are articulated, all suggest that we may be witnessing a great turning point in human history — perhaps we could even call it an axial moment — one characterized by profound economic, technological, social, cultural, and political transformations. To be sure, we are living in a time of world-changing events. Historical conditions are changing at an almost unimaginable rate, forcing us to redefine our ways of thinking, feeling, and acting. We are witnessing, indeed participating in, not only the acceleration of history but a profoundly uneven — not to say, deeply contradictory and contested — transformation of that history. This distinctly late-modern experience has many names: integration and fragmentation, combined and uneven development, transnationalization — if not globalization — of the market and of capital, multiculturalism and retribalization. Many of these transformations have caused deep imbalances and injustices, such as poverty in the so-called Four Fifths World, violence and nihilism in both the rich and poor nations, the concentration of wealth and power in a few "postindustrial," "high-tech," and "advanced" societies, to name only a few. Such transformations have had inherent dangers and possibilities as well.

In this context we would like to ask the question of an ecumenical future for Christian theology and ethics. This question not only will not go away; it requires giving critical attention to this context of incessant, profound transformations. As we enter this discourse, however, we are confronted immediately with a number of dilemmas that are situated at the center of our disciplines, if not our personal commitments. These cannot be ignored, avoided, or denied.

First, there is the *substantive* and *definitional* dilemma. Just what do we mean by "an ecumenical future"? What is "the challenge to Christian theology and ethics to create an ecumenical future"? There will be little doubt that, especially today, Christian theology and ethics cannot be regarded as a singular, much less unitary, totalized reality. To be sure, common threads form part of the tapestry that is Christian theology and ethics: for example, our recognition of the Bible as the fountainhead of our faith, the importance of Christian communities and their tradition, the Trinitarian foundation of Christian life. Yet, there are as many "Christian theologies" today as there are individual authors in this volume. We are in a position now that makes us more ready and able than a generation ago to recognize it as a truism that Christian theology and ethics is a pastiche of political, economic, cultural, religious, and historical specificities and pluralities and lies therefore in the realm of the human sciences.

Second, there is the *methodological* dilemma. Just how do we get at our definitions, theoretical perspectives, and methods? But also, how do we engage the questions of human survival and suffering — indeed, the so-called things themselves? If no reality comes to us unmediated, how do we get to the realities we wish to transform, given the changing language games, concepts, and ideas that mediate them? What methods and strategies do we deploy, knowing that these are profoundly shaped by cultural, ideological, and even social and economic assumptions and practices? Where does one go for the building blocks of an ecumenical future that are adequate to the experience of human life in general and of the Christian community in particular in the last decade of this century (and perhaps for the first decade of the next)?

Third, there is the *metatheoretical* dilemma. Since our definitions, theoretical perspectives, and methods are always and already implicated in the structures and processes alluded to above, can we practically and theoretically arrive at adequate definitions, theoretical perspectives, and methods without dealing with such issues as gender, class, and race as

6

relations of power? In what ways are our theories and practices shaped by power relations even before we have had a chance to touch, feel, taste, and eat them? Conversely, how do our concerns, particularly our Christian hopes and commitments, shape these metatheoretical issues? Phrased practically, one might ask, How do we as the ministers of the saving Word of God bear witness to the gospel of Christ in a world implicated in racial domination, class oppression, and gender inequality? Equally important, how do we begin to articulate a Christian theology and ethics horizoned by a commitment to a genuinely ecumenical future, given the context noted above?

The Essays: Embodiments of an Ecumenical Style

The writers of the essays in this book are concerned both with what it now means to talk about Christian theology and ethics and with the character and potentialities of Christian communities in a context fraught with profound difficulties. They all take it for granted that Christian theology and ethics must be understood as more than just critical reflection on the praxis of Christians and the Christian church. Hence, the juxtaposition of Christian theology and ethics with religions, cultures, and politics. They take it for granted that Christian theology and ethics must be oriented beyond Christian life and piety, which is to say, toward the revelatory, saving, and cosmic events of Christ in the Cross, Resurrection, and Second Coming. That Christ died for us sinners, he was resurrected on the third day, and he is coming again constitutes the sine qua non of Christian theology and ethics. Hence, the emphasis on the *ecumenical* and *evangelical* character of Christian theology and ethics.

Part 1 shows "an ecumenical journey" that Professor Charles C. West himself has undertaken since he went out to China after World War II to serve as a young missionary to Chinese students. He had firsthand experience with the Chinese Communist Revolution of 1949. There is no doubt that Professor West's experience with the emergence of the Communist regime in China has served as the backdrop for his best-known book, *Communism and the Theologians* (1958). This book was a "missionary" undertaking. It wrestled with the frontier question of theology and politics in the postwar context. It is by no means an accident that Professor West is now concerned with an entirely new topic in the newly emerged situation: the possibility of a viable Christian ethics in the post-Communist era.

We are grateful to Dr. Ruth C. West and the *Princeton Seminary*

7

INTRODUCTION

Bulletin for allowing us to republish her excellent interview with her husband regarding his ecumenical journey. This interview discloses in a personal and concrete manner the heart and soul of Professor Charles C. West's ecumenical journey both in theory and in praxis. We also are thankful to Paul Abrecht, a longtime friend and colleague of Professor West who collaborated with him at the World Council of Churches in Geneva particularly in the 1950s, its formative years, for his recollections of Professor West's contribution to ecumenical social thought.

Professor West's recent article contained in part 1, "Faith, Ideology, and Power: Toward an Ecumenical Post-Marxist Method in Christian Ethics" (1991), embodies his current "missionary" engagement with the post-state Communist situation in the fin-de-siècle context of the late twentieth century. Whether it was *Communism and the Theologians* or *The Power to Be Human* (1971) or "Faith, Ideology, and Power: Toward an Ecumenical, Post-Marxist Method in Christian Ethics," one basic theme reverberates: his ongoing and abiding ecumenical, evangelical, and missionary concern. The three essays in part 1 articulate this basic theme in personal, practical, and theoretical ways. They also define in broad terms many of the issues and concerns that the rest of the volume discusses in greater detail.

Part 2 contains ten essays that focus more explicitly on a number of theological, ethical, historical, and social questions, as they pose challenges for Christians and churches in the last decade of the twentieth century. The authors address the problems raised by the post-Christendom situation in the West; they grapple with the challenges posed by a pluralist, multicultural society; and they address the intensely problematic questions concerning social justice confronting both developed and developing countries. Whether the author is recognizing a pluralizing, if not a postmodern, world to be emerging, or deeply concerned with the injustices of an asymmetrical global system, each of them wrestles in a unique manner both with the need to reformulate theology and ethics in the light of the significance of the gospel message in a world of great transformations and with the imperative to engage in dialogue with various intellectual traditions and sociocultural, political realities.

Moreover, the essays in this section seem to share a number of methodological and substantive premises. First, Christian communities today face multidimensional dilemmas both within and without themselves. While the authors do not all agree as to the nature of these dilemmas, not to mention their order of importance, all identify difficult theological, ethical, historical, epistemological, sociocultural, or political problems with which Christians and churches need to deal as part of their identity. Second, all Christian communities — not merely those of the Reformed tradition — ought to be the *ecclesia reformata semper reformanda*. As such, they are always on the move, bearing and birthing a *theologia viatorum* toward an ecumenical future. Here one should take seriously the original meaning of *oikoumene* — "the whole inhabited world" — not just as a goal, but as a process. Third, Christians and Christian communities, if they are engaged in the creation of an ecumenical future, understand that ecumenical collaboration for the present age is not only the sine qua non of both theological reflection and praxis but needs to be informed by an evangelical, mission-oriented commitment.

Indeed, the Christian church is not the church if it does not have a mission, and the phrase *ecclesia reformata semper reformanda* finds its meaning and significance only within such a mission. At the same time, the church's mission is not a telos that is constituted apart from the structures and processes of its conditions of possibility. Thus, one might suggest that this volume can be interpreted as an ecumenical undertaking in which the authors, who come from diverse traditions of Christian faith, who carry with them different theological perspectives and commitments, and who represent different parts of the world, are nonetheless attempting to bear joint witness to the living presence of Christ in the midst of this turbulent world.

Part 3 presents eight essays that deal with the interrelated themes of religions, cultures, and politics. From different perspectives the authors focus on individual concerns that together constitute a shared, often implicit, understanding of what is at stake in understanding Christian theology and ethics in an ecumenical context. These essays can be divided into two main groups. One explores either methodologically or theoretically the transformative potentials of theology and religion, with the essays pursuing this in view of the sociopolitical significance of theological or religious perspectives for liberation, social justice, peace, and environmental ethics. The other group of essays articulates their concerns around either the theme of keeping one's own identity while respecting differences and diversities of the other, or the theme of forging solidarities in a confederative manner out of these differences and diversities in multireligious or multicultural contexts. There is no doubt that today these themes are increasingly important, not only in the former Yugoslavia and in India (with which three essays in part 3 specifically deal), but also in many other parts of the world.

Moreover, it is important to note that not unlike the essays in the previous section, these essays are also concerned with the increasing importance of an ecumenical undertaking for theology and religion today. In this section, this ecumenicity seems to be expressed in three basic ways: first, as an intrareligious or, more accurately, intra-Christian collaboration; second, as an interreligious dialogue and cooperation; and finally, as a critical dialogue and engagement of Christian theology with other ideologies, other disciplines, and other realms of life. These essays in part 3 are ecumenical, evangelical, and "missionary" also insofar as they seek to explore seriously, not only the ways in which the pressing issues of the contemporary world impinge on Christian theology and ethics, but also how these issues require of Christian theology and ethics a critical, creative, and daring response.

To be sure, it remains an open question whether these essays have grappled adequately and persuasively with these critical issues of our age. From one perspective, one can make the case that there is nothing new in this volume. Yet, newness is not the strength of this book. Rather, its contribution may well reside in suggesting, if not demonstrating, that Christian theology and ethics today must be situated in an ecumenical and evangelical context.

Summary

Overall, then, this volume seeks to respond to the challenge posed by the pressing issues of the present age with the following four messages. First, Christian theology and ethics as a *theologia viatorum* must by the guidance of the Holy Spirit be "missionary" always in its courageous attempt to confront unflinchingly the critical issues of the present age, whether it is a biblical and theological issue such as the reformulation of the gospel message, or whether it is a historical issue such as the ecological crisis.

Second, Christian theology and ethics must be faithful to the Lord Jesus by listening attentively to the thin voice of the Spirit, so that Christian communities may be not a human-made artifact but a Spirit-filled *ecclesia reformata semper reformanda*. What is at stake here is not only the desirability of a "permanent revolution" but a "revolutionary partnership" between God and humanity in the nurture of a more just, more humane *oikoumene*.

Third, such a partnership requires the daring attempt of Christian communities to engage by the Spirit in a creative *agōn* on both theoretical and practical levels between the past and the future, as well as the attempt to discern by the Spirit unmistakably the locus of this *agōn*. This theological struggle also not only determines the missionary quality of Christian theology and ethics, but it also shapes the character of an ecumenical and evangelical Christianity.

Finally, this volume suggests that the search for peace, reconciliation, solidarity, and coexistence among religions, cultures, nations, races, and polities must be the constitutive and defining horizon for Christian theology and ethics tomorrow.

It is our hope that the theoretical essays may reveal enough of their ecumenical, evangelical, and missionary quality in exploring the frontier of the present that they may be of some meaning and relevance for the readers of this volume. We trust that readers will find the various arguments and understandings to be stimulating and useful pointers toward our ecumenical future.

PART ONE

AN ECUMENICAL JOURNEY

· 1 ·

An Ecumenical Journey: A Conversation between Ruth and Charles West

RUTH C. WEST

IN THE FALLING DUSK of a warm spring night in 1942, a lanky Columbia senior, majoring in political science, slipped into the quiet quadrangle of Union Theological Seminary. The pressures of his college experience had been heavy. He remembers that "at the end I broke down in sheer exhaustion from the effort of trying to promote all good causes and stand for all good things. It was then I realized that our value as human beings, my value as a human being, was not in what I could accomplish, not in my virtues or something like that, but the fact that there is an overwhelming and forgiving love of God that reaches into my life and that upholds me regardless of my own failures and weaknesses and sins." This realization played a major role in his decision, made that evening, to enter the ministry.

Four years later, having completed his bachelor of divinity degree and a postgraduate year of work in ethics at Yale, he was ordained into the Presbyterian ministry and almost simultaneously commissioned by the then Presbyterian Board of Foreign Missions of the Presbyterian Church, U.S.A., to go to China as a missionary.

In the following conversation, I asked him to reflect on the people and experiences that have had a significant influence on his life.

RUTH WEST: In 1967, in your inaugural address, you linked mission and ethics together. Can you tie these in with your career's heavy emphasis on the ecumenical movement as well?

CHARLES WEST: Yes, I think I see three elements in your question: ethics, ecumenical fellowship, and mission. I tried to demonstrate in that inaugural address that Christian ethics has a missionary context. It is the effort to be faithful to the reality of Jesus Christ at work in the world and, in being faithful, to bear witness to it. I don't think that there is or should be a separation between the words we use to proclaim the gospel and the way we live in response to the gospel. The one should point to the other. The things we do are not good and exemplary always in themselves. But if they point beyond themselves to the one whom we obey and to whom we respond in our fallible and sinful way, then the witness is borne.

RUTH WEST: Let me ask a follow-up. In *Outside the Camp* you say that the church is missionary in its very existence, and that from the church Christ's love and power flow out into all other human relationships. Is that perhaps how you link ethics, mission, and ecumenics together in one witness?

CHARLES WEST: Yes. History is not closed. Communities are not self-sufficient. Those that close in on themselves become pockets of enmity toward other communities. In the long run it is the community of Christian believers united in Christ that undergirds all other human communities, because the church is the one community that depends finally, not on the good-will or the virtue or the special affections of a particular group of people, but on the love of Christ that binds us all, that forgives us all, that gives the whole world new life. In that community, then, other communities — of the family, nation, neighborhoods, and working groups — find their place, their significance, and their inspiration. So the reality of the church bearing witness to other communities about their true openness is, I think, the very heart of Christian mission.

Let me give you two examples: one out of the far-distant past, and one fairly recent. When I landed in China, I was very much aware that we were Americans in a country undergoing profound suffering and profound revolution. Many of the things that were said about Americans in those days were unfair. We were blamed for almost everything that was wrong in China. When the Communists came into power, America was a symbol of the whole imperialist power from which the country needed to be liberated. But I soon found out that it was not a Christian witness to try to defend America. It was my witness to listen to my Chinese friends and colleagues, to sympathize with their situation, to point beyond that to the reason why we were there, which was simply to serve the God who is their savior and ours, and who offers hope, forgiveness, and new life to us all. So, if you like, the Christian mission, or at least my part in it, was a mission of repentance for national and social sins and an attempt to point to a gracious God who gives life meaning beyond our human conflicts.

Another example, much more recent. In Christian-Marxist dialogues we have often found ourselves in ambivalent situations. How far can we trust our partners in an Eastern European country, knowing to whom they may have to report? How far can they trust us not to manipulate them for Western propaganda purposes? Establishing trust as a basis for dialogue is the first problem to face. We do it by trying to understand each other as persons behind the ideologies and powers that condition us. Then we can move to a second level, inquiring about the reality each of us confesses in this relation with one another. Truth does not emerge from winning the argument. It comes from mutual witness. It is a matter of inviting another person to see the world in the context of the ultimate reality that we confess, and of listening when they do the same for us. I remember a comment by a well-known partner in this dialogue, Professor Milan Machovec of Czechoslovakia, who once said, "I don't trust a Christian who isn't interested in converting me." That's exactly the point. Not converting in the sense of manipulating, but in the sense of wishing with all our heart and soul that the partner in dialogue might understand the reality that motivates and controls us.

RUTH WEST: It seems to me that the ecumenical movement has always had a special influence in your life. Why is that the case?

CHARLES WEST: Well, let me go back a bit. I became a Christian out of my experience with the ecumenical movement. I was in the unbelievably fortunate situation of being a member of the University Christian Association at Columbia during a time when we were receiving a stream of visitors from overseas who were real leaders of the church and spiritual guides from whom one could continually learn. We could call Reinhold Niebuhr across the street from Union Seminary anytime. D. T. Niles came through. Robert Mackie came through. In the end Visser 't Hooft came through. One could go on to name others. One was continually aware that one was part of a worldwide Christian community that was living by faith and bearing its witness in the most diverse situations on both sides of the battleline in the Second World War, in places like China and India, Indonesia and elsewhere. I remember reading the *Student World* in that light. Robert Mackie's travel diaries were especially illuminating. He would visit a part of the world, talk with Christians there, and bring out in his report the character of their faith, the kind of problems they had, what they were praying for, what dangers they were subject to, and above all their sense of being upheld by the prayers and the fellowship of the church around the world. I was converted to the Christian faith as an intellectually respectable and spiritually powerful ecumenical movement in the world. Therefore I decided to join a particular church, to study theology, to seek ordination to the Christian ministry, and to become a missionary. My commitment to the local church has always been a function of my awareness that it is part of that worldwide Christian community.

So, of course, I constantly sought wisdom and insight from the ecumenical movement and tried to meet people who were involved in it. I wrote a long and passionate letter, I remember, from China to M. M. Thomas, who was then a secretary of the World Student Christian Federation and who had written something in the *Student World* that I both agreed and disagreed with. So started one friendship. When we left China, and only one part of our first term as missionaries was over, we asked to serve in Europe and had the enormous good fortune of spending some time in Geneva, then going to Germany, where the people with whom we lived were also a part of this ecumenical movement, and knew it. The *Oekumene,* as the East Germans called it, was a reality to them in their daily Christian witness to a Marxist-Leninist society in a way that simply isn't the case in the United States. There I learned to sense what it meant that the church ecumenical and the local church were supporting and strengthening each other.

A qualification, however: a particular program, a particular person, a particular office in the World Council of Churches never lived up to the ideal. I learned to understand that there is a movement of the Holy Spirit in and through the ecumenical movement that is not to be identified with the sanctity or the wisdom of any particular leader or with the success of any particular conference but is present with us all, informing, inspiring, and correcting us from beyond. I discovered that to be the case in all the years we were in Bossey. I'm sure you felt it, too. Many of the conferences were not particularly successful in reaching human agreement — about theology, about social policy, or even about the Bible or the form of worship. But something always happened because, disagreement or no, we studied and prayed together. We did so, questioning and challenging each other on every level — theology, politics, Bible study, and even forms of worship. We learned from that questioning and confrontation because we were surrounded by the confidence that the word of God had something to say to us that is beyond us all. That's the reality of the ecumenical movement, and that's what I felt was happening at Bossey, at least in the years I was there.

RUTH WEST: When you entered seminary, you did so with the goal of becoming a student pastor. Winning the traveling fellowship in your senior year made it possible for you to spend a year at Yale in graduate work. Why did you select ethics as your focus of study and as your life's work?

CHARLES WEST: Because my questions always, from the very earliest years right on to today, have been more ethical than metaphysical. Not truth in itself but true understanding of human relations with each other and with God, truth in the sense of what is hopeful, what is promising, what is redeeming — this has been the object of my search. I have mentioned that I came to college all fired up to try to reform the world, and it was a long time before I learned that there is a certain pride in being ethical that way. But it means that I came to the Christian faith by way of ethics, asking about what is right and what is good, what will redeem the world, what gives us hope, and where the power is on which one can really count.

RUTH WEST: You learned both from your experiences and from the people with whom you studied. I noticed in reading *Communism and the Theologians* that you were working with the ideas of many people under whom you had studied. How did these people influence you as you began then to deal with the theological problems that have been your lifelong interest and concern?

CHARLES WEST: When I was a college student, Union Seminary was the Mecca of theological thought and the point of vision from which one could look out over world Christendom. Reinhold Niebuhr was the first real theologian with whom I came into contact. Well, not quite, because as a college sophomore I wrote a paper on Christianity for a course in the philosophy of religion with Irwin Edman. I read lots of liberal theologians, and Edman said when he handed it back, "Mr. West has struck a doughty blow for liberal Christianity." But it was Niebuhr's insight and Niebuhr's dialectic that pushed me theologically a step further.

When I got to Union, however, there's no doubt about who was the greatest influence on my thought. It was David Roberts. His course on the philosophy of religion led me step-by-step through all the complexities and problems of philosophy up to the point where I could see philosophically that revelation was respectable. I remember the rejoicing with which I discovered that fact. Roberts was a believing philosopher who agonized over the problem of unbelief. That's just about where I was at that point. And it helped me. It brought me intellectually into the Christian faith.

Reinhold Niebuhr was quite a different matter. He was brilliant. He was overwhelming. The first few lectures were completely beyond me until I began to get the rhythm of his thinking. I will never forget the time I raised my hand in class and asked something — I've forgotten what it was — and Niebuhr looked at me and said, "That's a very profound question." And then he proceeded to make it profound by the way he answered it. He was, in that sense, enormously encouraging, helpful, and, I always felt, humble, although one of the characteristics of his humility was that he never stopped to think that the force of his opinion might be overriding somebody. He was just too humble to think of himself as being that big. Paul Tillich was also influential. I took the history of philosophy with him and, like everybody else, was amazed at his brilliance, his insight, and the way in which the dialectic of his mind worked. I never really became a Tillichian, partly I think because my struggle was too intense for his system. He was a reconciler. He wanted to reconcile theology and philosophy. His own childhood experience was of a too-dogmatic Lutheran pastoral household. Mine was of a too-liberal secular home. I wanted to know more intensely what was true, what I could proclaim, what I could believe and give my life to. That was not his major problem. That may be one reason why Tillich's philosophy, although fascinating and useful and helpful in many ways, was never my ultimate guide.

Then there was John Bennett. The clarity and the simplicity and the toughness of his mind always impressed me. But I remember most of all his personal encouragement and his willingness to enter into dialogue with a student as an equal. I can't say that I ever had much dialogue with Reinhold Niebuhr, certainly not with Paul Tillich, but with Bennett I had a great many conversations in which we explored things together. I think that's been the experience of many, many generations of students with him.

One other thing about John Bennett from much later. I remember my friend David Paton saying one time that when ecumenical history is written, one will have to take account of the quiet presence of John Bennett. In one ecumenical meeting after another, his suggestions gave form and structure to what people were thinking, drawing their ideas together in a report so that something solid came out of it. John Bennett was a craftsman, an ecumenical craftsman, and a sweet, encouraging, mediating spirit, and older friend.

I could mention others at Union who played a role, but let me go on to H. Richard Niebuhr, who was my principal adviser in doctoral study and to whom I owe more than to anyone else an understanding of what scholarship means. Reinhold Niebuhr was quick to admit he was no scholar in that sense of the word, and Tillich was too much of a prima donna. For Richard Niebuhr, examining someone's thought from all the angles, looking at it in an unusual light, delighting in the new perspectives and ideas that can come out of it — this was the great joy of learning, and he communicated it to all of us who were his students. He made us love reading the great philosophers and theologians of history by the way he helped us think about them and by the way he thought with us. I never thought of Richard Niebuhr as a "great theologian," although in a way he was, but as a concerned Christian scholar, as one who opened the world of the mind to us, whose insight one could trust. That was his profound influence. I realize that in my teaching ever since then, especially on the Ph.D. level, I have more or less reproduced his understanding of what scholarship is, how students ought to learn, and how we ought to think about the great figures of history.

I was not able to follow him at certain points. He was so afraid of making an affirmation of faith that might be dogmatic and therefore express human pride rather than true obedience to the Lord, that he was self-questioning to a fault. The time when he really nourished us spiritually was when he preached. But that didn't happen very often. I think his hesitancy at that point was a wrong understanding of humility. It was more like anxiety, one might almost say, and I always disagreed with his disagreement with Karl Barth at just that point. But that perhaps is the other side of the great and sensitive scholar.

RUTH WEST: How have the settings in which you have worked influenced your thinking? Your experience in China, for example, came as the country was going through a shattering transformation. In fact, you actually spent time living under a Communist regime. In Europe you served in a church that had endured the war and that was now facing the challenge of Marxist thought. Your experiences in these widely differing worlds surely had a profound influence on your life and faith.

CHARLES WEST: I'm not all that proud of my record as a missionary in China. I was very young and a lot more self-righteous than I thought. I was constantly trying to push people into argument or discussion beyond where they were ready to be pushed. I wasn't sufficiently sensitive to the very real menace of the Communist world and the desperate efforts people were making to accommodate to it because they would have to live with it for the next forty-five years, whereas I was able to leave.

Berlin was another experience. There I was really an apprentice. I was learning about the resources of the gospel for everyday life from pastors, church leaders, and church members as they shared with me their life and theology in the face of Communist power in a very special way. I was blessed to have had such teachers. The orientation and structure of my theology really goes back to those days in Berlin.

RUTH WEST: You went out to China with a strong sense of a missionary calling, but with very little knowledge of what such a calling might involve. Can you describe how your studies and experiences in Asia and in Europe shaped your thinking about missions?

CHARLES WEST: The question of the mission of the church was not a high priority for any of my earlier teachers. They were thinkers in Christendom, and they were concerned, very much concerned, that Christendom should be faithful, but not as strongly that the gospel should be proclaimed throughout the world. But I felt that if the Christian faith is true, it is true precisely for people outside traditional Christendom. That is one of the main reasons for seeking service in overseas mission. I wanted to get out of the Christian context and to talk about the triune God in a non-Christian place, to non-Christian people, where it was something new, something exciting, something that would bring a new perspective and new hope to people who hadn't heard it for centuries.

The question of mission was on my mind all the time I was in China. It was certainly sharpened by the fact that China was taken over by a Communist government that was explicitly atheist in its orientation and that had very definite reasons for rejecting the Christian faith. I was searching at that time among Chinese Christians for what they thought the gospel was. I was disappointed that I didn't hear more from them about that. But I now realize that I was probably listening in the wrong way. I did hear some things that were hopeful and encouraging. But really in the forty-five years when Communism was dominant, the Christian church survived among people who found a community of love and mutual caring in their relation to God in Christ that broke through the brutal regimented poverty of their lives. It was not an intellectual reality. They did not theologize much about it. But it was there, and it outlasted the Communist dream. It was one answer to the question of mission that has been mine all my life long: What is the truth that is truly redemptive, speaks to and corrects our distorted perspectives and insights, and points us to a new, healing reality in human struggles? How is Christ made known in such a way that we participate in Christ's redeeming work? I could discover how this was happening in East Germany day by day by talking with Christian people there. Much later, it became clear that, in different ways, it was happening in China too.

In that connection, let me come back to Germany. I must bring in two other great figures who are probably more influential in my thought today than any of the ones we have mentioned so far: Karl Barth and Dietrich Bonhoeffer. What was it about Karl Barth that was so helpful to a church in a Communist-dominated society? One word, I think, is key: freedom. The conventional wisdom was that a Communist society is one of oppression, and as far as political and even ideological power goes, that was the case. But for the Christian the first reality in the world is not political power; it is the work of the risen Christ. That was the central truth from which one lived and in the light of which one then understood the power of Communists, the power of their ideology, the economic and political forces that were at work. So one was free to exercise a ministry both to Communist oppressors and to those who were oppressed by these new lords, who hated them, and who wanted to withdraw from their domain. Freedom from hate, freedom from fear, freedom to be constructive in a society that was dominated by an alien ideology: that was what the church in East Germany was learning from Karl Barth. So I knew I had to study his theology in the light of that experience. When I did so, I discovered that Barth had laid hold of the basic problem of the modern world: the problem of a human, self-centered struggle to realize a good society and then to incorporate God into it. *Kulturchristentum*, the Germans called it. Wars were fought in its name, sometimes against "atheist" Communism, sometimes against other "Christian" cultures.

The basic message of Karl Barth was that there is no way by which human beings can think themselves up to God. When God speaks, when God breaks into our lives, something new comes in that reorients us entirely and saves us from having to think about ourselves, our own ideals, our own principles, and our own cultures. That's freedom. And out of that comes a whole range of new possibilities for human life in fellowship with God in Christ. This is, I think, the wonder and the joy of Barth.

Then there was Dietrich Bonhoeffer. That's a somewhat different story. In Berlin we had a little group called the *Unterwegskreis*, a circle of those who are "on the way." We were advertising the fact that we were not in firm and fixed positions. This group, some of whose members were former students of Dietrich Bonhoeffer, were kind enough to invite me to share in their meetings. One of those was Eberhard Bethge, who was Bonhoeffer's closest friend, and who has been his editor and interpreter for these last forty years. He brought letters to that group. They were eventually published as *Letters and Papers from Prison,* and they were exciting. They suggested a whole new perspective on the modern world and the presence of Christ in it and for it. How does Christ take form in a world come of age, no longer dependent on the working hypothesis of God, a world free from religious concerns and premises for a genuinely worldly responsibility? What is the judgment and grace of God in such a world?

We spent our time in that circle, as I have spent my time in years since, trying to get a hold on what Bonhoeffer really meant in all its implications, not only in those prison letters but throughout his writings and his ministry. If I were asked who my favorite theologian is today, it would have to be Dietrich Bonhoeffer. The reason is very simple: every time I go back to read him, I learn something new, I see a new perspective, I find myself challenged in a new way to look at the world and at myself in the light of God, in ways I hadn't thought of before.

Not only that, every time I teach the course on Bonhoeffer, I learn new things from the students who write papers and go through the same experience. His combination of affirming the world and of understanding Christ's presence in the world as one who serves and suffers, and in that serving and suffering is also risen — in other words, his perception of how the biblical story works in modern civilization — is endlessly fertile.

RUTH WEST: In addition to these "great theologians," are there other persons who influenced you greatly?

CHARLES WEST: Yes, let me mention three to whom I owe an enormous debt. They were my fathers in the ecumenical movement. One was J. H. Oldham. I met him in his old age. He had been secretary of the first World Mission Conference in Edinburgh in 1910, chairman of the International Missionary Council, and principal architect of the 1937 Oxford Conference on Church, Society, and State. He was editor of the *Christian Newsletter.* When I came out of China in 1950, a report that I had written about the church there, based on my experience, fell into his hands, and he told the editor of the SCM Press that it ought to be published. It was, under the title *Christian Witness in Communist China,* with the pseudonym Barnabas.

But he didn't stop there. He invited me to a small conversation to which he also invited three or four other carefully chosen persons. We talked about China. We talked about the Christian faith and its relation to the events of the postwar world. And I came away from the conversation with my head spinning from all the new and different perspectives that had been brought out.

That was the first of a half dozen such meetings that Joe Oldham called, at which he presided, and in which he was the catalyst and we were invited to explore the frontiers of Christian faith. In my first years at Bossey, he brought a few of us together on theology and science, which first opened my eyes to that field.

Oldham was an explorer on the intellectual frontiers of the Christian mission, relating it to the major philosophical and social trends of the day, finding the persons who were the leaders in those fields, and bringing them together to talk with one another, always along with a few young learners like me. I was enormously privileged to have been allowed to take part in that process. It transformed my understanding of Christian mission. From then on I saw it, not just as the growth of churches in a non-Christian world, important as that is, but also as the relation of Christian faith to the major intellectual trends and problems as presented by the major thinkers of the day. That was Oldham, already in his eighties, but always on the frontier of Christian thought.

The second person was W. A. Visser 't Hooft. I was persuaded in a special way of the cogency and challenge of the Christian faith by reading in college a book of his: *None Other Gods*. I knew him by reputation as a student leader, as an interpreter of the Christian faith, as an evangelist on the social and intellectual frontiers of his time. But it was by working with him on the staff of the World Council of Churches that I learned most deeply about the balance and poise of the ecumenical movement: the way in which differences are to be respected and yet never allowed to go un-challenged; the way in which the work of the Holy Spirit in quite different traditions from our own is to be understood and brought into the dialogue; the way in which the major philosophies and ideologies of the world are to be challenged: in short, the way the gospel is to be proclaimed in the ferment of Europe and the world after the Second World War.

Visser 't Hooft had an absolute genius for listening to the discussion in a meeting, then coming in and not only summing up but taking us one step beyond toward new policy, new issues, and new directions. In a real sense he embodied the ecumenical enterprise from his position as general secretary of the World Council of Churches. There was a genius there that still needs to be captured and realized in the generation after him, if we want ecumenical dialogue and the mission of the church to be fruitful.

The third person is still very much alive and somewhat closer to my own age: J. E. Lesslie Newbigin. The first book of his I read was *A South India Diary*. It was simply the chronicle of his daily life as a newly ordained bishop in South India, reflecting the interaction of the Christian message and the life of the Christian church with the culture and society of his time and place. Newbigin is a missionary from his very soul. He lives it. I have always listened to him, hoping to learn myself how to capture something of that style, spirit, and poise in mission that he seems to come by so naturally. He also was one of those who tackled every intellectual frontier as it came along and tried to make sense of it in terms of the Christian gospel. He told me that he liked my book *Communism and the Theologians*. I think it was because it showed him another frontier on which to work.

His greatness is in the combination of serious thought and faithfulness of spirit that runs through everything he writes and everything he says. I'm still learning how to be a faithful and intelligent Christian from the things he writes and does, even in his old age, as he goes back to England and tries to tackle the question of the form of mission to Western culture.

RUTH WEST: I know that you have found working at Princeton Seminary to be a rich and rewarding experience, and you have often spoken of the privilege of working with its faculty and students. Can you comment on that and on other aspects of your work that have been equally rewarding?

CHARLES WEST: There are several different strands in the Princeton experience. One major strand was getting involved, almost from the moment we landed on these shores, in helping the Presbyterian Church to formulate a new confession of faith: the Confession of 1967. Our object was to prepare a teaching instrument that could be used by confirmation classes and that would introduce people to the Christian faith for our time. It was not designed to be a system of theology. It didn't cover all the bases. It was a confession. If you were challenged by someone outside the faith and asked: "What do you believe? What is the Christian faith all about?" where would you start, and what would you say? The Confession of 1967 was intended to help the believer respond. It did do that, I think, for that period and, in a way, for all periods. There is insight there that must not be lost, even though emphases may change: God the reconciler in Jesus Christ, and the implication of that reconciliation for the Christian life, for the mission of the church, and for the life of society.

"Reconciliation" was almost immediately attacked as being too mild a word. Is it a substitute for justice, for instance? Does it undermine the struggle for liberation? Not if you really understand it. Rather it puts the struggle for justice in a proper context: the overwhelming grace of God and therefore God's judgment on all that denies the character, spirit, and teaching of Jesus Christ. Reconciliation, in other words, involves dying and rising

26

with Christ, surrendering oneself and finding oneself again. I think anyone who reads the Confession of 1967 will realize that's what it's about.

The committee worked together as a group, and in the process I learned to appreciate the Presbyterian Church more deeply than I had before. On the committee were pastors who brought their own experiences and working theology, college teachers, seminary teachers, and one ruling elder. We had some rough times. Some of us felt at times that our strongest convictions were being submerged in the group process. But on the whole we grew in spirit as a group trying to be faithful to the church, to one another, and to the way we were thinking together as we tried to discover the form of what we were constructing.

I know much has happened since then with which the confession does not deal. Our understanding of the relation between men and women in the church and in society has changed profoundly. Problems of sexual ethics have been posed with more intensity than before. We are more deeply aware of our responsibility to God for the environment in which we live. But there is a basic orientation in the Confession of 1967 that is still a guide for faith and life.

To take another strand, the encounter with Marxism has played a fundamental role in my thinking through all of these years. In 1964 I was persuaded to go to the Christian Peace Conference in Prague. The following year I was chair of a group that formed what was then the U.S. Committee for the Christian Peace Conference. I was a part of that wonderful, exhilarating bloom of Christian-Marxist dialogue in 1966–68 when some of the profoundest questions of difference between us, and the way in which we interact, were posed by dissident Marxist philosophers and Christian theologians together. That was crushed in 1968 by the invasion of Czechoslovakia by Soviet troops. But through all of the seventies and the eighties we kept right on trying to cultivate relations wherever we could with the churches in Eastern Europe and with the people there, to support their ministry in any way we could. This is beginning to bear fruit once again now that the Marxism-Leninism of Eastern Europe has collapsed. We face a whole new horizon that we're going to have to explore in the next few years. I have ventured the conviction that although the Marxist-Leninist system is dead, Marxism is going to continue to be relevant and challenging in a number of ways. We are going to have to think as Christians more constructively about a social ethic because we no longer have the Marxist system to bounce off of.

Finally, there is the faculty of Princeton Seminary itself. It has changed enormously in the time I have been here. When I arrived, George Hendry was an intellectual guide and pillar to whom we all deferred, to whom we all referred. He just simply knew more than any of us did. Since he has left, the rest of us have developed a new and somewhat different kind of theological community that I would say is ripening now. Dan Migliore, David Willis-Watkins, Dick Allen, Mark Taylor, and Sang Lee are five extremely different persons with different emphases, and yet somewhere in the place where they meet a new theological direction for the church is emerging. It's rather exciting to watch that happen. In ethics, mission, and ecumenics, things have also changed. It's a distinguishable field interacting with theology, of course, and the swings in it have sometimes been wild. Dick Shaull was an exciting colleague, stimulus, and dialogue partner as long as he was here. We are still wrestling with the radical challenge he represented. When he left, Sam Moffett came. That brought quite a different experience and perspective. Sam is an old friend. I have known him ever since we were housemates in China. It is an honor to count him, Dick Shaull, and Alan Neely, his successor, as friends and dialogue partners in defining the mission of the church. None of us can do it alone.

I remember Sam Blizzard with his extremely detailed and careful sociological knowledge and the depth and care with which he trained his doctoral candidates. One of my early intellectual treats was to talk to those doctoral candidates about the relation between the science of sociology, the science of theology, and the field of Christian ethics. We were constantly defining an important intellectual frontier there. With Gib Winter, the frontier was also there, but it was more ideological. Gib was a sociologist with a very definite philosophy that interacted with his understanding of the Christian faith. Now, in Dick Fenn, we have another sociologist with another philosophical and theological orientation. This constant interaction with a discipline outside the theological circle is extremely important and fruitful, I think, for our whole enterprise. I am grateful to all of my colleagues who have questioned my thought and kept it moving, from that perspective.

Let me mention a more recent incident in this connection. When Dick Fenn and Peter Paris first joined the faculty, we had a retreat of the Church and Society Committee, in which we asked each other what our various convictions, disciplines, and orientations are. Besides Dick, Peter, and myself, there was Lois Livezey, Charlie Ryerson, and Bennie Ollenberger from Bible. We worked intensely for two years trying to define the Church and Society Program. We learned an enormous amount from each other about our emphases, our prejudices, and our points of view, and we managed to work out a curriculum, I think, in which we all could meaningfully participate. I think that's an enormous achievement. It has bound us all closer and made us understand each other more deeply in the community of the faculty than was my experience in the earlier years.

I could go on, of course. There are all my colleagues in the other departments. Let me say this in general. I have a feeling about the seminary that we are now a closer, more understanding community of scholars and teachers than we ever were before. That doesn't mean that we always talk the same language, but it does mean that we can talk to each other and we can work out problems and questions together. So I guess this is a great time to be retiring and let the process go on.

· 2 ·

The Contribution of Charles West
to Ecumenical Social Thought

PAUL ABRECHT

IT IS NO EASY assignment to describe and interpret Charles West's contribution to the ecumenical movement and very especially to its social thought. He has served this work in so many different roles over more than forty years: as a key interpreter of the ideological conflict at the height of the Cold War, 1950–54; as co-opted staff at the Second WCC Assembly, Evanston, 1954; as staff member of the Ecumenical Institute, Bossey, 1956–61; as member of the Working Committee for Church and Society, 1962–68; and as an active participant in the ecumenical program on science and faith, 1970–79. He was, in fact, a consultant, group leader, speaker, and report drafter at more ecumenical conferences and consultations between 1949 and 1990 than any other single churchman or theologian from America.

These were tumultuous years, and Charlie served as a kind of theological handyman ready to undertake difficult jobs for the ecumenical movement. In the process he made a large and lasting contribution to ecumenical reflection on social issues, mission and evangelism, racism, human rights, science and faith, the Christian-Marxist dialogue, and international affairs. Only a few persons from any country have served the ecumenical movement in so many capacities over so many years and have been so deeply involved in its consideration of theological and ethical issues. It is to be hoped that he or a student of ecumenical history will assemble his numerous contributions and properly evaluate his unique role as one of the molders of ecumenical thought and policy in this period. In this brief account I can only call attention to the highlights.

Contribution to the Christian Witness amid the Ideological Tension of the Cold War

I suppose it was inevitable that Charlie's most important and longest-lasting contribution would be in relation to the Christian response to the challenge of Communism. Arriving in Europe in 1950 after his experience with Chinese Communism, he plunged into the ecumenical debate about the churches' encounter with Communism in the context of the Cold War in Europe in the years 1950–54. It became the central theme of his writing and his many presentations to ecumenical meetings in these tense years.

Charlie entered into the World Council's discussion of these questions in November 1950, as a participant in a consultation on the churches and Communism organized by the WCC study department at the Ecumenical Institute in Bossey. It was a small but elite group, including, as I recall, Hendrik Kraemer, W. A. Visser 't Hooft, Stephen Neill, Nils Ehrenstrom, Bob Tobias, Max Alain Chevallier (France), Keith Bridston (WSCF), Charlie, and a few others. The purpose was to review the WCC's response to the situation facing its member churches as a result of increasing Cold War tensions. At the same time the growth of militant anti-Communism in many Western countries posed difficulties of another kind for the churches there. The only practical result was a decision to produce occasional confidential reports on the church situation in the Communist countries (later called *Background Information* [on church and society]).

In 1950 Charlie produced a remarkable study paper that was published under the pseudonym Barnabas with the title *The Christian Witness in Communist China* by the WCC Programme on the Responsible Society. This work established him as a lucid thinker on these issues, and he quickly became a major contributor to the European discussion of Christianity and Communism and member of a group of Christian specialists in this field, which came to include such eminent theologian commentators as H. Gollwitzer of Berlin, J. Hamel of East Germany, and J. Hromádka of Czechoslovakia. His Ph.D. thesis, published in 1955 as *Communism and the Theologians,* was a further testimony to his scholarly understanding of the theological-ethical issues.

Charlie had no illusions about the tendency of Communists to overstate their capacity to realize justice in history, or their distorted view of Christian faith, or their inability to grasp the illusions about human nature in their worldview. But he insisted that Christians must also understand Communism as a judgment upon their own involvement in outdated and unjust social and political systems. He developed this theme in a challenging essay for the 1952 World Conference of the International Missionary Council, in Willingen, Germany, entitled "China and the World Mission of the Church: The Lessons of a Failure." He declared that God had used Communism in China to do his will and overcome the glaring weaknesses in the witness of the Christian missionary movement. In his view,

> The events of history are in God's hand. They serve the purposes of His judgment and His grace. God is in Christ reconciling the world to Himself, including the Chinese world under Communism. Christ is the missionary even when the Church and the missionary movement of our time falsifies the message or empties it of its meaning. In the light of this work of God we have to understand the failure of our attempt at Christian mission in China. What is His Word to us in that He has crushed our institutions, crossed out our plans, and raised up Communism against us? How have we now, as chastened and repentant sinners, to preach the Gospel, to build our institutions and to make our plans?

Such statements brought him to the forefront of the discussion of these questions in missionary and church circles.

The outbreak of the Korean War had heightened the ecumenical debate on this theme. Some perceived it as a further attempt of the West to stop the triumph of justice in history. Against the objections of many Christians, the WCC in 1950 supported the UN-sanctioned resolution opposing the North Korean invasion of South Korea. The resulting war was bitter and costly. In the midst of this increasingly tense political and ideological situation, with all the anti-Communist passion that this aroused in the West and the deepening crisis of the churches in the East, the WCC began preparations for the Second WCC Assembly. Inevitably, the Communist–non-Communist problem was high on the list of social questions facing the assembly when it met in the United States in 1954.

The Preparatory Commission for the assembly's discussion of social questions, meeting in August 1953 in Switzerland, included a remarkable group of Christian social scholars and theologians, among them John Bennett and Charles West from the United States, M. M. Thomas from India, Denys Munby from the United Kingdom, Egbert de Vries and C. L. Patijn from Holland, Prof. H. D. Wendland and Dr. Walter Bauer from Germany, and Pierre Burgelin, a Christian philosopher from Strasbourg. Their task was to prepare a draft statement to be called "Social Questions: The Responsible Society in a World Perspective," which was to include an analysis of tensions between Communists and non-Communists. Since no one from the churches in the Communist countries was able to attend the meeting, the discussion of this latter theme was entrusted to Charlie and others familiar with the problems of the churches in Communist countries. Their draft helped greatly to avoid the kind of self-righteous criticism of the situation in Eastern Europe so common in the Western world. It also led to Charlie's being invited to serve as co-opted staff for Section III at the Evanston Assembly, where again he became a member of the section's drafting committee responsible for preparing the assembly message on the ecumenical approach to East-West ideological and political tensions.

These tensions were at their peak, and the assembly, meeting in the United States, was under pressure to denounce Communism. But the WCC remained faithful to its idea of responsible society, refusing to allow the conflict with Communism to divide the churches on East-West ideological and political lines. The statement also helped Western Christians to understand the witness of the churches in the East in their encounter with Communism. Again Charlie was responsible for formulating questions that the churches in the East and West should ask each other in relation to their witness to justice. As the Section III report to the assembly made clear, "Enemies of essential human freedom appear on both the political right and the political left"; Christians have "a duty to strengthen the forces of freedom which fight on both fronts."

The Ecumenical Debate about Christian Social Ethics

After 1954 two developments substantially altered the ecumenical discussion of the East-West conflict and the struggle for justice and freedom. The first was the 1956 revolt against Communism in Hungary and the subsequent Russian intervention, which greatly diminished the credibility of the Communist system in its struggle for justice and freedom. The second development was the growing demand of the independent countries of Africa and Asia and the Middle East for political freedom and economic justice, which challenged the Western colonial system.

Not until 1961, with the entry of the churches of the USSR and other Eastern European countries into membership in the WCC, did the Communist and non-Communist issue reappear significantly on the ecumenical agenda, exacerbated this time by the wars in Algeria and in Vietnam. Once again the superpowers were major protagonists, and throughout the 1960s East-West ideological conflicts became increasingly entangled with North-South issues.

The ecumenical examination of this new complex of issues inevitably raised the question of Christian involvement in the demands for "revolutionary change," especially in the countries of the Third World. This developed into a generalized revolutionary movement as Western youth and students joined in a revolt against their own Western consumer cultures. Clearly there was need for a new ecumenical reflection on the substance of Christian social thought in view of the changing world social-ideological situation. From this came the proposal in 1962 for a world study conference on issues of church and society. This conference was eventually convened in Geneva in 1966.

If Charlie did not play a large role in the preparations, it was because one of the three U.S. seats on the preparatory committee was taken by his fellow U.S. Presbyterian theologian and ethicist, Dr. Richard Shaull. (The other two were held by John Bennett and Margaret Mead.) Dick Shaull had become prominent as an American Presbyterian missionary working with students in Latin America, concerned with the Christian response to the Third World struggle for radical social change. His essay "Revolutionary Change in Theological Perspective," written for the preparatory volume for the 1966 conference, *Christian Social Ethics in a Changing World,* had so impressed the editor John Bennett that he recommended that it be the opening chapter. On the strength of this contribution he was invited to address the 1966 World Conference on this theme. However Charlie attended the conference in Geneva as a representative of his church and was made co-chairperson (with H. D. Wendland of Germany) of the special Working Group on Theological Issues in Social Ethics. In this role he made one of his most important contributions to ecumenical social thought.

There is need for a comparative study of the thought of these two eminent Presbyterian social thinkers: both eventually professors at Princeton seminary, both lucid and compelling writers and speakers, both influential participants in ecumenical social thought, both, though in different ways, concerned to make a positive use of Marxism in Christian action for social justice. Yet they were very different in their theology, in their approach to ideology, and in their influence on the ecumenical movement and its social thought and policy.

Charlie's contribution to the 1966 conference on the effect of the changing social context of Christian social ethics remains today one of the clearest and most helpful statements on this matter in ecumenical literature. Those familiar with the Charles West style of theological-ethical reasoning will recognize his hand in the draft that came to the conference plenary (with minor amendments, it was approved). It included a remarkable section entitled "The Intelligibility and Knowledge of Nature in Theological

Perspective," which, if remembered, would have helped to avoid much of the confusion that arose in later years in connection with such terms as "the integrity of creation" in the ecumenical program Justice, Peace, and the Integrity of Creation. A further section entitled "A Theological Understanding of Social Change" dealt with the implications of the revolutionary social context for Christian social ethics and social action.

> The Christian knows by faith that no structure of society, no system of human power and security is perfectly just, and that every system falls under the judgement of God in so far as it is unable to reform itself in response to the call for justice of those who are under its power. There is no divinely ordained social order, and not every change, as such, nor every status quo, as such, is necessarily good. There are only relative, secular structures subject to constant revision in the light of new human needs. There is in history a dynamic of evil as well as a dynamic of good. . . .
>
> The Christian is therefore called to speak a radical "No" — and to act accordingly — to structures of power which perpetuate and strengthen the status quo at the cost of justice to those who are its victims. The task of bringing about effective social change, and of discerning in the protest of the poor and oppressed the relative historical justice at work, is especially his. It may be his task to express the repentance to which he calls his own ruling group. Only then is he prepared for the witness he owes to the revolutionary: freedom from hatred — freedom to build a new world in which also the enemy will find a just place; freedom from self-righteousness — freedom to accept the give-and-take which must modify even revolutionary plans and power. For revolutions are also under judgement when they make their cause absolute and promise final salvation. (1966 Report, p. 200)

A further passage affirms the role of the social sciences in the "discernment of what is just and unjust, human and inhuman in the complexities of political and economic change" and concludes with a paraphrase of a well-known declaration: "The object [of Christian social thought] is not simply to understand the world but to respond to the power of God which is re-creating it."

The report proposed a new, more positive approach to the problems posed for theology "by the formation of ideologies."

> Ideology as we use it here is the theoretical and analytical structure of thought which undergirds successful action to realize revolutionary change in society or to undergird and justify its status quo. . . . Christians,

35

like all human beings, are affected by ideological perspectives. But their witness is the way in which they show themselves to be constantly corrected in their encounter with God and their neighbours while acting on their faith.

In its report "Economic Development in a World Perspective," the World Conference in fact used this understanding of ideology in its examination of contemporary economic systems. To my knowledge, however, this kind of analysis was not continued after the populist, activist "ideology" seized hold of ecumenical social thought in the 1970s.

Two specific recommendations of this working group were fulfilled: to sponsor an informal dialogue with two "non-Christian social ideologies" — one with Marxists, the other with "right-wing ideologies." Charlie had no role in the second, which took the form of a series of meetings with conservative business leaders in Europe who had been angered by the World Conference criticisms of the free-market economy. But he had a large role in the dialogue with Marxists, which was convened in Geneva in April 1967. This brought together a remarkable group of Marxists from Czechoslovakia, France, Spain, and Italy and an equally strong group of Christian theologians from Europe, Latin America, North America, and the Middle East.

Charles was one of the leaders and helped save the meeting from great confusion. At that moment, in the midst of the reform of Communism in Czechoslovakia, some Marxists (especially those from Czechoslovakia) were more Christian than the Christians, while radical Christians (especially some of those from France and from Latin America) were more Marxist than the Marxists. The meeting produced no great statement on the Christian insight into Marxism, but the exchange was extremely worthwhile in humanizing the debate. After 1968 and the Russian intervention in Czechoslovakia, the WCC sponsored no further dialogue with Marxists. Was this because ecumenical social thought had, in the years after the Uppsala Assembly (1968), moved to the Left and accepted Marxism as an alternative "economic science," so that dialogue had become pointless? In addition, by 1972 Dick Shaull had brought Marxist ideology into a commanding position in the thought and action of the World Student Christian Federation. Who could ask for more?

But as we now know by hindsight, just a decade later, Marxists were beginning to be a dying race, whether inside or outside Eastern Europe and China. Charlie is one of the few persons to have followed the permutations of the "dialogue" debate closely in these years, and he needs to give us his reflections on all that happened in this crucial period.

Charlie's Contribution to the Ecumenical Discussion of Science and Faith

In 1969 ecumenical social thought took several new turns, one of which was to lead to concentration on the future of man and society in a world of science-based technology. This theme had been proposed by the 1966 conference and endorsed by the Uppsala Assembly in 1968. In 1970 the WCC convened an exploratory study conference including one hundred persons from science, technology, philosophy, and theology. Charlie was again one of the theologians to which we turned for help. At the same time he was invited to participate in another Church and Society study project on the subject "Violence and Non-Violence in the Struggle for Social Justice."

There is not space here to report in detail his contribution to both these ecumenical programs. The first resulted in a series of ecumenical study conferences between 1971 and 1977. No doubt the most important was his contribution to the 1979 World Conference on Faith, Science, and the Future at MIT, where he was one of the staff of Section II, assigned to prepare a statement under the title "Nature, Humanity, and God." Judging again by the clear and articulate formulation of the issues, I have no doubt that Charlie had an influence on this statement. It follows closely the ideas developed in the 1966 conference regarding the problems raised by the theme of man's mastery and stewardship of nature. Thirteen years later, however, because of the advance of science and technology, their power was seen as much more threatening. This is eloquently set out in the report from the conference at MIT:

> The cultural context has radically changed since biblical times. In the biblical period humanity was confronted with an overpowering nature. The command to rule the animals and to subdue the earth delivered people from fear and from the temptation to divinize or demonize nature, and encouraged them to overcome suffering and to build culture. The power relations have since been reversed by science and technology. A desacralized nature is in the power of humanity, which is now able to destroy its own species and perhaps even all life on the earth. Our own technological inventions and our social process are threatening to get the upper hand and to become as overpowering as nature once was. What needs to be emphasized today, therefore, is the relatedness between God and his creation rather than their separateness. The dignity of nature as creation needs to be stressed, and humanity's *dominium* must be bound up with our responsibility for the preservation of life.

37

This report and the conference report entitled "The Nature of Science and the Nature of Faith" are the two most important theological statements to come out of the 1979 conference.

Conclusion

My last "official" ecumenical link with Charlie was at the Sixth WCC Assembly in Vancouver, in 1983. Charlie had come this time as press to report on the assembly for *Theology Today*. We both felt keenly the decline of substance in the assembly, and we had many opportunities to discuss the causes of this weakness. We agreed that it was due very largely to the exclusive emphasis on the populist or participatory method in ecumenical work. His subsequent account and evaluation of the Vancouver Assembly accurately and succinctly summed up the problematic situation of ecumenical social thought and action. Some of those with whom we disagreed would no doubt say that we are both incorrigible elitists. And they would no doubt add that we are also unredeemable Niebuhrians. But after the Seventh Assembly in Canberra, Australia, in February 1991, which was organized in the same populist style, it is clear that the downward trend continues; the substance and impact of ecumenical social thought continue to diminish. Theologians and ethicists like Charlie, committed to the struggle for substance and quality (as well as passion) in ecumenical social thought, are today in short supply.

· 3 ·

Faith, Ideology, and Power:
Toward an Ecumenical, Post-Marxist
Method in Christian Ethics

CHARLES C. WEST

THE WORD "post-Marxist" in this title has a double meaning. As an economic system, designed to express the creative vitality of the human species in control at last of the power of its own labor, and liberated from the dehumanizing oppression of capital, money, and private property, Marxism has collapsed. With it, a dream has also vanished. It was the vision of a new humanity unlimited in its horizons and achievements, wherein compulsion and control would disappear because each individual would identify self with the public good. It is hard to remember today how intoxicating that vision once was and how long it lasted, distorting power and excusing oppression, yet inspiring superhuman devotion and sacrifice. Just a generation ago, in the midst of the Khrushchev era, the Soviet philosopher Schischkin could anticipate, in a textbook on ethics, the coming of the Communist society and reflect on the way in which the students before his eyes were being prepared for it:

> The new man [and woman, the Russian word is generic] forms himself by active participation in the building of Communism by developing Communist principles in economic and social life under the influence of the whole system of education through the party, the state, and social organizations.[1]

---

1. A. F. Schischkin, *Grundlagen der marxistischen Ethik* (Berlin: Dietz Verlag, 1965). The English here is my translation of Schischkin's German translation of the original Russian.

Communism would arrive, Schischkin told his students, within their lifetime. They should begin to prepare themselves to live in it.

In a few pockets of the world this dream still inspires the hope of revolutionaries: the mountains of Peru and the Philippines, perhaps. But as a system of social power, planning to bring in utopia, it has crumbled under the weight of its own pretensions, crumbled so completely in fact that many in Eastern Europe who have suffered under it reject even the questions — of social justice, of community beyond class and nation, and of control over economic power for the public good — that the Marxist-Leninists tried to answer. We are left with a few Christians and social democrats combing the rubble for moral bricks with which to build a new ethos. This is post-Marxist society.

But the world today is post-Marxist in another, profounder sense. Karl Marx and his followers have changed the terms in which social ethics is done in ways that can never be reversed. The core of this change lies, I believe, in a new relation between consciousness and existence, between social analysis and social commitment — that is, between theory and practice, and between human responsibility and human hope. This essay will examine each of these aspects briefly in turn. The theme that unites them all is the ancient yet contemporary biblical question of the knowledge of truth in the context of response to the living truth pointing toward the promise by which we live.

The Question of Ideology

Karl Marx's formulation is classic:

> In the social production of their life, men enter into definite relations that are indispensable and independent of their will, relations of production which correspond to a definite stage of development of their material productive forces. The sum total of these relations of production constitutes the economic structure of society, the real foundation, on which rises a legal and political superstructure and to which correspond definite forms of social consciousness. The mode of production of material life conditions the social, political and intellectual life processes in general. It is not the consciousness of men that determines their being, but on the contrary their social being that determines their consciousness.[2]

2. Karl Marx, preface to *A Contribution to the Critique of Political Economy* (Chicago: Charles H. Kerr, 1904).

Thought, therefore, is a function of the social struggle. The system of ideas by which one grasps the world arises out of the struggle of one's group — Marx would say class — in the world to achieve or maintain its power and subdue its enemies. All pretensions to universal truth and morality are themselves ideological in this sense. This is the condition of human consciousness in a history characterized by the division of labor before the revolution produces a universal consciousness in a classless society.

Marx's own work deals primarily with the consciousness of this alienated humanity, which expresses itself in various ways: as *religion,* which protests yet sanctifies and offers escape from the oppressions of this world by referring us to another, purer one; as *philosophy,* which revolutionizes the world in the realm of ideas without ever changing material conditions (e.g., "the German Ideology"); as *political morality,* which turns class-dominated nation, state, and law into ultimate principles of order; and, above all, as *economic theory,* which turns exploitation into a law of nature (the fetishism of property, money, and capital). But Marx's successors were quick to see that his own historical materialism was, in a positive sense, an ideology: that of the masses of poor, exploited workers seeking liberation from the inhuman conditions of their lives. It both guided and reflected their struggle. It analyzed the powers of this world as part of the strategy and tactic of their overthrow and the promise of a new, undivided, classless humanity to come. In the light of this mass foundation, this praxis, and this universal hope, these followers of Marx could say with Lenin that, as an ideology, "Marxism is omnipotent because it is true."

An ideology, then, has five characteristics according to this model. First, it is the reflection of the life and struggle of a particular group in society. Second, it is an analysis of both the history and the structure of reality from the perspective of that group. Third, it is a guide to the group in bending the powers of the world to its social purposes in the search for peace, prosperity, and justice. Fourth, it claims to be true not only for the group but for all people; it claims to be a universal expression of reality and justice. Finally, it offers hope to all of society at the end of the process and the struggle.

To ideology so defined, three things need to be said. First, it is clear that ideological elements have been present in major structures of religious and philosophical thought from the beginning of recorded history. Confucianism in ancient China reflected the struggles of a scholarly officialdom against the more aggressive military philosophies of its time. Plato's *Republic* was in one dimension an aristocratic protest against democracy gone wild. Aristotle's *Politics* enshrined in the structure of being itself the social order of a city-state that was disappearing even as he wrote. Norman K. Gottwald and others have taken it as their project "to give an account of how theological representations relate to their material base and social sites over the whole course of Israelite-Jewish-Christian history."[3] In so doing, they have uncovered ideological elements in the biblical message itself and have at the same time imported their own ideological bias into the interpretation of Scripture.

Nor are the greatest of Christian theologians free of it: Ambrose wielding the power of the church in the court of the emperor, Thomas Aquinas qualifying feudalism with the values of the growing culture in the towns, Martin Luther expressing German independence of a far-off papacy, or John Calvin, to quote R. H. Tawney, approaching the new world of business and finance "in the spirit of a conqueror organizing a new province, not of a suppliant arranging a compromise with a still powerful foe."[4] All of these were much more than ideologies. They contained within themselves a transcendent reference, an openness to truth breaking into the social context from beyond, or in the Hebrew-Christian tradition, a response to revelation, which make them lasting resources for people in societies other than their own. Nevertheless after Marx, we cannot appropriate them or their successors without careful critical attention to their ideological dimension.

Second, humanity has always been aware, and the awareness is carried in its many religious traditions and classical philosophies, that the perception of truth is possible only within the context of relationships with others and with God, which also determine human behavior. Consciousness does emerge from social existence, thus broadly conceived. Perceived truth and lived truth depend upon and reinforce one another. Metaphysics and moral discipline are one seamless whole in classical philosophy from Socrates to the Stoics. The reality of God was known to the Hebrew people in the covenant relation through the Torah. Truth for the New Testament church is found in the community whose head is Christ. Despite the use made by natural theologians of Thomas Aquinas's adaptation of Aristotelian philosophy, it is doubtful that Thomas himself seriously contemplated the separation of faith and sacramental grace from the operation of human reason that his philosophy permits.

3. Norman K. Gottwald, *The Bible and Liberation* (Maryknoll, N.Y.: Orbis Books, 1983), p. 198.
4. R. H. Tawney, *Religion and the Rise of Capitalism* (Gloucester, Mass.: Peter Smith, 1962), p. 119.

The problem that confronted Karl Marx, however, was such a separation. It was rooted in the great rival ideology to Marxism in the modern world, which also preceded Marx by at least two hundred years: the philosophy known as liberal humanism. This term describes an ethos so pervasive that even many who reject the word live by its assumptions. In the United States today it is taken to mean strong government action on behalf of human rights and welfare and thus, by implication, bureaucratic interference in the private lives of citizens. In nineteenth-century England it meant free speech, free trade, and minimal government. In Europe it has stood for a secular humanist perspective. In Britain and America it has often described the social ethic of the established churches. I mean by it here roughly what Alasdair MacIntyre calls the "Enlightenment project,"[5] the structure of individualist humanism that underlies the science, the technology, the industry, the education, and the politics of much of the Western world.

The basic methodological premise of this ideology is confidence in the ability of human reason operating by empirical analysis (the scientific method) to discover ever-increasing horizons of relevant truth. It is a critical, not a naive, rationalism. Hume and Kant exploded the illusion that the human mind could discover the structure of things in themselves. But it is a critical confidence in the unlimited ability of the human mind to solve problems, to discover and make use of the laws of nature to expand the possibilities of human life. In Kant's words, "*Sapere aude!* dare to know! 'Have the courage to use your own understanding,' is the slogan of the Enlightenment."[6]

This is an ideological confidence as surely as is Marx's doctrine of the social determination of the consciousness. It is a functional way of thinking, whose object is control over reality and the enhancement of human power in the service of human needs or desires and not, as early modern scientists often believed, the contemplation of divine reality in the laws of nature. Human power is at its center, with the paradox that scientific knowledge and control may produce power from the atom or from the environment that can lead to human self-destruction.

Spiritually it is rooted in the primacy of the autonomous, free human individual. This, too, is sometimes paradoxical because it can be based on

5. Alasdair MacIntyre, *After Virtue* (Notre Dame, Ind.: University of Notre Dame Press, 1981).

6. Immanuel Kant, "Beantwortung der Frage: Was ist Aufklärung?" in *German Essays*, vol. 1, ed. Max Dufner and Valentine C. Hubbs (New York: Macmillan, 1964). My translation.

an epistemology of sensations (John Locke) or on a mechanical calculation of pleasures and pains (Jeremy Bentham). It is not inconsistent with determinism in psychology, sociology, or economics. Nevertheless the assumption is that individuals are primary autonomous realities whose choices and actions mold history.

One consequence of this view is that controls of individual behavior should be minimal and should be aimed not at realizing some common good or desirable community but at maximizing the opportunities for individual self-determination and choice. Education should provide the tools to do this. Democratic politics should regulate the process and prevent violations. Culture should be tolerant and pluralistic without limit. The goals of life should be set by individuals and private groups.

A further consequence of this view is that the behavior of individuals in the process of pursuing their own ends is subject to scientific study, which should be the basis of public policy. The primary example of this is the science of economics. It is pointless to intervene in the process to achieve socially defined goals because this is only self-defeating. The market must decide what goods and services are produced and consumed by whom, and when and where.

The faith of liberal ideology is a curious one, that in the process of pursuing private interests, myriad individuals will produce a harmonious and creative society that will continually enlarge the welfare and creative possibilities for all. The only public common good worth having is the result of the interaction of private interests, desires, and goals. Human beings can be trusted when trained in the scientific method to understand the necessary harmony between the individual and the general interest. Missing in all of this is the insight into the contextual character of human knowledge and the centrality of ethics to it that characterized an earlier age. This is the ethos in which Marx was educated, which he absorbed, and against which he revolted by taking its own humanist commitment to its logical conclusion.

The third thing we can say about Marx's understanding of "ideology" is that it contributed a fundamental exposé of the social and epistemological illusions not only of the liberal worldview but of all previous metaphysical worldviews. The human consciousness is not only limited and relative, it is distorted by the human social interests it serves. Knowledge is indeed functional and proves itself in practice, as the liberal methodology maintains. But the practice that validates it is the success of the social group out of which it arose in maintaining its dominant power or in overthrowing the power that it believes oppresses it.

Marxism was also paradoxical in its view of human knowledge and human nature. If one takes its doctrine of ideology with final seriousness, the result is complete relativism both moral and metaphysical. The Marxists avoided this conclusion because they trusted that the materially determined laws of history would lead humanity through class struggle and revolution to the total emancipation of humankind. It also measured truth by the power of results. Its version of critical self-confidence was the strategy and tactic of revolution and the building of socialist society toward Communism. It too believed, more naively than the liberals, that in human nature, once freed from private property, there would be no distinction between the universal goals of collective humanity and the desires of each human being. The result, as we know, has been new forms of tyranny and exploitation.

Nevertheless the question remains, and since Karl Marx no structure of thought that claims to give meaning and guidance to human life can avoid it, How far and in what way do our theology, our ethics, our science and technology, and our social analysis reflect the interests of our social group at the expense of others? In the post-Marxist world, this question has been diversified. Black consciousness, feminist perspectives, and multiple ethnic and religious worldviews from the Two-Thirds World have joined the traditional class conflict in raising it. Nor is it only a confrontation between these and the traditional white male bourgeois establishment of the industrialized countries in Europe and North America. Arab and Jew, Tamil and Sinhalese in Sri Lanka, Hindu and Muslim on the Indian subcontinent — all face it even more acutely. In all of these cases, traditional conflicts of culture, power, and exploitation are compounded by the ideological character of universal claims, on the one hand, and by a hermeneutic of suspicion that attributes bad faith to those claims, on the other.

How, then, in the light of the persistent searching question of ideology, is a Christian ethic possible? How can a believer bear faithful and convincing witness to a judging and redeeming God from within the limits and distortions of his or her ideological context? By what grace, to call the matter by its name, can the ideologizing sinner be justified? To this, let me offer two suggestions.

First, truth as we know it by faith is not a system of ideas but a relationship. It is furthermore a relationship we do not control, one that has grasped us and demands our response both in thought and in action. For Christians, it is the reality of Christ taking form in the world, to use Dietrich Bonhoeffer's words. It is the revelation of the mystery, therefore,

45

in which and by which we live, which we are always exploring but never fully understand. We are listeners and responders.

Because that is so, we must be listeners and responders also among those who challenge the bona fides of our faith, our ethics, or our social policy and call it ideology. We are here continually in a three-way relationship between ourselves, our neighbors, whether enemies or friends, and God, wherein the controlling and revealing reality is neither ourselves nor our neighbors but God. Therefore as we struggle with each other's ideologies, we do not break the relationship. We do not define our ideological opponents as creatures of their systems. Rather, we are called to repentance by them as we also call them to repentance. Both ways, we refer them and ourselves to that third partner, through whose word we are all judged and redeemed. Truth is a living relationship that we are called to explore with one another, recognizing that our national, class, ethnic, and other ideologies will be changed in the process.

Second, we are called not to be infallibly accurate in our social analyses or morally pure in our actions but to be responsible. Our analysis will be ideological and our actions will not be pure because we are human beings of limited experience and social bias, and because we can never wholly rid ourselves of the tendency to grant to our analysis of reality and its demands more universality than is due. If we allow ourselves to be paralyzed by the guilt of this condition, or if we try to repent of the ideology in our own perspective by adopting the ideology of our accusers, we fail both them and God. By particular acts — of conscientious objection or military service, of negotiation with unjust powers or mass demonstration against them, of support for or opposition to a particular plan for national health insurance, for example — we commit ourselves to what we believe is right, calling others to join us, knowing at the same time that there are elements of wrongness in the right action we choose, that we may have been mistaken, even ideologically biased, in our assessment of the situation and the moral demand it placed on us. A responsible action is action in a relationship, subject to further correction and guidance by our neighbors and God. It is precisely this firm commitment to fallible action that pulls us out of our ideological prism into serious encounter with both.

The Question of Power

Marxism has changed permanently the way the operations of human power are understood in social ethics. It is not that the Christian tradition has been unaware of anonymous power rooted in human will and desire yet transcending and enslaving human beings by its structures. The *exousiai* of the New Testament are expressions of these powers, created by God, destined to be subjected to the lordship of Christ despite themselves, yet meanwhile pursuing the enslaving logic of their own power. The New Testament concept of *kosmos* expresses the same insight throughout Christian history.

Nor is it the case that Christian history has been without adequate awareness of economic greed and exploitation and the structures of injustice to which they lead. The church through the centuries has made valiant efforts to uphold the biblical vision of material and spiritual community reaching out to include the poor. It approached the rising commercial civilization of the Middle Ages with strong condemnation of avarice and greed, usury and monopoly, and attempted to establish a responsible system of just wages, prices, and profits. Calvinism provided early modern Europe and America with a strong system of social controls over business practice and of care for those in need. There has been a strong socialist tradition in the Christian church throughout history, as John Cort in his book *Christian Socialism* has so extensively documented.

The problem of historical Christian ethics in this area was not its unawareness of the social, enslaving dimension of sinful power but its tendency to concentrate on the visible personalized expressions of political power and to neglect analysis of the anonymous forces, rooted in human greed and enhanced by expanding energy sources, that built our industrial system in the nineteenth century. A part of the Christian community was captured by liberal economics and sanctified this power. Another part withdrew from public power analysis altogether into the realm of private faith and motivation. A few proclaimed socialism as a Christian ideal. But there was little realistic analysis of the actual operation of the institutions of economic power. This was Marx's contribution.

The stage, to be sure, had already been set by the liberal economics of Malthus and Ricardo. The science of economics had already been established as that of the relations between commodities and money rather than human beings themselves. The labor theory of value, originally a moral concept concerned with the right of the worker, had become a theory about commodity prices. Labor itself had become a commodity, the basic price of which was the minimum physical maintenance and reproduction of the worker, modified only by supply and demand. The inherent conflict of interest between worker and employer (in other words, class war) and the drive of the system toward ever more intensive exploitation of the worker, limited only by the starvation and therefore shortage of laborers — all this was present in the science of liberal economics itself. There, however, it was mixed with unbounded optimism about the progress of a developing economy as a whole toward ever-greater prosperity and possibilities for human life.

It was Marx who cut through this strange marriage of inhumanity with humanism, with his catastrophic analysis of the same economic forces that the liberal economists had defined. In so doing, he developed an alternative, more realistic picture of the conflict of powers at work in the economic sphere. It was the picture of an idolatry, or, in his word, fetishism, whereby human products — commodities, money, and capital — are given the status of absolute value and truth, which real human beings must serve and obey. He revealed the inhumanity of such a world, both of the exploiters and the exploited. He traced its conflicts to their ultimate destructive consequences and raised in all seriousness the question, What power can save us from this demonic system? For Christians who took him seriously, he exposed both of their illusions: (1) that the exploitation and injustices of technological capitalistic expansion throughout the world can be defended or excused by the philanthropic use we make of their fruits, or (2) that the economic powers in our world can be brought to responsible service of the public good by ideals and moral persuasion. The full force of this last point did not really penetrate Christian ethical thinking until the depression of the 1930s, when Reinhold Niebuhr developed a realistic power analysis, both economic and political, as a guide to Christian action in the context of the judgment and the forgiving grace of God.

Today we know that Marxist analysis of capitalist accumulation and the class struggle it caused is also not adequate to the complex realities of power in modern technological society. Dependency theory, for example, does not adequately explain the persistent economic underdevelopment of large parts of the world. Transnational corporations maintain themselves and wield their power in ways that often cannot be explained by the exploitation of labor or the maximization of profit. Cultural factors, customs, and traditions wield an influence far beyond that which Marx foresaw. Most of Marx's predictions concerning the fate of advanced capitalist economies have not come true, partly because of the creative response of those economies to power struggle initiated by Marxist social democrats. Much has been made of the failure of socialist societies developed on Marxist-Leninist principles to release the forces of human productivity or to eliminate economic greed and exploitation.

Nevertheless, the basic challenge remains. Whatever its inadequacies as a total explanation of human behavior, Marxism remains a reminder of, and one tool for understanding, the way in which human greed and lust for power express themselves in the powers and principalities of the economic sphere, distorting the human consciousness as well as social relations in all their dimensions, including the religious dimension. The paradox of Marxist economics, which brings it so close to Christian thought, is that a ruthlessly objective analysis of human economic behavior in a sinful world is combined with an implicit confession of the underlying realities that will bring judgment upon that behavior. Marx's humanism misperceived those realities. His task has been passed to Christians. It takes, I think, three forms.

First is the discernment of the concrete varieties of human power structures, and the motivations that underlie them, in a technological bureaucratic world. Conspiracy theories are no longer adequate to this analysis. Nor can we leave it to the liberal economists. The desire for gain, the fear of economic insecurity or loss, and the structures of exploitation take changing forms that require continual sensitivity to new ways in which economic power is being used and needs to be controlled.

Second, it is our task to improve upon Marx's understanding of the proletariat by discerning, in their variety, groups in society that are powerless and victimized by others, in order to empower them to play an effective public role in defense of their interests. Once again, no romanticism about the poor and no demonization of the present power structures will help us in this. Reinhold Niebuhr was right many years ago: the achievement of a relative justice depends upon the balancing of power with power so that a higher level of mutuality emerges. This means that the controversy between a planned and a free enterprise economy cannot be solved in general but only by asking the question where and how private power must be controlled in the interest of others in the community, and where freedom should be allowed for the benefit of the community. The balance of public power with private power is inevitable, because no public power is as devoted to the general interest as it pretends to be, yet it alone can represent the interests and the decisions of the community as a whole.

Third, in Christian understanding, power is covenantal. It is rooted in the commitment of God to the people in a relationship that affirms, forgives, and redeems them all. This covenant community creates freedom, and only within it does freedom have meaning. Analogically, in the secular community free enterprise is chartered within the context of social relations to which it is responsible. To suggest the forms and the possibilities of that context and the possible redefinition of human interests and motivations within it is the service of the church to the community of human powers, both visible and anonymous.

49

PART TWO

THEOLOGY, ETHICS, AND SOCIETY

• 4 •

Cutting the Christendom Knot

GEORGE R. HUNSBERGER

W HAT ARE WE in the Gospel and Our Culture Network (GOCN) doing when we sound the call to the churches to engage in a "missionary encounter of the gospel with our Western culture"?[1] What are we doing when we alert the churches to the radical social dislocation we have experienced in the last several decades? What are we doing when we point to the need for "a fundamental repositioning of the churches' life and ministry in the North American context"? What kind of urges do we tap? What kind of impulses do we elicit?

Our companion movement in the United Kingdom has raised similar questions in regard to calls by a number of churches for the 1990s to be set aside as a Decade of Evangelism: "But what will this mean? Is it a revival of old-time religion? Is it an attempt to reestablish the churches' authority and control in society, to re-found Christendom? Or will it involve a willingness to examine and question many of the assumptions and beliefs of Western culture in the light of the Christian gospel? In other words, are we prepared to look at our own culture through the eyes of an overseas missionary?"

---

1. These comments were addressed to the first consultative gathering of the Gospel and Our Culture Network in North America. The GOCN defines itself as "a collaborative association of Christian leaders from diverse communions, working together to help the church explore and engage the newly emerging missionary encounter of the gospel in the cultures of North America." The author serves as the coordinator of the network and the editor of its quarterly newsletter. From its inception, Charles West has been a central figure in the network and has helped guide the formation of its agenda. He is a member of the Theology Work Group.

The form of these questions wisely disavows an intention to reassert a lost or failed Christendom. But is it that easy for the churches — or any of us — to set aside images and instincts that have been so deeply bred for centuries? How difficult that is, is evident from another comment from the U.K. movement in the same brochure that contained the one just quoted. The brochure announced a national consultation on the topic "The Gospel as Public Truth" planned for July 1992, the aim of which was said to be: "to test the thesis that the Christian Gospel can provide a positive critique of contemporary Western culture, the basis of unity and coherence, and the possibility of a hopeful future for the public life of our society." I'm sure there is much that I do not know or understand about the United Kingdom that might make such an aim more appropriate there than it would be here in North America. But the proposal that the gospel provide the basis of unity and coherence for the society, along with the hope — stated in another brochure — that the consultation "will help Christians in our society to 'reclaim the high ground' from its present captivity" puts a decidedly Christendom face on the direction of the movement there. Whatever its appropriateness in the United Kingdom, I cannot conceive that we would make a similar proposal here in North America.

It is not that I disbelieve that a society would be enriched by allowing the gospel to provide the basis of meaning, unity, and hope for its public life. Nor am I merely a realist who sees no possibility that our society would accept that idea. And I am not pretending that we Americans are above having Christendom impulses and urges. That would be ludicrous. To the contrary, such impulses are evident and powerful at every turn. What I wish to assert is that it is precisely this Christendom hangover that thwarts the recovery of the church's missionary identity in North America.

I am assuming the diagnosis that in fact we have found ourselves lacking genuine missionary character. What is lacking in actuality corresponds with deficiencies in our thinking. I agree with the important exploratory studies of my colleague Craig Van Gelder, who has noted that we have not developed in North America a missiology for our own context. (Douglas John Hall is making a similar point in regard to the absence of a North American contextual theology in his book *Thinking the Faith* [1989].) But while there is an absence of any rigorous approach to such a missiology, there is certainly an operational missiology present in the thinking and action of the churches. It is first an "overseas" missiology that construes mission as "over there" somewhere, among people who live in darkness and need our light. When forced to answer the question of mission here in North America, the focus turns inevitably toward efforts to help "the poor" out of our abundance and as an act of benevolence. If one pushes further to probe concerning any way in which the church has a mission to represent and commend the gospel, the answer describes programs designed to recruit new members (the nearest the answer ever gets to evangelism). Alternatively, one hears about efforts to exert influence on the society regarding issues of social justice or public morality.

What all of these elements of our functional missiology have in common is the feature of Christendom Douglas John Hall has so well described in his book *Has the Church a Future?* (1980). Our Christendom heritage has conditioned us to "tell our Christian story as a success story."[2] We tell it as those who have enjoyed the privileges of an ascendency shared with political power. We tell it, as Stanley Hauerwas has put it, with "a Constantinian set of presumptions that the Church should determine a world in which it is safe."[3] We have the light for the other inhabitants of the globe (an Enlightenment that is only partially religious!), we have the abundance from which to give them things they need, we have the understanding to guide their ethical standards. (The "we" in all this is of course a Western "we," not the whole church, spread as it is among the societies of the world.) Here is a missiology of the haves to the have-nots, of the empowered to the weak, and of the winners to the losers. Actually, in the end this operative missiology shows itself to be a very highly contextualized North American missiology, rooted in North American Christendom ways of thinking! But it is not critically contextualized, and that is the element we must engage.

These Christendom-oriented notions of mission have left us with what is more and more obviously a paltry and limp experience of anything like a missionary character, evidenced not only by the crisis of decreasing size in the mainline denominations but by the crisis of focus and identity in the wider expanse of churches. That in itself should force us to reexamine the Christendom roots of our images. But there is an even more important reason to do so. We have found ourselves, on the one hand, reeling from the ways we have felt the pinch of our disestablishment from what Martin Marty has called the "controlled secularity" arrangement in America, whereby the churches had for a long time enjoyed the permission "to do some monitoring, some inspiring, some legitimatizing of the larger culture."[4] While this was done largely by "devotional intrusions and not sub-

2. Douglas John Hall, *Has the Church a Future?* (Philadelphia: Westminster Press, 1980), p. 41.
3. Stanley Hauerwas, *After Christendom?* (Nashville: Abingdon Press, 1991), p. 18.
4. Martin Marty, *The Modern Schism* (London: SCM Press, 1969), p. 98.

stantive ones" and while it involved being "essentially relegated to the private realm," it was only with more recent "disestablishments" that we have felt how marginal we have become to American life. Individual liberty was once an American value legitimated by the churches and their theology of a God who endowed all with certain inalienable rights; now our right to hold that or any other belief is legitimated by the fundamental American myth of individual freedom.[5] In a more thorough way than ever, we have been relegated to the private realm of beliefs and values, where pluralism and relativity reign.

On the other hand, the dismay over our disestablishment — the near complete loss of our Christendom birthright — has awakened us rudely to how thoroughly domesticated we have become. Our willing acceptance of relegation to the private realm (the engine behind our proliferating denominationalism, according to Lesslie Newbigin)[6] has been an accommodation of far-reaching proportions. It has made us vulnerable to successive stages of intensity in the privatization of faith and the individualization of religious life. Sociologists have long noted the breakdown of denominational loyalty as a factor in church membership. Then, even commitment to a particular congregation has weakened in a consumer environment where folks shop for the best collection of religious services and programs from a variety of vendors. And now, as Catherine Albanese points out, that pattern too is giving way to one in which "Americans are going it alone in religious terms." They still claim to be religious but now pursue their religiosity apart from institutions or communities, a trend that Albanese says is the sign of "an entry into a new religious age."[7]

Our lingering Christendom urge for success pushes us to play to these changes, but the pattern of accommodation is even more wide-ranging than that. Accommodations of the Left and of the Right have left us essentially domesticated. We are tame, sometimes playful, companionable, but unthreatening to the quests and values pursued by the society and its people, largely because we share those values and beliefs unquestioningly. To be sure, every incarnation of the gospel, including those we most wish to foster in this network, is vulnerable to the possibility of domestication. Incarnation becomes domestication when the ultimate principles governing the

5. Robert Wuthnow, *The Restructuring of American Religion: Society and Faith since World War II* (Princeton: Princeton University Press, 1988), p. 13.
6. Lesslie Newbigin, *Foolishness to the Greeks* (Grand Rapids: Eerdmans, 1986), p. 145.
7. Catherine L. Albanese, "Forum: The Decline of Mainline Religion in American Culture," *Religion and American Culture* 1, no. 2 (Spring 1991): 139.

interaction of the church with its culture are set by the culture. When the church's incarnation of the gospel is made subject to the terms of the environment, established according to its principles, validated by its evaluations, and made subservient to its ends, its incarnation has been domesticated.

I suggest that we will be unable to shed our domestication and become an alternative community so long as we retain our Christendom ways of thinking. We either must accept the loss of Christendom — Christendom understood not only as a historical fact but as an element in the structure of our thought and self-perception — or we must continue to accept the terms laid down by the dominant culture. In Hall's words, we must begin where we are, "recognizing our new status in the world, especially the formerly 'Christian' world of the Western Hemisphere. We are a minority. We are few. . . . Christendom as Western Christianity imagined it and tried to create it for some sixteen centuries has come to an end. The church as a 'mighty army' is no more, and no manner of Christian revivalism can put Humpty Dumpty together again." But beginning where we are forms for Hall a new kind of hope: "The end of Christendom might be the beginning of the church!"[8]

What does all this mean for the Gospel and Our Culture Network and the fostering of the genuinely missionary character of the churches of North America? First of all it warns us that we must get at the radically fundamental root of the issue, our Christendom mind-set. Will the missiology of this movement be any better than that now operating in the churches if it wells up from the same spring, operating from Christendom impulses and with Christendom trajectories? Here our language may betray us. Newbigin, for all his assertions about the demise of Christendom and the fact that we can never go back to it,[9] continues to speak of "reseizing the high moral ground." The Christendom cast of the language is no less sharp when we are tempted to identify our agenda as "rewinning the West." George Hunter's recent book *How to Reach Secular People* (1992) is an important and sensitive introduction to ways we need to take seriously the people we seek to evangelize. But when it is assumed that secular people are "out there" and when it is not acknowledged that the cultural dynamics of secularity are as present in and among ourselves in the churches, such evangelism easily becomes an effort toward regaining the strength of a majority position, toward restoring a lost monopoly in the situation. Just as the culture's myth of individual freedom finds

8. Hall, *Has the Church a Future?* pp. 31–37.
9. Newbigin, *Foolishness to the Greeks,* pp. 102, 104.

verification in the material success of the social order, so we easily seek to affirm the rightness of our beliefs by the successful recruitment of converts. The more fundamental problem is to convert evangelism from recruitment geared toward institutional aggrandizement to announcement geared toward giving the news away.

To suggest that our agenda lies in the repositioning of the church (as Van Gelder has done) is certainly more to the point because it recognizes that the basic issue we face in our context is ecclesiological. The first order of business, before we engage the issues of evangelizing secular people or approaching the principalities and powers, is discerning who we are. We have lost our way on that. We await rediscovery. But here we must also be careful. Are we eager to reposition ourselves simply to ward off the uncomfortable effects of being marginalized? Are we most interested in finding new images for our identity so that we may again capture a place of importance and prominence in the social scheme of things? Is the reimaging driven by the need to be successful again?

I am suggesting in all of this that a self-conscious break with Christendom patterns of mission impulse must be the pervasive thread characterizing the Gospel and Our Culture agenda, in particular the strategies and forms we envision for the life of the local church as missionary congregation. Rather than a plan for reseizing, rewinning, and repositioning, we need a deeper revising (and "re-visioning").

In what follows I will venture to suggest the lines along which I have come to believe such re-visioning must take place, particularly in regard to the shape of the congregation as missionary. I will identify seven features for that reshaping and will try to show in each case how they represent a de-Christendomizing approach. I assume the general notion, made so vivid by Will Willimon and Stanley Hauerwas in *Resident Aliens* (1989) and shared by many, that we desperately need to learn how to be alternative communities. I am adding a stress on how much that must mean being alternative not only over against the dominant culture but also deliberately alternative to our own Christendom-become-accommodated past.

I speak as a missiologist (i.e., a scientist/participant/poet of the thing called mission) involved in preparing people for mission leadership. But academic though I am, I must confess here that there lurks deep down inside of me a pastor that always wants to break loose. That is both frightful and exciting. It is frightful because by memory and by observation I know the incredible pressures pastors face, especially in light of the shock waves of crisis currently rippling throughout the experience of our churches in North America. But somehow it is also exciting, perhaps because I can hardly conceive of a greater challenge at the present moment than discipling a Christian community. And I confess, I seem to have a strange confidence that a genuine, indigenous, faithful missionary ecclesiology really can grow from the stump of a church that has come to be, at one and the same time, both painfully disestablished and hopelessly domesticated. In that hope I offer these suggestions.

Visionary Leadership

I begin by speaking about pastoral leadership, not because I believe that churches are mere extensions of their pastors, but because pastoral styles can either break loose the logjams or bind them more tightly. I believe, as I have written in more detail elsewhere, that today's pastoral leader needs to give primary attention to four basic tasks.[10] These four do not describe discrete bits and pieces of a job description or strategic plan but represent pervasive tasks that undergird and inform all of the daily and weekly practicalities of the job of being "pastor."

The first, and perhaps most comprehensive, is *forming a communal "world."* We give shape to the "world" inhabited by the Christian community, and we do that in the most subtle of ways. At the heart of the pastoral task lies a concern with what Peter Berger has called the "social construction of reality." That is to say, we are engaged in the process normal to the life of human societies by which we construe the nature of our "reality," of our "life-world." World-construction is both subjective and objective in that it not only perceives the world in a certain way, but it also brings into being that very "world" as the one that people inhabit.

Walter Brueggemann contends that "for the community gathered around Jesus, it is precisely the act of worship that is the act of world-formation." It is in the act of praise that "the community of faith creates, orders, shapes, imagines, and patterns the world of God, the world of faith, the world of life, in which we are to act in joy and obedience." It is especially the task of ministry "to convene, evoke, form and re-form a community of praise and obedience . . . , an alternative community."[11]

A pastor's work touches on that world-formation at every turn, but

10. George R. Hunsberger, "The Changing Face of Ministry: Christian Leadership for the Twenty-First Century," *Reformed Review* 44, no. 3 (Summer 1991): 224–45.

11. Walter Brueggemann, *Israel's Praise: Doxology against Idolatry and Ideology* (Philadelphia: Fortress Press, 1987), pp. 26–28.

perhaps nowhere more directly or frequently than in worship. Our liturgical practices have tended to be either trivially personal or irrelevantly theological, but rarely a good marriage of life and gospel. There is a great need for us to indigenize the gospel content of our liturgies. What if, for instance, we said in our worship, "Lord, lighten our darkness" and allowed that to transfix us throughout as we touched open our darknesses. What if we said, "We have gathered to oppose the forces of evil, disavowing them by confessing the sin of our participation with them." Or, "What we are about to do subverts the political process. We acknowledge the forgiveness of God and forgive one another." Or when we come to the time of intercession, "We have come to the most radical and revolutionary moment in our worship. We are about to pray!"

It must be remembered that pastors engage in world-formation in and for a community. That means fully inviting, welcoming, and nurturing the companionship of the community in that casting. This begins to get at what I mean by "visionary leadership." It has become standard fare in church growth thinking to describe the "effective" pastor as the one who is a "vision leader." This usually conjures up the image of the pastor who has a well-defined idea of where the congregation needs to go and sees the path that will take them there. Such a leader rallies the troops around the vision and motivates a commitment to achieve that goal.

But that notion of vision has more to do with a plan of action or a tangible goal toward which to strive. There is a place for the kind of leadership that can help shape a congregation's aims in a crisp way. But that view of vision leadership is more tactical than strategic, no matter how grand the specifically envisioned goal may be. It misses what is more fundamental for the church, namely, its need to mature its vision of the world and of its own life as a gospeled community within it. In a post-Christendom, post-Enlightenment age, it is that which has become fuzzy, and for want of vision the people perish, even while pursuing someone's grand schemes. I propose a deepening refinement in the way we define the pastor as vision leader. The pastor's role involves (1) enabling the congregation (2) to reenvision itself (3) in a changed (and changing) environment. In other words, the pastor helps and encourages the congregation in the business of world-formation.

The other necessary pastoral tasks are really corollaries to the first. The second is casting a "wider rationality." The phrase is Newbigin's and refers to his sense that the gospel provides precisely what our modern scientific worldview does not, an indication of purpose, the purpose of God for the destiny of the world and the meaning of its history. Believing the

Bible's rendering of the character, actions, and purposes of that God does not mean, as the intimidating pressures of the culture tend to indicate, that we are less rational or irrational. It is right for us to understand that we embrace another rationality than that of the reigning culture, one that is wider and larger in its scope of explanation. This, and Newbigin's use of Michael Polanyi's account of *Personal Knowledge* in the first sixty-five pages of *The Gospel in a Pluralist Society* (1989), provides a way for the failure of nerve often noted as characteristic of the Western churches (which is really a failure of faith underneath it all) to be turned toward a growing confidence in the gospel.

Third, the pastor works toward *healing our fragmentary "worlds."* As Peter Berger observes in this highly pluralistic age, there is a kind of "base world" we all share together, certain ways of defining plausibility and providing places for our particular worlds. In actuality, however, we live in a multiplicity of "worlds." As we inhabit them in daily living, we experience two kinds of pluralism. One type is what Christopher Kaiser calls a horizontal pluralism, a plurality of communities, regions, and ethnicities in which are embodied distinctive subcultures within the larger culture. But each of us also experiences a vertical pluralism. We inhabit a number of distinct worlds — social constructions of reality — more or less simultaneously in our everyday lives. When we move from the factory world to our home world to the world of our children's schooling to a night out with our bowling league, we encounter worlds whose fundamental perspectives, principles, assumptions, and values are uniquely fashioned. Here our experience of pluralism becomes the most deeply personal. Negotiating pluralism is not just getting along with people who are different from me. It has to do with my own sense of identity in the midst of my fragmentary worlds.

Given this fragmentation, pastoring the church in a pluralistic society means giving attention to the need for healing along three fracture lines. First, healing is needed for the internal fracturing each of us experiences. Second, healing is needed between us; the fracture lines run between your worlds and mine. Third, the fracture line that segments off the church from other worlds and construes it to the larger society as simply another social world for the choosing begs for healing. (A major implication in all of this is that the work-worlds we inhabit must become primary agenda items within our gatherings. Only by engaging them directly will healing be possible in ourselves and our communities. The work of Marketplace Ministries and other similar emphases on the laity are crucial.)

Fourth, the pastor works at *igniting a subversive witness.* Most important here is the formation of the congregation's sense that in its life it is what Newbigin calls "the hermeneutic of the gospel."[12] This I will take up shortly as a major agenda item in its own right.

Disciplined Community

In his book *After Christendom?* Stanley Hauerwas asserts that in modern society the churches maintain their presence "by being communities of care," which has the effect of making it nearly impossible to be "a disciplined and disciplining community." That lost capacity is paralleled by the fact that the authority of ministers "is now primarily constituted by their ability to deliver pastoral services, rather than in liturgical leadership and the moral formation of the community."[13] His call for the recovery of disciplined community extends the call of *Resident Aliens* to be "an adventurous colony in a society of unbelief," a community of the cross, an alternative confessing community.[14]

The development of community is the primary tangible end that guides the pastor's work. We have for a long time emphasized discipling, but the notion was an individualized one. The same has tended to be true for our notions of education, evangelizing, equipping, training, and so forth. These are things we do to individual persons, one by one. Sometimes we do it in groups, but it is individuals being trained or equipped or educated in groups. What we need at this juncture, however, is the discipling of Christian communities, educating them to form as such, equipping them to live as such, evangelizing them into being disciple as group, as community.

David Bosch has put his finger on the nature of the shift this must entail. He notes the kind of paradigm we Protestants have inherited from our Reformation roots regarding the church. Because the Reformation churches emphasized so well that the marks of the true church are the right preaching of the gospel, the right administration of the sacraments, and (by some accounts) the exercise of church discipline, we have inherited the notion that the church is a place where certain things happen. This is in

12. Lesslie Newbigin, *The Gospel in a Pluralist Society* (Grand Rapids: Eerdmans, 1989), pp. 222–33.

13. Hauerwas, *After Christendom?* pp. 93–95.

14. Stanley Hauerwas and William H. Willimon, *Resident Aliens: Life in the Christian Colony* (Nashville: Abingdon Press, 1989), pp. 46–49.

sharp contrast to the notion that the church is a body of people sent on a mission, the notion that in many quarters is being recovered in the post-modern paradigm of mission. This recovery, however, is far from secured in the self-perception of congregations in North America. Different from the Reformation-induced model in only slight respects, we see the church as an institution where certain services are provided. The mission of the church, according to one part of a local congregation's mission statement, is to nurture and equip its members. The members, in that view, are the recipients of religious services and goods from an entity called church, not members together of a body called church which possesses a mission from God. The post-Christendom church will need to form itself as community in order to be missionary community.

Indwelling the Bible

How is such a community shaped? And how is its world to be cast? For the reshaping of the church as missionary community, there must be a recovery of the role of the Bible as formative of the community and the "world" it construes.

I recently read a sermon in which the preacher was reflecting back over the changes that had taken place during the forty years of his ministry.

> It was science then and the civilization that science was producing that was standard, and Christianity had to be accommodated to and made comfortable with that. . . . Today, however, looking back over forty years of ministry, I see an outstanding difference between then and now with regard to what is standard and who must do the adjusting. . . . Then we were trying to accommodate Christ to our scientific civilization; now we face the desperate need of accommodating our civilization to Christ. . . . Let the church stop its apologetic tone and face its gigantic task, unworthy though it is to face it, for the task is not to adjust Christ to this modern civilization but to adjust this modern civilization to Christ![15]

The Christendom confidence is still there. But the instinct to turn the tables is exactly right for the church itself today. Newbigin borrows from Polanyi the notion of indwelling to make a similar point. The church

---

15. Harry Emerson Fosdick, "After Forty Years of Ministry," in *A Great Time to Be Alive* (New York: Harper & Brothers, 1943), pp. 181–86.

"indwells" the biblical story as the clue to its own. "Its models and concepts are things which [the Christian believer] does not simply examine from the perspective of another set of models, but have become the models through which he or she understands the world. [The believer] has come to internalize them and to dwell in them."[16] This essential shift from looking *at* or *to* the Christian faith to looking *from* and *with* Christian faith focuses the goal for nurturing the Christian community.

Two corollaries follow. The first is that the community cannot indwell the Bible, any more than one can indwell a tool or instrument, without investing time. For the Christian community, it is a matter of time, time spent together, where talking happens. Second, if the Bible is indwelled so that it will become the lens through which the world is seen and understood, it must be used that way over and over again. The Bible, if indwelled, ceases to be the focus or object of study but becomes the tool for focusing on the dynamics of the surrounding (and internalized) culture, discerning the gospel's affirmation and critique of its features and hearing the call of God to be formed as an alternate community. As Willimon puts it in his helpful manual *Shaped by the Bible*, "How can we re-interpret the church to suit the demands of the Bible?" instead of vice versa.[17] In regard to both of these corollaries, the great importance of small groups, of "cells of Christianity" as the determining center of the life of our churches, should be immediately obvious.

Centered in the Reign of God

In a recent gathering of pastors and church leaders, I mentioned my sense of the great importance of the "reign of God" theme in the New Testament for understanding our mission. One pastor, known for his emphasis on missions and evangelism, asked what I meant by the reign of God, apparently sincere in the question and indicating that he just didn't know much about that. It is appalling that the central message of Jesus, "The reign of God is among you," is so strange-sounding on our lips and incomprehensible to our minds. Evangelism programs and models are bereft of even token acknowledgments of the notion. (A pleasant exception is *Joy to the World*, by Robert T. Henderson [1991].)

16. Newbigin, *The Gospel in a Pluralist Society*, p. 49. See also Lesslie Newbigin, *Truth to Tell: The Gospel as Public Truth* (Grand Rapids: Eerdmans, 1991), pp. 45ff.
17. William H. Willimon, *Shaped by the Bible* (Nashville: Abingdon Press, 1990), p. 63.

It seemed that Jesus expected the community of followers he shaped to thrive on the idea. I believe that is still so. And here, especially, we have important resources for shifting from our Christendom instincts. It might appear on the surface to be otherwise. After all, isn't the reign of God somewhat triumphalistic and maybe even militaristic? If Jesus himself is any example, however (and he said that he was), the reign of God rightly understood moves more toward humility, justice, gentleness, sacrifice, peace, suffering, and joy than the dynamics of our Christendom urges. What if we could learn that the reign of God is not present only when we reign, win, transform, fix, succeed, grow, or convince?

Paying attention to habitual biblical expressions regarding the reign of God may help us. In our day, we have come to recover the language of the reign/kingdom of God, but as we use the phrase in reference to the responsibilities of the Christian community, we commonly talk about "building" the kingdom, or "extending" the kingdom. To a certain extent, the first verb is the verb of choice for those more concerned for the social-ethical dimension of mission, the second for those more concerned for the evangelistic dimension. But both verbs express Christendom (colonial?) postures. And neither has precedent in the New Testament. Building imagery is used for the church, but not for the reign of God. There is growth imagery used for the reign of God, but not with any parallel injunction for us to extend it. Instead of these, the verbs used predominantly are "receive" and "enter." That is what we are told to "do" with the reign of God, which comes to us as gift and welcome.

Herein lies the prospect for a post-Christendom posture that does not need to succeed, except in the simple calling of being the people who are responding every day to the invitation of Jesus to be receiving and entering the reign of God that has come to be among us in himself. Evangelism is then not an effort to gain someone else's assent or recruit their loyalty but an offer of a gift, a welcome at the door — an invitation to come join us in receiving and entering the merciful and just reign of God.

Another example of the potential for centering the focus of the community lies in the Lord's Prayer. It has been suggested that the reference to the way "John taught his disciples" to pray in Luke 11:1 (in the request by Jesus' disciples that he teach them in the same way) should be understood as indicating the rabbinic practice of constructing a distinctive prayer as a summary of his most important teachings and thus a prayer that distinguished his disciples from those of other rabbis. If this is correct, it gives an important clue. The Lord's Prayer is then in the form of a summary of the gospel, the core of his teaching, the focus of his own praying and mission. It is also the badge of discipleship that marks us as distinctively his. It would obviously be his intention that it marked us not merely in the sounding of the words but in the living of its dynamics. Here, then, from the teaching of Jesus, we have his suggested centerpoint. I have often mused what it would be like if a congregation decided to suspend all of its many programs, events, meetings, committees, and groups for one year and would simply meet each Sunday morning around this prayer, hearing it, praying it, doing it, watching it, expecting it. What might happen and how might the church be redesigned from the ground up? I wonder.

The Hermeneutic of the Gospel

I have mentioned this notion of Newbigin's already. By it he means to indicate that the gospel can be known and understood only as it is being embodied in the life of some actual community of people who live by the Bible's story as their own. The only way that people can "come to believe that the power which has the last word in human affairs is represented by a man hanging on a cross" is through a "congregation of men and women who believe it and live by it." If this is true, evangelism emerges only as the congregation is prepared to give its life away to the world around it. All other evangelistic methods are purely secondary to this and have their power "only as they are rooted in and lead back to a believing community."[18]

In our pluralist environment, it has become especially crucial that evangelism be grounded not in an arguable logic but in a credible demonstration that life lived by the pattern of commitment to Jesus is imaginable, possible, and relevant in the modern and postmodern age. This requires more than what we meant previously when we called for verbal witness to rest on consistent Christian living. That tended to mean living exemplary, moral lives as upstanding citizens. It proved that Christianity measured up to the cultural requirements. The requirements of moral faithfulness are no less than they were, but another kind of demonstration is necessary now. It has become important to provide a demonstration that a faith in the gospel of God, against the grain of the culture's way of seeing, can be the genuine organizing center integrating the fragmented pieces of modern living. Only when that is seen lived out by someone who believes that way will the message about the reign of God have credibility. "The gospel will be perceived as a feasible alternative when those who do not know God

18. Newbigin, *The Gospel in a Pluralist Society*, p. 227.

have some positive, personal experiences with people who do."[19] (It is, perhaps, Donald Posterski's most important contribution to the "re-inventing" of evangelism that he seizes the horns of the pluralism dilemma and offers a way to witness by going into and through the culture's pluralist assumptions rather than by forming an evangelistic stance in resistance and opposition to those dynamics.)

It is mistaken to think that this somehow means that evangelism is stripped of its verbal, gospel-articulating character. The congregation is the hermeneutic, the lens through which the gospel will inevitably be read. But it will be the gospel that is read. A believing community gives voice to it. But this understanding of the congregation as hermeneutic does imply something about the style and manner of that voicing. Three images may serve as pointers toward a post-Christendom humility.

First, Newbigin suggests the image of a witness giving testimony "in a trial where it is contested" and where the verdict "will only be given at the end."[20] It is the function of such a witness "not to develop conclusions out of already known data, but simply to point to, report, affirm that which cannot come into the argument at all except simply as a new datum, a reality which is attested by a witness."[21] David Lowes Watson has suggested a shift from a sales model to a journalist model, keying on the recognition that evangelism is a global announcement that the reign of God is at hand.[22] Another model that commends itself in an age requiring that evangelists become meaning-makers[23] is that of docent, in the sense of its use in museums and the Atlanta Zoo. At the latter, docents are volunteers trained to mix among the crowds and be available to explain the various animal behaviors and habitats, providing interpretations of the worlds represented in the exhibits. Evangelism implies casting the "wider rationality" of a world seen as the location of the saving purposes of God.

19. Donald C. Posterski, *Reinventing Evangelism: New Strategies for Presenting Christ in Today's World* (Downers Grove, Ill.: InterVarsity Press, 1989), p. 32.

20. Newbigin, *Foolishness to the Greeks*, p. 68.

21. Lesslie Newbigin, *The Light Has Come: An Exposition of the Fourth Gospel* (Grand Rapids: Eerdmans, 1982), p. 18.

22. David Lowes Watson, "The Church as Journalist," *International Review of Mission* 72, no. 285 (1987): 57-74.

23. Cf. Posterski, *Reinventing Evangelism*, pp. 31-48.

GEORGE R. HUNSBERGER

Passion for the Common Good

For many, the image of exile (resident aliens, diaspora) grasps something of the heart of our contemporary experience and becomes suggestive for re-visioning our sense of identity in a post-Christendom era. It appears to some, however, that proposals such as these lead to insular sectarianism. The fear that an alternative community soon becomes an exclusive and closed community is based on good precedent. The concern is that the church not find in its need to be alternative a reason to excuse itself from responsibility for the world.

But here comes the rub. What categories do we have for the public responsibility of the church when it lives under new pluralistic rules and in a disestablished and peripherally privatized realm? What forms of "responsibility" are there that move beyond the Christendom baggage? The difficulty here lies in the easy presumption in our promotion of social justice that we know how things ought to be set up, and in our acts of charity and benevolence that we have what others need. In the WCC Commission on World Mission and Evangelism conference in San Antonio in 1989, it was interesting to watch the tone in the meetings and reports of two of the four sections. In the one dealing with evangelism and conversion, the report read with a necessary (and politically correct?) humility and respect for those of other convictions, religions, and cultures. The report expressed only with great care the continuing evangelistic mission of the church, which must be carried out with sensitivity in a spirit of dialogue. The other report was focused on several critical issues of justice in the world, most notably the Palestinians' cause and that of the Native Americans. The tone of the report was demanding and sure. There were no gray areas. The issues were clear and easily decided. The solutions called for were not presented for debate but for action. The report carried a tone of arrogant certainty.

In this area we may be on the most untested ground of all. I wish to suggest that we cast the issue in terms of the common good of our societies and that the requirement for the post-Christendom congregation is that it possess a passion for envisioning and seeking that common good. This stops short of requiring the Christendom mandate to transform the environment to correspond to the congregation's vision for it. But it disallows weak commitments that beg off because of the realities of the situation.

Within that framework, an exilic image may yet help, rather than hurt, the church's inclination toward seeking the common good, if properly understood. Jeremiah's letter to the exiles in Babylon provides a kind of guidance in this regard, especially because of its lack of Constantinian language (Jer. 29:1-14). The exiles were to seek the welfare of the city, but not from any impulse that they must somehow seize control of its policies and dictate its ideology. Nor was their welfare seeking to be done in order to justify themselves as pragmatically useful in the eyes of the ruling ethos, as the church has been pressed to do in modern American society. The impetus to seek the city's welfare was not even to be borne along by expectations of success in refashioning the shape of Babylon, but only by the recognition that their service announced greater realities than those upon which the Babylonian society was based (cf. Dan. 3:16-18).

If the Christendom image of our fit in the social scheme of things has played out and our prior sense of social responsibility was largely attached to it (in the espousal of both liberal and conservative agendas), what new sense must we gain of our God-given call to seek with passion the common good? In a religiously and ideologically plural setting, what is the place of Christian visions for what makes the common order "good"? How must they be sought or offered amid the alternate visions? If we seek the good not from a hope of success, then from what hope can we find motivation for representing the justice, peace, and joy of the reign of God?

A new cast to the very way we ask the questions is called for. While the carving of new paths for our thinking and action will not be easy and cannot be quickly achieved, at least several contours would appear to be important features for the way ahead. First, we must be self-conscious that *we offer our action for the common good within a pluralist setting and according to pluralist rules.* While the church seeks and finds its own identity beyond the definitions given by the culture, we cannot expect our participation in the social struggles to follow our rules. In this respect we will need to learn from the churches of the world that live out responsibility for the common good from their positions as minorities. The dynamics of mission in weakness and persistence at the margins will need to characterize our work.

Second, *our pursuit of the common good must be marked by a more rigorous holism.* The polarization between Christian action for social justice and Christian action for personal morality is problematic because both too easily represent an accommodation to the culture's individualist rights and interests. If the church only mimics the culture's loosening grip on the question about that which serves the *common* good and reflects the same tendency toward single-issue politics and constituency satisfaction, there will be little contribution that will distinguish the character of the coming reign of God the church represents.

Third, *our action for the common good requires more complete communal integrity within the church.* Whatever we espouse for the good of the society must be demonstrated by a living community that believes the vision enough to form its life around it. Ephraim Radner describes the shift implied as a movement from our tendency to think in terms of totalistic, theocratic transformation (a liberationist model) toward the recovery of a sense that it is "the growth and expansion of religious communities, separate but within the larger society, that will engender vehicles for noncoercive deliverance."[24] The church that pronounces concern for the homeless on the White House lawn, based on a set of values at odds with the culture, will welcome the homeless themselves into the shelter of their homes and houses of worship. For that integrity, Radner suggests, the image of exile serves better than one of liberation. In that image, the church becomes "a vessel of deliverance" rather than its agent.

Fourth, *our care for the common good must grow from a care-filled eschatology.* To say it that way is to distinguish such an eschatology from an overly "careful" — in the sense of reticent — eschatology that holds back from risk taking and vulnerability. On the other side, it distinguishes it from a "careless" — in the sense of reckless — eschatology that blusters on triumphalistically. We need to learn a pursuit of the common good that sets aside both our hand-wringing and our utopianisms, both our hand-washing self-justifications and our demanding impositions. It is the reign *of God,* after all, that is coming, and our assurance of that creates confident and humble action.

Intentional Pluriformity

A cluster of images crowd into my mind when I ask myself to imagine in what forms such churches as I have been attempting to describe might appear. The images tell me something about a bias I have. All of the images have some significant element of multiculturalism. I should have expected that.

If a student in preparation for ministry came to me and said, "I want to pastor a church in a way that responds to the challenges you have described. I want to learn how," where would I send her or him? At whose feet could someone learn? My first response would be that it would have

24. Ephraim Radner, "From 'Liberation' to 'Exile': A New Image for Church Mission," *Christian Century,* October 18, 1989, p. 933.

to be somewhere outside the comfort zones of our accustomed affluence. It will not be learned from rich Christians or churches, from the successful pastors. My next instinct would be to send them among the urban core, storefront, ethnic, charismatic churches. We will have to take our cues from such churches. In my view of things, these are the incipient twenty-first-century church of North America. They represent the future forms of the church's flowering in the postmodern world. (And they are the ones most like the coming churches of the Third World.)

There are reasons attached to this bias. William Myers has illustrated a major reason in his book *Black and White Styles in Youth Ministry* (1991). In it he compares the youth ministry programs in two churches, one black and one white. In the white church, the program "unreflectively strives to transmit a culture that . . . has blessed the members of the church"; in the black church, the program "critically distances itself from a culture that has proven . . . to be untrustworthy."[25] The resources for being alternative will have to come from those whose survival has long been bound up with being in community.

In line with that, several images of the future come to mind. In post-Christendom churches the staff will be multicultural. It will be diverse in gender, ethnicity, and nationality. Such churches will invite missionaries from other countries of the world, especially Third World countries. Reciprocal mission, a buzzword in many denominational bureaucracies, will take on real meaning as missionaries-in-reverse will come to do real missionary work, like pastoring, church planting, evangelism, ministries for the common good, continuing pastoral education, spiritual formation, and so forth (and not just cultural exchange and news from the overseas churches). These churches of the future will never engage in evangelism programs as single congregations. Evangelism will always consist of local ecumenical strategies in order to subvert mere recruitment and protect the genuineness of the Christian community's commitment to represent the gospel by announcement that the reign of God is at hand.

At the heart of these churches there will be the spirit of giving the gospel away, and therefore giving themselves away. The loss of things, the loss of time, and the loss of power and influence will be their common experience. They will know that if a church seeks to save its own life, it will lose it. And if a church loses its life for the sake of Christ, it will find it.

25. William R. Myers, *Black and White Styles in Youth Ministry* (New York: Pilgrim Press, 1991), p. 152.

• 5 •

Reformed Spirituality and the Moral Law

RICHARD L. SPENCER

A FASCINATING and revelatory conjunction has occurred in the life of the contemporary American Presbyterian Church: a series of scholarly analyses of American Presbyterianism[1] have appeared at approximately the same time as two influential books about Reformed spirituality written by prominent Presbyterian seminary professors.[2] The authors of the series attempt multidisciplinary analyses of the decline of Presbyterianism in North America. The authors of the two books seek to restore the vitality of the same Presbyterians.

The now-famous studies have been reviewed very critically by Edward A. Dowey and Richard K. Fenn, both of Princeton Theological Sem-

---

1. The seven volumes in the series, edited by Milton J. Coalter, John M. Mulder, and Louis B. Weeks, were published by Westminster/John Knox Press of Louisville: *The Presbyterian Predicament: Six Perspectives* (1990); *The Confessional Mosaic: Presbyterians and Twentieth-Century Theology* (1990); *The Mainstream Protestant "Decline": The Presbyterian Pattern* (1990); *The Diversity of Discipleship: Presbyterians and Twentieth-Century Christian Witness* (1991); *The Organizational Revolution: Presbyterians and American Denominationalism* (1992); *The Pluralistic Vision: Presbyterians and Mainstream Protestant Education and Leadership* (1992); and *The Re-Forming Tradition: Presbyterians and Mainstream Protestantism* (1992).

2. Robert H. Ramey, Jr., and Ben Campbell Johnson, *Living the Christian Life: A Guide to Reformed Spirituality* (Louisville: Westminster/John Knox Press, 1992); and Howard L. Rice, *Reformed Spirituality: An Introduction for Believers* (Louisville: Westminster/John Knox Press, 1991). Both of these works have philosophical and hermeneutical roots in Jungian psychology. Johnson acknowledges this debt in his earlier works. Rice reveals the (at least) secondary dependence on Jungian thought through his acknowledgment of the direct influence of Morton Kelsey, who, in turn, is profoundly indebted to Jung.

inary, who suggest that the failings of these studies are themselves diagnostic of the Presbyterian denomination's plight.[3]

As if answering the concerns raised by the studies of the denomination, Presbyterian teachers Howard L. Rice, Robert H. Ramey, Jr., and Ben Campbell Johnson address the church's need for fresh emphasis on Reformed spirituality and the Christian life. Though the authors approach their task in somewhat different ways, both fail to satisfy precisely at the points raised by Dowey and Fenn. In both cases, insufficient attention to Reformed confessional identity is at issue.[4]

The case will be made here that restoration of a fundamental theme of Reformed theology and ethics can address the concerns raised by Dowey and Fenn and can strengthen the recommendations made by Rice, Ramey, and Johnson in service of the renewal of the church. It is a theme that is found at the very heart of Calvin's theology and is substantially embodied in the Westminster documents — especially the Larger Catechism. That theme is the ordering work of the Holy Spirit and, more particularly, the role of the moral law in that ordering work.[5]

Two Defining Critiques

Dowey's critique paves the way for this theme. He complains in particular regarding the role of the terms "pluralism" and "re-formation" in the series edited by Coalter, Mulder, and Weeks. With reference to the first, Dowey

---

3. Edward A. Dowey, review of *The Re-Forming Tradition: Presbyterians and Mainstream Protestantism, Princeton Seminary Bulletin,* n.s., 14, no. 1 (1993): 1–10; and Richard K. Fenn, review of *The Mainstream Protestant "Decline": The Presbyterian Pattern,* ibid., pp. 11–17. Dowey, as Archibald Alexander Professor Emeritus of the History of Christian Doctrine at Princeton and as the principal architect of the Presbyterian Confession of 1967, is in a nearly unique position to evaluate these studies in light of our Reformed confessional heritage. Fenn, for his part, as Maxwell M. Upson Professor of Christianity and Society, is especially sensitive to questions of "relevance" in the church's efforts to promote a social and political agenda.

4. The urgent need for confessional-theological renewal is expressed by Allen C. McSween, Jr., in his article "The Possibility of the Renewal of Reformed Theology in the Church," in *Calvin Studies,* vol. 3, ed. John H. Leith (Davidson, N.C.: Davidson College, 1986), pp. 39–46. Though his recommendations are more general than those to be made here, the fundamental thrust of his argument supports the one made here.

5. Two works have been especially helpful at this point: M. Eugene Osterhaven, *The Faith of the Church: A Reformed Perspective on Its Historical Development* (Grand Rapids: Eerdmans, 1982); and Ronald S. Wallace, *Calvin's Doctrine of the Christian Life* (Grand Rapids: Eerdmans, 1959).

says that the variety of views and programs in the church has become a disjunctive pluralism that our confessionalism must reject. With reference to the second, he says that the use of the term "re-formation" may sound like "Reformation," but it refers not to the dynamic and ongoing renewal of the church according to the Word of God but rather to untheological criteria of success.[6] "The Protestant-Puritan-Presbyterian story, now nearly five centuries old, may be ending. We cannot tell. Our question now should not be 'are we successful?' but 'are we faithful?'"[7] In other words, the church's hope for authentic renewal is the same as it has always been: *ecclesia reformata, semper reformanda secundum verbum Dei*. Our current need for reformation (not "re-formation"!) can be met only by the one reality that first called us into being: the Word of God.

Fenn finds in the most constructively programmatic of the studies of denominational life evidence of "two very difficult trends" in the lives of typical Presbyterian church members.

> One places religion, the life of the spirit, and the possession of the soul well outside the jurisdiction of the church. The other trend makes it ever more likely that the laity's own commitments and obligations will be increasingly partial, particular, temporary, and negotiable. Neither of these trends augurs well for large-scale organizations that take themselves very seriously and are top-heavy with trained personnel and officials.[8]

Fenn sees a paradox in the church: chaotic fragmentation in the lives of the members has grown, even as the church has moved toward increased clericalization. The Presbyterian Church, he notes, has become top-heavy (especially in the denominational bureaucracies), at the same time that its members have drifted into marginally connected or integrated faith. The church has become for its members as permeable and chaotic as other human organizations have become under the impact of modernity. "Clerical imperialism," as he calls it, is not the answer. The people need worship and nurture that works to liberate and empower them. "Sunday morning may be the moment in their lives that helps them to make up for lost time

---

6. Dowey, review, pp. 9–10. "It is noteworthy, given the work we see, that this series is not claiming Reformed principles, but rather 're-formation,' a pusillanimous coinage that calls to mind its cognate, Reformed, without taking any position on what the Reformed tradition considers itself to be. Beware! We must not, like Stephen Leacock's hero, jump on a horse and gallop off madly in all directions. No polity could survive that, nor would it be worth the surviving" (p. 9).

7. Ibid., p. 10.

8. Fenn, review, p. 16.

and liberates them from the tyranny of organizational schedules, fiscal years, and the inexorable passage of time itself."[9]

Dowey and Fenn point the church beyond sociological and programmatic issues to the essential spiritual life of the people under the impact of the Word of God, understood according to our great confessions within the Presbyterian tradition.

Two Efforts in Support of Renewal

The Presbyterian seminaries are not failing to rise to the occasion of the church's need. Teachers at San Francisco Theological Seminary, on the one hand, and Columbia Theological Seminary (Decatur, Ga.), on the other, have very recently brought forth helpful guides on Reformed spirituality and the Christian life.

Howard Rice's *Reformed Spirituality,* on the one hand, and Robert Ramey and Ben Campbell Johnson's *Living the Christian Life,* on the other, do address the church's need for authentic renewal. Yet both works miss the mark at precisely the points raised by Dowey and Fenn.

Rice begins with experience as his basic concern and carries this theme forward throughout the book. "Because Reformed Protestants do not recognize and are not taught that there is a spiritual tradition within their own heritage, they have frequently had no basis to integrate their own experience into their faith or church life. They have been hesitant even to speak about their religious experiences for fear of being ridiculed or rejected."[10] Rice attempts to provide an authentically Reformed basis for having authentic spiritual experience and for integrating that experience into the larger matters of faith and into the life of the church. While his work provides a conceptual framework for spiritual experience, it misses the central genius of Calvin's theology of the Christian life, namely, the dynamic praxis of believer and fellowship, under the impact of the Holy Spirit's regenerating and reordering work, in which experience is always defined within the life-transformative agendas of God's commands. Without this agenda and dynamic praxis, personal experience tends to remain subjective and discrete — and vulnerable to the fragmenting influences of modernity referred to by Fenn.

When Rice does deal with the ongoing relevance of the divine com-

9. Ibid., p. 17.
10. Rice, *Reformed Spirituality,* p. 10.

mands (the "third use of the law"), he suggests that its principal value is as a guide to the conscience.[11] Having made this point, he immediately abandons the theme and moves on to complain of the moral standards of the Puritans. His subjectivization of the "third use" leaves the Presbyterian Christian in at best a "sub-Reformed" piety. The third use of the law in Reformed Christian living, as will be developed below, is both intensely spiritual and intensely practical. In fact, it cannot be authentic unless it is in an ongoing dynamic process of both discovery and realization (in the sense of giving substantial shape to lived reality). This version of Reformed spirituality is never abstractable from Reformed praxis, hence the difficulty Rice has of finding a conceptual basis for his agenda. (This is a major reason that the effort to bring "spiritual formation" to the life of the seminarian just does not ring true for Presbyterians. "Discipleship" is the better term for our tradition, for it connotes praxis as well as spiritual growth. For the Calvinist, spiritual growth will simply not go forward without the reordering of external life. In any case, "spiritual formation" is conceptually dependent on an Aristotelian-Thomistic teleology and a theology of virtue that carry with them a vision of maturity that is foreign to Calvin.)

Ramey and Johnson have a more auspicious beginning for their book. Their preface includes a splendid quote from John Mackay, late president of Princeton Theological Seminary: "Deep in the heart of Calvinism, and in Presbyterianism, in its truest and most classical form, resides a profound piety, that is, a passionate experience of God. . . . It is piety in this sense that provides the requisite dynamic for the conduct of church affairs and the application of Christianity to life in all its fulness."[12]

As theologian, administrator, and former missionary, Mackay surely grasped the essential praxis of Reformed faith and life when he connected piety and conduct. Ramey and Johnson do better than Rice in developing this theme in their book, especially in the chapter "Spirituality as Reconciliation in the World."[13] Yet nowhere in that chapter do they suggest that the divine commands have a role in the process. They have dealt with the commands seventy pages earlier under the heading "Scripture as Authority." They have not grasped Calvin's integration of the third use of the law into the larger pattern of the Spirit's work to restore order (including, of course, love and justice) to the life of the Christian, of the church, and of the larger

11. Ibid., p. 183.
12. John A Mackay, *The Presbyterian Way of Life* (Englewood Cliffs, N.J.: Prentice-Hall, 1960), p. 9, quoted in Ramey and Johnson, *Living the Christian Life*, p. 9.
13. Ramey and Johnson, *Living the Christian Life*, pp. 126–36.

community. Therefore they, like Rice, leave the Christian without one of the truly essential keys to Reformed faith and living.

It therefore seems especially timely to focus on this neglected theme in the Reformed faith and suggest how it may address these concerns.

Order, the Spirit, and the Law

Over 120 years ago, Charles Hodge wrote the following words, which distill a basic, systemic theme of John Calvin's theology: "All truth is enforced on the heart and conscience with more or less power by the Holy Spirit, wherever that truth is known. To this all-pervading influence we are indebted for all there is of morality and order in the world."[14] Three uses here of the word "all" and the use of the word "wherever" suggest how fundamental this theological affirmation is for Reformed theology and faith. It is the Holy Spirit who not only enforces the truth on the heart and conscience, as Reformed theologians universally acknowledge, but also brings about all of the morality and order that the world knows. This latter affirmation is usually made today only by those theologians who also affirm the Reformed theology of "common grace."[15] However, Hodge's affirmation is not limited to the common-grace theme. It brings into view more than order and morality. It draws our attention to the ways that order and morality come into human life — especially how they come most effectively in the life of the Christian and of the church.

It seems defensible to claim that the theme of order and the work of the Holy Spirit are at least as central to Calvin's whole theological work as any other theme. M. Eugene Osterhaven makes the case that this theme, though not a "system principle" for Calvin's theology, nonetheless provides a useful rubric by means of which to understand his most significant theological contribution.[16] Two aspects of Calvin's contribution will be treated here and are central

14. Charles Hodge, *Systematic Theology,* 3 vols. (New York: Charles Scribner & Sons, 1872), 1:532.

15. Usually Dutch Reformed theologians. See John H. Leith, *Introduction to the Reformed Tradition* (Atlanta: John Knox Press, 1977). A recent effort to construe common grace in terms of the "cosmic work of the Holy Spirit" is probably best found in Werner Krusche, *Das Wirken des Heiligen Geistes nach Calvin* (Göttingen: Vandenhoeck & Ruprecht, 1957).

16. M. Eugene Osterhaven, *The Faith of the Church: A Reformed Perspective on Its Historical Development* (Grand Rapids: Eerdmans, 1982), pp. 162–93. For supporting literature, see especially Josef Bohatec, *Calvin und das Recht* (Feudingen i. Westf.: Buchdruckerei und Verlangsanstalt G.m.b.H., 1934); I. John Hesselink, *Calvin's Concept of the Law* (Allison

for the purposes of this essay: (1) salvation as the restoration of order, and (2) the third use of the law as an essential element in that ordering work.

Salvation as the Restoration of Order

In his commentary on Psalm 96:10, Calvin wrote the following:

> So long as ungodliness has possession of the minds of men, the world, plunged as it is in darkness, must be considered as thrown into a state of confusion, and of horrible disorder and misrule; for there can be no stability apart from God. . . . No order can be said to prevail in the world, until God erect his throne and reign amongst men. What more monstrous disorder can be conceived of, than exists where the Creator himself is not acknowledged? . . . If God's method of governing men be to form and regulate their lives to righteousness, we may infer, that however easily men may be satisfied with themselves, all is necessarily wrong with them, till they have been made subject to Christ. And this righteousness has not reference merely to the outward actions. It comprehends a new heart, commencing as it does in the regeneration of the Spirit, by which we are formed again into the likeness of God.[17]

Four essential points emerge from this commentary by Calvin: (1) sin and ungodliness have left the world in a state of chaos and disorder; (2) only God can restore order to the fallen creation; (3) subjection to Christ is the key to that restoration of order; and (4) the process of restoration is a work of the Holy Spirit.[18] The original image of God in us was one of perfect and harmonious order, afterward disordered and thrown into chaos by sin and the Fall, and only through the mediation of Jesus Christ and the work of the Spirit is a restoration put in process in the life of the individual, of the church, and of the larger community.[19]

Park, Penn.: Pickwick Publications, 1992); Ronald S. Wallace, *Calvin's Doctrine of the Christian Life* (Grand Rapids: Eerdmans, 1959). See also Charles Partee, "Calvin's Central Dogma Again," in *Calvin Studies*, vol. 3, ed. John H. Leith (Davidson, N.C.: Davidson College, 1986), pp. 39–46. Partee finds "union with Christ" to be the most revelatory theme for all of Calvin's theology. This theme, when worked out in detail, may be seen as the substance of which "order and the Spirit" is the process.

17. Quoted in Osterhaven, *The Faith of the Church*, p. 169.
18. See Wallace, *Calvin's Doctrine of the Christian Life*, p. 107.
19. Osterhaven, *The Faith of the Church*, p. 171.

The Holy Spirit has an instrument that is used in making this salvation effective and in restoring order. That instrument is the Word of God. According to Osterhaven, "The broadest meaning of the Word is God's entire disclosure of Himself and his purposes, which was mediated through the prophets, apostles, and the Lord Jesus Christ. . . . Long in coming to its final fulness, but authoritative and endowed with divine power from its first utterance, the Word is the principle of order used by the Spirit in the formation of the body, the church, and in the nurture and edification of its individual members."[20] The proclamation of the Word is confirmed in the hearts of believers by the Holy Spirit. They are united to Christ by faith, hence initiating the great work of restoring the lost order. (Note the use of the word "formation" in this context, indicating reordering.) The individual Christian and the church, in turn, are used of God to bring a semblance of order to the larger community and to the life of the state. They are "salt" and "light" in the world.

The Third Use of the Law

Thus a process begins by the work of the Holy Spirit that continues throughout the life of the believer: a work of renewing the image of God, one that consists in righteousness and holiness. Ronald S. Wallace reveals the next logical step in Calvin's teaching.

> The renovation of man in the heavenly image is "manifested by the fruits produced by it, viz., justice, judgment and mercy." But this life of righteousness and holiness is simply life lived according to the law of God as summed up in the two tables of the Ten Commandments, which sum up the fruits of repentance and outline what the image of God consists in. Therefore to live a life ordered according to the image of God is to live according to the law of God.[21]

The life that reflects the Spirit's work in restoring the image of God is a life that is lived in active and prayerful conformity to the will of God as manifested in the commandments. I. John Hesselink has reminded us that for Calvin, the principal use of the law in the life of the believer was the so-called third use, that is, as a norm and guide for faith and conduct.[22]

20. Ibid.
21. Wallace, *Calvin's Doctrine of the Christian Life*, p. 112. The quotation from Calvin is from *Institutes* 3.3.8.
22. I. John Hesselink, "Law," in *Encyclopedia of the Reformed Faith*, ed. Donald M. McKim (Louisville: Westminster/John Knox Press, 1992), pp. 215–17.

The true Christian learns from the commands of God to live faithfully toward God and the neighbor. The first four commands of the Decalogue teach us of our duty to God and are summed up in the first Great Commandment. The final six teach us of our duty to our neighbor and are summed up in the second Great Commandment. The believer who contemplates these as essential counsels of God for the right living of this life finds the Spirit at work to weave them into the fabric of the heart as well as into the living of the outward life.[23] The disordered life is permeated with an ordering force, the Spirit of God, who uses the actual commands of God to give it a new and increasingly ordered quality.

Calvin did not leave his teaching general at this point. He provided a provocative and intensely practical hermeneutic of the commandments.[24] This hermeneutic is faithfully embodied in the Westminster Larger Catechism:

Q. 99. What rules are to be observed for the right understanding of the Ten Commandments?

A. For the right understanding of the Ten Commandments, these rules are to be observed:

1. That the law is perfect, and bindeth everyone to full conformity in the whole man unto the righteousness thereof, and unto entire obedience forever; so as to require the utmost perfection of every duty, and to forbid the least degree of every sin.

2. That it is spiritual, and so reacheth the understanding, will, affections, and all other powers of the soul; as well as words, works, and gestures.

3. That one and the same thing, in divers respects, is required or forbidden in several commandments.

4. That as, where a duty is commanded, the contrary sin is forbidden; and where a sin is forbidden, the contrary duty is commanded: so, where a promise is annexed, the contrary threatening is included; and where a threatening annexed, the contrary promise is included.

5. That what God forbids is at no time to be done; what he commands is always our duty; and yet every particular duty is not to be done at all times.

6. That, under one sin or duty, all of the same kind are forbidden or commanded; together with all the causes, means, occasions, and appearances thereof, and provocations thereunto.

23. *Institutes* 2.8.8–9.
24. *Institutes* 2.8.5.

7. That what is forbidden or commanded to ourselves, we are bound, according to our places, to endeavor that it may be avoided or performed by others, according to the duty of their places.

8. That in what is commanded to others, we are bound, according to our places and callings, to be helpful to them: and to take heed of partaking with others in what is forbidden to them.[25]

If the modern reader of these hermeneutical rules can resist the temptation to reject them out of hand as part and parcel of an old orthodox legalism (into which they certainly can be corrupted — as is the case with any form of ethical reasoning, including contextualism), then some wonderfully fruitful benefits can be discerned. These benefits are largely dependent on keeping fully in view that this counsel is set within the third use of the law, that is, the law as it is useful for those regenerated by the Spirit, no longer under the law's condemnation (Rom. 8:1-2).

First, they remind all who read them of the universality of God's commands, a universality that resists egocentric exceptions. Second, the commands are seen to be "spiritual," that is, part of the work of the Holy Spirit in reordering the inner and outer lives of believers. Third, they are to be observed by an engaged and informed mind. In other words, believers are to be fairly sophisticated in the processes of moral reasoning according to the commands of God.

This third quality fits well with the Reformed insistence on the "priesthood of all believers" and on the honoring of all proper vocations of whatever social standing. Believers are to engage moral questions with growing sophistication in a theological-spiritual version of what is called in our century "taking the moral point of view." They will then, inevitably, tend to form spiritual democracies of all citizens of the kingdom of Christ who are under the same and socially undifferentiated commands of God. This spiritual democracy then tends to shape a similar process in terms of the political citizenship of the same believers. The Holy Spirit's ordering work through the positive use of the law serves a socially transformative process by bringing into being morally self-directed people who make the commands of God indispensable residents and guides of their inner lives — and of their outer policies and habits.

25. The text of the Westminster Larger Catechism is from *The Constitution of the Presbyterian Church*, part 1, *Book of Confessions* (Louisville: Office of the General Assembly, 1991), 7.111–7.306 (pagination is not standard).

The third use of the law, contrary to its bad press in some quarters, actually lifts up "every person" as a precious and responsible keeper of the precious commands.

> There is no doubt that the perfect teaching of righteousness that the Lord claims for the law has a perpetual validity. Not content with it, however, we labor mightily to contrive and forge good works upon good works. The best remedy to cure that fault will be to fix this thought firmly in mind: the law has been divinely handed down to us to teach us perfect righteousness; there no other righteousness is taught than that which conforms to the requirements of God's will; in vain therefore do we attempt new forms of works to win the favor of God, whose lawful worship consists in obedience alone; rather, any zeal for good works that wanders outside God's law is an intolerable profanation of divine and true righteousness.[26]

For Calvin, the commands of God provide the fundamental structure of the moral life of the Christian. The Reformed vision of the faithful life simply cannot be grasped without this basic truth. The third use of the law provides the structure of engagement with personal life, the life of the church, and the life of the world.

The Third Use and the Contemporary Christian Life

In his *Institutes,* Calvin related the law to the expression of the image of God. "Now it will not be difficult to decide the purpose of the whole law: the fulfillment of righteousness to form human life to the archetype of divine purity. For God has so depicted his character in the law that if any man carries out in deeds whatever is enjoined there, he will express the image of God, as it were, in his own life."[27]

The process by which the Holy Spirit works to restore the effaced image of God in human life includes, indispensably, the intentional, diligent, and persistent use of the commands of God as guides for the conduct of life and for the agendas of piety and worship. For the Christian life to be effective in realizing God's purposes in church and world, that life must find in the law "all the duties of piety and love."

26. *Institutes* 2.8.5.
27. Ibid. 2.8.51.

It would, therefore, be a mistake for anyone to believe that the law teaches nothing but some rudiments and preliminaries of righteousness by which men begin their apprenticeship, and does not also guide them to the true goal, good works, since you cannot desire a greater perfection than that expressed in the statements of Moses and Paul. For whither, I submit, will any man wish to go who will not be content to be taught to fear God, to worship spiritually, to obey the commandments, to follow the Lord's upright way, and lastly, to have a pure conscience, sincere faith, and love? From this is confirmed that interpretation of the law which seeks and finds in the commandments of the law all the duties of piety and love. For those who follow only dry and bare rudiments — as if the law taught them only half of God's will — do not at all understand its purpose, as the apostle testifies.[28]

This use of the law, in other words, is as deep and as constantly relevant as any other dimension of Christian faith. A Reformed spirituality that does not fully account for this dimension, in the context of the Holy Spirit's reordering work, does not represent the heart of Calvin's own counsel.

In order to make this counsel more accessible to the contemporary person, an outline of its value to our time may be useful. Three aspects of the use of law are suggested: the heuristic, the pedagogical, and the programmatic.

The Heuristic Use of the Law

Calvin says that the law helps believers "to learn more thoroughly each day the nature of the Lord's will to which they aspire, and to confirm them in the understanding of it."[29] As the believer considers in depth the two Great Commandments and the Decalogue, now understood according to the hermeneutical principles outlined above, the believer has an interpretive grid for organizing the kinds of questions that may be posed regarding responsible behavior. God's will is not located in transcendent irrelevance but rather is concerned with life in the most mundane places of this world — places that can be examined and discerned when seen as the theater of the law's relevance.

The complaint is sometimes heard that the expression of the commandments found in the Westminster Larger Catechism is too detailed. Yet

28. Ibid.
29. Ibid. 2.7.12.

the catechism is more relevant precisely because it is bold in discerning how the general commands may be operationalized in the particular realities faced in everyday life. If one can avoid making its applications into pharisaical standards, then the confession's explication of the commands can be seen as a very creative and heuristically useful development.

The Pedagogical Use of the Law

Perhaps the best-known statement of this theme has been made by Helmut Thielicke in his magisterial *Theological Ethics*. "The justified man must inquire of the particular laws . . . whether and how far he has really given attention to the actualization of his faith in the particular spheres of life."[30] Yet Thielicke's Lutheran commitments restrain him from fully endorsing the Reformed "third use." Nonetheless, he provides a helpful conceptualization for us with his use of the terms "inquire" and "actualization." Thielicke is right in suggesting that the commands of God reveal our responsibilities in the "spheres of life." He is also right in suggesting that a process of actualization is at work. We have to look to Calvin, however, to learn the full meaning of the process of actualization under the impact of the Spirit's ordering work.

Each of the commands provides us with agendas: for learning, for growth in actualized obedience, and for experience of God's faithfulness as we seek to embody his manifest will. They provide for a divine pedagogy that includes discipline (Heb. 12:5-11) and an ongoing dynamic process of discovery and realization of the Spirit's work in us.

The Programmatic Use of the Law

The faithful believer is not content merely to understand "duty" abstractly but is driven by love and the ongoing dynamic of the Spirit's work (which never allows one to remain at a given point, satisfied that no further progess is to be made) to ever-fresh realizations of that duty in the relations of the common life. Therefore, when the fifth commandment is interpreted (as it is in the Westminster Larger Confession) as having as its scope "the performance of those duties which we mutually owe in our several relations,

---

30. Helmut Thielicke, *Theological Ethics*, vol. 1, *Foundations*, ed. William Lazareth (Philadelphia: Fortress Press, 1966), p. 138.

as inferiors, superiors, or equals,"[31] it declares criteria of mutuality that can become an active program for their realization. Standards become policy, and policy can become politics and law. Citizens nurtured by this counsel are likely to seek to embody in justice what God's law commands, including the very relevant counsel that "superiors" sin against "inferiors" by the "careless exposing or leaving them to wrong, temptation, and danger; provoking them to wrath; in any way dishonoring themselves, or lessening their authority, by an unjust, indiscreet, rigorous, or remiss behavior."[32]

This programmatic aspect of the law's use has a relentlessly forward-pressing quality that tends to resist any effort to establish institutions that can become "ontocratic."[33] The Spirit's work is always an ordering work that remains unfinished and therefore puts all realizations under pressure until the kingdom of God finally comes in fullness.

Conclusion

As Presbyterians and other Reformed Christians search for the keys to relevance and effective church life, they will do well to "look to the quarry from which they have been dug." There are yet resources in a balanced Calvinism for revitalizing Christian life today. They are resources that turn out to be burningly relevant and wonderfully applicable at the end of the twentieth century. Oliver O'Donovan summarizes the matter for us this way: "The command of God is not to be dismissed as an unevangelical *preparatio evangelii*. It is not a crutch; it is a life-giving command, 'Rise, take up your bed and walk!' "[34]

---

31. Westminster Larger Catechism, Q. 126.

32. Ibid., Q. 130.

33. For this concept, see Arend van Leeuwen, *Christianity in World History* (London: Edinburgh House Press, 1964); and Charles C. West, *The Power to Be Human* (New York: Macmillan, 1971).

34. Oliver O'Donovan, *Resurrection and Moral Order: An Outline for Evangelical Ethics* (Grand Rapids: Eerdmans, 1986), p. 154. See also p. 247: "Again, when we speak of the Christian moral life as lived in the Spirit, we declare that this life is itself part of the divine self-disclosure, and as such points us forward to the goal of that self-disclosure. The Holy Spirit, outside of whose field of operation the Christian moral life is unthinkable, is a signpost to the future, 'the earnest of our inheritance pointing to the redemption of God's possession' (Eph. 1:14)."

• 6 •

The Seventeenth-Century
Ecumenical Interchanges

ANRI MORIMOTO

For Reformed theology, the seventeenth century is the century of Scholastic orthodoxy. It is the fountain of a number of confessional formulas and creeds that have come to demarcate the outline of the present Reformed faith, and most of these forms were produced in polemical settings against the Roman Catholic or Lutheran faith. To that extent, the seventeenth-century Reformed theology may not look all that propitious to the cause of ecumenical dialogue. The purpose of the present article is to add to such a general perception a small footnote, to the effect that there were in fact significant crosscurrents that did transcend the confessional barrier in the seventeenth century and the next. As we commemorate the legacy of Professor Charles West, who has long been an ecumenist both in theology and practice while remaining distinctively Reformed in faith, it may not be totally out of place to take note of the pristine ecumenicity of Reformed theology. Reformed faith in the making was not as self-enclosed as might be supposed today. Even at the height of polemical exchanges, it remained open to recognizing and learning from the truths of other theological traditions. In that sense, ecumenical dialogue is not an exclusive property of our century.

The theologian we take up here as a sign of such ecumenical interchanges is François Turrettini (1623–87). Turrettini, perhaps the champion and grandmaster of Reformed polemics, is, among other theologians, frequently cited in Heppe's *Reformed Dogmatics*.[1] Born to the family of an

---

1. Heinrich Heppe, *Reformed Dogmatics: Set Out and Illustrated from the Sources*, ed.

86

immigrant Reformed orthodox theologian in Geneva, Turrettini was himself a pastor and professor of Reformed theology, whose teachings culminated in a three-volume set of argumentative theology, *Institutio theologiae elencticae* (1st ed., 1679–85),[2] as well as in the formation of *The Helvetic Consensus Formula* (1675). The formula is a product of Scholasticism expressly designed to defend orthodox Calvinism from the infiltration of Saumur teachings and marks the official closing of the period of Reformed creeds.[3] Turrettini is therefore not without reason described by historians of theology as "a stalwart" who did his best to halt "the growing rigidity" of Reformed theology "during what was virtually its last generation."[4]

What is less well known about Turrettini is that this defender and upholder of Reformed faith is at some important points profoundly indebted to Roman Catholic theology, and to the Thomist tradition in particular.[5] In a section we are to examine below, Turrettini bases his arguments entirely on Roman Catholic theology, with no reference at all to Calvin or other Reformed theologians. His theology thus exemplifies the fact that Protestant Scholasticism shares with medieval Scholasticism not only its method and framework but also its theological conception and insight, in a fundamental and substantial manner. Being "Scholastic" could of course be morbid for theology, but that does not mean that theology has nothing to learn from the Scholastic tradition, for the task of addressing the questions one faces in his or her own context. We first review a theological debate within Roman Catholicism, then see how it affected Turrettini's theology, with special reference to two distinctively Thomistic concepts involved in the debate, and finally take a glimpse of how Turrettini's

---

Ernst Bizer, trans. G. T. Thomson (reprint, Grand Rapids: Baker Book House, 1978), p. 715 and throughout.

2. The pagination in this article is based on the New York reprint edition (1847). The English translation is taken from George Musgrave Giger's unpublished manuscript deposited at the Speer Library, Princeton Theological Seminary.

3. For the details of the Helvetic Consensus Formula and its context, see Philip Schaff, ed., *The Creeds of Christendom, with a History and Critical Notes* (New York: Harper & Row, 1931; reprint, Grand Rapids: Baker Book House, 1985), 1:477–89; John H. Leith, ed., *Creeds of the Churches*, 3rd ed. (Atlanta: John Knox Press, 1982), pp. 309–23.

4. John W. Beardslee III, *Reformed Dogmatics* (New York: Oxford University Press, 1965), p. 14.

5. Beardslee has noted that Turrettini's Scholastic method is "often based explicitly on Aquinas" and that he "never gains strength by departing from Aquinas." He also notes, however, that Turrettini's "Calvinism is often lost in scholasticism" (John Walter Beardslee III, "Theological Development at Geneva under Francis and Jean-Alphonse Turretin, 1648–1737" [Ph.D. diss., Yale University, 1956]).

Thomism was carried into New England to be applied and utilized by Puritan theology.

De Auxiliis

Among the theological debates within Western Catholicism since the Council of Trent, none was as controversial as the one called *de auxiliis* that took place at the turn of the seventeenth century. The controversy was in fact one elevated stage of a series of theological debates concerning the way divine efficacious grace operates in humanity.[6] The question was originally raised by the Protestant understanding of divine grace and human depravity, and though Roman Catholic theologians did officially counter it with the canons and decrees issued by the Council of Trent, these Tridentine formulations were far from giving a definitive answer commensurate to the complexity of the question. The *de auxiliis* controversy in question now was thus occasioned when in 1588 a Spanish Jesuit, Luis de Molina (1536–1600), attempted to publish his commentary on part of Thomas's *Summa Theologica,* entitled *Concordia liberi arbitrii cum gratiae donis, divina praescientia, providentia, praedestinatione. . . .* With this publication he wished to clarify some of the persistent questions posed by Calvinism outside and Baianism within, but the resultant vigorous dispute surely proved contrary to his intention.[7]

Molina contended that divine grace and human freedom are not incompatible, since God foresees all future possibilities, even to the infinitesimal varieties, of human free reactions to proffered grace, and that with this infallible foreknowledge *(scientia media)* God ordains all circumstances so as to be conducive for the person to consent freely to grace by his or her own will. Molina's obvious intention was theologically to preserve human auton-

6. On the controversy and its relation to Baianism and Jansenism, see T. Ryan, "Congregatio de auxiliis," *New Catholic Encyclopedia;* Alister E. McGrath, *Iustitia Dei: A History of the Christian Doctrine of Justification* (Cambridge: Cambridge University Press, 1986), 2:86–97; James Brodrick, S.J., *The Life and Work of Blessed Robert Francis Cardinal Bellarmine, S.J., 1542-1621* (London: Burns, Oates & Washbourne, 1928), 2:1–69; idem, *Robert Bellarmine: Saint and Scholar* (Westminster, Md.: Newman Press, 1961), pp. 189–216. Brodrick's first book contains many revealing excerpts from the writings and correspondence of the time. His second book is a shorter but maturer rewriting of the first.

7. Brodrick remarks, "It is a piquant circumstance that this book, which was to rouse such a controversial storm as had never before swept through the dignified seclusion of the Catholic schools, should have begun with the word 'harmony' " (*Life and Work of Bellarmine,* 2:26).

omy vis-à-vis divine governance. But the Dominican theologian Domingo Báñez (1528–1604) and those who followed him were vigorously opposed to this manner of reconciling the two agents. Báñez believed that grace is efficacious, not because of God's foreordaining the circumstances favorable to human response, but intrinsically by its own nature. Báñez also affirmed God's omniscient foreknowledge, but for him it was not the cause of divine foreordination as Molina asserted. To the contrary, Báñez claimed, God foreknows because he foreordains. Divine foreknowledge is a logical conclusion, rather than a presupposition, of divine foreordination. God is the absolute cause and mover of all human actions, hence he knows how a person wills and reacts to the proffered grace. If Molina seemed to Báñez too Pelagian in attributing the principal cause of conversion to the human will, Báñez seemed to Molina too deterministic in denying the human will any role to play in the process of spiritual renewal.

Other Roman theologians of different traditions became involved in the controversy, but the ensuing details are of little significance to this article. The dispute became so heated that finally in 1597 Pope Clement VIII had to intervene and appoint a commission to settle the matter. After a year of strenuous deliberation of theology and ecclesiastical politics, the convened *Congregatio de auxiliis,* from which the name of the controversy derives, lined up ninety propositions from the writings of Molina to be condemned. Before securing papal approval, however, the condemnation was overturned by a Jesuit appeal. Measures were then taken (ultimately in vain) to encourage friendlier debate between the two groups, while the popes withheld giving approval to the proceedings of the *Congregatio.* It was only in 1607, two pontificates later, that the controversy came to an inconclusive settlement. Pope Paul V forbade further discussion, affirmed the orthodoxy of both Jesuits and Dominicans, and ordered both parties not to denounce each other as heretics.

François Turrettini

Turrettini refers to this controversy in his discussion of calling and efficacious grace. What is striking first of all here is that this expert in Reformed theology, who is especially prized for the strength of his polemics and disputations,[8] thought it appropriate to discuss the matter entirely depend-

8. See, for example, "Six Letters of Jonathan Edwards to Joseph Bellamy," ed. Stanley T. Williams, *New England Quarterly* 1 (1928): 230.

ing upon this Roman controversy, with an obvious tilt toward the Thomist understanding. He does so by reviewing a book of still another Roman theologian, Robert Bellarmine (1542–1621), who was to write the commissioned report on the controversy, *De Controversia Lovaniensi.*[9] In comparison with this unexpected rapport, Turrettini found not even a single line worth quoting from any Protestant theologian or confessional formula. Not that Protestants did not treat the subject; Calvin and other Reformed theologians, as well as the confessions they formulated, all treated the same subject thoughtfully and meaningfully. In Turrettini's judgment, however, they were not quite as important or illuminative or useful as the arguments exchanged during that Roman Catholic debate. This fact alone may be sufficient to reveal how open and appreciative Reformed theology could be toward other theological traditions, but the case can be further substantiated by an analysis of his theological claims.

The section that we are to review here is entitled *De vocatione et fide.* The question Turrettini had before him to answer is whether effectual calling consists of "moral suasion" or "physical operation." In seventeenth-century terminology, "moral suasion" means the operation of divine grace upon the human intellect, and "physical operation" refers to the same operation upon the human will. Sinners are first externally called by moral suasion, that is, illuminated with "rational teaching, offering, and persuading." Yet since they are spiritually dead before regeneration, just as Lazarus was in the tomb, this moral suasion is bound to fail unless the Holy Spirit penetrates to "implant in the heart or will . . . a new inclination or propensity" to willingly follow the call and convert oneself to God.[10] This "implanting" is called physical operation, or simply infusion.[11] Turrettini's initial answer to the title question, therefore, is to negate the moral suasion and affirm the physical operation as the cause of the efficacy of grace. He dictates this answer, in his words, "against the Romanists and Arminians."[12]

9. See Brodrick, *Life and Work of Bellarmine,* 2:18–22. For the text of *de gratia et libero arbitrio* on which Turrettini relied, see *Roberti Cardinalis Bellarmini Opera Omnia,* vol. 4 (Neapolis, 1856), pp. 267–459.

10. Turrettini, *Institutio theologiae elencticae,* 6.3.15.

11. Ibid., 6.3.6. Leonard Riissen reverberates Turrettini's terminology in his commentary on Turrettini's *Institutio.* "Is the whole act of God in converting a man nothing more than a moral one, namely illumination and persuasion by the Word? No! Does God infuse new life by a physical action of the Spirit? Yes" (*Francisci Turretini Compendium Theologiae didactico-elencticae ex theologorum nostrorum Institutionibus auctum et illustratum* [Amsterdam, 1695], quoted in Heppe, *Reformed Dogmatics,* p. 522).

12. Turrettini, *Instituto,* 15.4, title. As a matter of fact, Turrettini follows Bellarmine's description and differentiates within the Jesuit group two different positions on the issue. The

The denominator "Romanists" here, however, is not quite accurate. In the course of discussion the Romanists that he repudiates turn out to be Molinists, or those Jesuit followers of Molina in the *de auxiliis* controversy who asserted that the efficacy of grace consisted "in the assent and cooperation of man." Against this Jesuit view Turrettini takes sides with the Dominicans, and thus his argument goes on to overlap with the Roman controversy. If the efficacy of calling should consist in the moral suasion, then the divine operation would become dependent on human assent to and cooperation with it. Turrettini's criticism is directed to this synergistic idea implied in Molinism. He argues, in a manner similar to Bánez before him, that by transferring "the principal cause of conversion" from God to human free will, Molinists are trying to bring back "the very error of Pelagius."[13] Turrettini instead opts for the Dominican view and affirms "a real and physical action of God, which determines the will," not by "a simple and bare mere suasion," but by "an omnipotent and irresistible power."[14] The grace of calling is efficacious, not because human beings assent to it and cooperate with it, but because it is a physical action of God "which determines the will to will and select."

Inevitably, this conclusion invokes the charge of determinism. Bellarmine, on whose work Turrettini relies for the entire section, had also expressed his objection that this Dominican view would destroy human free will. But Turrettini confidently overrides this objection by saying that "physical predetermination" in no way leads to the exclusion or denial of the part to be played by the human will in the process of conversion. Three reasons are stated to support his argument: (1) the will is "the receptive subject of grace"; (2) the will is not forced to receive grace unwillingly; rather, grace is received "most sweetly" and "most suitably to the will"; and (3) the will, once renewed and acted upon, immediately acts, converting itself to God.[15]

What Turrettini seeks to do here is to safeguard the movement of human free will, while at the same time affirming the absolute prevenience of

---

first position, held by Molina, Lessius, Bucanus, and other Jesuits, is called *ab eventu* (from the event), which signifies that grace is efficacious because of "the vehemence of the persuasion." The second, held by Bellarmine himself and Suarez, is called *ab congruitate* (from congruity), which signifies that grace is efficacious because of the disposition of the heart that God foresees. In Turrettini's judgment, however, their difference is nominal (ibid., 15.4.4–8; Latin ed., p. 455).

13. Ibid., 15.4.2.
14. Ibid., 15.4.9.
15. Ibid., 15.4.16.

God's converting grace. He does this by making a distinction between "habitual or passive conversion" and "actual or active conversion." The former is also called regeneration, and the latter is conversion, in the narrower sense of the word. A person is first regenerated by the supernatural infusion of habits, and in that event the person is totally passive and dependent on divine initiative. But this regenerate person, now vivified and rightly disposed by the infused grace, exercises the infused habit and willingly turns himself or herself to God, which is conversion in its proper sense.[16] On this point Turrettini quotes a Scripture passage that Catholics also favor: "Convert us, O Lord, to thee, and we shall be converted" (Lam. 5:21),[17] and writes: "This habitual conversion consists in principles of action, which God confers upon the faculties of corrupt man, which are supernatural qualities, or habits, and dispositions, from which results an active power of converting himself, such as the Scriptures mean by the new heart, the seed of God, eyes, ears, mind, and the like, denoting something inherent and permanent."[18] Underlying his argument here is a distinctively Thomistic understanding of the structure of human freedom, to which I will soon return.

While Turrettini admits that this Dominican view "comes nearest to the truth," he does not forget to qualify his endorsement. He thinks the word "physical" misleading, as it may cause some to "confound the natural acts of providence with the supernatural acts of grace."[19] God's providential governance of the world is conducted according to natural causation, as is affirmed in medieval Scholasticism under the rubric *potentia ordinata*. But the work of calling and conversion is not in the realm of natural causation. It is carried out by the powerful and extraordinary infusion of grace, not by a chain of natural causations that ordinarily prevail in the world. The word "physical," therefore, should not imply "natural."

One must remember, however, that the affirmation of such a supernatural *causation* does not necessarily entail the denial of the ensuing creaturely *result* in humanity. The grace that is supernaturally infused by God's physical operation brings forth, in Turrettini's words, "qualities, or habits, and dispositions," that is, "something inherent and permanent."[20]

---

16. Ibid., 15.4.13.
17. See *The Canons and Decrees, Council of Trent,* Sixth Session, chap. 5; Thomas Aquinas, *Summa Theologica,* trans. Fathers of the English Dominican Province (New York: Benzinger Brothers, 1911; reprint, Westminster, Md.: Christian Classics, 1981), pt. I of II, q. 109, art. 6, reply obj. 1.
18. Turrettini, *Instituto,* 15.4.13.
19. Ibid.
20. Ibid.

The origin may indeed be supernatural, but the result of this supernatural operation does not remain only supernatural. It becomes a palpable and abiding reality of renewal within human nature. Affirming such an ensuing reality of salvation in humanity is not to "naturalize" — let alone "domesticate" — the supernatural grace. It is to affirm the powerful effect of the supernatural grace in the natural. This process of effectuation is important, in Turrettini's view, for grace operates "by way of principle."[21] That is, grace enables a person to act voluntarily. Efficacious grace "would flow into the will itself for its renewal and vivification, in order that, itself being renewed and acted upon by God, *it might act as a cause*."[22] Again, here is a peculiarly Thomistic idea of *gratia creata*, the kernel of Turrettini's Thomism.

At this juncture Turrettini invokes the Augustinian concept of the "delightful conqueror" *(victrix delectationis)*, who moves us "both powerfully and sweetly, pleasingly and invincibly."[23] What this means is that although the operation of grace is not a mere external "teaching" or "persuading" that can either be accepted or rejected, it is nonetheless not coercion. The soul is sweetly and pleasantly moved; better, the soul is inclined to move itself voluntarily, "such as becomes [the] intelligent and rational nature" of human beings.[24] As a consequence Turrettini modifies his initial answer to the title question on the operational mode of efficacious grace. He now affirms both moral suasion and physical predetermination: "The movement of efficacious grace is properly to be called *neither physical nor ethical*, but supernatural and divine, *which in a measure includes both these relations*."[25] Although the mode of operation is supernatural and physical, Turrettini believes, the infused grace creates an abiding and internal principle of action by which a person freely and voluntarily achieves his or her own conversion. The operation is certainly not "natural," nor is the grace "given over" to human control; yet it crystallizes into something that is intrinsic and abiding in human nature. Otherwise, conversion cannot be *our* conversion.

---

21. Ibid., 15.4.12.

22. Ibid. (emphasis added).

23. Ibid., 15.4.18 (Latin ed., p. 462).

24. Ibid. The expression is reminiscent of Thomas's definition of grace (see *Summa Theologica*, pt. I of II, q. 113, art. 3).

25. Turrettini, *Instituto*, 15.4.18 (emphasis added). See also 15.4.8: Efficacious grace moves the will "congruously to consent."

Thomas Aquinas

Interestingly enough, the Thomists with whom Turrettini was in accord were so insistent on divine predetermination that the opponents denounced them as Calvinists.[26] What an ecumenical-minded denunciation! At any rate, Calvinists — that is, Protestant Calvinists and Roman Catholic Calvinists alike — are often criticized for "making man into a log or a trunk," depriving them of their free will.[27] Whether Protestant Calvinists are culpable of these charges is not the question of the present study, but as far as Thomas himself and the later Thomists are concerned, the charge is unwarranted. Here I will take up two aspects that are closely related to Turrettini's argument. The first concerns the nature of human free will.

According to Thomas Aquinas, God the First Mover moves everything according to its own nature, just as in nature heavy things and light things are moved differently. Now human beings are rational creatures endowed with free will. It is "man's proper nature to have free will." Hence God respects this and moves men and women in their own manner; God does not move them without moving their free will.[28] It is in the nature of a stone to move downward (in the pre-Newtonian sense), but when the stone is moved upward by a person, the cause of the movement is not in the nature of the stone. Likewise, human beings can be sometimes moved by an exterior cause, but "that his voluntary movement be from an exterior principle that is not the cause of his will, is impossible."[29] In other words, it is impossible for human will to be merely moved by an exterior motive power, since it contradicts human nature. God moves human beings in such a way that they are moved by God but at the same time move themselves by their own will. How is it possible?

The classic definition of voluntariness, according to Thomas, is "to have a principle within the agent."[30] A similar definition can be found in

26. See Ryan, "Congregatio de auxiliis"; McGrath, *Iustitia Dei,* p. 95; Brodrick, *Life and Work of Bellarmine,* pp. 14, 32.

27. Turrettini, *Instituto,* 15.4.16, 21. In reply to the charge, the Synod of Dort asserted that the grace of regeneration "does not treat men as senseless stocks and blocks, or take away their will and its properties, neither does violence thereto" ("Third and Fourth Heads of Doctrine," art. 16, in Schaff, *The Creeds of Christendom,* 3:591). The Westminster Confession rejected the charge by affirming that human beings are "quickened and renewed by the Holy Spirit . . . thereby enabled to answer this call, and to embrace the grace offered and conveyed in it" (chap. 10, "Of Effectual Calling," in ibid., 3:625).

28. Thomas Aquinas, *Summa Theologica,* pt. I of II, q. 113, art. 3.

29. Ibid., pt. I of II, q. 9, art. 6.

30. Ibid., pt. I of II, q. 6, art. 1.

Aristotle and Gregory of Nyssa, but Thomas further elaborates upon it in relation to divine initiative. When the Scripture says, "Apart from me you can do nothing" (John 15:5), does it mean that there is nothing voluntary in human acts? Thomas replies:

> God moves man to act, not only by proposing the appetible to the senses, or by effecting a change in his body, but also by moving the will itself; because every movement either of the will or of nature, proceeds from God as the First Mover. And just as it is not incompatible with nature that the natural movement be from God as the First Mover, inasmuch as nature is an instrument of God moving it, so it is not contrary to the essence of a voluntary act that it proceed from God, inasmuch as the will is moved by God.[31]

God moves human beings by moving the will itself, but this does not mean a heteronomous domination, since the human will, once moved, becomes a mover in a secondary sense — just as nature can be moved by God and then move others as an instrument. Divine moving does not eradicate human moving but rather establishes it by providing it with the "principle" of the movement. The axiom of Thomist theology applies here beautifully: grace does not destroy but perfects nature. Human beings are free, and their actions voluntary, if and only when they have the "principle of action" within themselves.

Thomas further explains what this principle of action means with the concept of "intermediary habit," which makes the second point of my reference to Thomas. The concept originates in his critical reappraisal of a theological postulate assumed by Peter Lombard, whom Thomas reverently calls "the Master" in his writings. Lombard, in discussing the substance of Christian charity, asserted that charity is not something that is created in human nature but is the Holy Spirit himself (*gratia increata*) dwelling in the soul. By this assertion, according to Thomas's explication, Lombard did not mean to identify the Holy Spirit with the movement of love, but rather meant that the Spirit works "without any intermediary habit."[32] Lombard's concern was to distinguish charity and uphold it as the crowning virtue that is qualitatively different from other virtues.

Thomas, with all due respect to "the Master," did not quite concur. If the Holy Spirit moves the human mind in such a way that the mind "be merely moved, without also being the principle of this movement," Thomas con-

31. Ibid., reply obj. 3.
32. Ibid., pt. II of II, q. 23, art. 2.

tends, it would be "contrary to the nature of a voluntary act, whose principle needs to be in itself."[33] It would be like a stone's being moved by some extrinsic motive power. In order for the will to function as such, therefore, "there should be in us some habitual form superadded to the natural power, inclining that power to the act of charity."[34] The unmediated exercise of the indwelling Holy Spirit would destroy human spontaneity, which is essential for the movement of charity. The Holy Spirit ("uncreated grace") creates within the human subject a "created grace," or an intermediary habit, and this created grace functions as the principle by which the human subject acts spontaneously and voluntarily. Here again, the supernatural grace is to be "internalized." Turrettini, as we saw above, also affirmed the existence of such an abiding reality of salvation created in the form of a "new principle." He does not hesitate to describe it as "something inherent and permanent," and this new principle is the sum of Turrettini's concept of salvation.

It also has to be noted that, in Thomas's theology of merit, an action is deemed virtuous, and hence meritorious, only when it arises from the subject's free will.[35] Our hearts must be inclined by the hearts' own tendency, not dominated extrinsically or forced into service by an exterior agent, if our actions are to be meritorious.[36] Only insofar as it arises freely out of the agent's own principle, can love be counted as the agent's action and as such a virtue. Thomas's objection to the Lombardian position is grounded on the same consideration. Charity must be habitualized, Thomas insists, for it is the nature of a voluntary act to have within itself a principle with which it works, and love is such a voluntary act par excellence. A modern Thomist explains the point succinctly:

> The Lombardian solution denies what it attempts to affirm. . . . If the impulse of theological love were, as the Lombard maintained, a direct and extrinsic movement on the will by the Holy Spirit without a mediating virtue, then the uniqueness of the movement of the will would be annulled. It is in the nature of the will that it is never simply moved but also self-moving at the same time; there is no such thing as a voluntary movement whose cause is purely external.[37]

33. Ibid.
34. Ibid.
35. Ibid., pt. I of II, q. 114, art. 1.
36. See George Tavard, *Justification: An Ecumenical Study* (New York: Paulist Press, 1983), p. 41.
37. Robert Scharlemann, *Thomas Aquinas and John Gerhard* (New Haven: Yale University Press, 1964), p. 131.

The difference between Lombard and Thomas is not whether or not the Holy Spirit dwells in the regenerate as the principle of love, which they both affirm. The real difference between the two lies in whether or not they think this indwelling Holy Spirit issues forth an "intermediary habit" through which the movement of love occurs.[38] This action Lombard denies, and Thomas affirms. Put otherwise, Thomas too affirms the necessary presence of uncreated grace (the Holy Spirit), but in addition to this uncreated grace, he also affirms the existence of created grace.[39]

If we understand this distinction correctly, Turrettini's notion of the internal principle of action, as it stands in our perspective, emerges as a close correlative of Thomas's notion of the "intermediary habit," while not rejecting the Lombardian motif of the continual operation of the Spirit in and through this habit. The Holy Spirit himself never *becomes* or *turns into* created grace, and in that sense he is never domesticated or encapsulated by humanity. But the Spirit forms within the human nature a new habit through which he operates. Without this "intermediary habit," only the divine agent would be at work, with no participation from the side of the regenerate humanity. Human beings would then be merely moved — indeed as a stone is moved by an extrinsic motive power — which is obviously contrary to what the Holy Spirit achieves in humanity.

Thus I have explained two theories of Thomas Aquinas that surface in Turrettini's argument on efficacious grace: the definition of voluntariness, and the theory of "intermediary habit." Turrettini, taking the Dominican view on the *de auxiliis* controversy, agreed with Thomas, reviving the latter's theological insight in the seventeenth century.

I do not think it necessary here to point out that Turrettini's reasoning was by no means a matter-of-course path, especially under the shadow of the Reformation debate over the nature of regeneration. Calvin never spoke of the reality of regeneration in terms of "habit" or "internal principle," while the Council of Trent endorsed the Thomist view of justification by carefully describing the righteousness of the justified as "the justice by which God *makes us just*."[40] Turrettini, however, did not think it mandatory to follow in the wake of the Genevan Reformer on this matter. Nor did he think that he was betraying the pivotal doctrine of authentic Reformed theology. Learning from the "Angelic Doctor" of the twelfth century, in

---

38. Thomas Aquinas, *Summa Theologica*, pt. II of II, q. 23, art. 2.

39. Edward Yarnold, *The Second Gift: A Study of Grace* (Slough, England: St. Paul Publications, 1974), p. 53.

40. *Canons and Decrees of the Council of Trent*, Sixth Session, chap. 7.

Turrettini's judgment, does not threaten but rather enriches his Reformed faith.

The New England Setting

The *de auxiliis* controversy took on a new significance in the New England setting. It remains for us to see briefly how Turrettini's ecumenical learning was carried over into the American continent.

The New England Puritans are known for their avowed antagonism against everything that reminded them of Anglicanism and Roman Catholicism. They commonly identified the apocalyptic beast of the Book of Revelation with the Roman Church, and "papism," as they called it, was a scandal in the biblical sense of the word.[41] Yet for all the antagonism, their respect for the intellectual achievement of Roman Catholic theology was not low. At the seventeenth-century Harvard, Thomas Aquinas enjoyed no less repute than Calvin.[42] According to Norman Fiering, Thomas belonged to the standard learning of early New England intellectuals. He was "very well known in early seventeenth-century philosophy and was cited occasionally in student notebooks that have survived from Harvard in this period."[43] Not only Thomas but also such later Roman theologians as Cardinal Thomas Cajetan (1469–1534) and Robert Bellarmine — Turrettini's source — "were highly respected" among the New England Puritan divines.[44]

41. See, for example, Harry S. Stout, *The New England Soul: Preaching and Religious Culture in Colonial New England* (New York: Oxford University Press, 1986), pp. 48–49.

42. Samuel Eliot Morison, *Harvard College in the Seventeenth Century* (Cambridge, Mass.: Harvard University Press, 1936), pt. 1, p. 276. Morison also states that the students "were not necessarily conscious that they were aligning themselves with the traditional schools of Catholic theology, although ample materials for them to acquire the consciousness were in the College Library" (ibid., p. 277 n. 2).

43. Norman Fiering, "Will and Intellect in the New England Mind," *William and Mary Quarterly*, 3d ser., 29 (1972): 519–20. Fiering has surveyed many of these student notebooks from that period, but especially revealing is his survey on the books that Solomon Stoddard owned when he was a student at Harvard. Appointed "library keeper" in 1667, Stoddard was to become the first "librarian" of Harvard College, and the catalogue of his books is to date the oldest list that attests to the breadth of reading in early New England education. According to the list, Stoddard owned a couple of Thomas's works *(Quaestiones Disputatae* and *De Ente et Acte),* and one by Francis Suarez (1548–1617), a Jesuit who also has an expository commentary on Thomas *(Metaphysicarum Disputationum: In Quibus et Universa Naturalis Theologia Ordinate Traditur).* See also Norman Fiering, "Solomon Stoddard's Library at Harvard," *Harvard Library Bulletin* 20 (1972): 262–69.

44. Fiering, "Will and Intellect," pp. 519–20. Cajetan was the cardinal who summoned

Protestant theologians of Scholasticism must also have contributed to the influx of Roman theology into New England. Of those, Turrettini was the most influential, for his magnum opus, *Institutio theologiae elencticae*, was widely circulated on the American Continent, resulting in multiple reprints, including one published in New York. It was de facto *the* textbook of Calvinist theology in American Presbyterian seminaries until the late nineteenth century, when Princeton's Charles Hodge replaced it with his own three-volume set *Systematic Theology*.[45] There were other Continental Reformed theologians through whom the New Englanders were exposed to the thought of Thomas and later Thomists: Peter van Mastricht (1630–1706), a Dutch Reformed theologian, was one such, whose masterpiece work of theology, *Theoretico-Practica Theologia*, was placed at the center of Harvard divinity education in the early eighteenth century.[46] This bulky one-volume textbook of theology was even translated into English in part for more general readers in 1769.[47] Without doubt the New Englanders had glimpses of the theology of Bellarmine and other Roman theologians — and along with them of the *de auxiliis* controversy — through these Reformed theologians.

Actually, the New England Puritan divines had their own reasons to be interested in their writings. The Thomistic understanding of the operation of grace in relation to human freedom proved especially useful and valuable in the New England context. In the preface of Mastricht's English

---

and questioned Martin Luther at Augsburg in 1518. His monumental commentary on Thomas's *Summa Theologica* was instrumental in reviving Thomism in the sixteenth century.

45. Charles Hodge, *Systematic Theology* (New York, 1892; reprint, Grand Rapids: Eerdmans, 1989). For the relation of Hodge to Turrettini, see Beardslee, *Reformed Dogmatics*, p. 15.

46. Peter van Mastricht, *Theoretico-Practica Theologia, editio nova* (Amsterdam, 1724). According to Perry Miller, theological education at Harvard gradually shifted its standard textbook from Ames to Wollebius and Ursinus in the 1670s, and from there to Mastricht at the beginning of the eighteenth century (*The New England Mind: The Seventeenth Century* [Cambridge, Mass.: Harvard University Press, 1939], p. 96). Miller comments on Mastricht's meticulousness and precision, saying, "Beyond this limit no mortal could go" (ibid.). See also Cotton Mather's word of recommendation printed in the preface of the translation: "There is nothing that I can with so much plerophorie recommend unto you, as a Mastricht, his theologia. . . . I can heartily subscribe unto the commendation. . . . I hope you will, next unto the sacred scriptures, make a Mastricht the storehouse to which you may resort continually."

47. *A Treatise on Regeneration: Extracted from his system of divinity called theologia theoretico-practica and faithfully translated into English* (New Haven, [1769]). The translator shares Turrettini's apprehension that the adjective "physical" might be misleading. According to his editorial footnote, the word is used in Mastricht to mean "supernatural," in opposition to "moral" (ibid., pp. 18–19).

translation, the anonymous translator confesses wherein his concern lies. "The reason for translating and publishing the following Treatise at this time, is principally a hope, that it may have a tendency to put a stop to the controversy, which seems to be growing among us, relative to regeneration; whether it be wrought by the immediate influences of the divine Spirit, or by light as the means? and happily to unite us in the truth."[48]

By "the controversy which seems to be growing among us," the preface is referring not to the original *de auxiliis* controversy, which was officially settled more than a century and a half earlier. It is rather a variation of the same tune played by some new players, namely, those Arminians who were rapidly gaining ground on the American continent. They asserted that there is no such thing as the supernatural infusion of a new principle and that God's assistance does not exceed the domain of "natural assistance." The translator's intention is obviously to settle the matter in his favor, namely, with the same conclusion Turrettini and the Dominicans favored with regard to the original controversy. In the translated section of the *Theoretico-Practica*, Mastricht repeated afresh that the regenerating grace is "not a moral act, exercised in offering and inviting, as is the case with the external call," but it is "a physical act powerfully infusing spiritual life into the soul."[49] The sentence is meant to stand against what seemed to them a new form of semi-Pelagianism, and for that purpose they recycled the argument and terminology already familiar among them. The *de auxiliis* controversy thus continued to provide the basis of theology that Puritans could also make use of in the eighteenth century.

Other Continental theologians of Reformed Orthodoxy can also be quoted here. In fact, the English Mastricht has an appendix in which the translator ransacked virtually all Reformed theologians available to him in order to back up his point against the Arminians.[50] The list of consulted theologians includes Ridgley, Charnock, Willard, Flavel, Witsius, Le Blanc, Ames, Burmann, Braunius, and Brine. They all insisted in one way or another, as far as we can see from the quotations, that the grace of effectual calling consists not in the illumination of the faculty of understanding, as the Arminians assert, but in the powerful and sovereign act of infusion that implants a new will in the human mind.

However, the references to the Thomistic tradition in these theologians are less explicit than in Turrettini. Herman Witsius (1636–1708), for

48. Ibid., Preface, pp. v–vi.
49. Mastricht, *Theoretico-Practica Theologia,* 4.3.9.
50. Mastricht, *Treatise,* pp. 65ff.

example, a Dutch colleague of Mastricht, does refer to the distinction of "external call" by "moral suasion" and "internal call" by "a real supernatural efficacy." He also underscores that this grace of calling is not detrimental to "the liberty of the human will"; "on the contrary, [God] rescues and maintains it," since it is "a violence, indeed, but that of heavenly love, the greater the sweeter" (*victrix delectationis,* in Turrettini's conception).[51] The terms and concepts he uses accord with those of the *de auxiliis* controversy, but Witsius fails to show further understanding of the Thomist concern that underlies these terms and concepts. Turrettini's explanation, as we saw above, stands in relief precisely on this point.

The question of human free will was also made a focal point on the doctrine of original sin. John Taylor, a professed Arminian of New England, asserted that "*inwrought* virtue, if there were any such thing, would be no virtue; not being the effect of our own will, choice and design, but only of a sovereign act of God's power."[52] Again, the charge was not unfamiliar to the ears of those who knew the *de auxiliis* controversy. To them one may rehearse Thomas's conception of voluntariness: what God does is no more and no less than creating a new principle of the heart, or a new habit, by which the person acts freely and spontaneously. The person is therefore not compelled or manipulated by an alien force.

This is actually the answer Jonathan Edwards, the quintessential theologian of Puritan New England, gave to the question.[53] To be sure, virtues in the saints are first supernaturally infused, or "inwrought," to use Taylor's word, nonetheless they are real virtues of their own because it establishes in them a new principle by which they spontaneously and freely commit virtuous acts. Here Puritan theology shares a common vision with the Thomist theology, namely, human freedom is not endangered or alienated, but rather established, by divine infusion. Grace does not dominate our

51. See *De Oeconomia Foederum Dei cum Hominibus* (Utrecht, 1694); English translation, *The Oeconomy of the Covenants between God and Man: Comprehending a Complete Body of Divinity* (London, 1762), 2:457–75.

52. John Taylor, *The Scripture-Doctrine of Original Sin, Proposed to Free and Candid Examination* (London, 1738 [1740?]), pp. 245, 250, 180, quoted in Jonathan Edwards, *Original Sin* (New Haven: Yale University Press, 1970), p. 359. See also Shelton Smith, *Changing Conceptions of Original Sin: A Study in American Theology since 1750* (New York: Charles Scribner's Sons, 1955), pp. 13–19.

53. On the theology of Jonathan Edwards and his Thomistic reply to the Arminian charge, see my dissertation, "The Reality of Salvation in the Soteriology of Jonathan Edwards" (Princeton Theological Seminary, 1991), which has been published under the title *Jonathan Edwards and the Catholic Vision of Salvation* (University Park: Pennsylvania State University Press, 1995).

minds heteronomously. Rather, we are free only when we have an intrinsic principle within ourselves.

It is a pleasant surprise to realize how close Puritan and Roman Catholic theologies could be to each other in matters of salvation and its reality in humanity. Given the familiarity of Thomas's theology among the early New England intellectuals, it would indeed be surprising if they did not make use of this valuable tradition in pursuit of their own theological task of the day.

On Truth and Pluralism

SANDRA ELLIS-KILLIAN

The Problem

No age is without its screen of prejudices. The difficulty is that the screen tends to be invisible to those who are looking through it, but it is glaringly apparent to those who look back at it. Human reflection moves from one state of blithe confidence in the self-evidence of the accepted point of view to the next successive point of view.

However, an interesting new variation has developed in our day. There seems to be a certain sense of having achieved the superior state of being without prejudice. It is accompanied by a definite air of smug superiority. Where, all through benighted history, our predecessors have persevered in their unenlightened musings so deeply sunk in religious, cultural, ethnic, personal, and intellectual bias, we, in contrast, have not only identified such limitations but have freed ourselves from them. All that has really happened, of course, is what always happens: one set of prejudices has supplanted another. (I avoid here the lately much-abused term "paradigm.") In any case, the lesson is that the awareness of the blind assumptions of others is not always sufficient for opening our eyes to our own.

Here is the problem, illustrated. In the campus dining hall two students, Joe and Ruth, lingered over coffee. Both were seniors there, in an Eastern liberal arts college of the highest academic prestige. Their conversation took a turn toward impasse when Ruth disclosed in the natural course of the discussion that her Christian values influenced her position on the issue they were discussing. Joe drew back in dismay and amazement, exclaiming, "How can we even talk about this then? If you bring Christian beliefs into this, how can you possibly be open-minded?" Pressed by Ruth to justify the judgment that Christianity and open-mindedness were mutually exclusive, Joe was at somewhat of a loss to explain what he saw as self-evident: a person who held convictions was ipso facto closed-minded, impervious to new information, unable to reason outside of a preconfigured scheme. Debate is meaningless, he more or less argued; if one already has formed a commitment, one will not be able to give due consideration to all the possibilities.

This illustration isn't an invention. It's a true story, and easy enough to come by these days. Here we have an attitude that congratulates itself on its triumph over one kind of dogmatism by the unconscious imposition of another, namely, that the way to eliminate dogmatism and preserve an open forum is to eliminate convictions.

For Joe, to hold convictions at all, at least certain kinds of convictions, was the same as holding them with a rigid dogmatism, immune from examination. For this student it was a given, an axiom of intellectual life, that to have arrived at particular (in this case, Christian) conclusions and to form further judgments on the basis of them necessarily renders a person incapable of thoughtful, responsible review of them, or of openness to new or different ideas, and therefore simply disqualifies the person from the discussion.

Practical questions might occur to one who thought very far into this attitude. How does this system work, exactly? If we are all going to guarantee our tolerance of other points of view by not having any fixed point of view ourselves, then is there really going to be all that much to be tolerant of? Or, maybe there could be two separate groups, those who get to have opinions and those who get to hang around and be tolerant of them.

In fact, one does not go far in these conversations before the partisan spirit is discovered. As it turns out, the objection is not very democratically applied. It isn't *all* convictions, *any* point of view, that the thinking person cannot countenance. It's just that there are *certain* convictions that thinking people don't hold. That is to say, if one holds such a conviction (e.g., Christianity), then one is not a thinking person. One hardly knows which fallacy to attack first — the petitio principii or the ad hominem.

At the moment, I would like to focus on the commonplace assumption that being Christian means being closed-minded. For the student in the example, the fact that another person subscribed to Christian doctrines, and that such doctrines were seen to have a bearing upon moral judgments, meant that no genuine, in the sense of reasonably objective and open, moral discussion could take place. Here is a prejudice as offensive as any held by medieval Crusaders toward the infidel, and the logic-impaired people who hold it in the name of enlightenment seem equally resistant to attempts to point out that it does not compel assent. Just because there have been and are intolerant, closed-minded Christians does not mean Christianity entails intolerance and closed-mindedness. But this is a distinction largely lost on the modern mind.

Still, there lurks here a genuine philosophical issue. Underneath the superficial matter of the currently popular anti-Christian bias lies a very real and very old philosophical conundrum. If one is of the conviction that one has found Truth (e.g., Jesus Christ), is the search for Truth over? Can such a person seriously entertain challenges to that Truth? Can that person be meaningfully said to be open to new ideas, new truths? Recognizable in the amorphous nature of this latter-day attitude are variations on the problem of the One and the Many. Is there one Truth or many truths? If there are many truths, how can one of them be *the* truth? Is a unitary notion of Truth logically inconsistent with diverse truths? If one is committed to the truth of one idea, to what degree must one rule other possibilities out of one's universe? Can a person genuinely convinced that, for instance, Jesus Christ is the way, the truth and the life, tolerate — let alone thoughtfully consider — divergent perspectives, even denominational variations on the doctrines? Can one meaningfully be said to be able to evaluate critically one's own Christian point of view?

The Reverend Professor Charles West believes that such commitment means very little unless it continually searches out its challenges from within and without, in an attitude of healthy, uninhibited intellectual curiosity, genuine receptivity, through authentic dialogue in a cooperative, courteous spirit across lines of every sort of philosophical, political, and religious demarcation. Professor West has a history of explicitly urging upon others the necessity of the free and respectful exchange of ideas, which he sees as vital to two great Christian enterprises to which he has devoted himself: ecumenism and education. The career and example of Charles West give empirical evidence contradicting the contemporary notions about the incompatibility of Christian conviction with freedom of thought, and with rigorous thought. His point of view would be incomprehensible to Joe, the student in the example, who cannot imagine a combination of a frank and deep allegiance to certain specifically Christian convictions together with advocacy of sound reasoning and freedom of thought. There is much in the modern mind that resists the notion, dear to Professor West, that the integrity and vitality of one's Christianity is proportionate to the exercise of robust, free thought on the part of the Christian. For him, as for many

105

Christians, not only are reason and devotion not mutually exclusive, they are in fact mutually dependent.

There is, as I have said, a genuine puzzle in the incompatibility that is popularly supposed to exist between open-minded, healthy reason on the one hand and intensity of devotion to religious, most particularly Christian, truths on the other. Again, it is in fact not a new puzzle if one remembers, for instance, Cratylus, the Heraclitean, who believed the thing to do is to quit speaking altogether because it is not possible to say anything true about a world in flux. The dilemma is a species of *choice* between the One and the Many, rather than a *relationship* between the One and the Many, a choice to which many seem to feel they are pressed by force of logic: they must choose between being open to new ideas or espousing eternal verities. One must decide if one believes in Truth and has an idea about what it is, in which case one is presumed to operate within a closed system. Or, one can choose the alternative, which is to operate with an open system of acquisition and processing of knowledge, abandoning the notion of a unitary Truth, but embracing a proper pluralism. These are perceived as two different and more or less mutually exclusive orientations.

From the side of the sciences, particularly physics, there is plenty of extremely intriguing evidence and some fascinating models of systems that are committed but open. Their evidence suggests that we are not forced to such a choice. But we can't go into all of that here. What we can do within these limits is to examine a bit of the logic of the issue. What I want to show philosophically is that one does not have to accept that there is a logical contradiction between these two positions, as is often uncritically assumed to exist. I would like to look at a couple of ideas that support a view held by Professor West and many others among us, namely, the view that it is not only perfectly consistent for Professor West to preach and teach the truth of Christianity, at the same time demanding a fair-minded evaluation of it *by those who hold it,* but that moreover it is actually a fulfillment of Christian teachings that those who hold them to be true do not do so uncritically. Once again, the problem is the assumption that some sort of antithesis exists between Christian conviction and good thinking with its self-critical capacities and its openness to new ideas.

A recurring theme of Professor West's is that to be a Christian means being the enemy of prejudice and narrow-mindedness. The pursuit of understanding requires the sympathetic entertainment of ideas divergent from, even contrary to, one's own, and being Christian requires that one pursue understanding. That Christian conviction requires reason, tolerance, and intellectual acuity is a principle he has defended in word and deed, and in so gracious a spirit of appeal to the gospel teachings of reconciliation, love, and forgiveness that, especially knowing him, it is hard to resist the notion that tough, clear thinking and open exchange of ideas are indeed Christian virtues, in spite of popular opinion to the contrary. The theology classroom, Professor West has said in a discussion of teaching method, must be a place where challenges to the Christian faith are encountered on their own terms. Students must enter into dialogue with secular views — scientific, economic, political, and philosophical — as well as with rival religious worldviews in their full strength, a requirement that sometimes necessitates that the instructor "act as the protagonist for an uncomfortable or unfamiliar point of view."[1] Oddly enough, it would seem to some, he views it as his *Christian* duty to "try to encourage students to rethink their own traditions and their own convictions, theological and social," a process that may demand "digging more deeply into a position espoused but not adequately understood," or it may demand "exploring a new enthusiasm critically"; in any case, he expects "every paper to be a critical dialogue."[2] Here is an attitude congenial to and welcoming of a pluralistic world, yet focused upon training in a very specific allegiance. I take my theme from some of his own words:

> In a world where major ideologies are breaking down and religious-cultural nationalisms are rising, the time is past when we can coerce each other's consciences with moral absolutes. Past is also the time when we can dismiss each other's theology or social analysis with a hermeneutic of suspicion. . . . This does not mean that the struggle for justice and liberation should be less intense or that bad theology should go unchallenged. It means rather that this struggle and this challenge become truly serious, because it does not come from the hopes and desires of the challenger but from the calling and command of God who corrects and directs us all. The church, and hence the ecumenical movement, is a place where we struggle for one another's souls often with conflicting views of that calling and command.[3]

The question is, in light of the incomprehensibility of such a combination to many minds today, on what grounds may such a combination

---

1. Charles C. West, "Ecumenics, Church, and Society: The Tradition of Life and Work," *Ecumenical Review* 39 (October 1987): 468–69.
2. Ibid.
3. Charles C. West, "Ecumenical and Social Ethic beyond Socialism and Capitalism," *Ecumenical Review* 43 (July 1991): 338.

(of hospitality toward pluralism together with deep religious, particularly Christian, commitment) be supported? By way of tribute to Professor West, there is a thought or two I would like to propose on this subject of the compatibility of the notion of Truth with the endorsement of pluralism in our society and in our theological discussion. The idea I would like to defend is that, not only is the notion of truth in a nonrelative and ultimate sense compatible with tolerant pluralism in a society, but such tolerance is a condition of, and such pluralism an asset to, the search for truth. Furthermore, a condition of a meaningful conviction about truth is that there is freedom to believe otherwise.

Cultural pluralism does not logically imply philosophical or ethical relativism. The fact that there are many different points of view does not mean either that all of them have an equal claim to validity or that (1) tolerating the variety or (2) fair consideration of their claims requires a liquidation of personal convictions.

I would like to show that this problem results in part from confusion of an epistemological principle with what I will call a process of learning psychology. By examining and maintaining this distinction, maybe we can see the logical compatibility of confidence in the existence of Truth in an ultimate sense, even a conviction about its content or nature, with the permissibility — even necessity — of doubting it, questioning it, critically reviewing it, and of honest exploration of alternatives. Failure to maintain this distinction between the *principle* and the *process* has unfortunate consequences for moral dialogue. Where this distinction goes unrecognized, the idea begins to take hold that having a tolerant pluralism, with its open forum for debate, entails ethical relativism, and that idea is what successfully aborted the discussion between the two students in the example.

The distinction to be drawn between the epistemological principle and this learning psychology process is along these lines: The epistemological fact of assumptions about truth that govern and make possible discourse, especially moral discourse, is not the same thing as the process whereby we learn truth. What we assume, or place faith in, in order to know is different from how we learn. It is one thing to assume that Truth exists and that the idea of truth adjudicates among claims and conclusions. It is another thing to make one's way in the understanding of Truth. To seek to know what is true, one assumes some things about it, including that it is in some sense and to some degree knowable. But the process by which we increase our proximity to it, clarify, deepen, and extend our understanding of it, is a process of practicing uncertainty. Behind the willingness to entertain the provisional nature of all our ideas lies a presupposition about the trustworthiness of truth together with a healthy humility about the notorious unreliability of our grasp of it. You will recognize here the old argument against radical skepticism: one must presuppose truth in order to debate even the question of truth. Recent studies of the ancient skeptics show that although they did offer a "critique of the human ability to establish truth," still even among them there were "no unmitigated sceptics," for they were perfectly prepared to find many claims true, even though they could not be rationally established beyond disagreement or beyond doubt.[4] Furthermore, they ventured into constructive positions of their own. However, an immutable Truth may require a dynamic learning process. It may thus be that, as Richard Popkin aptly says, " 'sceptic' and 'believer' are not opposing classifications."[5] The connection is that a *learner* has to be both. In order to learn, one must both believe and practice skepticism; the point of this essay could perhaps be expressed by the observation that the literal meaning of "disciple" from both Greek and Latin is "learner."

We thus have a principle and a process — an epistemological platform from which to launch a method of learning, and the need to avoid confusing them. How can we get a better look at the distinction between them? I would like to turn to two resources in order to discuss these two ideas. First, I'd like to borrow from the moral philosophy of Iris Murdoch in order to get a closer look at the idea of an epistemological sovereign concept. Then, against that backdrop, if we look at the method of persuasion used in certain cult groups contrasted with that used in more ordinary forms of Christian formation and reflection, we may find that even in the most intense loyalties there must be a place for sufferance, doubt, and inquiry.

The Principle: The Sovereign Truth

Iris Murdoch is more widely known for her fiction than for her philosophy, but the achievements of her moral philosophy may be more important. In her work of roughly the last thirty years, she has reasoned out a recovery of the notion of a transcendent ideal in ethics.

True, most people probably never noticed it was missing. However,

4. Leo Groarke, *Greek Scepticism: Anti-Realist Trends in Ancient Thought* (Montreal: McGill-Queens University Press, 1990), pp. 14, 5, 12–13. The distinction between "mitigated" and "unmitigated" skeptics is Hume's.

5. Richard H. Popkin, *The History of Scepticism from Erasmus to Spinoza* (Berkeley: University of California Press, 1979), p. xix.

those acquainted with the history of twentieth-century Anglo-American philosophy, such as the theologians who, as always, must reckon with contemporary philosophical trends, know that various modern rejections have arisen of the traditional philosophical enterprise. The net effect of several emerging schools of thought was to eliminate much of what had for centuries constituted the primary activity of philosophy, particularly moral philosophy. Metaphysical models and concepts were discarded, and discredited with them was the old, respected concept of a supreme value in ethics. None of the old standards such as Love, Freedom, Pleasure, Reason, History, God, and so forth could any longer serve as a governing moral ideal in a philosophy because the very notion of a governing moral ideal was no longer taken seriously. For a while, it fell into such disrepute as almost to defy resuscitation. Murdoch's contribution, however, has been to restore that notion and to give it greater plausibility by answering the criticisms of it. The gains of Murdoch's work include some philosophical advantages for Christian moral philosophy.

The sovereign concept for Murdoch is the Good. It is an abstract ideal, nonrepresentable and elusive, but she argues that this idea of the Good is epistemologically necessary and is presupposed in all moral cognition and discussion. The way we lost entitlement to a sovereign ideal had to do with the way in which behaviorist, empiricist, analytic, and existentialist schools, in spite of their differences, coalesced in divesting moral philosophy of a transcendent, metaphysical background of meaning and in relocating moral values in the choice-making activity of the individual. The appeal of such a view came in part from its ability to resolve the problem illustrated by Joe, the student in the example, who could not see a way to reconcile freedom of thought with the authority of an external source of value. The old question, How is freedom compatible with the authority of the Good? is difficult, Murdoch herself admits, because establishing definitions or appealing to revelations of the ideal seem to preempt the "value of a free adherence."[6] Moral choices, in order to be moral and to be choices, must be free. Freedom, so this thinking goes, is not compatible with obedience to authority or persuasion of some kind, for insofar as any of these influence the choice, it is not freely chosen. We create our own values in a vacuum of moral neutrality. Thus it is necessary to moral maturity that we eliminate those cumbersome "fictions" that previously served as sources of value that were transcendent and objectively real (from a minimal sense of being an abstract principle independent of our choice, to the fullest sense of being,

6. Iris Murdoch, "The Darkness of Practical Reason," *Encounter* 27 (July 1966): 46–47.

for example, one of the Forms or an extant personal deity). Although the schools of thought that produced this view are in varying degrees passé, their assumptions took hold. The continuing grip of this point of view is seen in the antipathy of Joe to the admission of Ruth, his college classmate, that her Christian conviction informed her moral reflection.

Murdoch critiques the pretensions of this view and exposes the problems in the arguments used to establish it. Of the analytic-behaviorist orientation, Murdoch says that the desire to remove moral philosophy into an aloof, sterile neutrality is misguided, and that in any case the attempt fails. Murdoch refers to this attempt to separate fact from value as the "antinaturalistic" argument that appears in various forms in modern ethics. The goal was to confine ethics to the examination of value-neutral empirical facts in the publicly observable behaviorist world; for the analytic school, it was to study only "the logical structure of moral language" with the "neutrality of logic."[7] But Murdoch believes that neutrality in moral philosophy is both logically absurd and, in practice, impossible. "Moral philosophy cannot avoid taking sides, and would-be neutral philosophers merely take sides surreptitiously."[8] What happens is that arguments in ethics take place within a milieu in which a certain concept operates unacknowledged as the sovereign value and "decides the relevance of the facts and may, indeed, render them observable."[9] Philosophers thus subvert their own claims to neutrality in that they "have done their moralizing unconsciously instead of consciously."[10]

Two hidden premises operate in the antinaturalistic stance, Murdoch says. If morality is viewed as attached to the substance of the world (facts), then there is danger that morality will become dogma. It is further assumed that dogma is bad. As Murdoch points out, however, these are moral, not logical, objections.

> This is not a logical or philosophical objection, it is a straight moral objection to the effect that certain bad results follow in practice from thinking about morality in a certain way. We may agree with this. But to say it is of course *not* to say that morality cannot under any circumstances

7. Iris Murdoch, "Metaphysics and Ethics," in *The Nature of Metaphysics,* ed. D. F. Pears (1957; reprint, New York: St. Martin's Press, 1965), p. 121.

8. Iris Murdoch, *The Sovereignty of the Good* (London: Routledge & Kegan Paul, 1970), p. 78; see also p. 52.

9. Iris Murdoch, "Vision and Choice in Morality," in *Dreams and Self-Knowledge* (= *Proceedings of the Aristotelian Society,* supp. 30 [1956]), p. 54.

10. Murdoch, "Metaphysics and Ethics," p. 121.

be a part of a general system of belief about how the world is, or about transcendent entities . . . it is merely to maintain that the holding of such beliefs is morally and socially dangerous.[11]

The irony of this argument is that in a covert attempt to secure ethics from dogma, it has created another dogma: that this kind of fact-value neutrality together with a rejection of belief systems or transcendent principles is the only way to ensure sound moral reasoning. Murdoch herself does not escape this characteristically modern dread of dogma. But the point she makes is that in the study of morality, no compelling logical reasons force us to affect a neutrality that we in any case cannot and do not actually attain. Tell *that* to Joe.

Likewise, Murdoch's critical work finds the twentieth-century divorce of ethics from metaphysics much overrated. This divorce may appear "in a strong form which claims that all concepts of metaphysical entities are empty, or in a weak form which merely holds that the existence of such entities cannot be philosophically established."[12] The "antimetaphysical argument," as she terms it, claims that since "we cannot establish transcendent metaphysical structures by philosophical argument, then such structures cannot be the basis of ethics."[13]

But, Murdoch replies, the fact that certain metaphysical structures or transcendent concepts cannot be irrefutably verified by logical constructions means only that they cannot be proven. To show that the acceptance of some particular transcendent idea cannot be forced upon us out of logical necessity proves neither that it doesn't exist nor that it is irrelevant or invalid for use in ethics. Murdoch therefore accepts the weaker form of the antimetaphysical argument, that is, that metaphysical entities or concepts cannot be established deductively or definitively, as philosophers have often tried to do. But she is saying that it is still consistent with that weaker form to grant the meaningfulness and relevance of transcendent, metaphysical concepts or entities. For example, she says that there may not be any conclusive philosophical proofs for the existence of God, "but it is not senseless to believe in God."[14] Thus Murdoch, a perfectly frank atheist, is quite prepared to accept the reasonableness of a position she herself rejects. That a position may not be logically compelling does not mean it is illogical. An idea may be reasonable and well thought out without forcing

11. Ibid., pp. 109–10.
12. Murdoch, "Vision and Choice in Morality," p. 52.
13. Murdoch, "Metaphysics and Ethics," pp. 107–8.
14. Murdoch, "Vision and Choice in Morality," p. 53.

assent or even persuading. It is necessary and inevitable that we form conceptions of reality. That such conceptions of reality are going to be mixtures of more-or-less objective description and of personal conviction does not necessarily make them false, and it certainly does not make them illegitimate.

Notice here another way the student Joe might be answered. The very fact that a commitment is held may enable, rather than impede, the debate, for in the absence of the kind of QED proofs that simply are not achievable for such things, a position remains subject to scrutiny, exploration, and evaluation of the sort that takes place in dialogue. In her recent *Metaphysics as a Guide to Morals,* Murdoch repeats a point of importance to her, namely, that a metaphysical system ought not to be some rigid piece of machinery deterministically sorting and shutting out data; rather, it should operate as a "big complicated heuristic image" that assists the weighing and review of ideas and perceptions.[15] The very fact that a metaphysical scheme, or more loosely, just a transcendent governing idea, cannot be proven is what makes it *arguable.* That is, such a commitment, rather than obstructing debate, actually enables it. It naturally invites it, feeds it, and enlivens it. In an age of pseudoskepticism this point is worthy of reflection; a sovereign or guiding principle does just as much to raise questions as to answer them. An intelligent commitment is more likely to elevate than to foreclose the discussion.

Murdoch argues, then, that while much of the modern criticism of traditional metaphysics and of past loyalties to transcendent principles must be accepted and take its toll, nevertheless it has produced no proof that compels us to reject (1) the existence of a transcendent source of values or metaphysical entities or outlines that we feel command our loyalty, or (2) their relevance and appropriateness in the development of an ethic based on them. Nothing in all the philosophies hostile to metaphysical concepts proves "that *belief* in the transcendent can form no point of a system of morality."[16] Murdoch thus exposes what she calls a conspiracy to render inadmissible, even inexpressible, some of the trusty old familiar philosophical notions. She is able to bring these concepts, albeit in a reduced and humbler form, down out of the attic to which recent modern thought had relegated them. Murdoch makes a case for the viability of a nonneutral transcendent principle in moral philosophy, which in the constructive portion of her work she seeks to identify and rehabilitate as "the Good."

15. Iris Murdoch, *Metaphysics as a Guide to Morals* (New York: Allen Lane, Penguin Press, 1992), p. 196.
16. Murdoch, "Vision and Choice in Morality," p. 55, her emphasis.

At this point, what we have is this: none of these rejections (the antimetaphysical and the antinaturalistic arguments, as she dubs them) can be validly invoked (or, as may be more often the case these days, as in Joe's case, unreflectively assumed) to ignore or exclude commitment to a transcendent ideal or frame of reference, for example, a Christian one, in moral discussion. So, without giving up gains honestly made by modern critiques, Murdoch has shown how, on their own terms, they fail to establish the extreme conclusions to which they have popularly been pushed. In so arguing, she has created a place for her own and others' constructive position in which the epistemology of morality operates under a sovereign, transcendent metaphysical principle. An interesting advantage of her critique is that while it makes it permissible to develop a metaphysically based ethic, we still have the benefit of the modern critiques in that we are unburdened of the old obligation or compunction to prove the sovereign principle. A Christian, such as Ruth, does not have to prove her point of view to justify it in a moral discussion. Making a case for it is enough. Even a tentative, exploratory, or experimental case is enough; moreover, doing so promotes the very dialectic that Joe says it deters.

Let's turn now to Murdoch's own intriguing constructive argument. She is in an interesting border position. On the one hand, she rejects the modern rejection of metaphysics and transcendent ideals in moral thought; on the other hand, she seeks to avoid the grandiose system-building of days past, and especially anything on the order of religious truth claims. She steers a narrow course between no metaphysics and too much, between no transcendent point of ultimacy and a religionlike but strictly nonreligious transcendent sovereign concept. The initial exposition of her idea of a sovereign moral concept is presented in *The Sovereignty of the Good*. Then, in the recent *Metaphysics as a Guide to Morals,* she extends her critical analysis to structuralism, deconstruction, and others; expands her apologia for the Good; gives a more aggressive and sustained separation of it from religious doctrine, particularly from Christian theology; and continues the discussion of the role of art as a medium of moral growth toward the Good.

What Murdoch proposes in the concept of the "Good" is something on the order of a secular, postmodern Platonist ideal. What Murdoch wants is a "transcendent good outside human imperfections and vanities, in some way beyond the operations of time, chance, and necessity,"[17] but one that avoids the anachronistic errors of dogmatism and intolerance, as well as

17. A. S. Byatt, *Iris Murdoch*, Writers and Their Work Series (London: Longman Group, 1976), p. 9.

the subjective psychological defenses of wishful thinking. It must therefore be "a kind of inconclusive non-dogmatic naturalism."[18] What is needed, she says, is a "non-metaphysical [in the sense of not being embedded in an inflexible, overly structured system], non-totalitarian, non-religious way" of dealing with "the transcendence of reality."[19] It is an attempt to provide the anchorage of the old classical metaphysics and of Christianity, but in a modern, secular, skeptical, atheistic, nondogmatic form.

Murdoch's version is largely a transposition of Simone Weil's Christian Platonist idea of perfection. The Good also owes much to G. E. Moore. It is a supersensible reality, mysterious and indefinable. It is apprehensible but not comprehensible. It cannot be reduced to or exchanged for any other concept; that is, one cannot substitute another value, such as love or freedom or duty, for the Good because all such other ideas are valued in terms of the Good.

This hierarchy of values is the chief point in her argument for the sovereignty of the Good. Reminiscent of Aquinas's Fourth Way, the moral argument for the existence of God, the appeal is made to our cognizance of degrees of goodness, which presupposes the idea of perfection. We do not endow objects or actions with moral values (as many modern ethicists have supposed); we try to discern the values that are in them. What our moral experience shows us is the operation of a standard that is real and external to us, that is wholly indifferent to our will or choice, the reality of which we know because we perceive comparative degrees of value. Degrees of value point to perfection without ever measuring up to it, and point to it *because* they do not measure up to it. We intuit perfection as always lying still beyond even the very best or the greatest. The Good, then, is not some sort of arbitrary ephemeral label, a function of our choices, pointing backward to an act of the will, as some ethicists would have us believe. Rather, Murdoch says, it is moral discernment (not choice) that points beyond to a distant, incorruptible ideal.

The supremacy of the concept of the Good is further supported, in Murdoch's view, by applied linguistic analysis. The term "good," she says, must enter into the definition of any other virtue, insofar as its value is measured, and measuring values is what morality is. "Asking what Good is, is not like asking what Truth is or what Courage is, since in explaining the latter the idea of Good must enter in; it is that in the light of which the explanation must proceed."[20] For example, if we identify courage as a value,

18. Murdoch, *The Sovereignty of the Good*, p. 44.
19. Murdoch, "Against Dryness: A Polemical Sketch," *Encounter* 27 (July 1966): 19.
20. Murdoch, *The Sovereignty of the Good*, p. 98.

we must say what kind of courage is *good*. If we say that love is the supreme ideal, we have to explain types of love and point to that which has the highest *good*. "And if we try to define Good as *x* we have to add that we mean of course a good *x*. If we say that Good is reason we have to talk about good judgment."[21] Murdoch believes the Good, therefore, can be shown to be truly the sovereign moral concept, implying a standard that is not reducible to psychological or empirical terms, which is the transcendent ideal that orders and adjudicates our perception of value. "Good as absolute, above courage and generosity and all the plural virtues, is to be seen as unshadowed and separate, a pure source, the principle which creatively relates the virtues to each other in our moral lives."[22]

Murdoch's program includes much of the doctrinal equipment of Christian theology in her form of "demythologized" (it is ironic that she should be so fond of this word; she does not seem to be aware of theological critiques of it), de-dogmatized, secularized, but quite deliberate substitutes: the Good for God; self-delusion of egoism for original sin; Beauty for grace; and contemplation of the particular, especially art, for prayer. Her philosophy is as fascinating for the ways it fails as for the ways it succeeds. It has been hailed as marking a reversal of Feuerbach's ladder, suggesting that philosophical trends have begun to turn in the direction of religion, rather than away from it, as has been the case since the Enlightenment. Reason now seems to be facing round, implying now the very ideas of the transcendent and the divine from which it was thought to have liberated itself.[23] Her critical work having cleared so inviting a path for the reintroduction of metaphysics and transcendent realities, followed by her constructive work, which goes to such lengths to provide ethics with all the resources of Christianity but without being religious, combine in their effect (1) to make the philosophical arena "safe" once again for Christian moral philosophy and (2) to recommend the Christian concepts where her alternatives for them fail to fulfill her own persuasive requirements for them. Tempting as it is to go into this subject (my view is that in its shortcomings, her program attracts more favorable attention to a Christian moral philosophy than it does for her determinedly nonreligious moral philosophy), it lies beyond the purpose of this essay. Here I look briefly at what happens if we accept her critical arguments establishing the suitability and legitimacy of

21. Ibid.
22. Murdoch, *Metaphysics as a Guide to Morals*, p. 507.
23. Peter Hebblethwaite, "Feuerbach's Ladder: Leszek Kolakowski and Iris Murdoch," *Heythrop Journal* 13 (April 1972): 143.

commitment to a sovereign ideal, but change the identity of the ideal from the Good to Truth.

Consider the linguistic analysis by which she establishes the Good as the concept of highest value. I believe her demonstration is incorrect. A parallel analysis will show Truth, not the Good, to have the final authority. When we delineate degrees of value, we in fact do so by reference not to goodness but to truth. We do not normally say "good courage is . . ." or "good wisdom is. . . ." Instead we talk about what is "true courage" or "real wisdom." Indeed, some of Murdoch's own examples actually insert the term "true" or a contextual equivalent of "true" (e.g., "real") as a measurement of goodness. When determining moral values, we thus refer not to a good-ness standard, although she is of course right that there are degrees of goodness. We actually (note that "actually" itself is a truth-measurement term) refer to a standard of truth or validity. Finally, the decisive test in an analysis of this kind is that when we define "Good," *we do so likewise in terms of truth.* We reckon goodness by truth, but not truth by goodness. We speak of what is "truly good," but we do not speak of "good truth." "Good truth" is a redundancy, for we conceive of knowledge of truth as by nature good (even if we experience it as unpleasant or painful), whereas what we identify as good remains to be authenticated (note that "authentic" is another truth-measurement term) as truly good.

We *know what is good by knowing what is true.* (In fact this point is the very substance of Murdoch's moral method, namely, the truer our perceptions, the better we become.) We inquire after what is the "true good" or what is "really good" as opposed to what appears to be good but is not, or what is illusory, false, or partially good. Here, linguistic analysis supports the significant conclusion that moral value is determined by truth value. It shows that even the Good is penultimate and remains to be tested against a more final standard, Truth. I do not believe the importance of this can be overstated: Truth, not the Good, is the sovereign concept. Moral judg-ments, appreciation of moral value, and goodness take place under the authority of the epistemological principle of truth value. The implication is that moral value is not ultimately a function of goodness, but that goodness is ultimately a function of truth. Moral reasoning operates under the epistemological principle of truth. The authority that Murdoch at-tributes to the Good actually belongs to the Truth.

An example might even be drawn from the criticism of one of Mur-doch's arguments in favor of moral theories that are based on beliefs, or, to put it another way, based on working from a "metaphysical picture" of reality. We have seen how she defends the legitimacy of metaphysical pictures by pointing out the faulty arguments that have been used to reject them. But she also has a positive argument in favor of them, namely, that beliefs or metaphysical pictures are psychologically useful and can be morally uplifting. As an aspect of moral theorizing, they constitute an activity that "is not the discovery of bogus 'facts' but is an activity whose purpose and justification are moral."[24] But it is clear that those who develop and apply such theories or pictures, including Murdoch, do so because they believe the one they use to be true, not because it may be uplifting.[25] Belief in a metaphysical frame of reference is held not because it gives moral inspiration; rather, it is capable of giving moral inspiration because it is accepted as true. And because it is accepted as true, it can do more than inspire — it is expected to reveal what is moral. For the people who believe in a transcendent source of value, its impact upon ethics derives from its status as truth claim; it represents the *reality from which value derives*, the *is* from which *ought* is determined. Belief systems are believed in, not because they are good for one, as if belief systems were health food one didn't care for but ate anyway. Rather, belief systems are the result of convictions about their truth, and they are cherished for the sake of their perceived truth.

Murdoch has her own reasons for steering away from Truth as the sovereign ideal. They are interesting in light of the question at hand (whether conviction is compatible with freedom of thought). The idea of truth and truth-seeking is quite central to Murdoch's work. But she cannot make it the sovereign ideal because for her it raises the specter of dogma, by which is meant intolerance and closed-mindedness, with the propensity to uncompromising systemization. It seems to Murdoch to pose a threat to freedom. To avoid the danger, Murdoch confines the notion of truth to instances of historical particularity. In this role, however, the idea of seeking the truth becomes indispensable to Murdoch's moral philosophy as her

24. Iris Murdoch, "A House of Theory," in *Conviction,* ed. Norman Mackenzie (London: MacGibbon & Kee, 1959), p. 226. See also "Hegel in Modern Dress," *New Statesman* 53 (May 25, 1957): 675.

25. Some remarks along this line may be found in Basil Mitchell's discussion in *Morality Religious and Secular: The Dilemma of the Traditional Conscience* (Oxford: Clarendon Press, 1980) and also in Eric Osborne, *Ethical Patterns in Early Christian Thought* (New York: Cambridge University Press, 1976). Murdoch's consistent hope is to detach religious method from its truth claims. In *Metaphysics as a Guide to Morals,* for instance, where Murdoch remarks, "Praise and worship are not just expressive attitudes, they arise in very various cognitive contexts and are themselves a grasp of reality" (p. 418), the reference is to the resource provided in religious devices for training attention, not a concession to the veracity or existence of the object of worship.

variation on the Socratic theme that knowledge is virtue. The idea is that the basis of morality is the cultivation of the individual's perception of reality. What is crucial is that the illusions of our natural egoism be disrupted and corrected by the recognition of the reality of that which is other-than-self. "'Good is a transcendent reality' means that virtue is the attempt to pierce the veil of selfish consciousness and join the world as it really is."[26] The moral agent is "compelled by obedience to the reality he can see."[27]

The Cave Allegory, Plato's story of ascent from ignorance to knowledge of truth, from illusion to reality, is a thematic image throughout her work, and its merging of the concepts of truth and goodness, of Reality and the Good, has for her the same appeal for the same reasons as the ontological proof. But there is enough of the twentieth-century aversion to doctrine of any sort out of fear of its tendency to become imperialistic that Murdoch ties these ideas of "obedience to reality" strictly to instances of space-time particularity and rejects for truth the role she assigns to the Good. Thus, in spite of her absorption in the concepts of truth (reality vs. illusion), she misappropriates the Good, which is the moral goal, as the sovereign ideal, when the sovereign ideal is in fact Truth. Much of her own extraordinary work goes far to support this conclusion. Ironically, every argument she makes for the role of the Good as the transcendent governing principle in moral thought leads beyond the Good to Truth, while her focus upon the discernment of reality (what is true) — namely, deliverance out of self-deception into cognizance of the truth, as the very essence of moral method — likewise points to the role of Truth as the sovereign principle rather than a subsidiary one.

The relationship of truth and truth-seeking to the Good receives deeper study in *Metaphysics as a Guide to Morals.* Her critique of structuralism, for instance, is its "radical separation of meaning from truth," resulting in the removal of the "idea of truth and truth-seeking as moral value," which she views with dismay, "not only as philosophically baseless and morally intolerable, but as politically suicidal."[28] Here Murdoch seems to see, but does not go quite so far as to claim, that freedom is threatened not

26. Murdoch, *The Sovereignty of the Good,* p. 93. The best place to read Murdoch's account of moral method is *The Fire and the Sun: Why Plato Banished the Artists* (New York: Oxford University Press, 1977), but see also "The Sublime and the Beautiful Revisited," *Yale Review* 49 (December 1959): 247–55; and *Metaphysics as a Guide to Morals,* especially chaps. 4 and 11, "Art and Religion" and "Imagination."

27. Murdoch, *The Sovereignty of the Good,* p. 42.

28. Murdoch, *Metaphysics as a Guide to Morals,* pp. 193, 194, 214.

by people with commitments to truth but rather by the absence of the checks and balances that can flow only when the ideal of Truth prevails as the sovereign principle of accountability in discourse among people with (or without) commitments, and prevails over what is to be judged good.

Throughout her work, Murdoch has reanimated the classical arguments against skepticism, enlivening our understanding of them by demonstrating their application to new questions. "The phenomena of rationality and morality are involved in the very attempt to banish them."[29] Further analysis, however, reveals that rationality (truth) has an antecedent relationship to morality (goodness) in quite the sense of the original observation of antiskepticism: the very existence of moral debate, of the development and evaluation of a moral philosophy or position on a moral issue, *presupposes* the operation of standards of rationality — issues of intelligibility, of coherence, of reasoning that is true or false, valid or invalid, sound or faulty. The apparatus of truth-seeking logically underlies the processes of morality, namely, good-seeking.

Fascinated in earlier years by the ontological proof, with its idea of perfection, Murdoch returns to the proof at length in *Metaphysics as a Guide to Morals*. She surveys its history and concludes with her own variation of J. N. Findlay's reversal of the proof: God's necessary nonexistence. In Murdoch's view, by demonstrating the necessary nonexistence of God, and then by combining this argument with the moral argument (the hierarchy of values, Thomas's Fourth Way), the ontological proof demonstrates instead the necessary existence of the Good.[30] If we change the term "Good" to "Perfection," its equivalent in the ontological proof, an interesting thing occurs in the linguistic analysis of "Truth." Where it would be an aberrant use of words to say "good truth," it would not be to say "perfect truth," although in this expression "perfect" takes on a Greek sense of "complete," "full," or "finished," rather than the sense of merit. But that we can say "true perfection" tells us that perfection is proven by truth, which, you will recognize, is the basis of the ontological argument. The primacy of Truth again suggests itself.

For Christians, the Trinity unites Perfection and Truth, which are incarnated in Jesus Christ, one of whose names is Truth (John 14:6); who is the embodiment of the (Christian) sovereign moral "Good," God; and who is the Logos, God knowable in human being. Suppose we let Murdoch's work establish for us the "right" to a commitment to a transcendent

29. Ibid., p. 203.
30. Ibid., see chap. 13, "The Ontological Proof," and also p. 508.

sovereign concept or metaphysical picture. Suppose we furthermore take over the case she makes for the concept as the Good, but as actually applying to the Truth as the sovereign principle. Perhaps it can also be admitted that these present-day elaborations of the old argument against radical skepticism (that pursuit of truth is the inescapable assumption behind the articulation of a stance, even one that denies the existence of truth or denies that it is knowable or can be agreed upon — for to make such claims is to assert that something is or is not the case, and that the object is to *know* what is the case) remind us that the epistemological idea of truth figures in a governing way in moral discourse and debate. Suppose we next, heartened by Murdoch's gallant and exacting philosophical rescue of the role of such beliefs in ethics, consider it philosophically permissible for the Christian to identify the Truth as Christ, the sovereign ideal and governing epistemological principle in the quest for moral understanding. We might easily go further and defend it as fulfilling more effectively and more economically all of Murdoch's requirements of the Good. Given Murdoch's critical preparation for, and outline of, the role of the Good, I would propose that the Christian version answers more effectively to every need.

However, the purpose of this essay is to show that having convictions is logically and practically compatible with freedom of thought. To that end, a distinction is made between, on the one hand, a governing principle (Truth) that is at barest minimum an epistemological presupposition necessary to the acquisition and discussion of knowledge and, on the other hand, the process of learning. In other words, how we go about learning and what is assumed by that act are two different, although related, things. While it would be satisfying to prove that Jesus Christ is, by being the Truth, better at being the Good (a better sovereign ideal by Murdoch's own standards) than the Good that Murdoch designs, I will confine the matter to an attempt to illustrate how such a conviction does not necessarily entail the danger of dogmatism and the threat to dialogue feared by both Murdoch and by Joe from our example. Up to this point, Murdoch has supplied quite a bit of correction and enlightenment for the attitude Joe represents. But Murdoch herself shares the extreme distrust, characteristic of Western postmodern mentality and exhibited in crude form by Joe, of religious, especially Christian, asseveration. Yet, in our culture today we have some extraordinary examples of extreme and abusive dogmatization, which might clarify some of the issues of freedom of thought as related to conviction, if we were to contrast them with the more ordinary methods of Christian learning.

The Process: Learning by Questioning

The phenomenon of destructive cults has received some media attention and mixed reactions from the academic community, but regardless of one's views about thought reform (mind control, coercive influence, coercive persuasion, brainwashing, etc.), we have here an opportunity to look at an instructive variation on the theme of conviction. An identifiable pattern of persuasion in use by some groups involves the following features: tightly controlled flow of information restricted to the viewpoint of the group and to their interpretations of any criticisms of it; "saturation" exposure to the group's point of view to the exclusion of all others; cultivation of psychological and material dependency; interpretation of resistance, opposition, or disagreement as morally evil; contrived guilt and exploitation of guilt; deliberate deception (sometimes called "heavenly deception" in the cultic ethic of end-justifies-means, e.g., if lying is what it takes to get a person into the salvation that is possible only in our group, it is right — not wrong — to deceive you); increasing isolation from outside influences (e.g., resources, activities, friends, family, information); a systematic invasion of privacy; and prevention of conditions that permit personal, private reflection.

Those being recruited find that the response to any expressed doubts or questions is either the immediate temporary disapproval and withdrawal of the initial excessive friendliness and welcome, pity for one's ignorance, or the insinuation of stupidity, or all three. Those who join find that to doubt or question the received doctrine is treated as sinful, as a moral violation, an act of betrayal. The assumptions, often enough straightforwardly expressed within the group, include the belief that it is this group alone that has the truth, and all the truth; whatever is outside the purview of the group must be rejected as belonging to the opposing world of ignorance, falsehood, and evil. There's more to it than this condensed inventory can reveal, but this much will be more than some are prepared to believe actually takes place. For the purposes of the present argument, it will be sufficient to entertain the idea of such a group for the sake of the contrast I want to draw. Those who have studied or had experience with cults will recognize the description.[31]

31. For the reader interested in the subject, the following references are particularly relevant to the present discussion: Robert Jay Lifton, *Thought Reform and the Psychology of Totalism* (New York: W. W. Norton, 1961; reprint, Chapel Hill: University of North Carolina Press, 1989); idem, "Cult Formation," *Harvard Mental Health Letter,* February 1991, reprinted in *Cultic Studies Journal* 8, no. 1 (1991): 1–6; Thomas W. Keiser and Jacqueline L. Keiser, *The Anatomy of an Illusion* (Springfield, Ill.: Charles C. Thomas, 1987); Arthur J. Deikman, "The Evaluation of Spiritual and Utopian Groups," *Journal of Humanistic Psychology* 23 (Summer

/On/ Truth and Pluralism

A combination of behavior modification techniques, together with a sophisticated, earnest-sounding appeal to a recruit's highest ideals and simultaneous gratification of basic psychological needs, produces an inter-locking system of psychosocial manipulation that has the potential to es-tablish control of thought and decision without need for recourse to crude old-fashioned external physical coercion (although physical abuse may occur). The effect of a successful sustained application of this system of simultaneous, multilateral pressures is the detachment of one's capacity for critical thinking and the transfer of one's capacity for independent decision making to the control of the group's leader(s). What takes place is what Stanley Milgram described in his famous study *Obedience to Authority* as the "agentic shift"; that is, moral and intellectual agency is transferred from the individual to an authority figure, who assumes these responsibilities on behalf of the subordinates.[32] Being moral then becomes simply a matter of obeying and conforming. Using good judgment becomes practicing the judgment that one is given. Groups that ply this system of manipulation directed at control and suppression of independent thought are referred to as destructive cults. Note that such groups are so identified not by their doctrine but by their method of recruiting and retaining followers.[33]

1983): 8–18; and Marc Galanter, *Cults: Faith, Healing, and Coercion* (New York: Oxford University Press, 1989). See also the American Psychiatric Association report *Cults and New Religious Movements*, ed. Marc Galanter (Washington, D.C.: APA, 1989); Richard Delgado, "Religious Totalism: Gentle and Ungentle Persuasion under the First Amendment," *Southern California Law Review* 51 (1977): 1–98; "The Vatican Report: Sects, Cults, and New Religious Movements," most easily available in *Origins* 16, no. 1 (May 22, 1986): 1, 3–10, and in *Cultic Studies Journal* 3 (Spring/Summer 1986): 93–116; Michael D. Langone, ed. *Recovery from Cults* (New York: W. W. Norton, 1993). Directed more toward popular readership are Robert B. Cialdini, *Influence: The New Psychology of Modern Persuasion* (New York: Quill, 1984); Ronald M. Enroth, *Churches That Abuse* (Grand Rapids: Zondervan, 1992); and Arthur Deikman, *The Wrong Way Home: Uncovering the Patterns of Cult Behavior in American Society* (Boston: Beacon Press, 1990). A number of autobiographical accounts of cult recruitment and exit are available. One such account can be found in Steven Hassan's *Combatting Cult Mind Control* (Rochester, Vt.: Park Street Press, 1988).

32. Stanley Milgram, *Obedience to Authority: An Experimental View* (New York: Harper & Row, 1974), pp. 132–55, esp. pp. 147–48. Milgram also applies his findings to studies of compliance with Third Reich Nazis. Milgram believes his experiments support Hannah Arendt's contention in *Eichmann in Jerusalem* (Magnolia, Mass.: Peter Smith, 1983) about the "banality of evil." Eichmann was deadly, she says, not because he was the evil, sadistic genius that the prosecution made him out to be. What made him the war criminal he was, was his abdication of critical thinking and moral responsibility; he was just doing his job, just following orders — which is what made him a "good" soldier, citizen, and patriot.

33. This is why the most tiresome attempt to leap to the defense of cults ("Well, wasn't

Even from this abbreviated description of a complex phenomenon, it may not be too difficult to trace an illuminating contrast. What are the conditions of an authentic conviction, the kind of conviction we respect because it is what a conviction is supposed to be? It turns out to be the opposite of what we find in the cult experience. Most of us, if we think about it, would concur that a conviction is meaningful as a conviction only insofar as it is the result of genuine interior assent on the part of the person who holds it, moreover, that the assent follows some form of personal engagement with relevant inquiry. Some hard-to-express but necessary element of "conviction" is missing to the extent that the conviction is superimposed somehow from without, manipulated, held unreflectively or without being understood or without awareness of its ramifications, and certainly if it is coerced in any way. Conviction that we are likely to regard as genuine tends to be the product jointly of training in, or exposure to, a point of view, into which is incorporated, over time, personal exploration, uncensored contact with disagreement or alternatives, discussion within and without, together with private reflection and the validating or contradicting experience of one's life. It is a process in which ideas are both frankly debated and also isolated for solitary pondering, where they are mulled over and weighed in light of many things. Curiosity and contemplation, which take time, are tools leading to increasing ownership of an idea and thus to an informed and genuinely personal acceptance or rejection. Whatever encouragement the individual may receive to make a commitment, we are likely to find the commitment somehow more real if questions, puzzlement, and reservations are respected and welcomed, not condemned or maneuvered for advantage.

Christianity once regarded as a cult? These new groups are just the same: persecuted, unpopular minorities whose success is envied by established religions") is a complete misunderstanding of what is at issue. What is at stake is not the right of people to subscribe to a cult's doctrine but the right to do so *freely*. What is to be scrutinized is the extent to which commitment in a cult group is achieved through deception, manipulation, or exploitation. It is not the content of a cult's beliefs that is criticized as "cultic" (although the content of belief certainly ought to be open to critical discussion among any who are interested). Rather, it is the extent to which deliberate deception and manipulation thwart freedom of thought and choice. In fact, one of the dividends of the study of cults is a refinement in our understanding and classification of techniques of persuasion, so that we acquire much greater acuity in identifying the subtle points at which a legitimate device of rhetoric or solicitation begins to corrupt, rather than invite, assist, or guide the thinking process requisite to unobstructed decision making. A close look at how cults recruit and retain their followers will equip one to evaluate strategies of persuasion in other contexts, such as Christian evangelism, where Christians ought to be very sure that the method does not compromise the message.

In cults, in contrast, attempts are made to ferret out any suspected reservations on the part of a recruit, not in order to help the recruit pay attention to them and think them through to the recruit's own satisfaction, but rather to forestall that very process by bulldozing any caution, reluctance, or question with cult fast-talk or "sacred science."[34] A person's honest doubts, we feel, ought to be tolerated; they may or may not find reassurance, but we usually think it less than healthy when proselytizers try to deny or repress doubts and certainly unhealthy if they try to punish them. Cult "conviction" may be intense, but it survives only by taboos that keep it stagnant; there is no genuine interchange either with the world outside or with the inner world of one's own private deliberations. In such an atmosphere it is impossible to preserve such useful notions as "loyal opposition," which remind us that within human limitations of knowing, a deep, viable commitment may have healthy tensions. In cult-controlled isolation, conviction is frozen.

Doesn't it damage the idea of free adherence if a conviction is not permitted to be a dynamic, ongoing process, to an ever-increasing extent under the self-direction of the adherent? Ideally, shouldn't Christian conviction, for example, be free to become richer and more complex with challenges worked through, with intellectual growth? Shouldn't it be possible to take into consideration new experience and data as they flow in, to interact with them in light of one's belief, if the belief is really held freely? Learning is not to be capped. A conviction that we think of as truly belonging to the one who holds it is marked by a willingness to entertain the impact on it of new ideas, new angles as they present themselves. A conviction tends to lose its value in our eyes if it can be maintained only in an information vacuum. A conviction is less impressive to us as such if we discover that conflicting or challenging ideas are avoided, either by one's own choice, or on one's behalf by another to prevent dissent or defection. When people hold a conviction naively or dogmatically, they might be silly and harmless, or part of a formidable political force; they may intimidate, or we may condescend. But whatever power or appearance it may wield, a conviction that is withheld from the arena where ideas are challenged and subject to modification and correction, a conviction that is not explored or examined honestly, however hesitantly, a conviction that is sheltered from criticism, lacks some essential ligature by which it is vitally connected to the mind of the person who holds it. A person who clings to a belief in

---

34. See Robert Jay Lifton, *Thought Reform and the Psychology of Totalism: A Study of "Brainwashing" in China* (1961; reprint, New York: W. W. Norton, 1969), pp. 419-29.

response to pressures that he or she has not scrutinized begins to look less like a person holding a belief and more like a robot, responding according to programming rather than engaging the world out of an integrated center of consciousness and moral responsibility. Indeed, "personal closure" is the term used to describe the shutdown of critical faculties that can be achieved by cult manipulation.

Call to mind instances in which claims to conviction are held suspect. A teenager eagerly embraces an idea that we suspect has more to do with the need for peer acceptance than with a reasoned review of its intrinsic merits. A mother is alone in insisting that her son, a convicted serial-killer, is a good boy who would never do such things. An untraveled village man living in isolation takes for granted the self-evidence and universality of his worldview. A consumer who succumbed to a "hard sell" defends the shrewdness of his purchase. A Christian fundamentalist refuses to take required college courses in religion from the department's faculty members, all of whom are Protestant clergy, because such exposure might tempt him from the "wisdom of God" with their "worldly wisdom." In these examples we see how riddled with liabilities are our powers of reasoning. A need to belong may cloud judgment. Yearnings may serve us for facts when facts are too painful. A view held in all innocence may be the product of an unwitting ethnocentrism. The need to justify an action may motivate a rationalization. Where belief is too fragile, it can be compensated for and shielded by a ferocious anti-intellectual orthodoxy. The need to resolve the experience of cognitive dissonance may subconsciously prompt us to interpretations that reconcile contradictions so that we never actually have to face them. The method of recruitment used by cults cunningly exploits all such all-too-human vulnerabilities, creating around desires and dreams a sealed system of rationale that becomes impervious to examination as involvement with the group increasingly compromises the ability to maintain boundaries — between what is relevant and irrelevant to a question, between psychological needs and logical reasons, between self and the group.

So beneath what looks like a level playing field for cult and noncult religious commitment is in fact a deep fault line running the length of the ground. The difference is the systemic, totalist way cults practice the repression of critical thought and the individual person's independent analysis and self-determination. The difference between cult and noncult conviction has to do with the individual's freedom to question. Significantly, this freedom to question is not at all a freedom from influence or a freedom from persuasion. Our lives are saturated from birth to death with physical, educational, psychological, and sociocultural influences that shape the way we think and over which we have virtually no control. In addition, we are ceaselessly targeted for quite calculated persuasion by every sort of political, fund-raising, and marketing special interest. Cicero, Kauṭilya, the apostle Paul, the Pelagians, Anselm, David Hume, Sigmund Freud, Martin Bormann, Gandhi, Billy Graham, Washington lobbyists, Mothers Against Drunk Drivers, drug dealers, and the Pillsbury Doughboy all seek to influence us. There's no escape from persuasion.

Freedom consists not in removal to some airtight island impenetrable to forms of influence. There is no such place, even in the imagination. It certainly does not consist in the illusion people cherish that they are not susceptible to influence, insidious or otherwise. Freedom consists not in being unpersuaded or uninfluenced but in the capacities we manage to exercise in order to question, namely, to know about and evaluate the overt and subtle forces at work on us, to be informed, to keep a rhythm of discourse with many others, alternating with our own private thought. Of the ideas that recommend themselves to us, some may be right and true, but which ones? and to what degree? Why do we believe what we believe? How do I come to be persuaded of the truth of my convictions? The freedom that gives conviction its meaning and validity as a conviction (whether or not it is true or we agree with it) is not a freedom to be untouched but a freedom to become cognizant of the nature of the influence in order to weigh its legitimacy and relevance. It is a freedom to probe and test one's conviction by a constant two-directional movement of going deeply into it and of standing back from it. It is a freedom to plunge devotedly into one's ideal, seeking by its methods the insights it gives, while interacting without undue constraint with new and different ideas. It's a freedom to find a broader context, a freedom to enter the lists. This is a freedom that cults must abort. Failure to activate an individual's own psychological mechanisms to foreclose on the exercise of such freedom will mean a failure to retain centralized control over the member's behavior and allegiance.

No one will deny that abuses of influence take place within Christian groups, and indeed some become cults. But the interest of cult methods of persuasion is that they model an extreme form in which a whole encyclopedic list of exploitative, psychologically subversive tactics coalesce into a system of psychological coercion that is capable of liquidating the ability to think independently or to interact genuinely with influences outside the cult. By studying cults, we become much better able to identify abusive persuasion in other contexts where abuses may be incipient or partial and therefore less obvious. Not all persuasion is abusive, and in any case persuasion is ubiquitous in human experience. But some forms of persuasion that are abusive can, when coordinated toward a single objective, cross the line into forms of psychological coercion. To the degree that such elements determine what a person's convictions are, the person's conscious, informed, and voluntary connection to the conviction is intercepted. That connection of the individual thinking, deciding mind with the beliefs it holds is exactly what is at stake. The telling factor revolves around the extent to which that mind can of its own accord interact with information and input from the world around it in relationship to the beliefs it holds. What needs to be retained by the individual is the final role of conscious, informed agency in decisions about commitments, and the means of doing so is to exercise the freedom to question.[35]

May we come to some general agreement that such is the nature of meaningful conviction? Seeking truth involves the exchange of information and ideas, review, engaging in trials of argument and practice, attempting to persuade and responding to persuasion, facing the implications of doubt, searching out one's own motives, and giving attention to perplexities. These are basic ingredients in the learning process by which we come to conviction and retain conviction. In its essence, it is a process of considering questions. The fact that very few people, if any, on even fewer subjects actually fulfill this ideal of the alert, honest, thoughtful mind does not change the fact that we think conviction is properly the result of some such process of questioning.

The issue now at hand is, How is the sovereign principle of truth (as discussed above in the section "The Principle: The Sovereign Truth") related to this process of learning by questioning? The answer is that the principle of sovereign truth (1) founds the search, makes the process of questioning possible, guides it, and is the goal of it; even while (2) it itself is subject to it.

The original problem was the perceived incompatibility of conviction about truth with the freedom to question it. Is belief, particularly Christian belief, necessarily held uncritically and dogmatically? Are we forced to a choice between either unbelief or dogmatism, between being modern pluralist or anachronistic catechumen? Is genuine conviction inimical to the process of debate and questioning? Acquaintance with cult methods of recruiting and retaining followers suggests exactly the opposite: conviction

---

35. Interestingly, this very observation is the focus of two of the documents of Vatican II: "Declaration on the Relation of the Church to Non-Christian Religions" (Nostra Aetate) and "Declaration on Religious Liberty" (Dignitatis Humanae).

about truth counts as conviction only when it involves honest attention to questions that arise. A belief that must remain uncritical in order to be believed has already failed to be worthy of commitment. A distinction that will help keep us out of this trouble is the distinction involving the principle of truth that underlies the process of learning. This distinction lets us separate the immutability of Truth from the mutability of our knowledge of it. Sovereign Truth may be trustworthy; our understanding of it is always suspect. What we hold to be true, therefore, always must be open to scrutiny.

All this brazen use of "truth" and "Truth" would scandalize the Oxford analysts and the assorted modern antirealists. So, just to keep our bearings here nearing the finish, let's review how we arrived at these uses of the word. We have appropriated Murdoch's criticisms of the antinaturalism and antimetaphysical positions, so she can run interference for us with the objections of the analysts and antirealists. She has made a plausible case, which we are accepting, for a sovereign principle in moral philosophy. However, it has been argued that epistemological and moral sovereignty lies not with her choice, the Good, but rather with the concept of truth. For good measure, we have thrown in the centuries-old argument against radical skepticism, to the effect that the ideal of truth is presupposed in any attempt at discourse or discovery, including doubt. To doubt presupposes truth. Finally, considering that some religious traditions identify their ideal as the supreme Truth (Truth, now capitalized as a specified ideal, as Murdoch uses the Good), I have begged indulgence to do so as well. How might we relate the process of questioning to the principle of truth if we identify that sovereign epistemological and moral concept of truth with a particular religious ideal, namely, Jesus Christ.

Christ as Truth is a familiar theme in Christian Scripture and tradition. He is the way, the truth and the life; he is the Logos, the rationality underlying creation, the one through whom all things were made; it is his Spirit of truth whom he will send to guide disciples into all the truth; he is the light that overcomes the darkness; he is the one to whom all authority in heaven and on earth has been given. It is he who invites us to ask, seek, and knock with the promise that we will receive, find, and be answered. The Epistles speak of his Spirit who searches everything, even the depths of God; this Truth is the image of the invisible God, in whom all the fullness of God was pleased to dwell, through whom all things hold together. In apocalyptic vision he is Alpha and Omega, the beginning and the end. Devout Christians are often especially fond of these and other passages of variations on the theme of Christ as the supreme source of truth, the source of knowledge of truth, the light of life. For Christians, Jesus incarnates Truth and guides us in knowing it.

Classical Christian theology elaborates the theme philosophically. Most interesting in this context is perhaps the epistemology of Augustine, for whom Christ is the light of the mind,[36] through whom we are awakened, in the Platonic sense of anamnesis, to truth. Christ is God incarnate, the truth by virtue of which anything true is true, and also the active power of illumination by which we see truth. It is Christ who illumines the mind wherever and in whatever medium knowledge of truth is pursued. The Truth of Christ can thus be conceived of, for instance, as the light behind even word analysis in philosophy in the best tradition of J. L. Austin, so that our very usage of "truth" is critiqued and refined, confusions sorted out. Christ is the source of intelligibility itself. Christ is the true Teacher, the wisdom of God, dwelling within the mind, who makes possible the quest of truth and also its discovery. If we take some such interpretation of Christ as the light of the mind, the means to truth because he is Truth, as some theologians and even ordinary Christians have liked to do, what freedom does that give us to enter, with our Christian convictions, the pluralistic ring?

Murdoch's objection to the identification of the sovereign moral principle with any particular content or doctrine is its peril of dogmatism. No sooner do we get some notion in our heads about what the ultimate Truth is or who the Good is — whatever messiah or ideology we think it is, Jesus, Allah, Marx, Mao, or Moon — than we promptly start abusing other people in every conceivable way in the name of it. Human history up to and especially including the present gives credibility to these fears. But the question may be asked, Must it always be so? Or, to direct the question precisely to the philosophical point, Is it *necessarily* so?

I argue that, although Jesus has been made the excuse for every sort of persecution, the real nature of Christ as the sovereign Truth is to invite the learning processes of the sincere seeker after truth, in which doubt and questions, honestly acknowledged, advance education, and in which intellectual occlusions have no place. This trust in Truth to reveal itself militates against fanaticism, intolerance, and milder forms of narrow-mindedness. But this trust in Truth likewise mitigates against credulity and simple-mindedness. It may be anchored and oriented by doctrinal confession, but the learning process it begins is continually fed by ambiguities, apparent

---

36. Ronald Nash takes the phrase for the title of his exposition of Augustine's epistemology (*The Light of the Mind: St. Augustine's Theory of Knowledge* [Lexington: University of Kentucky Press, 1969]). Of special interest here is his attention to the neglected Epistle 120 (pp. 92–93).

inconsistencies, inconclusiveness, unfinished business, unassimilated data, and existential experience. We need to have a way to understand how we keep the faith, that is, to hold the Christian conviction of trust in this Truth, while always keeping our conclusions subject to amendment in view of our irremediable predicament of historical contingency, human limitations, and fallibility. Preserving the distinction between the epistemological principle of truth, as identified here with Christ, and the process by which we learn about this truth lets us separate the unchanging and perfect nature of Christ from our developing and imperfect knowledge of him. The distinction lets us confess Christ as Truth, while practicing a humility appropriate to learning readiness at whatever stage of personal pilgrimage we may be, open at that level to new ideas.

In short, conviction of Christ as the sovereign Truth, in such terms of faith and trust as let us acknowledge his nature as Truth at the same time we remember the incompleteness and unreliability of our grasp of any truth, including his, gives us the *freedom to welcome pluralism,* with all of its opportunities to expand and deepen our knowledge. This is the very freedom that Murdoch and so many others of our day believe is threatened by commitment to an ideal of Truth. With the distinction between the epistemological principle or guide and the process of our following it, it is harder to twist the sovereign Truth into the role of bully. In fact, once we get this distinction clearly in mind, it is possible to endorse pluralistic tolerance, not just from the standpoint of a necessary but perhaps grudging respect for diversity and individual conscience, but to endorse it enthusiastically as a valuable resource for the Christian life of the mind.

Endorsement of pluralism has not historically been a high-visibility Christian virtue. Nor, for that matter, has it been a general practice of humankind over the millennia. Again, however, studies of skepticism help us understand the problems. The fear has ever been that if the doctrine may be challenged at any point, the surety of the whole is shaken. The fear is that any questioning impugns the object of inquiry rather than the certainty of our understanding of it.[37] So, the logical extreme (to which this idea has indeed been pressed at the opposing poles of cults and religious fundamentalism on the one end and postmodern noncommital pluralism on the other) is (1) if one has a commitment, any questioning of it amounts to an essential denial of or departure from it (cults, right-wing fundamen-

37. For a good illustration, see Popkin, *The History of Scepticism,* pp. 69–70. He discusses the criticisms of the Reformers' questioning by Francis de Sales, who saw it as necessarily reducing them to "sceptical despair."

talism); or (2) the fact that everything can be questioned implies that there is nothing stable enough to commit to (postmodern pluralist). The distinction I am talking about makes it possible to transfer the implication of fallibility from the object of knowledge, in this case Christ as the sovereign Truth, to the human mind trying to know it, leaving the possibility of a logical compatibility between conviction of Truth and doubt about it, and even suggesting their mutually supportive relationship in the acquisition of knowledge.

The moderate skeptical observation is surely right: nothing can be established beyond disagreement. Everything probably ought to be at one time or another, in one way or another, subject to question. Our understanding is at least always either incomplete or inconsistent; this is a lesson we may carry over from the sciences. Godel's theorems demonstrate that no system that is internally consistent can be complete, and that any system that is complete contains inconsistencies. Murdoch is fond of commenting that the useful metaphysical picture is always an incomplete, open-ended one.[38] Dorothy Sayers puts the idea pithily: "There's nothing you can't prove if your outlook is only sufficiently limited."[39] Such is precisely the situation in cults. Sustaining an impregnable doctrine requires a very narrow and tightly sealed perimeter. The process of questioning natural to those who sense the possibilities of both error and progress in human understanding is the process cults must obviate.

If one is prepared to say, however, that Christ is the same yesterday, today, and tomorrow, although my knowledge and certainties about Christ are not necessarily the same from one day to the next, then we have made room for the questioning process that is consistent with deep and abiding conviction. We have room for seasons of spiritual desolation and doubt. We have room for the spiritual-epistemological duty of relentless self-examination, to search to the bottom of the motives of our beliefs. We have room for dialogue and exploration of other traditions and points of view. It becomes possible for the church to change its mind on issues such as its relationship to temporal powers, the ordination of women, or uses of technology, without impugning the reliability and consistency of Christ. It is not Christ whose position has changed. It is not the Truth that has changed, but through the questioning process, with research, prayer, and debate, *we* have refined our discernment of it. Revisions are not necessarily

38. For example, Murdoch, *Metaphysics as a Guide to Morals,* p. 89.
39. Dorothy Sayers, *A Matter of Eternity: Selections from the Writings of Dorothy L. Sayers,* ed. Rosamond Kent Sprague (Grand Rapids: Eerdmans, 1973), p. 52.

improvements, but as long as we continue to compile experience, ask questions, and enter discussion with an interest in other views, there is hope for improvement.

What I have tried to work on here philosophically is something that I think many Christians intuitively believe, and that some theologically minded Christians have discussed, along the lines of Augustine's "I believe in order to understand." My judgment differs, however, from Tertullian's in that I think that Athens has a great deal to do with Jerusalem. We may indeed know in whom we have believed and be persuaded that he is able to keep that which we have committed unto him, but such belief, persuasion, and commitment require that we go deeply into the study of them and of their object. The kind of trust in a sovereign Truth we are looking at here has become quite foreign to philosophical debate.[40] The climate is not hospitable to an exploration of the interesting ways such a sovereign Truth functions epistemologically. The sovereign epistemological principle of Truth, Jesus Christ, anchors and enables the search for truth in a process of inquiry, the basis of which is the integrity of the individual intellect in its commerce with life.

One philosophical function of the sovereign Truth of Christ is an axiomatic first principle that generates whole systems, moral programs with personal, social, and political corollaries. But at another time, Christ as sovereign Truth may function philosophically as more of a heuristic device, sponsoring a debate that may return to question his sovereignty. A Christian may, for the sake of pursuit of truth, temporarily bracket personal faith without repudiating it in order to follow out an argument in thought or to enter fully into one with others. Christ as Truth may function in argument "temporarily unsupported" while the argument may lead to or away from support for the initial "assumption" of Christ as Truth.[41] The Christian who keeps the distinction between the principle (Christ) and the process of learning (of which such arguments are components) need not fear the outcome of the argument because the outcome of such an argument may be accepted as "temporarily" valid and therefore constituting an as yet unanswered question, but regarded as provisional within a larger context. Faith may wax and wane in such a process, often with an overall direction of forward progress. But if we remember the distinction between trust in

---

40. So much so that this antipathy was the subject of Nicolas Rescher's editorial "Postmodernity and Paranoia," *American Philosophical Quarterly* 27 (January 1990): 89–90.

41. See Jonathan Barnes's description of Aristotelian and Platonic forms of hypotheses in his *Toils of Scepticism* (New York: Cambridge University Press, 1990), pp. 92–95.

the principle (of Christ as Truth) and the flexibility of the give-and-take learning process, faith need not be made to stand or fall in encounter with such challenges to it. Charles Converse West is thus able to assert:

> The Christian therefore is the guardian of the human question in the university and society against all the systems of ideas. He encourages empirical sciences to remain truly empirical, in order better to serve human welfare. He drives home ever again the point that we know what a human being is only by meeting him, recognizing his claims on us, and living with him, as God meets us in the man Jesus. There is no conclusion to this learning process. But it is a process of living which knowledge was made to serve and illuminate.[42]

A Christian therefore has homework in any and every field. One who is a disciple of this sovereign Truth ought to recognize an obligation to be accurately informed, to think and rethink. If Christ is the sovereign Truth, then spiritual pilgrimage must also be intellectual pilgrimage. I have attempted here to use some philosophical tools in defense of a very old idea, one that finds itself presently in uncongenial times. It is the idea so beautifully, and succinctly, expressed by Simone Weil: "One can never wrestle enough with God if one does so out of pure regard for the truth. Christ likes us to prefer truth to him because, before being Christ, he is truth. If one turns aside from him to go toward the truth, one will not go far before falling into his arms."[43]

42. Charles C. West, *Outside the Camp: The Christian and the World* (Garden City, N.Y.: Doubleday, 1959), p. 165.

43. See Simone Weil, "Spiritual Autobiography," in *Waiting for God,* trans. Emma Craufurd (1951; reprint, San Francisco: Harper & Row, 1973), p. 69.

• 8 •

The Christian Base Communities and the
Ecclesia Reformata Semper Reformanda

RICHARD SHAULL

M Y CALVINIST HERITAGE awakened in me, early on, a passionate concern for and commitment to the church as the instrument of God's
redemptive purpose in history. That same heritage also led me to believe
that the church, in order to be faithful to this calling, must always be open
to renewal and willing to respond time and again, in new ways, to the
guidance of the Holy Spirit in new historical situations. I have been proud
of the fact that I belong to a church that, since its beginning, has declared
itself to be an *ecclesia reformata semper reformanda*.

These convictions played an important part in my decision to return
to Princeton in 1962. After my return, I was happy to find, in Charles West,
a colleague with similar concerns and greatly appreciated the opportunity
we had to work together for a number of years in courses on the mission
of the church in the modern world. I was encouraged not only by the
response of students to these issues but also by the possibilities I saw for
the renewal of mainline Protestant churches in the United States.

In recent years, however, I have come to the conclusion that these
churches, by and large, hold out few prospects for the radical renewal called
for at this time. In fact, precisely when the changing human situation calls
for new and creative responses, they seem to be turning their backs on these
challenges, dedicating more and more of their energies to the struggle for
self-preservation. In various denominations, small but well-organized
groups energetically defend patterns of church life and mission from the
past, while those in positions of leadership, who once encouraged and

135

created space for new ventures in mission, seem more and more reluctant to do so.

Upon returning to Latin America after an absence of nearly two decades, I was thus quite surprised by what I found there. What I had most hoped for but failed to see in the United States was happening: the re-formation, or, as some there would call it, the "reinvention" of the church. But it was not taking place among the historical Protestant churches, but rather in Roman Catholic circles; it was occurring not as the result of the initiative and struggle of distinguished church leaders and scholars but among poor and marginal people and those living in solidarity with them in the Christian Base Communities (CBCs).

The church as described in the New Testament was a "happening." The poorest people were sharing the little they had and learning how to work together to transform their world in the direction of the reign of God. Those considered powerless were struggling courageously in the face of overwhelming destructive power, as they willingly offered their lives in the struggle for justice. Among those denied everything most of us consider indispensable for human life, I found an amazing spirit of joyfulness and of hope. In their midst, I could understand what Paul meant when he spoke of the church as the firstfruits of a new age.

In the Christian Base Communities, I recognized a new historical manifestation of the *ecclesia reformata semper reformanda,* of such central importance in our Calvinist heritage. Consequently, I came to the conclusion that it is from the vantage point of this new reformation that we can best understand who we are as heirs of the Reformation of the sixteenth century. In this encounter, the Spirit may lead us to discover how we can recover and incarnate that heritage once again.

As a result of my contacts with a number of CBCs, I'm convinced that we in North America can learn a great deal from them. We cannot import and copy what they have done, but we can get clues from them about essential elements in the re-formation of the church that we should take into account. Here I would like to examine those I consider to be most important.

Connecting with a "New Historical Subject"

Central American and South African Christians speak of a *kairos.* By the use of this word, they call attention to the specific historical situation in which they are living, as a time when "God is passing through," a time of

136

unique opportunity, a moment in which the time is ripe for new initiatives and movements. For them, at the center of this new situation is the emergence of the poor and marginal Third World people as "the new historical subject." The Christian Base Communities in Latin America represent a creative response to this kairos.

I share the opinion of many Latin American social scientists and theologians that the emergence of this new historical subject in and through the popular movements is the most important development that has taken place in the last decade in Central and South America. Everywhere such movements are springing up and growing in strength and importance, primarily among the poorest people: movements of peasants and industrial workers, Indian and Afro-American movements, women's movements, movements of the mothers and wives of the "disappeared," movements for alternative health care and popular education, and small cooperatives for production and distribution. In some places, the entire populace seems to be on the move for life, health, culture, dignity, and freedom.

The victims of exploitation and injustice are not only becoming more aware of what is happening to them but are also perceiving why they are suffering. More than this, they are emerging from their silence and passivity of centuries and are deciding to take into their own hands the struggle to change society. They represent a new social class that is coming to the fore as protagonists in the struggle for liberation.

In many places, the primary motivating force in all this is Christian faith. As small groups of peasants or residents of slums gathered to study the Bible, they discovered that the biblical story was their story and that its language became their language. A new experience of the presence and power of God in their lives gave them a new sense of their worth as human beings and a new experience of community. And as they began to work together to meet some of their most immediate needs, they found themselves energized and organized for action. A profoundly religious people found, in their religious heritage, rich resources enabling them to become subjects, taking responsibility for their life and destiny.

If we look at the history of the church from this vantage point, we can perceive how frequently a new form of church has emerged in response to the needs and aspirations of a new social class. This happened as the newly organized Lutheran and Reformed Churches connected with the emerging "middle class" in Europe in the sixteenth century, and as the Wesleyan movement developed among industrial workers and other marginal people in eighteenth-century England. In both instances, those in the forefront of these movements faced the spiritual crisis of their time and found, in the gospel, a message of good news that spoke directly to the needs and aspirations of a new historical subject. They also re-formed the church as this newly discovered message became incarnate in another cultural world and thus became a dynamic force not only in shaping that culture but also in transforming society. Today, something similar is happening through a new reformation in Latin America.

In the Beginning: An Initiative from Outside

The Base Communities are frequently referred to as *the church of the poor,* and rightly so. But I have discovered that the original response to the kairos mentioned above, which led to the birth of the CBCs, came not from the poor themselves but from men and women belonging to the more privileged classes who decided to live and work in solidarity with the poor.

My wife and I lived for several months in Colonia Nicarao, in Managua, Nicaragua, and were closely associated with members of the Base Community there. This CBC early on served as an inspiration and model for other CBCs in Nicaragua, from Managua to the island of Solentiname. Its members trace its origin, in the early 1970s, to the arrival of a young Spanish priest who lived in their midst, helped them to look at their situation through eyes of faith, and brought them together in small groups in their homes to study the Bible and reflect on what was happening in their daily lives.

In an extremely poor neighborhood in Canoas, in southern Brazil, I found a dynamic CBC, whose members were working together to bake bread, care for the health of their children, secure basic services for their community from the government, and deal with larger social and political issues. This all began twenty years ago, when a Marist brother decided to leave the school for wealthy children in which he was teaching and move into this neighborhood, a decision that led to his arrest and imprisonment by the military on several occasions.

Across an entire continent several thousand priests, lay brothers and sisters, as well as women and men from diverse professional backgrounds, took this step. As they moved closer to the poor, they frequently found themselves regarded with suspicion by those in power. Many were arrested or forced to leave when their lives and the lives of those with whom they were working were threatened; a number were killed by death squads and the military.

We have here something similar to what happened in the early stages of the modern missionary enterprise. Those early pioneers saw a world of millions of men, women, and children living and dying without Christ and felt called to dedicate their lives to carrying the gospel to them. They decided to go to other lands and peoples, with little concern for economic well-being or security for themselves or their families, even if it meant begging for the money they needed from friends and from interested congregations. It involved entering an unknown and strange world, learning another language, and getting to know a culture not their own in order to discover how to present the Christian message in that language and culture and how to express it in life and community.

The new company of missionary pioneers in Latin America had this same spirit. Their eyes had been opened to the suffering around them. Their conscience had been awakened, and they knew that God was calling them to respond. They also knew that they could not wait for the religious institution to which they belonged to recognize this need and set up mission programs in line with this new vision. If their religious order or diocese was ready to send and support them, they rejoiced in that fact. Otherwise, they had no choice but to go ahead on their own. Priests went to live in poor urban or rural neighborhoods, working in the community to support themselves. Small groups of nuns got together to do the same. Often a few young women and men trained as doctors, teachers, or social workers took a similar step and offered their professional services to their new neighbors.

They knew that the world of the poor was not their world. They did not speak their language or understand their culture. They realized that they could not be content to pass on their own religious language or reproduce the patterns of congregational life developed elsewhere. That would alienate the poor even further from themselves and their own history and culture. It would also increase their sense of inferiority and powerlessness. On this new missionary frontier, missioners were called upon to enter an unknown world, identify themselves with the suffering and struggle of the poor, listen to them, and learn from them and with them. This meant learning how to honor their culture and their religious faith, helping them to understand better their own world and name it, discover their own ability to think and to act, and thus participate in a creative process out of which a new language of faith and new forms of community life might emerge.

Living and working in this way, the early missioners set in motion a process that is often being carried forward by the poor themselves. On a recent visit to Nicaragua, I met with a number of grassroots CBC leaders from isolated rural areas, most of them with little formal education, who are products of this early work and continue it in other communities. I was amazed to discover the contribution they were making, which went far beyond anything an outsider from another culture and class could do. They were able to relate to the poorest rural folk, help them understand their situation, and discover what they might do to change it; they were able to draw on the rich language and imagery of their culture to speak of their faith and the depth of their understanding of the gospel.

Becoming a Community of Faith in the Struggle for Life

In our traditional work of evangelism, we have tended to pull people away from the immediacy of family and community, as well as the struggle with daily problems, into a church sanctuary. There we present a "spiritual" message that may have little or no direct relationship to the overwhelming problems of suffering people.

The Christian Base Communities have adopted an approach that turns this all around. Those responsible for organizing them go directly to the people *where they live their daily lives,* bringing them together in homes, or under a tree in rural areas, or in any available community building. There those who gather focus attention on their immediate problems, learn to speak of them with each other, and explore what the Bible has to say about them.

Some groups begin their meetings with Bible study, seeking to discover what guidance it may offer them for dealing with these concrete problems. In others, those present begin by talking with each other about the things that have happened to them in the past week, striving to understand them and deal with them in the light of what the Bible has to say.

With both approaches, the important thing is that the cultivation of the spiritual life is set in the context of the daily struggle of the poor to get enough food to eat, to find ways of caring for their small children while working, to improve the conditions of the shacks in which they live, to improve relations in the family, to rehabilitate young people on drugs, or to deal with violence in their neighborhood. And each of these problems is dealt with in light of the Word of God. As one member of a Base Community in a favela in São Paulo put it, "A Base Ecclesial Community is a group of people who reflect on the Word of God as a family. They discover together the needs of their street, their neighborhood, and their people and use the Word of God as a mirror in which to see their situation."

With time, these informal groups often become vital faith communities because their members discover that God is present precisely in the midst of all this. They speak of God as being very close to them, of God "passing through their street" and "gracing" their lives. Those who share in their life together often sense this presence of God among them in a compelling way. Here are people who are struggling with overwhelming problems with an amazing spirit of hopefulness and often of joyfulness. Women and men who have nothing seem willing to share everything, take on impossible tasks and get surprising results, and face persecution and death threats without fear.

The CBCs expose the spiritual bankruptcy of those who seek to find God in a "spiritual" realm far removed from the human struggle in which the God of the Bible is present. They challenge us to enter into the mystery of the divine as we open our eyes and tune our ears to the moving of the Spirit in the midst of the struggle for authentic life as the world is transformed. They also suggest to us that grace abounds in the hells of this earth, that the Spirit of God is present most dynamically where men, women, and children are dying because of exploitation and injustice, that Christ is to be found in the midst of those who dare to share his suffering and run the risks of crucifixion.

Moreover, the fact that this new experience of the presence of God has come to us as a gift from the poorest and most marginal people, those considered to be of little worth, may indicate that we can hope to enter this realm of the Spirit only as we live in solidarity with them and make their struggle our own as well. When I immerse myself in the life of a vital Base Community, it provides me with a vantage point from which to look more critically at much that goes on in many of our churches. I see more clearly the barrenness of any type of evangelism that disassociates the spiritual quest from the hard realities of daily life. I realize how much money we waste maintaining large church buildings that contribute little or nothing to the development of faith communities in neighborhoods, and how much time and energy we spend on church programs that could be used to bring people together in community. And I realize that even our sincere efforts to break out of this by starting Bible study groups in homes or even forming "house churches" can fail because they focus primarily on the individual "spiritual" journey rather than on the discovery of God's grace in the midst of life in the world.

Honoring the Religious World of the People

As the members of the CBCs met God at the heart of their struggle for life in their local communities, something else happened. The God who related to them where they were also provided them, through the Scriptures, with a means by which *they could articulate their own faith and speak their own word*. This represents another major break with our traditional approach to evangelism and Christian education.

When I graduated from seminary, and especially after I had completed my doctoral studies in theology, I felt certain that the theological concepts I had learned, and which served so well to orient my thought and life, could mean the same thing to others. Gradually, I was forced to see that this was not the case. In Brazil, university students eventually succeeded in showing me that my theological categories did not help them to name their world; some years later, women students at Princeton Seminary helped me to see that they could not use my theological concepts to express their faith. More recently, teaching courses in theology for laypeople in local churches, I have been forced to realize that, while they are struggling to put their world together in a meaningful way, each must find his or her own way of doing so. If I convince them to accept and use my theological language, I may draw them away from their own resources for thought or lead them to believe that they are really incapable of thinking creatively.

When the poor in Latin America began to read the Bible in the CBCs, many of them for the first time, they were amazed to discover that many of the people figuring in the biblical story were people like themselves: poor and oppressed women, fisherpersons and peasants, people living in exile, lepers, and other outcasts. They came to see that the biblical story was their story, the struggle there described, their struggle. As they spoke with each other about what they read in the Bible, they found themselves speaking articulately and authentically about their own situation and thus finding their own word. In fact, since their struggle was so similar to that described in many parts of the Bible, they often arrived at a depth of understanding of it that others of us, including biblical scholars, have failed to achieve.

As pastoral agents working with the CBCs encouraged their members in this type of reflection, something else happened. They became more aware of the religious imagery and symbols that were so much a part of their own history and culture, paid more attention to them, and began to reflect on them in dialogue with the Bible. Out of this interaction has come new confessions of faith and new liturgies; a number of Masses expressing the religious faith and experience of peasants, the poor, and indigenous people; as well as new developments in theological reflection that are affecting the thought of professional theologians.

Living in a Caring, Sharing, Empowering Community

In the Christian Base Communities, those who have no place in our modern society are beginning to live a new quality of life in community. Those who have nothing are showing us what can happen when we share our material possessions. As they read the Bible in their small communities and feel compelled to live by the Word, they realize that they are called to share the very little they have with others engaged in the same desperate struggle for life. This may mean sharing their last kilo of rice with a mother whose children have not had anything at all to eat, or welcoming a homeless family into their one-room shack.

A community of Salvadoran refugees who lived for a number of years in Honduras have recently returned to their country and settled in a region completely destroyed by the war. They have organized themselves to work together to create a new life for themselves. The first houses they build are for the widows with small children, the sick, and the disabled. And the food they grow is shared with all on the basis of need.

As those who have always struggled alone, convinced that there was no other way to survive, learn to share in this way, they are often surprised to experience God's closeness as they share. As one theologian has put it, the God who is manifest only in love breathes on people who have learned how to share. Living by the love in which God is present, they bring down grace upon themselves and their community and thus learn how to share more, love more, and live for others.

This extraordinary willingness to share is not to be found everywhere in the CBCs, and there is no guarantee that this revolutionary breakthrough will be sustained indefinitely. But whatever happens in the future, the CBCs witness to the power of the gospel to shape life in community. They point to a quality of life that is radically different from what we usually experience in the church. They call into question the individualism of our middle-class way of life, in which we strive to be self-sufficient and dedicate our time and energy to the pursuit of our personal goals of material enrichment and professional advancement. And they expose the spiritual bankruptcy of our congregational life, where we refuse even to deal with these issues.

At a time when the passion for acquisition of more and more consumer goods seems to be captivating people of all classes around the world, the CBCs remind us that there is another way, they help to keep alive the hope that human beings can find a richer life as they learn to share with each other, and they demonstrate the power of Christian faith to transform our common life.

143

The members of the CBCs have discovered another dimension of the *koinonia* of the Holy Spirit. Those who have learned to share their material possessions have also found that they can live and work together in such a way that they *raise up and empower each other*. As they do this, those who had no place in society discover their own worth. Those who were convinced that they could do nothing recognize that they can think and act and develop their talents. And those who were powerless take responsibility to work with others to try to solve some of their immediate problems and change their world.

In a society structured hierarchically, in which a few have power over the vast majority and everyone strives for such power at the expense of others, this development is indeed revolutionary. Those who have been powerless are calling for a fundamental restructuring of power throughout society and are becoming a subversive force in it. And in a church also structured hierarchically, the CBCs represent a new model of community life in the body of Christ that calls for a re-formation of both Catholic and Protestant churches today as radical as that coming out of the Reformation initiated by Luther and Calvin in the sixteenth century.

How did this happen? From the beginning, priests as well as laywomen and laymen who moved toward the poor were very much influenced by the pedagogical approach articulated by Paulo Freire in his *Pedagogy of the Oppressed*. Rather than giving something to the poor or doing something for them, they were determined to help them discover their own potential, create space for them to emerge as subjects and thus to be empowered and empower each other. As persons moving in this direction gathered around the Bible, they began to discover what the apostle Paul had to say about the charismata, or gifts of the Spirit present in each community for the building up of the body.

Gradually, it became clear that a CBC could function well only as its members took responsibility for a wide variety of tasks. People were needed who would take the initiative in working with others to prepare the liturgy, direct Bible study, engage in evangelism, care for the most urgent needs of the sick and those in trouble, organize people to work toward the solution of urgent community problems, and discover how to act politically. And one or more persons were needed to coordinate these various activities. It also became clear that members of each CBC had the charismata needed for these ministries and that the community had the responsibility of recognizing those who had these various "gifts."

Out of this experience, new patterns of ministry are developing. Ministries are arising from below, as the community decides what specific tasks need to be undertaken and chooses those who should carry them out for a limited period of time. A few natural leaders often emerge and are given opportunities for further training, but they are encouraged to serve the community and help to train others rather than control and dominate it. One or more persons from outside — a priest, a nun, a pastoral agent — may play an important role in the organization and development of the community. But his or her role is that of helping its members take full responsibility for all aspects of its life.

While the CBCs are committed to the development of this new vision of ministry, they often fall short of their goal. The men and women chosen for specific ministries may fail to carry them out. After a few years, people in the Base Communities fall victims of routine, just as in any other organization. And those who emerge as leaders are not immune to the temptations of power. At the same time, the CBCs have been structured in such a way that their members are challenged to take responsibility. People are energized and are learning how to empower each other; they are discovering that they can work together to solve some formidable problems. In many instances, their vitality witnesses to the dynamic presence of the Holy Spirit creating a new model of church more in line with the New Testament witness.

Moreover, as a result of this reality, the church is becoming, once again, the firstfruits of a new order. As a wide range of popular movements develop, inspired in many places by the CBCs, new patterns of social organization are emerging that move in the direction of economic self-reliance and participatory democracy and that offer an exciting possibility for radical social transformation by nonviolent means. As this happens, the CBCs and the popular movements are rightly seen as the major threat to the established order of privilege and exploitation and are often singled out for brutal repression. At the same time, Marxist parties and revolutionary movements are being challenged to look critically at their structures and undertake the type of restructuring by which power will flow from the bottom up more than from the top down.

Compelled by the Gospel to Struggle for Liberation

Critics of the CBCs often claim that they are more oriented toward political action than toward spiritual growth, that they have reduced the gospel to politics. On the basis of my experience, I'm convinced that such charges completely distort the picture. In fact, I would claim that we cannot understand CBCs unless we recognize that their orientation and motivation are fundamentally religious. Emphasizing this point, Cardinal Arns of São Paulo, Brazil, once remarked that if the priests in his diocese tried to bring the poor people together to discuss politics, the people would never come back a second time.

The poor people in both rural and urban areas were attracted to the CBCs because of their religious concerns. Most of the communities I have visited began as small Bible study groups. In them, people got more in touch with the religious traditions and symbols so central in their lives, which then became revitalized and transformed through their study of the Bible. Out of this came a new experience of the presence of God and of the power of Christ to transform their lives.

As I have pointed out earlier, however, at the heart of this *spiritual* experience was the discovery of the presence and power of the divine *in the midst of their daily life in family and neighborhood and in their struggle for survival.* As a result of this basic experience of the gospel, the members of the CBCs were able to grasp what the Bible has to say about the nature of God's redemptive action in history. As their perception was not distorted by an ideology separating the personal and the social, the spiritual and the material, they realized that God's salvific action has to do with the fullness of human life as it is lived in the world.

Consequently, their faith turned their attention toward the world around them; the more vital and profound their faith, the stronger their compulsion to express it in their daily life in society. Moreover, standing where they stood as poor and marginal people, they were able to grasp something else at the heart of the gospel, namely, discipleship calls for commitment to the struggle to change the world. The poor, according to Jesus, are blessed because they cannot tolerate the unjust present and keep alive the hope for its transformation. Thus, their witness may help us as Calvinists to recover something of Calvin's passion for the transformation of all realms of society in line with the Word of God.

The poor in the Base Communities, starting out from this spiritual experience, have much in common with "born-again" Christians. As a result of their discovery of the nature of God's redemptive action, however, their spiritual pilgrimage moves in a different direction, as has been pointed out by a number of recent sociological studies of the CBCs. According to these studies, the CBCs tend to follow a certain process of development in their attempts to live out their faith. Their members begin by discovering that, in community, they can work together to solve some of their most imme-diate problems. Working mothers can take turns caring for small children

146

of the community, rather than leaving them untended or locking them in their houses when they go to work. By joining together to bake bread or set up a soup kitchen, their families will have more to eat. Working together, they can improve the shacks in which they live and deal with some of their most basic health problems.

Before long, however, members of a faith-motivated community decide that they must do something to get titles to the land on which they live, try to have electricity and running water installed in their neighborhood, and get the local government to open schools and provide some sort of health care. These goals can be achieved only if they are organized to present their needs to the government and bring pressure on it. And when these small efforts meet strong if not violent opposition on the part of those in power, members of the CBCs begin to raise questions about the structures of power under which they live and become interested in social analysis. This often leads them to join a variety of popular movements, including labor unions, in order to work for more fundamental structural change.

Spiritual rebirth, grounded in biblical faith, leads to this type of social and political involvement. Precisely because it is grounded in faith and sustained by a faith community, their witness is so strong. At the same time, these struggles are so demanding that some of those caught up in them may no longer give the attention they once did to the spiritual life of the CBC. If the church authorities not only cut off their support of these communities but also try to isolate them from the rest of the church, this is more likely to happen.

In this situation, the future development of the CBCs will definitely be affected by the presence or absence of evangelical Protestants. For Protestantism in Latin America, especially through the Pentecostal movements, continues to grow because of the central importance it gives to a personal experience of Christ and because of its sensitivity to the deep spiritual longing of those who are suffering the worst deprivation. As these churches made up of poor people pay more attention to what the Bible has to say about God's concern for the poor, and as they relate more closely to the poor in the CBCs, as is already happening in some places, Catholics and Protestants may help each other find the resources they need for their renewal in a new ecumenical era.

In these pages, I have tried to show that the Christian Base Communities, with all of their limitations, are a contemporary expression of an *ecclesia reformata semper reformanda*. As such, they present a tremendous challenge to any Reformed church to recover and live its heritage. Moreover,

I believe that the CBCs can help us to understand what this means by identifying issues with which we must struggle and by demonstrating that nothing short of re-creation or reinvention will suffice. The question before us is whether our Presbyterian and Reformed Churches, so at home in the dominant middle-class culture and so structured for self-preservation, can find ways to move toward this goal.

Immanental and Prophetic: Shaping Reformed Theology for Late Twentieth-Century Struggle

MARK K. TAYLOR

Reubem Alves has said that "theology is our effort to bring together the petals of our flower that is continuously torn apart by a world that does not love flowers,"[1] a comment that applies to our effort to do Reformed theology in the context of our era. Alves's image actually works better for me if I can add that bringing together the flower might also require some careful pruning of the plant and some creative grafting. Within the purview of this image I am less interested in "the fundamentals" of Reformed theology and more concerned with what Christians who count themselves members of "Reformed" traditions might think and practice in the late twentieth century. I am engaged here in "traditioning," that is, in the study, retrieving, and recasting of a tradition for our lives in this time.[2]

Although I appreciate many things about the Reformed tradition, there are times when I also wonder whether it is a good thing that the world is graced with Reformed and Presbyterian Christians. I have learned to see what many of our African-American brothers and sisters,[3] and a large

---

1. Reubem Alves, "From Paradise to Desert: Autobiographical Musings," in *Frontiers of Theology in Liberation Theology*, ed. Rosino Gibellini (Maryknoll, N.Y.: Orbis Books, 1979), p. 293.

2. On this "traditioning" as itself a dimension of Reformed traditions, see B. A. Gerrish, *Tradition and the Modern World: Reformed Theology in the Nineteenth Century* (Chicago: University of Chicago Press, 1978), pp. 181–88.

3. Elsewhere, I have developed my position on why these groups need to be heard and

number of our Christian feminist sisters, diagnose in it as fundamentally resistant to changes they consider essential for the practice of their full, God-given freedom and wholeness.[4] Such conversations always leave me saying both Yes and No to my tradition; they therefore set me working to take up one task of theologians: "to make the heritage more effective by selectively constituting it as tradition."[5]

I am grateful for the opportunity to offer this theological reconstruction in a text honoring the work of theologian and ethicist Charles C. West. Not only did I serve with him for almost ten years on the faculty of a Reformed institution, Princeton Theological Seminary, I also came to respect and value his collegiality and friendship. Even our profound theological disagreements always felt like exercises in mutual respect. As I recall them, the nature of our disagreements usually pivoted around two debates: first, whether Christian faith and theology needs to acknowledge its own ideologies and then foster its own more profound ideology (my position), or whether it is to occupy a place outside of ideology so as to critique ideologies; and second, whether a Christian's prophetic critique can be rooted in a profoundly immanental understanding of God (my position), or whether it needs always to be based on stronger notions of a transcendent God. This essay focuses on the second debate and works toward a view of the Reformed tradition that presents prophetic critique as much more closely linked to divine immanence than many theologians of the Reformed tradition (e.g., Calvin and Barth) might tolerate. I suspect that I am also again developing a theological position here in marked contrast to the theological stance of West, but I offer this as another phase of my ongoing respect for him.

Seeking "the Reformed Tradition"

When we seek to focus on something called "the Reformed tradition," what we seek can be very elusive. We have been hesitant, it seems to me, in

on the senses in which their critiques need to be given priority in Christian theology. See "In Praise of Shaky Ground: The Liminal Christ and Cultural Pluralism," *Theology Today* 43 (April 1996): 136–51.

4. For just a few of many examples, see Gayraud Wilmore, *Black and Presbyterian: The Heritage and the Hope* (Philadelphia: Westminster Press, 1983); and Beverly Harrison, "The Electric Circuits," in *God's Fierce Whimsy: Christian Feminism and Theological Education* (New York: Pilgrim Press, 1985), pp. 108–13.

5. Gerrish, *Tradition and the Modern World*, p. 188.

pointing out the kind of human face we Reformed Christians have presented to our world since the days of the Reformation or since the particular reforms of John Calvin. We often instead take some things that are true of the Reformed tradition and make them distinctively descriptive of the Reformed tradition, when in fact they also are traits of other Christian religious traditions and institutions.

Karl Barth, for example, was helpful in reminding us that the uniqueness of the Reformed tradition does not lie only in a particular set of religious experiences, forms of faith, polity forms, even doctrines — but rather in its faithful pointing to God who stands as other and so judges and extends mercy to all that is religious and human.[6] Few Christian traditions would deny this view. The main problem, however, is that even pointing to a God of this sort, distinguished from the human realm, is embedded in a distinctive communal tradition that needs to be described in more detail.

Similarly, it has been said that it is very un-Reformed to say particularly what it is to be Reformed, especially if one is distinguishing Reformed from other types of Christian communion. Allegedly, so this claim goes, to be Reformed is to be ecumenical — and so it is non-Reformed to describe the Reformed place as other than this ecumenicity.[7] The problem with this claim is that however ecumenical a person or tradition may be, there are still different, distinctive ways of assuming that ecumenical posture. It begs the question of whether the Reformed tradition features a distinctive way of being ecumenical.

Or maybe we recite the phrase *ecclesia reformata semper reformanda* (the church reformed and always to be reformed), noting that it is of the essence of our tradition to be in a state of reformation, transformation, and change. It has been suggested, on the basis of this slogan, that to say what the Reformed tradition is, is really quite impossible, for it would be to fix in place something that cannot be fixed, something that by its very essence is in motion.

Now, on the side of all of these observations, I would affirm that the Reformed tradition is indeed marked by a unique, essential view of God, by a striking ecumenicity, and by an affirmation of change and development. But those affirmations tell us very little about two things: (1) what

---

6. Karl Barth, *The Word of God and the Word of Man* (New York: Harper & Row, 1956; orig. pub., 1928), pp. 234-35.

7. I am here recalling a position regularly articulated in the setting of Princeton Theological Seminary, where I have taught for eleven years.

forms these affirmations of God, ecumenicity, and transformation actually took in particular sociohistorical contexts, and (2) what form these affirmations might take for us today in our particular settings.

Let me proceed, therefore, to a level where I think a more concrete reading of the Reformed tradition is accessible and in relation to which, ultimately, a more meaningful Reformed theology might be discussed. The level I have in mind is the sociocultural level, where distinctive marks of the tradition are looked for on the plane of historical and cultural development. Rather than being an atheological or pretheological move, it is one intrinsic to good theology. It is an example of Clodovis Boff's notion of theology's "socio-analytic mediation,"[8] that is, a delineation of theology's embodiment in the social worlds of its faithful.

A great deal can be said about Reformed theology's embodiment in this way. I will select just a few observations and group them around two general statements about the Reformed tradition — one positive and one negative. To anticipate the argument to come, these positive and negative traits of the Reformed tradition are so mutually connected that taking steps to mitigate the harshness of the negative will suggest we change some of our almost unquestioned ways of achieving the positive. That is to say, mitigating the evil in our tradition will require revisioning the way Reformed Christians have often seen themselves as contributing to the good.

A Tradition of Social Transformation

First, my positive statement. *The Reformed tradition has been and is a world-formative and world-reformative mode of religious life and Christian faith.* The language here is that of Nicholas Wolterstorff. He argues, as have others, that "the emergence of original Calvinism represented a fundamental alteration in Christian sensibility, from the vision and sensibility of turning away from the social order to seek closer union with God to the vision and practice of working to reform the social world in obedience to God."[9]

The original Calvinists were a people of suspicion — suspicious of the acceptance of social structures as an inviolable reflection of natural or

8. Clodovis Boff, *Theology and Praxis: Epistemological Foundations* (Maryknoll, N.Y.: Orbis Books, 1987), pp. 1–66.
9. Nicholas Wolterstorff, *Until Justice and Peace Embrace* (Grand Rapids: Eerdmans, 1983), p. 11.

cosmic hierarchy. They were a people of interruption — interrupting any easy chants, such as "God in his heaven, the bishop in his chair, the Lord in his castle."[10] (Today, a good Reformed theologian will also insist, I believe, that the male pronouns also warrant suspicion, interruption, and change.)

Concerning economic disparities, in Calvin's Geneva or elsewhere, we can see Calvinist suspicion and interruption issuing in world-reformative activity. Calvin considered the disfranchisement of the poor and their suffering to be a violation of humans who were the image of God.[11] In sermons, the rich were not spared Calvin's biting critique. It was a duty to love and so to order social life that the wealthy would not be reinforcing the plight of the hungry but rather would be offering food to the hungry.[12] The Calvinist world-reformative impulse was often adjusted — either to adapt to new and ever-changing situations or to strengthen and refine understandings of how Christians are to engage the social order in faithfulness to God.[13]

Many examples might be given to portray the world-formative and reformative character of the Reformed tradition. Let me simply allow two well-known students to conclude my point. Ernst Troeltsch writes in his *Social Teaching of the Christian Churches*:

> This leads Calvinism everywhere to an organized and aggressive effort to form associations, to a systematic endeavor to mould the life of Society as a whole, to a kind of "Christian Socialism" . . . it lays down the principle that the Church ought to be interested in all sides of life, and it neither isolates the religious element over against the other elements, like Lutheranism, nor does it permit this sense of collective responsibility to express itself merely in particular institutions and occasional interventions in affairs, as in Catholicism.[14]

In 1965, Michael Walzar wrote:

10. Ibid., p. 7.

11. John Calvin, *Institutes of the Christian Religion*, ed. John T. McNeill (Philadelphia: Westminster Press, 1960), 3.7.6.

12. John Calvin, *Commentaries on the First Twenty Chapters of the Book of the Prophet Ezekiel*, trans. Thomas Myers (Grand Rapids: Eerdmans, 1948), 2:224 (Ezek. 18:7).

13. Wolterstorff's examples of this process of refinement include Abraham Kuyper, who directed Reformed theology along a socialist path, similar at points to Marx's class analysis, but disavowing any identification of that path with Marxist-Leninism or socialist political parties (Wolterstorff, *Until Justice and Peace Embrace*, pp. 79–81).

14. Ernst Troeltsch, *The Social Teaching of the Christian Churches*, vol. 2 (Chicago: University of Chicago Press, 1931), p. 602.

It was the Calvinists who first switched the emphasis of political thought from the prince to the saint (or the band of saints) and then constructed a theoretical justification for independent political action. . . . This is surely the most significant outcome of the Calvinist theory of worldly activity, preceding in time any infusion of religious worldliness into the economic order.[15]

It is important to stress that this world-reformative impulse was no mere addendum to Calvinist piety. World-formation and reformation, through concrete institutional life, were intrinsic to Christian faith and practice.

A World-Repressive Tradition?

I offer the following negative statement about the Reformed tradition because the tradition's very world-reformative impulse requires it. Any commitment to the church as *ecclesia reformata semper reformanda* will require reformers' capacities to turn icy but passionate gazes upon their tradition. The negative statement is that the Reformed tradition has been and is often a "world-repressive" model of religious life and Christian faith.

Wolterstorff acknowledges this repressiveness at points, though he does not examine it as much as I would like. He does note two failings of "early Calvinism" that may be a starting point for us. First, while often speaking of a just social order, early Calvinists "failed to think through how they could live together in a just society with those with whom they disagreed." Although this was not unique to Calvinists, "this was their great and tragic failing."[16]

A second related failing was a "recurrent triumphalism." A triumphalist Calvinist is, according to Wolterstorff, "that most insufferable of all human beings . . . one who believes that the revolution instituting the holy commonwealth has already occurred and that his or her task is now simply to keep it in place. Of these triumphalist Calvinists the United States and Holland have both had their share. South Africa provides them in their purest form."[17] U.S. Presbyterians displayed their own deadly leadership in the decade after World War II, which is usually seen as the halcyon period of mainstream Presbyterianism. During that time, two respected Presby-

15. Cited in Wolterstorff, *Until Justice and Peace Embrace*, p. 9.
16. Ibid., p. 22.
17. Ibid., p. 21.

terian laymen, one the U.S. secretary of state (John Foster Dulles), another the director of the Central Intelligence Agency (Allen Dulles), conspired in Eisenhower's administration to set in place the CIA-led coup that overthrew the only real democracy Guatemala has had since the Conquest — all in an effort to protect U.S. business interests in that small country. That coup set the stage for decades of ruthless military rule and for what the United Nations has called genocide.[18]

We may like to think, and perhaps rightly, that this repressive, tri-umphalist Calvinism is not in us, the rank-and-file members of Presbyterian/Reformed communions; nor, we trust, is that incapacity to live together justly. Before assuming this, however, we need to take a closer look at the repressive impulse — especially in its incipient, less extreme, tri-umphalist forms.

My best example is one of John Calvin's "Draft Ordinances," a legal document meant to guide political and ecclesial life with respect to the needs of the poor in sixteenth-century Geneva. In large measure, the document displays the world-formative character I have already highlighted: the solemn, religious duty to set in place structures that shape social renewal, that meet the needs of the sick, people unable to work, widows, orphans, and any others deemed "worthy of special charity."[19] This is all planned with an admirable eye to detail. The document is an example of a concrete reformative ministry for any contemporary church seeking to be more than an occasional giver of charity, wishing to construct and sustain structures that meet tangible need.

This section of the 1541 Ecclesiastical Ordinances ends with a paragraph, seemingly harmless, but perhaps a signal of a deep-running fault beneath the mountainous range of Calvinist social piety. The paragraph is a warning against "mendicancy," an admonition to discourage all begging as "contrary to good order." So important is this "total prohibition of begging" that official sentries were ordered at church entrances to prevent and remove loiterers and other insolent ones who give offense.[20]

Even though these ordinances are exemplary in their intent to meet

18. On the Eisenhower administration's links to this overthrow, see Richard Immerman, *The CIA in Guatemala: The Foreign Policy of Intervention* (Austin: University of Texas Press, 1982); and Piero Gleijses, *Shattered Hope: The Guatemala Revolution and the U.S., 1944-1954* (Princeton: Princeton University Press, 1991).

19. "Draft Ecclesiastical Ordinances, September and October 1541," in *Calvin: Theological Treatises,* ed. J. K. S. Reid, The Library of Christian Classics, vol. 22 (Philadelphia: Westminster Press, 1954), p. 65.

20. Ibid., p. 66.

need, this guarding of church doors to keep beggars away is a sign of how the Reformed "will to order" often limits its embrace of the world in all its need. This limitation may be seen in the social piety of our contemporary churches — not only Reformed churches, but surely in our Reformed churches. All too often, we presume that our social piety must take place through our order of things. The beggar with gumption enough to ask for money violates not only the ordered social pattern for gaining money through work and compensation but also our ordered ecclesial pattern for dispensing support to "the truly needy."

The problem is that to be in need *is* to be out of the dominant order of things. If a Reformed Christianity limits its social piety to that which is consonant with good order, the truly disadvantaged are not going to be significantly engaged by that kind of Christianity. And so we might lament with the young H. R. Niebuhr: the middle-class denominations add organization upon organization to meet the needs of the disordered and disinherited, but still the church at best reinforces the distance between the middle-class churches and the churches of the disinherited.[21] However energetic, this social piety seems unable to forge genuine solidarity and participation between the orders of preferred classes and the disordered poor.

I am not suggesting a naive spurning of every structure and pattern we know, so that we meet every request that comes our way. But the choice is not simply between maintaining our good order and naively abandoning order. There can be an imagination that seeks ever-new orders and ecclesial reforms, by envisioning Christians meeting with the homeless and hungry out on the church steps, in the streets, or in various forms of community organizing. Working out a vision of this sort would be a way toward real solidarity.

Our tendency in the Reformed tradition, however, has all too often been to do only that which can be done "in good order." Because of the cultural practices of ordered middle- to upper-class life, and in spite of all our announced concern and effort, U.S. Presbyterians tend to exclude from their midst the real presence of those who live within the lower ranges of economic and cultural life. In so doing, our social piety tends to reinforce established orders, strengthening the ethos of well-ordered respectability. This is an old problem. When facing the demands of the frontier, the Presbyterian Church often "judged the needs of the frontier by standards

21. H. R. Niebuhr, *The Social Sources of Denominationalism* (New York: Henry Holt, 1929), pp. 77–105, 264–69.

of Philadelphia and insisted on making men Gentlemen before it made them ministers."[22] We have been and often are reinforcers of established orders — of church, of nation, of government.

Our social piety is built on a sense of order, and certain elements of our theology reinforce that bias. I suggest that what is lacking is a theology motivating us to see that God's presence, power, and grace are already in and with the poor in all their disordered state, so that God is experienced as beckoning us Christians there, to solidarity with them, in their struggles for a new order. If our world-formative impulse is to be refined, so as to check world-repressive effects of our reinforcement of established orders, then we need to consider some theological revisions.

Revisioning Reformed Theology

The general theological revision needed to check the world-repressive elements of Reformed tradition is one that recasts God's "sovereignty" so that the divine presence is understood as more immanent to every personal and social dimension of our history (ordered or disordered) than has often been confessed by Presbyterian/Reformed communions. In short, I suggest that we *recast God's sovereignty so that we envision divine transcendence as less a matter of God coming "down on" or "to" society, nature, and history in order to work redemption, and more a matter of God "arising from" and "within" society, nature, and history.* Without some such general revision, talk about God's lordship and sovereignty — however loving and merciful we take a sovereign God to be — all too easily is envisioned in our Reformed communities as the divine God-on-top creating order below and maintaining a cult of order, the members of which will rarely embrace and participate in the revolutionary struggle of those outside their order. Ultimately what is at stake here, then, is not just our view of God's relation to world but that relation as open also to the marginalized and those dominated by the order of things.

I will not be proposing a departure from a healthy sense of transcendence that we in the Reformed tradition have often received from theologians Calvin, Barth, and others. Our tradition's "world-reformative" impulse and our critique of the social order as "fallen" are postures in large part attributable to Christians and theologians such as Calvin and Barth who could point to a word of judgment and grace that is *other than* our

22. Ibid., p. 161.

social and historical life. That sense of the otherness of God's being and address does need preserving.

Preserving the otherness of God's being and address, however, does not mean pointing *away from* or *outside* our social and historical life. Wolterstorff is descriptively accurate when he says that Reformed movements of resistance against social injustice were "grounded in the conviction that there is a world from outside our existence that calls us to the actions of love."[23] Descriptively accurate as this comment is, however, it is not the only way to marshal and sustain impulses of reformation and resistance. In fact, as I will be suggesting, it might be better to sustain our world-reformative impulses by pointing to the "otherness" of God's being and address, not as coming from outside our existence but as *arising from and within our existence.* In this way, to respond to God's distinctive call and to be in communion with God will entail our being in the dynamics of struggle between orders and between order and disorder. It is from within these dynamics of struggle that God "calls" us and for which God empowers us.

Beyond the "Flow Model" of Grace and Vocation

With this notion of "call" we come to the more specific revision I wish to suggest. A more immanental Reformed theology needs to be worked out especially regarding Christian vocation, if we Reformed Christians are to be led beyond the confines of our ordered existence into the threatening regions of disorder and radical suffering. The crucial question concerns how we relate our experience of God's grace to our experience of vocation, or "calling."

The early Calvinist notion of vocation was one of the most powerful elements in Calvinist social piety. With Reformed teaching came the affirmation that ordinary occupations, whether that of chambermaid or prince, were ways through which all Christians, not just religious professionals, responded to God's call and exercised a grateful obedience to the God of grace. For reform of the social fabric, Calvinists exercised "obedience motivated by gratitude and expressed in vocation."[24] This flow of grace from God through gratitude, obedience, and into vocation was a powerful theology of Christian practice to which can be traced many of our tradition's most impressive reforms.

23. Wolterstorff, *Until Justice and Peace Embrace*, p. 144.
24. Ibid., p. 15.

Again, however, we need to examine the logic relating our experience of divine grace to Christian calling. The basic logic of the Reformed tradition concerning vocation may be thought of as a flow model. It is one that begins with the pre-given grace of God operative in believers, which then, as a second phase, "motivates" obedient actions, these latter being "expressions" of a person's grateful obedience. The dynamic of transformation is down from God, through individual gratitude, out to actions with and for others.

This way of ordering grace to vocation, though it clearly relates God to the Christian's world of action and witness, keeps us Christians thinking of movements *from* God's realm of grace *to* humans who need that grace. The cost of thinking this way is that this logic reinforces the very dualism that a theology of God incarnate in Jesus Christ is meant to overcome. Though it may claim to be connecting realms, this flow from divine grace to Christian vocation in the world actually keeps us busy exercising dualistic muscles: first the vertical relation with God, then horizontal relations with humankind; first the love of God, then love of neighbor; first an experience of grace, and then the obedient active giving of gifts in the realm of nature, society, and history. Thus so ordered, although we may intend to reform the world, the world can easily become the last region to receive watering from the river flow of God's grace. All too easily the intensity of grace's power is left swirling in the headwaters of the relation between the God of grace and grateful Christians, with only a trickle making it through to the Christians organized for action in solidarity with world and society. We might say that the Reformed tradition has suffered from a trickle-down theology of divine grace that ultimately possesses little power to save us from the trickle-down theories of economic justice that all too many of us U.S. Christians accepted in the 1980s.

Maybe we could say that the problem lies not in the logic of the flow of grace but in the failure of the Christians to be full and open channels of God's graceful action. Maybe there's nothing wrong with the theology; maybe there are simply too many economic and political forces to which many Christians have yielded, thus deflecting the right flow of God's grace. No doubt this is partly true. But we need to also ask if this flow model of God's grace really works for Christian participation in struggle, or whether it allows Christians all too easily to regard that participation as only a gratuitous addendum.

This flow model of God's grace and Christian vocation is insufficient for encouraging believers toward solidarity with those whose life is disordered or outside our established orders. This view of our vocation in relation to God's grace makes it too easy for us to think that God's grace is flowing through us before, or apart from, solidarity with the lives of the disordered poor. The vision of *first* God's grace, *then* vocational practice tends to make a vocational practice of solidarity with "the disinherited" a subordinate or optional dimension — however much we may say it is not.

I am suggesting, then, that we recast our vision of how our Christian vocation, wherein we heed God's call wherever we work and live, is related to divine grace. What I am suggesting is not some pure innovation but a vision implicit in some elements of Reformed tradition and in the Scriptures — especially as the Scriptures are being read by large numbers of Christians in the Base Communities of Central and South America, where reform and growth of the church is occurring at a breathtaking pace and in ways that feature a striking fusion of the spiritual and the social.

My suggestion is that we view Christian vocation and good works not as obedient and grateful responses to God's grace, with grace happening "behind" Christians, as they then "march forward" into society and history. Instead, our vocation and good works might be viewed as the forms of life or places in which we receive God's grace. This would mean that we do not know God's grace and then do, but that in the doing, we are knowing the God of grace. Knowing and doing become much more simultaneous aspects of our relationship to God. In fact, God's being might best be experienced by us, in the words of Duns Scotus, as "the doable knowable" *(cognoscibile operabile)*.[25]

This does not mean that our good works, vocations, or callings become preconditions or causes of God's grace, which only then can be conferred on us. By no means. The Reformation tradition's *sola gratia* (by grace alone through faith) can remain. But this does mean that we shift our view of the locus of divine grace. Our calling is the grace-full beckoning to us from the worlds of nature, society, and history, drawing us to participate in those worlds and thus with God. In responding to those worlds, in our entering into them with the God who lures us there, who gives us to the tasks of healing there — in all this, and not prior to or apart from this, we experience the gift of God's grace. Being given to solidarity with the needs of those in disorder, being given to reconnecting people broken apart from one another, and being graced with the task of reweaving the fabric that holds people together in a frayed and tangled world order — all this

25. Duns Scotus, *Ordinatio*, prologus, 5.6, cited in Nicholas Lobkowicz, *Theory and Practice: History of a Concept from Aristotle to Marx* (Notre Dame, Ind.: University of Notre Dame Press, 1967), p. 74.

is what is meant by being given the grace of the God of Jesus Christ. God has so radically graced nature, society, and history that for us to be given God's grace is to be given to those worlds. In being given to this grace, we know the God of Jesus Christ. Ideally, this should open our eyes to think critically on what Latin American theologians and Christians have been suggesting, namely, that the poor are the "theophany of God." In their struggle for healing, and in solidarities with them, is to be found the revelation of God shining in history.[26]

Reshaping the Reformed Tradition

A transcending God who is thus radically immanent to nature, society, and history is often hard to glimpse through the lenses of the Reformed tradition. We have been too much under the spell of "first God and God's grace, then the world and our vocation," leaving us vulnerable to the subordination, or even denigration and neglect, of world and vocation. This can be seen in Calvin, whose notion of vocation is one of obedient response to our experience of God's founding grace.[27]

Barth too, great as his theological contribution is, and as impossible as it is for us to ever think apart from his work, I have not yet found very helpful on this issue. Barth's theology, even in its later phases, when supposedly he stressed more "the humanity of God," does not encourage a view of God as having graced humanity in nature, society, and history. Instead he proposes a radical "self-denial," a taking-leave of one's remembrance of place in society and history.[28] The flow between divine grace and Christian vocational practice in obedient faithfulness to Christ is consistently *from* grace received *to* obedient action in the world. In a somewhat frightful militarization of the God/world relation and of the Christian's heeding the call of Christ, Barth summons Christians to acknowledge this direction of that flow through their self-denial and so to be "witnesses of the great assault which is directed against the world." Christians in vocation "stand in the service of this great onslaught."[29]

The Reformed tradition, though, does contain elements that might

26. Victor Araya, *God of the Poor* (Maryknoll, N.Y.: Orbis Books, 1987), pp. 125ff.
27. *Institutes* 3.10.6.
28. Karl Barth, *Church Dogmatics* (Edinburgh: T. & T. Clark, 1958), IV/2, pp. 539–40.
29. Ibid., p. 543. I cannot develop this idea here, but I believe that vigorous theologies of self-denial and of grace as given first, prior to action, tend also to slide toward use of militarization metaphors for characterizing Christian participation and witness to the world.

orient our lives to a God of grace rising within so as to lure us into healing solidarity with a groaning nature, and a struggling humanity in social and historical life. Calvin confessed, for example, that with qualifications a reverent mind could say that "nature is God."[30] And even Barth, though declaring it as only included in the deity of God, struggled to say, "God is human."[31] One might conceivably work hard to mine these statements for a more immanental Reformed theology.

One striking step within the Reformed tradition, toward recasting divine presence and grace as immanent to nature and to human social and historical life, was taken by the nineteenth-century Reformed pastor, educator, and theologian Friedrich Schleiermacher. Although he seems barely read in Reformed communions and theological institutions, this theologian is noteworthy for interweaving divine grace and causality with the nature system, and with the social and political dynamics of history.[32] For some, this may seem a risk-laden venture, and because of Schleiermacher's move, the early Barth explicitly announced that Schleiermacher be set outside the Reformed line of thought.[33] Later in life, however, when looking back over his lifelong struggle with this "church father of the nineteenth century," Barth never gave up on Schleiermacher, writing, "Could he not perhaps be understood differently so I would not have to reject his theology, but rather might be joyfully conscious of proceeding in fundamental agreement with him?"[34]

Yes, it is possible to read Schleiermacher "differently" — at least differently from usual readings by Barth portraying him as the divinizer of human self, community, and religious life. However coextensive with natural and human process Schleiermacher made the divine causality and grace, he never made them identical or equal in kind.[35] This holds true for the kind of intimacy he saw between God and world, and also for the way

30. *Institutes* 1.5.5.

31. Karl Barth, "The Humanity of God," address given September 25, 1956, published as Essay Two in *The Humanity of God* (Richmond: John Knox Press, 1960), pp. 37–65.

32. The two best brief introductions to Schleiermacher's thought are Martin Redeker, *Schleiermacher: Life and Thought,* trans. John Wallhauser (Philadelphia: Fortress Press, 1973); and B. A. Gerrish, *A Prince of the Church: Schleiermacher and the Beginnings of Modern Theology* (Philadelphia: Fortress Press, 1984).

33. Barth, *The Word of God and the Word of Man,* pp. 195–96.

34. Karl Barth, "Concluding Unscientific Postscript on Schleiermacher," in *Karl Barth: The Theology of Schleiermacher,* Lectures at Göttingen, Winter 1923–1924, ed. D. Ritschl (Grand Rapids: Eerdmans, 1982), pp. 261–70.

35. Friedrich Schleiermacher, *Christian Faith,* ed. H. R. Mackintosh and J. S. Stewart (Philadelphia: Fortress, 1976), p. 51, and "Postscript" to p. 54.

he connected our experience of divine grace and the vocation of Christian "good works." Let me comment on this latter theological connection in Schleiermacher, since I have highlighted it already as essential for understanding our retreat from a significant embrace of those who are beyond our good order.

Schleiermacher connected our experience of divine grace and vocation in such a way that there really could be no experience of divine grace apart from our being embedded in community, in history, in our vocational practice of good works. Regarding our vocation, the Reformed pastor and theologian Schleiermacher says something that I have yet to read Calvin or our Reformed confessions to say. He interpreted the good works of Christian vocation as "a means of grace." Schleiermacher writes, "We recognize no means of grace but such as are at the same time good works, and that all good works must likewise be means of grace."[36] There is here very little theology suggesting "*first* God's grace through faith in Jesus Christ and *then* obedient action through vocation." No, he says, "Our union with Christ in faith *is* . . . an active obedience."[37] For Schleiermacher, this is to locate the experience of divine grace where Christ's redemptive community is embracing or removing the world's corporate misery in all its forms.[38] This way of relating our experience of divine grace to our experiences of being vocationally in the struggles of history yields a view of divine grace that is more intimate to historical life and world-struggle than is articulated in the theological or confessional documents I know in the Reformed tradition.

Perhaps some formulations in the Confession of 1967 of the Presbyterian Church (U.S.A.) come close. The confession pivots on a key sentence: "To be reconciled to God *is* to be sent into the world as God's reconciling community."[39] Moreover, the confession understands our call to ministry as a call of Christ beckoning to us from the sufferings of humanity — so much so, in fact, that the very "face of Christ" is what the church sees in the faces of people in need. Christ is not seen first, known or celebrated somehow first, only afterward issuing in ministry to suffering humanity; no, seeing and ministering to people in need is itself to see the face of Christ.

One senses that the Confession of 1967 here has rightly and courageously reached back behind Calvin, Barth, Schleiermacher, and any

36. Ibid., sec. 112, p. 522.
37. Ibid., sec. 112, p. 519.
38. Ibid., secs. 86, 87, esp. pp. 359-60.
39. Confession of 1967, A.1, Inclusive Language Text prepared by Freda A. Gardner and Cynthia A. Jarvis, in *Reconciliation and Liberation: The Confession of 1967* (= *Journal of Presbyterian History* 61 [Spring 1983]), p. 190.

other Reformed theologians or documents to retrieve that surprising insight from Matthew 25 (vv. 35-46) that when we see and do unto the hungry, the thirsty, the imprisoned in precisely *this* praxis, we are seeing and doing unto Jesus Christ. The God of the Reformed tradition might occasion yet more grace-full world-reformative actions if that tradition stresses that the divine one can only be encountered here — in the theophany of God in the poor of the earth, luring all of us to encounter the God of grace in the struggle with and among the poor, whether they be a part of our order or not. This is part of the surprise of Matthew's gospel about where we find the God of Jesus Christ, and where we can know and serve that God.[40]

One thus doesn't need a Schleiermacher in order to urge the church along toward the insight that the Christ of God dwells immanently in ministries to and for those in radical need. In fact, Schleiermacher himself warrants critique in several ways. Episcopal Divinity School theologian Carter Heyward has suggested that although Schleiermacher helpfully turns the theological enterprise toward human experience and struggle, he still needs critique concerning his bourgeois liberalism and his insufficient attending to the realities of radical evil.[41] Nevertheless Schleiermacher can still serve theologians well, keeping every element of theological construction and doctrine trained to the life-process and struggles within which God abides.

From the perspective of a Reformed tradition that is both immanental and prophetic, there is still much to do, beyond the Presbyterian Church's Confession of 1967. This confession is still very much like the Genevan ecclesiastical ordinance that, for all its world-reformative agenda, pulls back from authentic embrace of the disinherited in all their disorderly need. It often hovers only on the brink of really acknowledging the intimacy of God and Christ with the lives of the poor and in the processes of society and history.

In the Confession of 1967, for example, the divine presence and Christian vocation are allowed to intertwine intimately with the full plurality of the human situation, and it suggests that this position implies a faithful stand against racial divisions. But then it only affirms a general

40. My theme in "La Sorpresa de San Mateo" (The surprise of St. Matthew), lecture, Seminario Evangélico Presbiteriano, San Felipe, Retalhuleu, Guatemala, June 21, 1987. For just one selection from the biblical studies of Matthew 25:35–46, see Joseph A. Grassi, "The Divine Identification Ethic in Matthew," *Biblical Theological Bulletin* 11, no. 3 (1981): 81–84 (with bibliography).

41. Isabel Carter Heyward, *The Redemption of God: A Theology of Mutual Relation* (Lanham, Md.: University Press of America, 1982), pp. 185–88.

posture of reconciliation, suggesting that we are "one universal family." It holds back from explicitly affirming liberation movements of particular black Christians engaged in the struggle for justice. Similarly, in the document we confess the Creator God as the God of all nature and human physical life. Our distinctive sexual natures, however, as men and women, are discussed not as created gifts or as modes of expression of our spirituality. The entire section on sexuality knows only how to talk of God's ordering of our life, of threats posed by anarchy in sexual relationships, and of the importance of order of marriage.

In the first case, there is little confession and call to solidarity with a divine presence nurturing and sustaining liberation of African-Americans, and in the second, there is little or no accepting and affirming of the human self, nature, sexuality, or sensuality. If the God of grace isn't confessed as intimate to these, how can that God be the one of Jesus Christ, in whom God is poured out into life and world?[42] The confession is too constrained by its leading metaphor of reconciliation and thus blunts the church's primary need to address the many questions of "liberalism" in late twentieth-century struggle.[43]

* * *

Theology's intellectual revisioning alone will not prevent a Reformed Christianity from being world-repressive, because that repressiveness is often born of social, historic, and economic practices that press in upon the Reformed people of faith and with which Christians often compromise. Theology can assess, however, how it may be reinforcing, with its theological language, our compromising practices, and it may take steps to resist those practices.

What I have suggested here is that the Reformed tradition's praiseworthy world-formative impulse has been guided by a theology that all too easily, perhaps unwittingly, accepts a world-repressive compromise with established orders. It does this, in spite of all its talk about doing good and practicing vocation, in part because its adherents think it possible to expe-

---

42. For a more systematic assessment of the Confession of 1967 in relation to contemporary liberation theologies and for development of themes not taken up here, see Daniel L. Migliore, "Jesus Christ the Reconciling Liberator: The Confession of 1967 and Theologies of Liberation," in *Reconciliation and Liberation: The Confession of 1967* (= *Journal of Presbyterian History* 61 [Spring 1983]), pp. 33–42.

43. For my own proposals on relating liberation to reconciliation, see Mark Kline Taylor, *Remembering Esperanza: Toward a Cultural-Political Theology for North American Praxis* (Maryknoll, N.Y.: Orbis Books, 1990), pp. 175–81.

rience God's grace before, or apart, from encountering radical struggle in society and history. What is needed is an appropriation by us of those elements in our tradition that teach that God's presence and our receiving of God's grace are immanent to social and historical struggle. I am aware that this immanental turn may feel like a move against Protestant theology's notions of so-called prevenient grace, if by that phrase we mean a grace for individuals that "comes before" action and vocation; but it does not compromise the *preeminence* of grace as the power of God that lures us to, and meets us in, social and historical struggle, above all in the cries of those suffering in our midst.[44]

Can a Reformed tradition make such an immanental turn, away from prevenient grace but still highlighting the preeminent power of grace in history? If it is to sustain its own best world-reformative impulses in ways that foster radical solidarity with people in need outside established orders, I believe it must. It needs resources for assuring that the God of grace cannot be known and experienced apart from where that God already is at work powerfully — in the struggles and hopes of those in radical need. It is this kind of God of grace who can lead us out of the well-ordered places of Reformed world-repression and into the places from which new emancipating world-transformative impulses are emerging. Where are these places? As an answer, I offer the short poem-prayer written by a Presbyterian and exiled Guatemalan woman, Julia Esquivel.

> In the most obscure and sordid place,
> in the most hostile and harshest,
> in the most corrupt and nauseating places,
> there You do Your work.
> That is why Your Son
> descended into hell,
> in order to transform what is NOT
> and to purify that which IS BECOMING.
> This is hope![45]

44. See the helpful commentary on the *prevenience* and *preeminence* of grace in John W. de Gruchy, *Liberating Reformed Theology: A South African Contribution to an Ecumenical Debate* (Grand Rapids: Eerdmans, 1991), pp. 181-82.

45. Julia Esquivel, "Esperanza" (Hope), in *Threatened with Resurrection: Prayers and Poems from an Exiled Guatemalan* (Elgin, Ill.: Brethren Press, 1982), p. 105.

• 10 •

Christianity on the Eve of Postmodernity:
Karl Barth and Dietrich Bonhoeffer

SHIN CHIBA

Postmodernity and Christianity

Japan and Postmodernity

It has long been pointed out that the last few decades of the twentieth century represent a great turning point in world history. To be sure, one can discern some unmistakable signs here and there in the fin-de-siècle context that attest to the arrival of the postmodern situation in the so-called late capitalist societies or the postindustrial societies in North America, Western Europe, and Japan.[1] When looking closely at current trends in the intellectual, sociocultural, and political situation of my own society, Japan, I cannot but recognize that what is conspicuous about the contemporary Japanese situation is not the emergence of the so-called new human species *(shin jinrui)* among the youth but that middle-aged and old people as well as the young are gradually becoming engulfed in the historical wave of postmodernity.

1. Throughout this study I use the term "postmodernity" in reference to the "postmodern" situation or age, while I mean by "postmodernism" a contemporary school of thought, whether poststructuralism or revisionist Marxism, neopragmatism or neo-Nietzscheanism, which directly deals with the implications of the presupposed arrival of "postmodernity." I take as some of the defining characteristics of postmodernity the following tendencies of the "high-tech," consumer, and information society: the sense of meaninglessness, the sense of aimlessness or flatness, the loss of confidence in normative judgment, and the like.

As a matter of fact, some acute observers of the current "high-tech," "information," and "consumer" society of Japan insist that it represents a most exemplary instance of the postmodern situation of reaction, where "resistance" has been virtually wiped out and "politics" has been practically abolished.[2] Even though one may not totally agree with their somewhat extreme and pessimistic analyses of current Japanese society, one must admit that they have at least captured a glimpse of some undeniable trends of postmodernity observable in Japan today.

It is neither feasible nor advisable, however, to apply unthinkingly or directly to Japan the arguments of such French and American postmodern theorists as Michel Foucault, Jacques Derrida, Jean-François Lyotard, Jean Baudrillard, Frederic Jameson, or Richard Rorty. As is often noted, modern Japan has shown a general tendency to observe the continuous arrival of Western ideas and ideologies without seriously confronting them or assimilating them into traditional Japanese ideas. While ideas or "isms" of Western origin have been enthusiastically imported one after another, they are sooner or later used up, disappearing into oblivion. At the same time, there are obviously some aspects of peculiar Japaneseness that remain untouched in the whole matter of importing Western ideas and isms. This very fact makes it difficult to assess the Japanese situation in an unambiguous and outright manner. For instance, it is reported that Japanese theorists Kojin Karatani and Akira Asada not so long ago shocked and intrigued Derrida in their roundtable discussion by boasting that there is no need for deconstruction, as there has not been a construct in Japan.[3]

The best one can say with confidence about current Japanese society is the following: while the premodern still lingers so heavily on every aspect of Japanese sociocultural life that the modern has not reached its maturity, the postmodern has already begun to take shape gradually in some aspects of the sociocultural life, such as in the lifestyle of the consumer society and an efficient high-tech, information society. What one can expect from contemporary Japan is a possible complicity to be formed between the premodern and the postmodern. In this sense the Japanese situation can rightly be described as extremely treacherous and complicated.

2. Masao Miyoshi and H. D. Harootunian, "Introduction," in *Postmodernism and Japan*, ed. Masao Miyoshi and H. D. Harootunian (Durham, N.C.: Duke University Press), pp. ix–xv; Masao Miyoshi, "Against the Native Grain: The Japanese Novel and the 'Postmodern' West," in ibid., p. 148; Alan Wolfe, "Suicide and the Japanese Postmodern: A Postnarrative Paradigm?" in ibid., pp. 220–29; Kôjin Karatani, "One Spirit, Two Nineteenth Centuries," in ibid., pp. 271–72.

3. Miyoshi, "Against the Native Grain," p. 148.

Nonetheless, the recent argument concerning the dominance of postmodernity in Europe and North America does illuminate in part a gradual change taking place in the sociocultural life of today's Japan, especially the dimension emphasizing the loss of the value basis of present-day life and its concomitant meaninglessness and aimlessness. According to postmodernism, in the postmodern world the modern idea of humanity, which had been considered to possess universal value, has collapsed. Furthermore, it proclaims that the postmodern situation has witnessed the collapse of the idea of modern subjecthood, as it is simply "the age in which the subject is dead" (Jean Baudrillard). Lyotard argues that the discrediting of the grand narratives of modernity leads to the disintegration of the social aggregates, which in turn changes people into a mass of individual atoms. Thus, "each individual is referred to himself," and yet "each of us knows that our self does not amount to much."[4] The self cannot eliminate the sense of being insignificant and fragmented, while incorporated into a system of some sort or other. Nevertheless, Lyotard maintains that the self is by no means isolated from that system or organization: "Young or old, man or woman, rich or poor, a person is always located at 'nodal points' of specific communication circuits. . . . A self does not amount to much, but no self is an island."[5] We can see here the gist of postmodernity, which is variously characterized as foundationless, empty, flat, depthless, and meaningless.[6] This is one of the most serious challenges facing Japanese society today.

Allow me to portray briefly the postmodernity of Japan in a somewhat pessimistic manner. Excessive materialism and what we might call comfortism grounded in the modern ideology of "progress" and "growth" have now become so dominant a lifestyle in Japan as to have become a prevailing ideology. The mode in which this postmodern ideology attempts to realize itself is typically "the changing of change," as Sheldon S. Wolin indicated as the defining mode of postmodernity, which is to say, "the intensification and rationalization of change, the continuous reproduction of the new and the simultaneous subversion of the old."[7] Con-

---

4. Jean-François Lyotard, *The Postmodern Condition,* trans. Geoff Bennington and Brian Massumi (Minneapolis: University of Minnesota Press, 1984), p. 15.

5. Ibid.

6. Cf. Sheldon S. Wolin, *Seijigaku Hihan* (A critique of political science), ed. and trans. Shin Chiba, Takafumi Nakamura, and Makoto Saitô (Tokyo: Misuzu Shobô Publishers, 1988), pp. xv–xx; Miyoshi and Harootunian, "Introduction," pp. vii–viii; Frederic Jameson, *Postmodernism; or, The Cultural Logic of Late Capitalism* (Durham, N.C.: Duke University Press, 1991), pp. 6–9.

7. Sheldon S. Wolin, *The Presence of the Past: Essays on the State and the Constitution*

temporary Japan is indeed a characteristically postmodernizing society of rapid, incessant change.

As a result, the formal rationalization and control of human life has increasingly permeated the society, so that victory may be won over ordinary people by state and corporate bureaucracies. Politics is taken away from common people's hands to be delivered to elite experts, while democracy is acclaimed only as rhetoric.[8] Economic power is concentrated in the hands of technocrats, so that the so-called rational choice theory extensively pervades social planning and policy making, whereby economic inequality and injustice are rationalized and incorporated into the social structure. Culture suffers the vulgarizing impacts of philistinism and commercialism; its basis of value is jeopardized and weakened by consumerism. Traditional learning, knowledge, and thought are increasingly looked down upon as a relic of the previous (i.e., modern) age. Supreme intelligence (*sophia*), wisdom of life, and knowledge of matters that are all concerned with the *Bildung* of human personality are replaced by a massive amount of technical information and data. Thoughtlessness spreads out among men and women, old and young, in sharp contrast with the rise of technical knowledge and information. Religion and faith tend to be regarded either as fitting artifacts ready to enter the museum or as archaic objects for archaeological investigation. When it comes to the *human* situation of postmodernity, there is a certain increase of diversity in tastes and hobbies, although the lifestyle becomes all the more standardized and normalized, so that the human *Typus*, uninteresting and unoriginal, may become predominant.

Excessive materialism and comfortism have become an ideological screen to veil this serious and critical situation. A lucid illustration can be obtained, for instance, by looking into the recent phenomenon referred to as "becoming a playland" — a kind of huge adult Disney World — of such megalopoleis as Tokyo, where an affluent and cute little cosmos for the enjoyment of leisure is played out. No matter how real this performance may appear, its illusoriness and falsity become obvious when one juxtaposes

---

(Baltimore: Johns Hopkins University Press, 1989), p. 77. Cf. Shin Chiba, "Gendai Kokka to Seitôsei no Kiki: S. S. Wolin no Democracy Ron" (The modern state and the crisis of legitimacy: S. S. Wolin's ideas on democracy), *Shisô* (Thought), no. 784 (October 1989): 44.

8. Highly suggestive is John McGowan's argument that postmodern foundationlessness leads neither to chaos nor to liberation but to rigidified social order. See John McGowan, *Postmodernism and Its Critics* (Ithaca, N.Y.: Cornell University Press, 1991), pp. 23–24. Cf. Jameson, *Postmodernism*, pp. viii–xxii.

it against the real world. For this juxtaposition exposes the inherent fictitiousness of this performance by contrasting it with today's realities in the world and Japan, namely, threat of hunger and nuclear disaster, anomie, anxiety neurosis, and a sense of loss spreading widely in the populace.[9]

What meaning, then, does religion or faith have in this postmodern situation, when the great majority of people today have little interest in them? What meaning in particular does the transcendence of Christian faith come to have? Is the Genesis story of Noah's ark as narrated in Genesis 6–9 a suitable metaphor to express the contemporary situation? Noah devoted himself to the task of building an ark for many days and nights, as God had ordered him. He diligently set out to this task under the burning hot sun in the midst of people's derision and ridicule. For he believed in the promise of the Lord and took seriously the unseen as a reality of life. Is this image of the faithful Noah an appropriate metaphor to express the way in which a Christian believer lives in postmodernity? Or is a more fitting metaphor Jesus' parables of heaven as described in Matthew 13:44-46, the stories of treasure hidden in a field and of a merchant in search of fine pearls? Is Christian faith increasingly becoming a rare and priceless treasure in the dark and muddy sea of postmodernity?

Postmodernity Defined as Post-Christendom

It was an inspiring and grateful experience for me to have recently gained acquaintance with The Gospel and Our Culture Network (GOCN). This theological network represents a North American quest for reformulating the gospel message in a postmodern context that is also defined, in an important sense, as post-Christendom. This project is headed by a group of theologians, pastors, and lay believers, among whom our coeditor George R. Hunsberger serves as coordinator, and our teacher Charles C. West as a theological collaborator. While the participants in the project cross the boundaries of denominations and theological positions, they are united in perceiving that a Christendom model has become outdated in North America, that North America should be addressed more emphatically as a new mission field, and that a radical reformulation of the gospel message and the church's mission is needed. They insist that Christians and

9. Cf. Shin Chiba, "Joshô: Seiji Shisô no Genzai" (Introduction: The present-day perspectives of political thought), in *Seiji Shisô no Genzai*, ed. Yasunobu Fujiwara and Shin Chiba (Tokyo: Waseda Daigaku Shuppanbu Publishers, 1990), pp. 5–6.

the church should live vigorously the life of witness to the gospel and should perceive themselves as "resident aliens" and as "a colony of the kingdom" in a post-Christendom culture and society.[10]

This postmodern, post-Christendom challenge represents the crisis not simply for human society at large but also for the Christian community in particular. Theologically stated, the crisis of postmodernity portrays both the judgment of God over the Christian community and wider society and God's invitation to repent and to start anew. The crisis of postmodernity should be understood as posing not a dead end for the Christian community but a new opportunity for it to engage in rigorous self-criticism and self-examination of its past failures and inadequacies. Without a serious attempt at deconstruction, no creative work of construction is possible. Without genuine *metanoia* there can be no renewal of the Christian community, and without a renewal of the Christian community there will be no transformation of our society. Genuine repentance and self-examination should be the only point of departure in our search for a new form of evangelical and prophetic Christianity amid a society heading toward the decentered, deconstructed, and fragmented world of postmodernity.

Certainly the Christian community in non-Western societies is by no means immune from the postmodern crisis. We all are involved in the global wave of the postmodern crisis. It is my opinion, however, that the postmodern crisis first and foremost discloses the historical failures and inadequacies of the leading Western churches and the other non-Western churches entangled with them. These historical failures and inadequacies of the main Western churches are sharply and accurately seen both by the hitherto repressed or unnoticed non-Western communities, which remain relatively uninfluenced from the impact of these leading Western churches, and by marginalized or fringe groups within the West. For instance, in the view of Leo Tolstoy, Kanzô Uchimura, Mohandas Gandhi, Martin Luther King, Jr., and Indian tribal peoples in Latin America, it is clear that a main inadequacy of Western Christendom is its historical failure to dissociate

---

10. For example, George R. Hunsberger, "The Newbigin Gauntlet: Developing a Domestic Missiology for North America," *Missiology* 19, no. 4 (October 1991): 394, 401; Craig van Gelder, "A Great New Fact of Our Day: America as Mission Field," ibid., p. 417; Stanley Hauerwas and William H. Willimon, "Why Resident Aliens Struck a Chord," ibid., pp. 419–29; Stanley Hauerwas and William H. Willimon, *Resident Aliens* (Nashville: Abingdon Press, 1989), pp. 12, 44–45, 49, 132; Wilbert R. Shenk, "Report on a European Assignment," *The Gospel and Our Culture Newsletter* 2, no. 2 (October 1990): 2. It is worth noting that a sister movement of The Gospel and Our Culture Network exists in Great Britain initially formed by Lesslie Newbigin, H. Dan Beeby, and others.

itself from the sociopolitical structure of war and violence, a conspicuous feature of Western civilization for centuries in the modern age. It is no exaggeration to say that for the first time in history a good opportunity has been made wide open on the eve of this post-Christendom age for Western Christians to enter a serious dialogue on an equal footing with non-Western traditions of faith as well as with marginalized fringe communities of faith within the West.

At the same time we now have a good opportunity to mine the rich and diverse Western Christian traditions for an alternative form of Christian existence. What immediately comes to my mind are those minor traditions or figures that helped form decentered communities of Christ within Western Christendom: Saint Francis of Assisi, the Anabaptist tradition of the Reformation period, the Mennonite tradition, the Quaker community, John Wesley, Jonathan Edwards, Søren Kierkegaard, father and son Johann Blumhardt and Christoph Blumhardt, and the like. The main purpose of this article, then, is to search for some insights and ingredients within the Western tradition itself that can help us envisage a genuine form of evangelical and prophetic Christianity in the works of the two most prominent theologians of the twentieth century: Karl Barth and Dietrich Bonhoeffer. They were the theologians who, some decades ago, self-consciously began doing theology in what they perceived to be a post-Christian Europe.[11]

Karl Barth

Karl Barth (1886-1968) is a profound theologian of the twentieth century whose impact is comparable both to Augustine, who exerted a great influence on the transitional period from antiquity to the Middle Ages, and to Martin Luther, who served to usher in the modern age while having been himself deeply rooted in medieval life. We need to take Barth seriously, because he was a theological thinker who, out of his experiences of World War I, continued to point to the inherent limitations of the Western project of modernization. Barth understood his theological task was to search for a form of theology capable of coping with the cultural crisis of the West. If postmodernity can be understood as "a crisis of cultural authority, specifi-

---

11. Incidentally, in the opinion of Charles C. West, Barth and Bonhoeffer are "two other great figures who are probably more influential in my thought today" than any others (Ruth C. West, "An Ecumenical Journey: A Conversation between Ruth and Charles West," *Princeton Seminary Bulletin*, n.s., 12, no. 2 [1991]: 126–27; see chap. 1 above).

cally of the authority vested in Western European culture and its institutions,"[12] then Barth's theology of revelation is a theological effort in the beginning of the twentieth century to foresee and cope with the postmodern crisis.

In short, he was a theological explorer on a quest for an evangelical and prophetic form of Christianity on the eve of postmodernity. Whatever aspect of his theological reflection is to be taken up, it reveals a dynamic theological response to the postmodern situation. Thus, Barth has to be understood as a theological thinker who creatively developed a postmodern theology of the Word based upon the event of God's self-revelation in Christ in the context of the Europe after World War I, which was undoubtedly for him a "post-Christendom" Europe.

Nietzsche and Barth

Friedrich Nietzsche represents a philosophical origin of postmodernism; for instance, it is well known that Michel Foucault picked up a Nietzschean method of genealogy to shed light on the mechanisms of invisible power operation vested in modern knowledge and institutions. Furthermore, Nietzsche's acute observation of the predicament of modern humanity and society was often a penetrating foresight of what can be termed a postmodern situation. The following famous observation in *Also sprach Zarathustra* (written 1883–91) is but an example of this: "No shepherd and one herd! Everybody wants the same, everybody is the same: whoever feels different goes voluntarily into a madhouse."[13]

Nietzsche's following penetrating, though rather lengthy, portrayal is a prognosticative proclamation concerning the postmodern turn of European civilization.

> What I relate is the history of the next two centuries. I describe what is coming, what can no longer come differently: *the advent of nihilism.* . . .

---

12. Craig Owens, "The Discourse of Others: Feminists and Postmodernism," in *The Anti-Aesthetic: Essays on Postmodern Culture,* ed. Hal Foster (Port Townsend, Wash.: Bay Press, 1983), p. 57.

13. Friedrich Nietzsche, "Also sprach Zarathustra," in *Friedrich Nietzsche Werke — in drei Bänden,* vol. 2, ed. Karl Schlechta (Munich: Karl Hanser Verlag, 1955), p. 284. An English translation of this passage appears in *Nietzsche,* ed. and trans. Walter Kaufmann (New York: Penguin Books, 1968), p. 130. (Hereafter, page numbers of English translations will be noted in parentheses following the citation in the original language.)

This future speaks even now in a hundred signs, this destiny announces itself everywhere; for this music of the future all ears are cocked even now. For some time now, our whole European culture has been moving as toward a catastrophe, with a tortured tension that is growing from decade to decade: restlessly, headlong, like a river that wants to reach the end, that no longer reflects, that is afraid to reflect.[14]

Nietzsche's declaration of "the advent of nihilism" should be understood not only as his premonition of what the coming age would be like but also as a manifesto of his own "active nihilism." After all, he welcomes this nihilistic turn and proclaims that he is "the first perfect nihilist of Europe."[15] We can see his analyses of "the advent of nihilism" and of historical Christianity's entanglement in it in his fragmentary notes and comments that were posthumously edited as *The Will to Power*. These notes and comments are sometimes permeated either with self-contradictory and hyperbolic remarks or with poorly or little argued series of statements. If we rightly decipher his genuine intent from these fragments, however, Nietzsche is maintaining here that such negative aspects of nihilism as insecurity, self-deception, self-shame, valuelessness, and loss of self-esteem are rooted in what he calls "Christian morality," the decadent historical development of European Christianity and its ecclesiastical institutions. Nietzsche devastatingly criticizes German Protestant Christianity's spiritual staleness and laxity; he insists that *"the Christian acts as all the world does* and possesses a Christianity of ceremonies and *moods."*[16] Thus, he openly declares "a war against Christianity" by claiming, "I regard Christianity as the most fatal seductive lie that has yet existed, as the great holy lie."[17]

To be sure, as we shall see more closely later on, there exists an essential chasm between Nietzsche, who is rightly referred to as the apostle of Antichrist, and Barth, who is sometimes misconstrued as the fideistic theologian for the catacombs. Curiously enough, however, there also exist some points of continuity between the two thinkers. The young Barth's ideas owed much

14. Friedrich Nietzsche, *The Will to Power*, ed. and trans. Walter Kaufmann and R. J. Hollingdale (New York: Random House, 1967), p. 3.

15. Ibid. Nietzsche stands for active nihilism as "a sign of increased power of spirit" and even as "a violent force of destruction" (ibid., pp. 17–18).

16. Friedrich Nietzsche, "Der Antichrist," in *Friedrich Nietzsche Werke*, II, p. 1198 (p. 610). For Nietzsche's criticism, see, for example, *The Will to Power*, pp. 7, 9, 12–13, 16, 20, 54–55, 113, 125.

17. "Der Antichrist," p. 117. Walter Kaufmann is right in indicating that in the history of Western philosophy, Nietzsche is one of the first thinkers to complete the break with religion ("Introduction," in *Nietzsche*, p. 17).

to an insightful diagnosis of nineteenth-century theology proffered by church historian Franz Overbeck, Nietzsche's colleague during his young, Basel years, and one of his few lifelong friends. Overbeck's influence on the young Barth should not be underestimated. His impact is comparable in its magnitude to the influence of Kierkegaard and of the older and the younger Blumhardt. Overbeck's criticism of historical Christianity, its theology, and church life shared common ground with Nietzsche's in some substantial respects. The young Barth was decisively influenced by Overbeck's profound theme of "the end of Christianity," as well as by his critical insight into an easy continuity between faith and culture, between Christianity and world history, as presupposed in many versions of contemporary dominant liberal theology.[18] One must conclude, then, that Barth's critical grasp of the modern age and its theology, at least in the early stage, was substantially shaped under the milieu of Nietzsche-Overbeckian philosophical diagnosis. Nietzsche, Overbeck, and Barth all stood on common ground when they critically regarded late modernity as replete with signs of the end of Western civilization and confronted themselves with "the advent of nihilism" as the most critical historical event that the Western world had ever encountered.

Barth shared with Nietzsche a recognition that nineteenth-century European civilization was facing a catastrophe. Moreover, Barth shared with him a recognition that the prospect for a catastrophe of Western civilization had outmoded some metaphysical assumptions dominant in the West for centuries, among which were the unwavering trust in the suprasensory world and the contempt for the human body — what Nietzsche called Christianity's Platonic biases.[19] At any rate, Barth did not fail to recognize Nietzsche's partial and yet profound insights into the predicaments of historical Christianity.

It should be noted, however, that Barth's treatment of Nietzsche was generally negative and critical. Yet this fact does not imply that Barth totally ignored or underestimated Nietzsche, for he did take seriously Nietzsche's devastating critique of historical Christianity. As we shall see later, Barth

18. Karl Barth, *Theology and Church*, trans. Louise P. Smith (New York: Harper & Row, 1962), pp. 55–73; Karl Barth, *The Epistle to the Romans*, 6th ed., trans. Edwyn C. Hoskyns (Oxford: Oxford University Press, 1933), pp. 3–4, 100, 118, 162, 204, 252, 268; Karl Barth, *Protestant Thought from Rousseau to Ritschl*, trans. Brian Cozens (New York: Harper & Brothers, 1959), p. 271. Cf. Eberhard Jüngel, *Barth-Studien* (Zurich: Benziger Verlag, 1982), pp. 64–72; Eberhard Busch, *Karl Barth*, trans. John Bowden (Philadelphia: Fortress Press, 1976), pp. 115–16; Thomas F. Torrance, *Karl Barth* (London: SCM Press, 1962), pp. 39–44.
19. For example, Nietzsche, *The Will to Power*, pp. 94–95, 131, 133.

felt that he had to attack Nietzsche fiercely, simply because Barth regarded his blame of the Crucified One as well as his advocacy of Dionysian *Übermensch* as nothing more than a seductive form of contemporary idolatry and thus likely to give way to various dehumanizing forms of ambiguous surrogate religions and false religions. However, Barth was not a champion of Nietzsche-bashing but rather stood with Karl Jaspers, Fritz Buri, and others in seeing that Nietzsche's fierce contestation against Christianity grew out of profoundly Christian soil. Nietzsche could grapple with, come to know, and reject Christianity, from within as it were, because he as a son of a pious Lutheran pastor was after all a thinker with a theological perspective and orientation. Close attention will enable one to recognize immediately that a biblical mode of inquiry, the spirit of an authentic, sustaining theological quest, breathes in even his well-known and most anti-Christian polemics such as *Also sprach Zarathustra, Der Antichrist* (1888), and *Ecce homo* (1888). Nietzsche thus has been constantly read and interpreted in the tension-filled twofold significance as simultaneously a destroyer of Christian faith and a reviver of the authentic Christian message.[20]

In this connection it is worth noting Nietzsche's highly ambivalent attitude toward Jesus of Nazareth and primitive Christianity. Nietzsche often sounds as if he is trying to rescue the authenticity of Jesus and primitive Christianity from the subsequent historical developments of Christianity, which are often equated by him with "mendaciousness" and "nausea." He argues that Christ denied everything that is today called Christian. "'Christianity' has become something fundamentally different from what its founder did and desired"; "in truth, there was only *one* Christian, and he died on the cross."[21] Nietzsche even refers to "genuine, original Christianity" and insists that it is possible at all times.[22]

20. Cf. Steven E. Aschheim, *The Nietzsche Legacy in Germany, 1890–1990* (Berkeley: University of California Press, 1992), pp. 201–5. Aschheim traced the historical process in which, immediately after Nietzsche's death, Protestant thinkers like Hans Gallwitz, Theodor Odenwald, and Albert Kathoff tried to appropriate Nietzsche into renewed forms of Christianity (pp. 203–8). He also delineated the way in which Nietzsche was incorporated into a pro-Nazi Germanic Christianity (pp. 208–13).

21. Nietzsche, *The Will to Power*, p. 114; Nietzsche, "Der Antichrist," p. 1200 (p. 612). See also Nietzsche, *The Will to Power*, pp. 97–98, 102, 115, 123. Concerning Nietzsche's ambivalent attitude toward Jesus, see Tracy B. Strong, *Friedrich Nietzsche and the Politics of Transfiguration*, expanded ed. (Berkeley: University of California Press, 1988), pp. 123–27.

22. Nietzsche, "Der Antichrist," p. 1200 (p. 613). Cf. Masao Nakamura, *Nietzsche to Kirisutokyô Rinri* (Nietzsche and Christian ethics) (Tokyo: Kôbundô Publishers, 1961), pp. 117, 140–47, 151–59, 227, 306–12, 374; Shôzô Shinobu, *Nietzsche Kenkyû* (Nietzsche studies)

But Nietzsche and Barth were a world apart. A decisive difference could be found especially in their understanding of the cross of Jesus. Nietzsche could not see the significance of the cross of Christ at all and dismissed it as "gruesome paganism": "God gave his son for the remission of sins, as a *sacrifice*. In one stroke, it was all over with the evangel! The *trespass sacrifice* — in its most revolting, most barbarous form at that, the sacrifice of the *guiltless* for the sins of the guilty!"[23] Nietzsche thus proceeded to speak of "the death of God" and proclaimed that he would rather adhere to the earth.

Barth, in contrast, moved in the diametrically opposite direction. Having undergone the so-called Feuerbachean experience by encountering an atheistic tradition of the West, he nonetheless began to perceive a "God's revolution" in the very atheistic forefront. This quest culminated in a new "discovery of God" based on the revelatory event of Christ in a post-Christendom Europe. In short, Barth, unlike Nietzsche, insisted that God is throughout a *living* God for humanity,[24] though Barth, like Nietzsche, broke away both from the metaphysical conception of God rooted in the suprasensory world of abstraction and from highly humanistic and culturally immanentistic premises of nineteenth-century theology.

Barth presented a long and intriguing analysis on Nietzsche in *Die kirchliche Dogmatik,* III/2. It was indeed a powerful critique of Nietzsche. Unlike his rather ambivalent treatment of Nietzsche in his formative years, Barth here appeared to embark upon the task of delineating his decisive difference from Nietzsche. The context in which this critique emerged was the section where Barth's view of human nature was discussed under the heading *Mitmenschlichkeit* (fellow humanity). It was Barth's attempt to come to grips with Nietzsche's Dionysian anthropology, that is, the absolute isolation of *Übermensch,* over against his own notion of *Mitmenschlichkeit,* that is, "person" being not in the singular but in pluralities — with others. Barth's analysis of Nietzsche was interesting, as it disclosed an unbridgeable chasm between the two thinkers with regard to the evaluation of the cross of Christ, which both of them took to be the central doctrine of Christianity.

(Tokyo: Seki Shobô Publishers, 1980), pp. 47–54, 69; Seiichi Yagi, *Jesus to Nihilism* (Jesus and nihilism) (Tokyo: Seidosha Publishers, 1982), pp. 56–58.

23. Nietzsche, "Der Antichrist," p. 1203 (p. 616).

24. Karl Barth, *The Humanity of God,* trans. John Newton Thomas (Richmond, Va.: John Knox Press, 1960), pp. 11–33. Cf. Hideo Ooki, *Barth* (in Japanese) (Tokyo: Kôdansha Publishers, 1984), pp. 25–28; Setsurô Oosaki, *Karl Barth no Rômasho no Kenkyû* (Karl Barth's studies in the Book of Romans) (Tokyo: Shinkyô Shuppansha Publishers, 1987), pp. 34, 60–62, 99–105, 167–84.

Though Nietzsche from the outset regarded Christian morality as a "system of cruelty," it was, in Barth's view, because Nietzsche himself was profoundly a moralist in his own right, having "the question of morality behind him." Nietzsche's amoralism, which professed to stand "beyond good and evil," was understood to be the other side of his inherent moralism.[25] As political theorist Bonnie Honig stated in her recent stimulating book, Nietzsche could be correctly described in a sense as an ethical recoverer of ancient virtù and responsibility.[26] But this ethics was an ethics of an *Übermensch,* a Dionysus-Zarathustra, and an ethics affirming fully the Dionysian life. In short, Nietzsche was "the most consistent champion and prophet of humanity without the fellow-person"; according to Barth, this aspect of Nietzsche's anthropology was closely linked with the fact that he "never spoke except of himself," and "how little he dealt with material and objective problems."[27] As Nietzsche rightly contrasted "the Crucified" with "Dionysus" in *Ecce homo,* Barth argued that Nietzsche could not understand at all the significance of the cross of Christ. To be sure, Nietzsche, unlike many ordinary Christians in his days, rightly understood the cross to be the central pillar of Christianity. It was nothing but a manifestation of Nietzsche's penetrating power of insight. But Barth maintained that one should adhere absolutely and unconditionally to the cross of Christ with the thoroughgoingness with which Nietzsche rejected "the Crucified."[28] Nietzsche could not comprehend either the true significance of the cross or such vital concepts as sin, guilt, repentance, atonement, or judgment. He regarded them simply as Judaic residues of Christianity.[29]

There is thus little doubt that a radical conflict here exists between these two thinkers. What bothers Barth is certainly not that the Nietzschean ethic of ancient virtù rouses enmity toward order, stability, and the status quo but that it cannot establish any democratic solidarity with other human beings. Nietzsche's hero is an isolated yet proud *Übermensch* who does not need others to be with and who is only interested in "becoming what he

---

25. Karl Barth, *Die kirchliche Dogmatik* (Zollikon and Zurich: Verlag der Evangelischen Buchhandlung/Evangelischer Verlag, 1938–55), III/2, pp. 284–86 (*Church Dogmatics,* trans. G. W. Bromiley et al. [Edinburgh: T. & T. Clark, 1958–60], III/2, pp. 235–38).

26. Bonnie Honig, *Political Theory and the Displacement of Politics* (Ithaca, N.Y.: Cornell University Press, 1993), pp. 42–75. Cf. Strong, *Friedrich Nietzsche and the Politics of Transfiguration,* pp. 192–95.

27. Barth, *Die kirchliche Dogmatik,* III/2, pp. 289–90 (pp. 241–42).

28. Ibid., pp. 288–90 (pp. 240–42).

29. For example, Nietzsche, *The Will to Power,* pp. 98, 102; Nietzsche, "Der Antichrist," p. 1195 (p. 606).

is" by perpetually conquering himself. Here we can see a strongly elitist and antidemocratic conception of human person on the part of Nietzsche. His endless disdain for the social and moral causes of the French Revolution and of modern socialism as well as of Christian ethics undoubtedly reflects in part at least his inherent antidemocratic, self-righteous, and even social Darwinist sentiment. For he had only contempt for women, the poor and the weak, the outcast and the deviant, the ill-constituted and the degenerate, the lowly and the meek in society.[30] Nietzsche did not have the slightest notion that self-sacrificial love and humble service for the needy and the afflicted could be the most courageous act that men and women were capable of. For he could only poorly and mistakenly understand such a morality as "slaves' consciousness" or "a denaturalization of herd-animal morality."[31] Barth understood all these shortfalls of Nietzsche and interpreted them as stemming from the self-contradictory project of becoming like an ancient Greek "philosophizing god," Dionysus (i.e., the lonely battle of perpetual self-conquest).

Against Nietzsche's Dionysian concept of person, Barth adhered to the image of Jesus the Crucified as the defining image of humanity: "humanity of person consists in the determination of his being a being with others."[32] Human significance resides for Barth in a person "being in encounter," in "mutual speech and hearing," and in "openness, seeing and being seen," which always happens spontaneously when one is receptive to others.[33] Barth also argues that the central gospel message, "God is for humanity," is disclosed in the person and event of Christ. Human beings, as God's covenant-partners, are defined not simply as personal beings who respond to God's call and invitation to participate in God's full essence and being — that is, his life and freedom.[34] More significantly, God in his perfect freedom has decided to stand with human beings and to love them in order to carry out his purpose of redemption.[35] This event of grace and redemption took place once for all and for all time in Christ, when he died for our sins on the cross and rose again on the third day. Moreover, Barth insists that in Christ was disclosed the highest possible image of humanity

30. For example, Nietzsche, *The Will to Power,* pp. 58, 79, 111, 115, 122–23, 126, 142, 144.

31. Ibid., pp. 82, 126.

32. Barth, *Die kirchliche Dogmatik,* III/2, p. 291 (p. 243).

33. Ibid., pp. 299–301 (pp. 252–53).

34. Ibid., II/2, pp. 564–65, 638–39.

35. Ibid., II/1, pp. 306–61. Cf. George S. Hendry, "The Freedom of God in the Theology of Karl Barth," *Scottish Journal of Theology* 31, no. 3 (June 1978): 229–44.

and its ultimate criterion as well. A truly human person encounters others and lives with and for them. The humanity disclosed in Christ simply means humanity as a communal being.[36]

Although Barth nowhere indicates it in his polemic against Nietzsche, the most radical critique of Nietzsche that can be drawn from the iconoclastic thrust of a Barthian viewpoint is that Nietzsche is helplessly unguarded against the emergence of many forms of surrogate faiths, false religions, and the occult, which are nothing more than the divinization or absolutization of human being. Nietzsche's declaration of the "death of God" as well as his desperate, solitary, and sorrowful task to become an *Übermensch,* a divine Dionysus-Zarathustra, can be shown to have easily given way to many ambiguous forms of false religions such as the Nietzschean philosophical stance of the cult of Nazism. That a considerable reactionary fragment of subsequent generations of Nietzscheans provided a fitting ideological backdrop for the spread of Nazism in the German Third Reich cannot be regarded either as accidental or as unrelated to Nietzsche's own Dionysus-Zarathustra project.[37] As is widely known, Barth throughout his life combatted every kind of modern project of divinization of human being, within and without Christianity, in all its forms. One of the principal premises of Barth's theology has been that every attempt, whether quasi-religious or secular, that refuses God as the sole and true God inescapably leads to the divinization of human being in one way or another. The consequence of this is the dehumanizing subjugation of everything authentically human. This is the primary reason why Barth felt it urgent to take issue with Nietzsche's Dionysian anthropology as sharply as possible, while accepting some of the latter's substantial criticisms of historical Christianity.

God's Transcendence and the Overcoming of Nothingness

On 1 August, 1914, the day Germany declared war, ninety-three German intellectuals published a manifesto in support of the war policy of Kaiser

36. For example, Barth, *Die kirchliche Dogmatik,* III/4, pp. 51, 713–14; III/2, pp. 242–63, 290–97. Cf. Herbert Hartwell, *The Theology of Karl Barth* (London: Gerald Duckworth, 1964), pp. 123, 129. The following sentence aptly illustrates what Barth means by "fellow-humanity": "It is not as he is for himself but with others, he achieves true humanity, that he corresponds to his determination to be God's covenant-partner, that he is the being for which the person Jesus is, and therefore real person" (*Die kirchliche Dogmatik,* III/2, p. 290 [p. 243]).

37. Aschheim, *The Nietzsche Legacy in Germany,* pp. 201–3, 209–58.

Wilhelm II and his counselors. Barth then seemed to have a shattering premonition that the modern project of nineteenth-century theology was finished. For among these intellectuals he discovered to his horror the names of eminent theologians of his day, almost all of his theological teachers, including Adolf von Harnack and Wilhelm Herrmann, whom he had greatly venerated. In later years Barth remembered the day as "a black day" and expressed his reaction as follows: "In despair over what this indicated about the signs of the time, I suddenly realized that I could not any longer follow either their ethics and dogmatics or their understanding of the Bible and of history. For me at least, 19th-century theology no longer held any future."[38]

Barth's decisive break with nineteenth-century liberal theology by now constitutes a well-known chapter in the history of Christian theology. According to his understanding, nineteenth-century theology was nothing else than a modern, humanistic, and subjectivist theology of the self. It was based on the inherent religiosity of person, whether it was a person's "supposedly innate and essential capacity to sense and taste the infinite" or the person's "religious *a priori*."[39] It was also an inheritor of eighteenth-century Enlightenment thought burdened with an all-pervasive rationalism, a consistent subjectivism, and a historical relativism. An emphasis was laid on a person's essential religiosity rather than God's self-revelation in Christ, on the person's faith rather than the message (gospel) of Christ, on the person's relation to God rather than vice versa. Barth's criticism was directed toward these very human-centered, subjectivist, and immanentistic assumptions of nineteenth-century theology.[40] In short, nineteenth-century theology had an inherent tendency to lose sight of the sovereignty, freedom, and transcendence of God, who encounters human beings as the Lord. Thus, Barth's repudiation of this subjectivist theology of the previous century could be understood to have been informed partly by a Feuerbachian project that saw that "God" there was ultimately a projection of "human essence" and that such theology was in the end nothing but an anthropology.

The publications of Barth's two editions of the commentary on the Book of Romans (1919, 1922) signaled his determined struggle to recover the

---

38. Barth, *The Humanity of God*, p. 14.
39. Ibid., p. 21.
40. Ibid., pp. 23–27. Cf. Karl Barth, *Der Römerbrief*, 2nd ed. (Munich: Chr. Kaiser Verlag, 1926), pp. 259–60; John Macquarrie, *Principles of Christian Theology* (London: SCM Press, 1969), p. 144.

freedom and sovereignty of God in the theological scene of Europe dominated by modern humanistic theology. He aimed at a thoroughgoing grasp of the biblical message that "God is in heaven, and thou art on earth." He also argued that God can be known only through the taking place *(Geschehen)* of the encounter *(Ereignis)* of the Word of God with men and women, that is, by God's revelation in Jesus Christ. Here one can detect a distinctively Barthian trait in the theology of revelation: a Christocentrism based on the transcendence of the Word of God. Only the lordship of the Word of God — God's revelation in freedom, sovereignty, and grace — creates and constitutes living objectivity, concrete actuality, and ultimate reality. Thus, Barth opposes the humanistic and subjectivist cosmology of nineteenth-century theology with the transcendent, sovereignly free, objective Word of God, which itself is simultaneously the *Ereignis* and the *Geschehen*.[41]

This basic trait of Barth's theology was again manifest in later years in his theological resistance to the nihilistic revolution of the 1930s, namely, National Socialism of the German Third Reich. He totally refused every endeavor to identify God's revelation in the law of nation, folk, blood, race, land, or history. Instead he attempted to listen to the Scriptures, to the Word of God, to Christ. To live a "theological existence" meant for Barth simply to respond and to adhere to the freedom of the Word of God in mission and in theology. The Word of God was for him the living words of God proclaimed to living men and women of all ages through the life and action of Christ as witnessed in the Scriptures. The Word of God is Christ the Crucified and the Risen; Christ's relation to us is God's free gift and grace.[42]

I would characterize Barth's theology as one of freedom, based upon the grace and freedom of God in Christ. Barth understands the "being of God" as the "subject who loves in freedom."[43] The question of ethics and the problem of human freedom arise only from this "freedom" of God, who freely takes the initiative to act in love toward humanity in Christ.

41. Cf. Charles C. West, *Communism and the Theologians* (Philadelphia: Westminster Press, 1958), pp. 196–99; Torrance, *Karl Barth*, pp. 97–99; Shin Chiba, *Gendai Protestantism no Seiji Shisô* (The political ideas of contemporary Protestantism) (Tokyo: Shinkyô Shuppansha Publishers, 1988), pp. 394–97.

42. Barth, *Die kirchliche Dogmatik*, I/2, pp. 886–89. Cf. Daniel L. Migliore, *Called to Freedom* (Philadelphia: Westminster Press, 1980), pp. 27–31.

43. For example, Barth, *Die kirchliche Dogmatik*, II/1, pp. 5, 288. Cf. Mitsumasa Ueda, *Karl Barth no Ningenron* (Karl Barth's understanding of human being) (Tokyo: Nihon Kirisuto Kyôdan Shuppankyoku Publishers, 1977), pp. 184–209; Clifford Green, *Karl Barth* (London: Collins Publishers, 1989), pp. 11–12.

Human freedom for Barth lies in the free and loving act of God in Christ, which sets us free once and for all from the bondage of sin, evil, and nothingness to live an authentically human life with God and with our fellow human beings.

Barth's point of departure for the question of ethics can be described as a dialectical recognition of the possibility/impossibility of human ethics, which he has constantly insisted on proclaiming since the publication of his *Der Römerbrief,* first and second editions. As human history is penetrated by the forces of sin and of "nothingness," the question of ethics is an impossible undertaking, simply being a "sickness unto death," a "fatal attack." Theological thinking, after experiencing the demonic calamities of World War I, can no longer affirm unequivocally the naive possibility of human ethic, since the overwhelming reality of "nothingness" or "emptiness" has been experienced as inescapably attached to everything human. Thus, Barth declares that World War I was an event in world history that signaled the end of every sort of ideology and of the triumph of human action, whether legitimism or revolutionism, modernistic ethics or theological ethic.[44] Here, paradoxically, "not-doing" alone can be acknowledged as a possible, legitimate action. For Barth insists that "not-doing" does not mean ethical quietism or negativism; rather, it means the sole possible point of departure as well as the fundamental premise for a legitimate action. "Not-doing," if properly understood and executed, can refer all human activities to the action of God so as to prepare the way for a "true revolution originated from God."

For Barth, the reality of "nothingness," however real its force might be, is never the last word for humanity. Barth argues in a manner reminiscent of Christoph Blumhardt that nothingness is made obsolete and extirpated in Christ, because Jesus is Victor. "Nothingness is the past, the ancient menace, danger and destruction, the ancient non-being which obscured and defaced the divine creation of God but which is consigned to the past in Jesus Christ, in whose death it has received its deserts, being destroyed with this consummation of the positive will of God which is as such the end of His non-willing."[45]

The impossible undertaking thus again becomes a possibility, and the question of ethics can become something that human being can bear, simply

44. Barth, *Der Römerbrief,* 2nd ed., pp. 469–73. Cf. Mitsuo Miyata, *Seiji to Shûkyô Rinri* (Politics and religious ethics) (Tokyo: Iwanami Shoten Publishers, 1975), pp. 158–59.
45. Barth, *Die kirchliche Dogmatik,* III/3, pp. 419–20 (p. 363). Cf. R. Lejeune, *Christoph Blumhardt and His Message,* trans. Hela Ehrlich and Nicoline Maas (Rifton, N.Y.: Plough Publishing House, 1963).

because the forgiveness of sin is *real* only in Christ because of his justification of sinners by the grace of God. The forgiveness of sin is a consequence of the "revolution of God" that has taken place, for Barth, in the events of Christ's *parousia* (advent) — his coming, his death and resurrection, and his return. Therefore, the task of ethics becomes a new possibility to human beings by God's grace and in Christ, who is truly divine and truly human. Barth recounts in a poetic manner that when the ethical question interrogates our whole conduct and casts a dark shadow over what we do in life, a new light is shed at the very point where it is darkest.[46] According to Barth, this new light is nothing but a light of God's grace, a light of forgiveness: "Since there is such a thing as forgiveness (which is always forgiveness of *sin!*), there is such a thing as human conduct which is justified."[47] An ethics is made possible by the forgiveness of sin; it should rightly be called an "ethics of grace." For the grace of God alone enables men and women to bear the question of an ethics that is inherently beyond the reach of their power. They are provided with the task *(Aufgabe)* of responding to God's grace *(Gabe)*, and an ethics is made possible in the very task.

In a more subjective perspective Barth often speaks of the forgiveness of sin in terms of the eschatological experience of "awakening from sleep." Commenting on Romans 13:11-14 in *Der Römerbrief*, he argues that insofar as no recollection of revelation, of the knowledge and freedom of God, is made available, human beings remain asleep, sold under time: "Men are asleep, even the apostle, even the saint, even the lover. . . . They lie like pebbles in the 'stream of time,' and backwards and forwards the ripples hurry over them. They do what they ought not; what they ought they do not."[48] The eternal moment of Now takes place in the flux of time as the high time for us to awake out of sleep. This hour of awakening, the striking of the last hour, is the eschatological moment of the *parousia*, the presence of Jesus Christ. According to Barth, this eschatological life of awakening is primarily expressed as the life of love for people, concrete, particular men and women. Love, as he defines the "great positive possibility," contains within itself what we call an eschatological radicalism. For love is not only the "new doing" that is the meaning and fulfillment of all "non-doing," but it is also "vertically concerned with the denial and breaking up of the

---

46. Karl Barth, *The Word of God and the Word of Man*, trans. Douglas Horton (New York: Harper & Row, 1956), p. 170.

47. Ibid., p. 172. Cf. Charles C. West, *The Power to Be Human* (New York: Macmillan, 1971), pp. 165, 226, 233–34.

48. Barth, *Der Römerbrief*, 2nd ed., p. 483 (p. 499).

existing order."[49] This vertical and eschatological radicalism of love places the reactionary finally in the wrong, while making the assertion of the revolutionary obsolete and banal: "Inasmuch as we love one another we cannot wish to uphold the present order as such, for by love we do the 'new' by which the 'old' is overthrown."[50]

Barth again and again returns to this eschatological theme of awakening out of sleep. In *Die kirchliche Dogmatik,* IV/2 (1955), he argues that the freedom of Christians is being renewed as they keep awakening from sleep in Christ, that is, in their continual reawakening. The sleep from which Christians awaken and continually reawaken is variously expressed, for instance, as "the sleep of death," "the relentless downward movement consequent upon their sloth," or "the sleep of all kinds of errors and phantasies and falsehoods."[51] The initial awakening from sleep and the consequent lifting up of ourselves take place in our repentance of sin and our conversion. In the subsequent, continual reawakening and lifting up, as much as in the initial repentance and conversion, we have to do with "a movement of the whole person," "a renewal in the totality of our being," not with an improvement but with a fundamental transformation.[52]

Yet Barth reminds us that this continual reawakening out of sleep and the consequent freedom of human beings are not ends in themselves, as it has often been represented in a far too egocentric Christianity. Instead this freedom leads one to "cross the threshold of one's private existence and move out into the open" in order to serve as God's witness in his cause and in the welfare of humanity on earth.[53] The perpetual reawakening of human beings from sleep in Christ by the power of the Holy Spirit is nothing other

49. Ibid., p. 477 (p. 493). Barth also maintains the following: "Love is the good work by which the evil is overcome (Rom. 12:21). Love is that denial and demolition of the existing order which no revolt can bring about. In this lies the strange novelty of love. In the cycle of evil unto evil, of reaction unto revolution, it plays no part. . . . Love, because it sets up no idol, is the demolition of every idol. Love is the destruction of everything that is — like God: the end of all hierarchies and authorities and intermediaries. . . . Love does not contradict; and therefore it cannot be refuted. Love does not enter into competition; and therefore it cannot be defeated. . . . No impossibility of my not doing good in the realm of evil — the only realm we know! — can rid me of the duty of love. If, therefore, as a protest against the course of this world, I cease to love, I thereby simply — do not love God, offer no sacrifice, and do not renew my mind (12:2). This is the relentless, impelling, earnestness of the command of love; and therefore love is the fulfilling of the law" (ibid., pp. 480–81 [pp. 496–97]).
50. Ibid., p. 477 (p. 493). Cf. Chiba, *Gendai Protestantism no Seiji Shisô,* p. 407.
51. Barth, *Die kirchliche Dogmatik,* IV/2, p. 628 (p. 555).
52. Ibid., pp. 626–44 (pp. 553–70).
53. Ibid., p. 639 (p. 565).

than the life in sanctification in which they are solidly set in the movement of conversion. There can be no denying that here God reveals himself to be for humanity, and humanity for God.[54]

A number of postmodern Nietzscheans today appear to shrink from advocating positively the human image of a Dionysus-Zarathustra. For example, they neither plead the life of an *Übermensch* — as Nietzsche understood to be a life of the highest being for the self — nor attempt to overcome the decadent by their active nihilism. There can be little doubt that a segment of contemporary postmodern Nietzscheans has begun to assume an aspect of reactionary force. For they positively assess the accelerated mode of modernizing processes and tend to align themselves with the intensification of rationalization observable in many areas of the current postmodern society.[55]

No matter how divergently contemporary Nietzscheans understand and absorb Nietzsche's message, Nietzsche himself insisted on the idea of an *Übermensch* and risked himself on "active nihilism," which purports to destroy all that is old and to create unceasingly what is new. But Barth, over against Nietzsche, attempted to fight gods that are not real God, bore witness to the real God, and articulated the gospel of Christ. He carried on all these works in the midst of the great events of the twentieth century, which was for him the apocalyptic century par excellence, faced with the monstrous force of nothingness in its manifold manifestation. For Barth was a theological thinker who wrestled with the challenges of the century that had witnessed the two great world wars and the appearance of nuclear weapons. Over against Nietzsche's Dionysian *Übermensch*, Barth continued to point to the single person Jesus Christ: "'Heaven and earth' and person in their centre. *Ecce homo!* is true in this respect. Here is the Son of Man. Here is humanity at the heart of the cosmos."[56]

While Barth looked straight at the vast force of nothingness making its abode in the modern world, he pursued a theological reflection that purported to become relevant to the situation of postmodernity in Europe after World War I. Nonetheless, he carried through a theological reflection

---

54. Ibid., p. 644 (p. 570).

55. The following works have critical references to reactionary Nietzschean postmodernists today: William E. Connolly, "Introduction: Legitimacy and Modernity," in *Legitimacy and Modernity*, ed. William E. Connolly (Oxford: Basil Blackwell, 1984), pp. 1–9; Mark Warren, *Nietzsche and Political Thought* (Cambridge, Mass.: MIT Press, 1988), pp. ix–xv, 1–45, 152–89, 207–48; Sheldon S. Wolin, "The Post-Modernity of American Politics and Theory," *Journal of Social Science* 27, no. 1 (October 1988): 7–9.

56. Barth, *Die kirchliche Dogmatik*, III/1, p. 29 (p. 28).

immune from the current postmodern parody or schizophrenia. A transcendent perspective of God's grace and freedom in Christ was opened up in the theological reflection of Karl Barth. A remarkable aspect of his theological reflection was the utter clarity with which the transcendence of God was understood to be revealed in Christ in the midst of, and for the sake of, humanity.

Dietrich Bonhoeffer

It is no exaggeration to say that Dietrich Bonhoeffer (1906-45) stood out as one of the few potent and seminal theologians in the twentieth century. He not only influenced the life of the church but also fired the imagination of men and women in the world after World War II. Like Barth before him, Bonhoeffer witnessed the historical collapse of Western Christendom and its structures, which was primarily brought about by two great world wars. He also laid down some seminal and intriguing, albeit inchoate and elusive, reflections on the future form of a "worldly, universal Christianity." In this connection what is noteworthy is Friedrich Nietzsche's influence on Bonhoeffer's understanding of the modern Western world and historical Christianity's entanglement with its dominant metaphysical conceptions. For the reader of Bonhoeffer cannot fail to recognize an inescapable presence of Nietzschean thought as well as style of language in Bonhoeffer's critique of the hitherto dominant metaphysical worldview of modern rationalism and idealism and in the style of his theological language, tinged with basic characteristics of *Lebensphilosophie.* Probably more seriously than Barth had done, Bonhoeffer took stock of Nietzsche's claim on modernity and Christianity as well as his plea for the earth; Bonhoeffer read substantially all of Nietzsche's works with great enthusiasm and care.[57]

The overall poor reception of Bonhoeffer in the subsequent postwar decade in Germany — especially in then Western Germany — can be accounted for first in light of the guilt associated with his involvement in the assassination conspiracy against Hitler. According to Eberhard Bethge, the German church in general immediately after the war refused to celebrate

57. Cf. Tiemo Rainer Peters, *Die Präsenz des Politischen in der Theologie Dietrich Bonhoeffers* (Munich: Chr. Kaiser Verlag, 1976), pp. 127–51; David H. Hopper, *A Dissent on Bonhoeffer* (Philadelphia: Westminster Press, 1975), pp. 99–131; Eberhard Bethge, "The Challenge of Dietrich Bonhoeffer's Life and Theology," in *World Come of Age,* ed. Ronald Gregor Smith (Philadelphia: Fortress Press, 1967), pp. 27–28; Elizabeth Mensch and Alan Freeman, *The Politics of Virtue* (Durham, N.C.: Duke University Press, 1993), pp. 59–61.

Bonhoeffer among Christian martyrs by acknowledging the basic difference between such "genuine" martyrs as Paul Schneider and Bonhoeffer.[58] This general disregard for Bonhoeffer in the decade immediately following the war in Germany can be explained secondly in light of the seminal nature of his theological reflection, the development of which was halted by his premature death. More important, he was not a systematic thinker but was basically a theologian of deep insight. Thus, his seminal but fragmentary theological reflections gave way to many diverse interpretations, some of which were simply deplorable distortions.[59]

Keeping in mind this interpretative fluidity and the limited space assigned here, it seems necessary to set forth at the outset as concisely as possible the point of my focus as well as the general scheme of my theoretical attempt at understanding Bonhoeffer. First, this study will concentrate on the theme of transcendence in Bonhoeffer's thought during the last years of his life, as seen particularly in the posthumously published books *Ethik* (1949) and *Widerstand und Ergebung: Briefe und Aufzeichnungen aus der Haft* (1951). When Bonhoeffer broke away from the dominant metaphysical tradition of Western thought as a response to the emergence of the postmodern, post-Christendom world, what sort of transcendence did he try to offer? What was Bonhoeffer's ontological foundation of transcendence in the postmodern world? These questions in turn will naturally lead us to reflect on one of Bonhoeffer's basic themes: the conception of "religionless Christianity" in "the world come of age" *(die mündige Welt)*.

58. Eberhard Bethge, "Turning Points in Bonhoeffer's Life and Thought," in *Bonhoeffer in a World Come of Age,* ed. Peter Vorkink II (Philadelphia: Fortress Press, 1968), pp. 73–78.

59. For example, John C. Godsey, "The Legacy of Dietrich Bonhoeffer," in *A Bonhoeffer Legacy,* ed. A. J. Klassen (Grand Rapids: Eerdmans, 1981), p. 161; Peter Vorkink II, "Preface," in *Bonhoeffer in a World Come of Age,* ed. Peter Vorkink II (Philadelphia: Fortress Press, 1968), p. ix; Paul M. van Buren, "Bonhoeffer's Paradox: Living with God without God," in ibid., pp. 2–3; Eberhard Bethge, "Bonhoeffer's Christology and 'Religionless Christianity,' " in ibid., pp. 47–48; Ronald Gregor Smith, "Introduction," in *World Come of Age,* ed. Ronald Gregor Smith (Philadelphia: Fortress Press, 1967), p. 20.

David H. Hopper rightly observes that each interpreter of Bonhoeffer can marshal weighty arguments from Bonhoeffer's own writings to lend credence to his or her particular interpretation. His following remark is worth quoting: "Müller, for example, is able to quote in a surprisingly effective manner a variety of passages from Bonhoeffer's writings to support his semi-Marxist interpretation. Ott does the same for his ontological personalism, Dumas for his Hegelian analysis, Mayer for his 'act-being unity' and so forth" (*A Dissent on Bonhoeffer,* p. 71).

I would count among deplorable distortions of Bonhoeffer's position, for instance, the theses of the death of God, Christian atheism, a sort of morbid pessimism or trauma, and the affirmation of whatever is worldly.

Barth and Bonhoeffer in the Quest for Transcendence without Metaphysical Premises

We have already seen Karl Barth's rejection of modern theological anthropocentrism and subjectivism. Barth's polemic against nineteenth-century theology should above all be understood as a repudiation of modern Cartesian transcendence in philosophy. Seen from the historical perspective, the change from the traditional, otherworldly transcendence of the Middle Ages to the modern Enlightenment transcendence of the Cartesian subjecthood implied an ontological shift in emphasis from the otherworldly and the transtemporal dimension of life to what is this-worldly and historical. Ironically, as Hannah Arendt showed in *The Human Condition*, this modern loss of otherworldly transcendence and of belief in a hereafter did not necessarily entail the attainment of the world. Arendt argued that modern human beings, when they lost the certainty of the other world and a world to come, were thrown back upon themselves and not upon this world; they were not only unable to believe that the world might be potentially immortal, but they even became uncertain that it was real. "Modern man at any rate did not gain this world when he lost the other world, and he did not gain life, strictly speaking, either; he was thrust back upon it, thrown into the closed inwardness of introspection."[60]

Arendt thus understands modern transcendence in terms of "an exclusive concern with the self"; she regards the modern person's introspection as a manifestation of this very preoccupation with the self. The modern subjective person, as she maintained, tends to reduce all experiences with the world as well as with other human beings to experiences between him and himself. This is because the modern person is no longer sure about the reality of the world.[61] We see a striking resemblance here between Barth's

---

60. Hannah Arendt, *The Human Condition* (Chicago: University of Chicago Press, 1958), p. 320. Cf. Shin Chiba, "Arendt to Kindai Sekai" (Arendt and the modern world), *Journal of Social Science* (International Christian University) 24, no. 1 (October 1985): 59.

61. Arendt, *The Human Condition*, pp. 254, 320. No doubt it was Descartes who provided modern transcendence with a normative philosophical expression. In the Cartesian project of *de omnibus dubitandum* the transcendent self of the cogito set itself to the task of examining all things in the universe. This modern transcendence of the cogito based on the human faculty of knowing and doubting apparently became an ontological springboard for the extraordinary advancement of modern science and technology. Arendt, however, regarded this modern Cartesian transcendence as amounting to nothing more than an introspective subjectivism; it was "the sheer cognitive concern of consciousness with its own content" (ibid., p. 280).

From this perspective she proffered an observation with regard to the destiny of this modern transcendence, a view of "modern man" that could be construed as an anticipation of

fierce polemic against the subjectivist language and thought form of the modern rationalistic theology of the self and Arendt's philosophical delineation of the problematics of modern Cartesian transcendence of the cogito.

It is easy to detect a partial influence of Nietzsche — and perhaps of Heidegger as well — in Arendt's understanding of the historical changes in perspective on transcendence. This impressive statement by Nietzsche in the *Götzen Dämmerung* seems to be of great importance to her: "We have abolished the true world. What has remained? The apparent one perhaps? Oh no! With the true world we have also abolished the apparent one."[62] Not only did Arendt cite Nietzsche's profound, albeit pessimistic, assumption that the sensory cannot survive the death of the suprasensory. She also endorsed the Nietzschean — and Heideggerian — verdict that both the metaphysical theory of two worlds, the sensory and the suprasensory, held in esteem since Parmenides and Plato, and the metaphysical theory of the ontological primacy of the suprasensory over the sensory had come to an end.[63]

In this connection it is striking to discover again the fundamental congruity, with regard to the modern demise of traditional ideas of God and metaphysics, of Arendt's assumptions (also those of Nietzsche and Heidegger) and those of Barth and Bonhoeffer. Barth and Bonhoeffer, however, conceiving that the deaths of "God" and of "metaphysics" are not simply a cultural and philosophical problem but a theological problem of the first order, emphatically launched into the theological task of seeking for a true and genuine form of transcendence in the post-Christendom context of twentieth-century Europe. The scientific and technological civilization of the modern age — that is, the positivism of modernity — seems to have left little room for human beings' experience of transcendence, that is, "a divine reality beyond natural, social, and cultural realities."[64] "Transcendence" here desig-

---

later postmodern argument: "The highest he could experience were the empty processes of reckoning of the mind, its play with itself. The only contents left were appetites and desires, the senseless urges of his body which he mistook for passion and which he deemed to be 'unreasonable' because he found he could not 'reason,' that is, not reckon with them" (ibid., pp. 320–21).

62. Friedrich Nietzsche, "Götzen Dämmerung," in *Nietzsche Werke*, vol. 6, pt. 3, ed. Giorgio Colli and Mazzino Montinari (Berlin: Walter de Gruyter, 1969), p. 75. This sentence is quoted in Arendt's posthumously published book *The Life of the Mind* (vol. 1 [London: Secker & Warburg, 1978], p. 11). Arendt also quotes Heidegger's reformulation of Nietzsche's statement in "Nietzsche's Wort 'Gott ist tot'": "The elimination of the suprasensory also eliminates the merely sensory and thereby the difference between them" (ibid.).

63. Arendt, *The Life of the Mind*, vol. 1, pp. 10–11.

64. Rainer Mayer, "Christology: The Genuine Form of Transcendence," in *A Bonhoeffer Legacy*, ed. A. J. Klassen (Grand Rapids: Eerdmans, 1981), p. 179.

nates a reality and presence of something beyond the human sensory universe as well as beyond the human experience of realities as immanence. As Rainer Mayer indicated, the concentration on the immanent coupled with the exclusion of the beyond has molded the habitual mind-set of the modern person.[65] How can one speak viably of transcendence in the context of scientific positivism and the loss of transcendence? The history of twentieth-century Christian theology seems to be in an important sense a history of theologians' various attempts to respond to this question.

We have already seen Barth's strenuous attempt to underscore the transcendence of God's freedom and sovereignty in terms of the event of the self-revelation of God in Christ. The characteristic feature of Barth's notion of transcendence is not only its Christocentric focus but also its dynamic and revolutionary nature, coupled with its consistent emphasis on the unique nature of divine transcendence. Thus, it is important to note that Barth totally rejected every attempt of human beings, in the name either of religion or of metaphysics, to fabricate, utilize, manipulate, or control divine transcendence for human purposes. For Barth, divine transcendence can be received by and mediated for human beings only in accordance with God's initiative and God's will.

Bonhoeffer shared with Barth the serious attempt to underscore the Christocentric and event-full, dynamic and unique character of divine transcendence. It is now almost axiomatic to acknowledge Bonhoeffer's substantial indebtedness to Barth's self-conscious and consistent effort to repudiate unqualifiedly traditional metaphysical, and hence religious, conceptions of God, whether they be Aristotelian concepts of "supreme being" and of "unmoved mover," or Enlightenment concepts of a "Deus ex machina," or a "God" of stopgaps, or a "God" of pure inwardness.[66] Bonhoeffer used the terms "metaphysical" and "religious" interchangeably, because both terms implied for him humankind's attempt to reach God without revelation, rather than God's reaching them, by turning God into an abstract idea or a carnal object of their egoistic religious eros.

---

65. Ibid.

66. For example, Dietrich Bonhoeffer, *Widerstand und Ergebung: Briefe und Aufzeichnungen aus der Haft*, ed. Eberhard Bethge (Munich: Chr. Kaiser Verlag, 1970), pp. 304–14, 373–94. (ET: *Letters and Papers from Prison*, 3rd ed., trans. Reginald Fuller et al. [London: SCM Press, 1971].) Cf. West, *Communism and the Theologians*, pp. 338–45. *Widerstand und Ergebung* and also *Ethik* (see n. 73 below) do not correspond exactly to English translations and contain many paragraphs that English translations do not have. Page references for the English translations have been supplied parenthetically wherever possible.

Bonhoeffer, however, wished to go further than Barth in his wrestling with the problem of the demise of the traditional metaphysical idea of God. For his well-known quest for a "religionless Christianity" or a "nonreligious interpretation of the gospel" involved his theological attempt to forge a genuine form of thoroughgoing *historical* transcendence. From his viewpoint Barth did not go far enough to formulate a solidly historical transcendence. Thus, during the period of his imprisonment (from spring 1943 to April 9, 1945), during the very last years of his life, Bonhoeffer began to speak critically of Barth's theology of revelation. This can be seen in his critical reference to Barth's "positivism of revelation" *(Offenbarungspositivismus)* in *Widerstand und Ergebung.*[67]

What did Bonhoeffer mean when he said that Barth's theology was subject to a "positivism of revelation"? This designation pointed to the tendency of the early Barth's theology to remain self-contained within the domain of the truths of revelation without any reference to the outside world. The truths of revelation then became self-authenticating and credal, without external test and evaluation, losing critical touch with the experiences of the things in the world.[68] For Bonhoeffer, Barth's positivistic doctrine of revelation was not only incongruous with the biblical position but also "too easy."[69] Furthermore, for him it simply succumbed to a notion of revelational transcendence devoid of genuine historicity and worldliness. Bonhoeffer's critique of the early Barth's theology of revelation prefigured in a significant way Jürgen Moltmann's later substantial criticism of it in terms of the proclamation of the *Deus dixit,* which was grounded only in itself as proving itself and thus was essentially defenseless, unprovable, and

67. Bonhoeffer, *Widerstand und Ergebung,* pp. 306, 312–13. Bonhoeffer argues as follows: "Barth was the first theologian to begin the criticism of religion, and that remains his really great merit; but he put in its place a positivist doctrine of revelation which says, in effect, 'Like it or lump it': virgin birth, Trinity, or anything else; each is an equally significant and necessary part of the whole, which must simply be swallowed as a whole or not at all. That isn't biblical. There are degrees of knowledge and degrees of significance; that means that a secret discipline must be restored whereby the mysteries of the Christian faith are protected from profanation. The positivism of revelation makes it too easy for itself, by setting up, as it does in the final analysis, a law of faith, and so mutilates what is — by Christ's incarnation! — a gift for us. In the place of religion there now stands the Church — that is in itself biblical — but the world is in some degree made to depend on itself and left to its own devices, and that's the mistake" (ibid., pp. 312–13 [p. 286]).

68. Similarly Eberhard Bethge expresses the charge of "positivism of revelation" in terms of "the absence of reference" of the truths of revelation to the world come of age ("The Challenge of Dietrich Bonhoeffer's Life and Theology," p. 85).

69. Bonhoeffer, *Widerstand und Ergebung,* p. 312.

nongroundable.[70] As one may rightly predict, Barth did not appreciate Bonhoeffer's charge of "positivism of revelation," though he was embarrassed by it.[71] But it is worth noting that the mature Barth himself sought for a more historical notion of revelation and eschatology by attempting to combine more solidly the history of covenant with the history of the world in *Die kirchlichen Dogmatik*, IV/1-4.[72] Thus, Bonhoeffer attempted to formulate an appropriate notion of Christocentric, historical transcendence by trying to evade the pitfalls of either traditional metaphysical otherworldliness or the early Barth's revelational transcendentalism.

The following key passage from Bonhoeffer's *Ethik* points toward the world's ontological change, as Bonhoeffer sees it, brought about by the event of the incarnation, crucifixion, and resurrection of Christ; this ontological shift of the world in turn has become the foundational basis for his notion of Christocentric historical transcendence: "In Jesus Christ the reality of God entered into the reality of this world."[73] Here we encounter Bonhoeffer's insight of great significance that because of the events of the incarnation, crucifixion and resurrection of Christ, there are no longer two separate realities — that is, the reality of God and the reality of the world, the holy and the profane — but only one reality. That is the reality of God manifest in Christ in the midst of the world. "Sharing in Christ we stand at once in both the reality of God and the reality of the world."[74] This is not a confusion or mixing up of the two realities but the unity of both in distinction. What is upheld in Christ is the dialectical unity between the reality of God and the reality of the world, between the holy and the profane, and between the sacred and the secular. One can justifiably observe here the Christocentric character of Bonhoeffer's theology. For it is presupposed that just as Christianity without Christ is nothing more than a groundless abstraction, so without the events of Christ's incarnation, crucifixion, and resurrection, there can be no substantial understanding made possible of

---

70. Jürgen Moltmann, *Theologie der Hoffnung* (Munich: Chr. Kaiser Verlag, 1964), pp. 43–47. Cf. Shin Chiba, "Transcendence and the Political: A Critical Comparison of Reinhold Niebuhr and Jürgen Moltmann" (Ph.D. diss., Princeton Theological Seminary, 1983), pp. 180–85.

71. Karl Barth, "From a Letter of Karl Barth to Landessuperintendent P. W. Herzenbrück, 21 December 1952," in *World Come of Age*, ed. Ronald Gregor Smith (Philadelphia: Fortress Press, 1967), pp. 89–92.

72. Cf. Chiba, "Transcendence and the Political," pp. 193–210.

73. Dietrich Bonhoeffer, *Ethik*, ed. Eberhard Bethge (Munich: Chr. Kaiser Verlag, 1985), p. 207 (*Ethics*, trans. Neville Horton Smith [London: SCM Press, 1971], p. 167).

74. Ibid., p. 240 (p. 197).

God and the world.[75] Furthermore, one can rightly argue that we have the ontological ground not only for the worldly and historical existence of God but also for the divine significance of the world.[76]

An important contribution of Bonhoeffer's theology is that his notion of historical transcendence based on the gospel of Christ engendered a perspective on ethical transcendence, that is, a transcendence of Christian existence as shown in the concrete relationships that Jesus' followers have with their neighbors in daily life. For the gospel of Christ, which is not of the world, exists for the service of the world.[77] Bonhoeffer insists that the genuine and ethical transcendence of Christianity is made manifest in "a new life in 'existence for others,' through participation in the being of Jesus . . . the man for others."[78] In other words, genuine and ethical transcendence is disclosed in Jesus' "being for others" and hence reenacted every time a follower of Jesus lives and exists in Jesus' way of being for others. Stating it in a somewhat different light, Bonhoeffer says that the transcendent is represented in the tangible neighbor who is given to us each time, who is within reach in any given situation.[79] For in Christ is disclosed the transcendence of "God in human form," that is, "being for others"; "in Jesus Christ we see the God who took the form of the poorest brethren."[80] According to Bethge, this "being for others" has become a new Christological title for Bonhoeffer that directs the follower of Jesus into concrete action, obedience, and service for others by prohibiting any flight from the world.[81]

75. For example, Wolf Krötke, "Der begegnende Gott und der Glaube," in *Bonhoeffer Studien,* ed. Albrecht Schönherr and Wolf Krötke (Berlin: Evangelische Verlagsanstalt, 1985), pp. 25–28; James Burtness, *Shaping the Future: The Ethics of Dietrich Bonhoeffer* (Philadelphia: Fortress Press, 1985), pp. 30–43; Ray Sherman Anderson, *Historical Transcendence and the Reality of God* (Grand Rapids: Eerdmans, 1975), pp. 72–100; John D. Godsey, *The Theology of Dietrich Bonhoeffer* (London: SCM Press, 1960), pp. 264–80.

76. Bonhoeffer, *Ethik,* pp. 207–11. Cf. Ernst Feil, *The Theology of Dietrich Bonhoeffer,* trans. Martin Rumscheidt (Philadelphia: Fortress Press, 1985), pp. 36, 60–83, 87–88, 139; Larry L. Rasmussen, *Dietrich Bonhoeffer: Reality and Resistance* (Nashville: Abingdon Press, 1972), pp. 16–17.

77. Bonhoeffer, *Widerstand und Ergebung,* p. 312.

78. Ibid., p. 414 (pp. 381–82). Cf. Godsey, "The Legacy of Dietrich Bonhoeffer," p. 169; Rainer Mayer, "Christology: The Genuine Form of Transcendence," in *A Bonhoeffer Legacy,* ed. A. J. Klassen (Grand Rapids: Eerdmans, 1981), pp. 188–89; Thomas I. Day, "Conviviality and Common Sense: The Meaning of Christian Community for Bonhoeffer," in ibid., pp. 221, 224.

79. Bonhoeffer, *Widerstand and Ergebung,* p. 414.

80. Bonhoeffer, *Ethik,* p. 235.

81. Eberhard Bethge, "Bonhoeffer's Christology," pp. 69–71. Cf. Larry Rasmussen, *Dietrich Bonhoeffer: His Significance for North Americans* (Minneapolis: Fortress Press, 1990), p. 26.

Here it is appropriate to ask two questions — one terminological, the other substantial — with regard to Barth's notion of revelational transcendence of God's freedom and Bonhoeffer's notion of historical and ethical transcendence. First, are not their respective notions of transcendence still in fact another form of metaphysics? Second, are not these notions of transcendence in fact impossible to maintain in the current situation of postmodernity? The answer to the first question depends on how one defines metaphysics. Paul M. van Buren confronted the first question in his stimulating article "Bonhoeffer's Paradox: Living with God without God." I concur with his suggestion that Bonhoeffer's notion of historical transcendence — together with Barth's notion of revelational transcendence — is a sort of metaphysics as every Christian theology is, if metaphysics is broadly defined as "an attempt to describe the structure of our understanding of how things are generally, that is, how the whole is, how everything taken together is."[82] According to this definition, every Christian theological affirmation, including Barth's and Bonhoeffer's, cannot escape being a sort of metaphysics in which "God is the single first principle, having linguistic and ontological priority."[83]

However, one must keep in mind that Barth and Bonhoeffer did not define the term "metaphysics" as broadly as the above definition suggests. Instead, they meant by this term a more specific form of static and rationalistic metaphysics that had dominated Western philosophical and theological thinking since Aristotle. They tried to do away with this static, rationalistic, and settled metaphysics of being and instead posited dynamic and event-full notions of theological ontology. In this endeavor their approach can be rightly compared to a parallel phenomenon in the field of modern philosophy where Martin Heidegger, Ernst Bloch, and others decidedly broke with the Western tradition of metaphysics that had embodied the tacit assumption of the world as something abstractly given and settled from the start in its foundational structure.

More important, Barth's and Bonhoeffer's revelational approach refused the basic epistemological method of metaphysics, that is, the method of representation of what is *(essentia)*. They were attempting not to represent but rather to receive the unfolding and the taking place of revelatory truths of Christ as proclaimed in the Scriptures. In other words, they repudiated the metaphysical way of doing theology, which, as it were, tries to extend its epistemological hands to get hold of God and to put him in

82. Van Buren, "Bonhoeffer's Paradox," p. 9.
83. Ibid., p. 13.

196

its pocket of neat formulas. These two considerations seem to be sufficient to support the suggestion that "transcendence" rather than "metaphysics" is an appropriate term to capture the gist of these two theologians' approaches.

As to the second question, I would argue that one would certainly endorse, from Barth's and Bonhoeffer's theological perspective, postmodernism's repudiation of both the traditional account of transcendence and the Enlightenment's grand narrative of rational and anthropocentric subjectivism. For they too perceived the postmodern predicament of meaninglessness of life and the aporia of anthropocentrism. They were aware of, and deeply sympathetic with, the postmodern human condition menaced by aimlessness and foundationlessness, but they would refuse postmodernism's apparent surrender to the modern worldview of positivism. Instead, they would demand a total and radical change from the modern preoccupation with the self to the life of Christocentric focus, which is beyond in the midst of our life. Therefore, one may justifiably maintain that in its rejection of whatever is transcendent or of normative value,[84] postmodernism has succumbed to the same thoroughgoing positivism of late modernity, whether philosophical or scientific. What cannot be endorsed is this anthropocentric, epistemological, and technological positivism of late modernity. For it has become the main cause of the postmodern predicament of meaninglessness by driving out everything that is beyond the comprehension of modern rationality.

Toward a Theology of Amor Mundi

As is often indicated, "Who is Christ in our world come of age?" was Bonhoeffer's theme in the last phase of his life. There is no settled account among interpreters concerning what was meant by "the world come of age" or "the world of adulthood" *(die mündige Welt)*. At least it is certain that Bonhoeffer's insight into the late modern age as "the world come of age" stemmed from Kant's understanding of the Enlightenment. As is well-known, Kant understood the Enlightenment as the exodus of human beings from their immature state of dependency on the guidance of others, so as

84. For example, McGowan, *Postmodernism and Its Critics*, p. 32. Cf. Adam B. Seligman, "Towards a Reinterpretation of Modernity in an Age of Postmodernity," in *Theories of Modernity and Postmodernity*, ed. Bryan S. Turner (London: Sage Publications, 1990), pp. 123-27.

to use their own reason and to become responsible. In accord with Kant's understanding of the Enlightenment, Bonhoeffer seems to have attempted to express by the usage of the phrase "the world come of age" the irreversible process of modern society becoming autonomous.[85] "The world come of age," then, means an autonomous human society, independent of metaphysical and religious hypotheses of the divine, as they had been functioning as the ontological foundation of traditional society. Bonhoeffer thus formulated the task of his "religionless Christianity" in "the world come of age" in the following paradoxical statement: "The God who lets us live in the world without the working hypothesis of God is the God before whom we stand continually. Before God and with God we live without God."[86]

According to Bonhoeffer, "God in the Bible" is not the God of *homo religiosus* or the God of philosophers but the God of Abraham, of Isaac, and of Jacob, the real and concrete God who discloses himself in Christ and who meets each man and woman in a particular time and space. Because of the revelatory events of Christ's incarnation, crucifixion, and resurrection, God is God, here and now, in our midst as "the most concrete existence." As Bonhoeffer put it, "God is the 'beyond' in the midst of our life."[87]

It would be obvious, then, that an increasing weight of significance is given to history and to the world in Bonhoeffer's thought. The concept of the world *(mundus)* is for Bonhoeffer not primarily a *kosmos,* which suggests the world of space, but rather a *saeculum,* which signifies the world of time. It is a concept that refers to the historical world, which has experienced an ontological change by the event of Christ, a world with new meaning and new potential. Because of the events of Christ's incarnation, crucifixion, and resurrection, the world, when seen in Christ, now stands before us with a new appearance and a new significance. Bonhoeffer no

85. Cf. André Dumas, *Dietrich Bonhoeffer: Theologian of Reality,* trans. Robert McAfee Brown (London: SCM Press, 1971), pp. 184–86.

86. Bonhoeffer, *Widerstand und Ergebung,* p. 394 (p. 360). It seems that one does not have to conceive Bonhoeffer's proposal for "religionless Christianity" or "nonreligious interpretation of the Gospel" as an accommodation with modernism. For by these expressions Bonhoeffer nowhere suggests an unqualified acceptance of secularization. Rather, they signify a thoroughgoing, Christological reinterpretation of the gospel. His approach is to be understood as an attempt to recover Jesus' affirmation of the genuine secularity as well as the humanness of the gospel, as seen in Jesus' polemic against various manifestations of Judaism's religious and inhuman legalism in his time.

87. Ibid., p. 308 (p. 282).

longer tries to understand the world as a self-sufficient and self-contained system. The world is consistently understood Christologically. Which is to say, the world is the *mundus* that "is loved, condemned, and reconciled in Christ."[88] The world is also in human terms *"the sphere of concrete responsibility* which is given to us in and through Jesus Christ."[89]

The follower of Christ also participates through faith in Christ's dialectical relation to the world and is encouraged to love the world with a great sense of responsibility and judgment and without any illusion. Because the world is ultimately reconciled to God in Christ through his death and resurrection, the kingdom of God, no matter how hidden it may be, is already beginning to be formed in the world. Thus, while being liberated from the fanatical temptation of trying to transform the world into God's kingdom by human power, the follower of Christ is encouraged to be hopeful, to love the world, and to participate together actively in the things of the world. There is no room for an otherworldly resignation, that is, a simple subjugation to the dominant forces of the world. This *amor mundi* (love of the world) is nothing else than an expression of what Bonhoeffer calls a "profound this-worldliness," an instance of which he finds in Luther's spirituality: "I have come to know and understand more and more the profound this-worldliness of Christianity. . . . I do not mean the shallow and banal this-worldliness of the enlightened, the busy, the comfortable, or the lascivious, but the profound this-worldliness, characterized by discipline and the constant knowledge of death and resurrection. I think Luther lived a this-worldly life in this sense."[90]

Bonhoeffer also speaks of *amor mundi* and *amor terrae* (love of the earth) by referring to the lordship of Christ over the world and the earth. What belongs to the lordship of Christ is not solely what is called a religious sphere or a sacred realm of the world but the entire world. Consonant with the lordship of Christ over the world in its wholeness the follower of Christ is given "a commission by the otherworldly to work in this world."[91] Bonhoeffer also maintains that "whoever loves the earth loves it as God's earth"

---

88. Bonhoeffer, *Ethik,* p. 247 (p. 232).

89. Ibid. (p. 233).

90. Bonhoeffer, *Widerstand und Ergebung,* p. 401 (p. 369). Jean Bethke Elshtain, for instance, correctly emphasizes Luther's affirmation of family life, women, the naturalness of human sexuality, together with labor and work, as remarkably enlightened for his time (*Public Man, Private Woman: Women in Social and Political Thought* [Princeton: Princeton University Press, 1981], pp. 84–90).

91. Dietrich Bonhoeffer, *Gesammelte Schriften,* ed. Eberhard Bethge (Munich: Chr. Kaiser Verlag, 1958–60), 3:31.

and that "whoever loves God's kingdom, loves it wholly as *God's* kingdom, but loves it also as God's *kingdom on earth.*"[92] The task of Christ's follower then consists in loving and serving both the world and the earth in a way most fitting to Christ, who is the Lord of the world and the earth.

It would be a misunderstanding to conceive of the *amor mundi* theology of Bonhoeffer's last years as an expression of unrestrained secularism. It should not be regarded as a direct and absolute affirmation of the creaturely world as such, as seems to be the case for Hannah Arendt, a stimulating political theorist of *amor mundi*. The world that Bonhoeffer wished to affirm was not the world of the first creation but rather the world of new creation, that is, the world of the second creation, made actual by Christ's cross and resurrection.[93] The relationship between the cross of Christ and the world is dialectical in the sense of their maintaining a "polemical attitude towards each other," to use Bonhoeffer's own words.[94] On the one hand, the cross of Christ judges the sins of the world and disqualifies the world's claim of its inherent goodness and absolute worthiness. The cross always stands as a reminder of the tenacity of evil, which still grips the world. In contrast, the crucified Christ, who bore upon himself the sins of the world, enables the world to be reconciled to God and thus endows the world with a new divine reality. Because of the cross the world is now ontologically changed, so that a new opening is made into the self-contained world, and a new possibility of overcoming its own evil is imparted. Thus, it is correct to assert that the cross does not alienate people from the world but instead propels them into the very midst of the world; the cross thus works as "the imperative for service to the world."[95]

Bonhoeffer's theology of *amor mundi*, perhaps more strongly than any other Christian theologies in the past could, activates people into service for the world with the dedicated sense of calling and responsibility. In this connection it is important to note that Bonhoeffer draws from the Scriptures five particular divine mandates that serve as the concrete, strategic, and concentrated loci for the fulfilling of human beings' daily responsibility of *amor mundi;* these are church, marriage (family), labor, culture, and political authority.[96] Following a suggestive remark on this score by Paul

92. Cf. Feil, *The Theology of Dietrich Bonhoeffer*, p. 118.
93. Bonhoeffer, *Gesammelte Schriften*, 1:137; Dietrich Bonhoeffer, *No Rusty Swords: Letters, Lectures, and Notes, 1928–1936, from the Collected Works*, ed. Edwin H. Robertson; trans. Edwin H. Robertson and John Bowden (New York: Harper & Row, 1965), p. 189.
94. Bonhoeffer, *Ethik*, p. 207.
95. Feil, *The Theology of Dietrich Bonhoeffer*, p. 116.
96. Bonhoeffer, *Ethik*, pp. 220, 303–9. There is a discrepancy in Bonhoeffer's descrip-

Lehmann,[97] it can be argued that a more active sense of freedom and responsibility is presupposed with the human agent in the shift from the traditional notion of God's commandment to that of mandate observable here. For as Bonhoeffer maintains, the notion of mandate implies the divine authorization for the human agent to carry out a specific historical task: "the conferment of divine authority on an earthly agent."[98] He seems to suggest here that human beings are deputies of God who, squarely placed in these specific structures of life particularly appropriate in a world come of age, are commissioned to carry out the historical task of love and service for the world.[99] Boldly stated, human beings in a world come of age are bestowed, in these particular loci of the earthly station, with a far greater freedom and responsibility as God's deputies. This can be understood as a particular human condition of freedom, responsibility, and risk, which men and women in a world of adulthood are supposed to assume. The term "responsibility" here should not be defined narrowly as a dutiful fulfillment of role or function. Rather, it must be defined broadly as something synonymous with "calling" *(Beruf)*, that is, a total response with one's whole being to the love of God for the world as well as to the entire reality of the world.[100]

Bonhoeffer maintains that the new form of Christian existence requires the ecclesiastical framework and institutional practices of the church to be substantially changed. "The church is the church only when it exists for others. . . . It must tell men of every calling what it means to live in Christ, to exist for others."[101] His suggestion for change in the church includes, among other things, a giving away of all the church's property to those in need, the clergy's living to be solely dependent on the free-will offerings of their congregations, the church's sharing in the common, mundane problems of

---

tion of divine mandates between the earlier section "Christ, Reality, and Good" and the later section "The 'Ethical' and the 'Christian' as a Theme." In the former Bonhoeffer talks about labor, marriage, political authority, and church as "divine mandates." In the latter he speaks of church, marriage and family, culture, and political authority. Here "labor" is dropped, while "culture" is added.

97. Paul L. Lehmann, "Faith and Worldliness in Bonhoeffer's Thought," in *Bonhoeffer in a World Come of Age*, ed. Peter Vorkink II (Philadelphia: Fortress Press, 1968), pp. 38–40.

98. Bonhoeffer, *Ethik*, p. 274.

99. Cf. Lehmann, "Faith and Worldliness in Bonhoeffer's Thought," p. 39.

100. Bonhoeffer, *Ethik*, p. 274. Cf. West, *The Power to Be Human*, pp. 261–65.

101. Bonhoeffer, *Widerstand und Ergebung*, pp. 415–16 (pp. 382–83). Concerning Bonhoeffer's critique of the churches, see Geffrey B. Kelly, "Radical Faith and Social Liberation of the 'Little People' in the Americas," *Princeton Seminary Bulletin*, n.s., 12, no. 2 (1991): 216–19.

society in the spirit of service.[102] To be the church of Christ and to be the follower of Christ, for Bonhoeffer, require being in communion with the Crucified, hence to participate in the sufferings of God in the life of the world.[103] To participate in God's sufferings in the godless world must mean our sharing with the suffering God the sins and injustices, the pains and miseries of this world, which he bears upon himself. In the very process of participating in God's sufferings in the world, the church and the believer learn to be "conformed with the unique figure of Christ," who was made man, was crucified, and rose again.[104] Here one may safely say that Luther's *theologia crucis* is acted out and incorporated into Bonhoeffer's theology of *amor mundi* in its specifically worldly and political context.[105]

Finally, I wish to take up a question as to what kind of experience led Bonhoeffer to formulate a new theology of *amor mundi*. Though one may justifiably point to other particular experiences that he had, I would like to draw particular attention to his growing disappointment with the Confessing Church and his growing appreciation of his political comrades of the conspiracy during the last years of his life. Bonhoeffer felt that the Confessing Church failed to develop its theological resistance into any sort of political resistance to Nazism. To be sure, one may say that the Confessing Church fulfilled theological responsibility as a church by courageously raising a voice of opposition to Nazism. But this carrying out of theological responsibility remained unworldly in nature, hence not sufficiently open toward the world. Especially after 1940, Bonhoeffer became increasingly dissatisfied with the Confessing Church's capacity to struggle against Nazism: "The Confessing Church has now largely forgotten all about the Barthian approach, and has lapsed from positivism into conservative restoration."[106]

In contrast, Bonhoeffer began to appreciate more and more "civil courage" that took up responsibility and guilt, manifest among a circle of political comrades who joined the assassination conspiracy against Hitler; these conspirators came from ideologically, socially, and culturally diverse backgrounds.[107] The experience of working with these political associates led Bonhoeffer to appreciate their (mostly non-Christian) fine character,

102. Bonhoeffer, *Widerstand und Ergebung*, p. 415.
103. Ibid., p. 395.
104. Bonhoeffer, *Ethik*, p. 28.
105. Cf. Peters, *Die Präsenz des Politischen in der Theologie Dietrich Bonhoeffers*, pp. 113–18.
106. Bonhoeffer, *Widerstand und Ergebung*, p. 359 (p. 328).
107. Cf. Eberhard Bethge, *Dietrich Bonhoeffer: Theologe, Christ, Zeitgenosse* (Munich: Chr. Kaiser Verlag, 1969), pp. 961–62.

sense of responsibility, and spirit of *amor mundi*. He has written: "Civil courage, in fact, can grow only out of the free responsibility of free men. Only now are the Germans beginning to discover the meaning of free responsibility. It depends on a God who demands responsible action in a bold venture of faith, and who promises forgiveness and consolation to the man who becomes a sinner in that venture."[108]

Epilogue

In this study we have considered Barth's and Bonhoeffer's notions of revelational and Christocentric transcendence. We have approached this theme by examining their respective notions of transcendence formulated on the eve of a postmodern, post-Christendom Europe in the early and mid twentieth century. Their theological endeavors were particularly of great significance for our purpose because their conceptions of transcendence were not only dynamic and pertinent to the aspirations of the age but also purported to underscore the unique character of God's transcendence.[109] In other words, both the identity and the relevance of divine transcendence were upheld in a persuasive manner by them. Their endeavors embodied not only a purely theoretical quest for divine transcendence but a life's existential search for it in the face of various historical threats of this century. Their theological endeavors thus remain a source of inspiration for us.

Bonhoeffer's quest for "a non-religious interpretation of the gospel" or a "religionless Christianity," which is also a theology of *amor mundi*, seems to be pertinent even to many non-Western societies and cultures where traditional religions are required to reformulate their messages under the modernizing impact of Cartesian transcendentalism. What is especially intriguing for Asian Christians is Bonhoeffer's lifelong interest in Mohandas Gandhi and in the religions of the Orient in his search for a "worldly, universal Christianity."[110]

---

108. Bonhoeffer, *Widerstand und Ergebung*, p. 15 (p. 6).

109. Bultmann correctly notes that twentieth-century theologians such as Tillich, Ebeling, Vahanian, R. G. Smith, and J. A. T. Robinson are agreed on the idea that the transcendent is to be sought in the midst of this world and history. He fails to indicate, however, that in most cases their efforts tend to sacrifice the sui generis character of God's transcendence for the affirmation of historical transcendence. Barth and Bonhoeffer are exceptional on this score. See Rudolf Bultmann, "The Idea of God and Modern Man," in *World Come of Age*, ed. Ronald Gregor Smith (Philadelphia: Fortress Press, 1967), p. 265.

110. Cf. Feil, *The Theology of Dietrich Bonhoeffer*, pp. 197-98; Ernst Feil, "Dietrich

René Girard, a contemporary French theorist, proposes from the perspective of social anthropology a "nonsacrificial reading of the gospel text," a proposal reminiscent of Bonhoeffer's "nonreligious interpretation of the gospel." According to Girard's diagnosis of the present age, what is left for us today is the validity of the gospel texts alone in the face of the apocalyptic situation of nuclear threat.[111] This can be seen as a strange consensus reached in the deciphering of our age and its agony between a contemporary theorist and a martyr-theologian of the twentieth century.

Bonhoeffer's Understanding of the World," in *A Bonhoeffer Legacy,* ed. A. J. Klassen (Grand Rapids: Eerdmans, 1981), p. 252.

It is especially surprising and even eye-opening to note the basic congruity of Bonhoeffer's message with the historical task of *Mukyôkai* (noninstitutional church) Christianity in Japan, founded by Kanzô Uchimura. Like Barth in the West, who was faced with the outbreak of World War I, Uchimura became acutely aware of the collapse of Western Christendom and began to explore a genuine, original Christianity without ecclesiastical institutions or rituals. A consistent quest for an evangelical and prophetic Christianity where prayer and the practice of social justice are intimately combined with one another, as in the case of Bonhoeffer, has been historically carried out in this Mukyôkai lineage. The expression "the gospel in the midst of the secular" (Masao Sekine) well captures the ethos of Mukyôkai. This expression suggests the idea that to believe in Jesus is to live as Jesus lived, that our daily life lived through communion with Jesus is itself the sacrament, and that the concrete place of the secular is the place where faith is tested, a witness to Jesus is carried on, and the worship of God is held. Cf. Masao Sekine, *Sezoku nonakano Fukuin* (The gospel in the midst of the secular) (Tokyo: Kirisutokyô Yakankôza Shuppankyoku Publishers, 1967).

111. For example, René Girard, *Things Hidden since the Foundation of the World,* trans. Stephen Bann and Michael Metteer (London: Athlone Press, 1987), pp. 180–262; René Girard, *Violence and the Sacred,* trans. Patrick Gregory (Baltimore: John Hopkins University Press, 1972), pp. 1–67, 250–73, 309–18; René Girard, *The Scapegoat,* trans. Yvonne Freccaro (Baltimore: Johns Hopkins University Press, 1986), pp. 101–11, 160–212. Cf. Hitoshi Imamura, *Tetsugaku no Postmodern* (Philosophical postmodernism) (Tokyo: Unite Publishers, 1985), pp. 120–40; Paul Dumouchel, "Introduction," in *Violence and Truth: On the Work of René Girard,* ed. Paul Dumouchel (Stanford, Calif.: Stanford University Press, 1988), pp. 17–20.

In the volume edited by Dumouchel, Lucien Scubla critically examines Girard's "nonsacrificial" understanding of Christianity ("The Christianity of René Girard and the Nature of Religion," pp. 160–78). Cf. William E. Connolly, *Identity/Difference: Democratic Negotiations of Political Paradox* (Ithaca, N.Y.: Cornell University Press, 1991), p. 231 n. 3. Scubla, however, fails to recognize the innovative and original aspect of Girard's revelational critique of the traditional-religious interpretation of the New Testament. One can justifiably see in it a parallelism with Barth's and Bonhoeffer's critique of religion.

· 11 ·

Environmentalists Read the Bible:
The Co-creation of a Community,
a Story, and a Virtue Ethic

LOUKE VAN WENSVEEN SIKER

THE LAST DECADE of our century is an unprecedented decade of decision. Entire life systems are closing down, and we are faced with the
responsibility of grasping fast-diminishing final opportunities to sustain
creation in at least a good part of its variety and with at least a degree of
dignity. As Christians around the world are facing up to this challenge, they
find their communities, faith, and ethics transformed by the newness of
the issues and the magnitude of the task. Where the environmental movement and the churches intersect, an ecumenical, evangelical (in the Barthian
sense), socially engaged Christian community is emerging as a witness to
the healing and sustaining power of the Holy Spirit in our age.

In this essay I trace the development of this new embodiment of the
church. My thesis consists of three parts: (1) the lively and ongoing practice
of interpreting the Bible in light of the environmental crisis is strengthening
the communal identity of the Christian environmental movement; (2) at
the same time, this practice is giving rise to a new articulation of the
Christian story; and (3) together, the emerging Christian ecological community and story are giving rise to a virtue ethic suited for Christian
existence in an ecological age. I gladly dedicate these pages to my teacher,
Charles C. West, who has tirelessly pursued the vision of a transformed and
transforming ecumenical Christianity.

In 1967 historian Lynn White published a landmark article in which
he accused the Christian tradition of carrying "an enormous burden of

205

guilt" regarding the environmental crisis. As a cornerstone of his argument, White linked the biblical creation accounts to Western anthropocentrism and dualism, which in turn he linked to the attitude of dominance over nature. Ever since White's article, the place of the Bible in environmental ethics has been a matter of debate. Three questions in particular have occupied the attention of Christian environmentalists:

1. Should the Bible be a central authority in a Christian environmental ethic?
2. Where should the burden of guilt be located: in the text itself, or in frameworks of interpretation?
3. Which biblical texts can be retrieved in support of an environmental ethic?

I will discuss the debates surrounding these three questions, showing how in the midst of disagreement there are significant points of agreement with important implications for Christian community and faith in an ecological age. First, I will suggest that the debates about authority and guilt (questions 1 and 2) have strengthened the communal identity of the Christian environmental movement by becoming occasions for ritual affirmation of commitment and confession of sin. Second, I will suggest that the debate about the retrieval of texts (question 3) has given rise to a new articulation of the Christian story. In the final section I will combine these observations and link them to the development of a Christian ecological virtue ethic.

Authority and Guilt: The Creation of a Community

Lynn White, Jr., labeled Saint Francis of Assisi as the patron saint of ecologists, but he saw no use for the Bible in changing Western attitudes toward nature. In making this choice, White essentially indicated that the only way for environmentalists to remain within the Christian tradition is to remove the Bible from its traditional place of authority. In other words, Christian environmentalism would imply a critique of bibliocentrism, especially the exclusive bibliocentrism of Protestant traditions.

This critique has become a major issue in Christian environmental circles.[1] Two basic positions have emerged. Some environmentalists, like

1. For the purpose of this study, I do not distinguish between the work of theologians

White, choose to remove the Bible from its pedestal. Others choose to keep the Bible as a central authority of Christian faith. I will briefly discuss these two positions and then address their implications for the communal character of the Christian environmental movement.

The strongest critiques of bibliocentrism have been voiced by ecofeminists and process theologians — both well represented in environmental circles. In her book *Models of God,* Sally McFague argues, for example, that an "aural tradition" that invests the Bible with ultimate authority is anthropocentric, for "we are the only ones who can 'hear the Word of the Lord.' "[2] McFague proposes that we see the Bible simply as a resource for doing heuristic theology, as one way to find out about God and God's work. Thus the Bible fulfills an important role, but its authority is not exclusive. In McFague's words, heuristic theology claims that "reality is not limited to its biblical or traditional metaphors, models, and concepts, though these do provide 'case studies,' previously successful metaphors and models that give invaluable assistance in the attempt to characterize 'demonstrable continuities' within the Christian paradigm."[3] Along similar lines, process theologian Jay McDaniel has argued that we show our appreciation for the Bible exactly by transcending "bibliolatry."[4]

By contrast, more traditional mainline Protestants and Roman Catholics continue to argue for a central role of the Bible in environmental ethics. Yet in these traditional circles also, one can discern two rather revolutionary shifts of understanding involving the Bible and its place in Christian faith. First of all, among Protestant environmentalists renewed interest in natural theology has led to a questioning of the Bible as the exclusive source of divine revelation. This questioning process indicates a conscious move beyond Barthian caution toward a conception of the Bible as the central, but not the only, authority for Christian faith. *Sola scriptura* is being reinterpreted as *pleraque scriptura,* so to speak.[5]

---

and that of ethicists. In the context of Christian environmentalism this distinction is hard to maintain.

The debate on the place of the Bible in environmental ethics is most evident in the work of individual theologians and ethicists. Official church documents generally follow accepted church teachings about the place of the Bible in ethics.

2. Sallie McFague, *Models of God: Theology for an Ecological, Nuclear Age* (Philadelphia: Fortress Press, 1987), p. 67.

3. Ibid., p. 37.

4. Jay McDaniel, "Christianity and the Need for New Vision," in *Religion and Environmental Crisis,* ed. Eugene C. Hargrove (Athens: University of Georgia Press, 1986), p. 204.

5. For another modern critique of *sola scriptura,* see Stanley Hauerwas, "Interpreting the Bible as a Political Act: Sola Scriptura as Heresy," 1992 Sprunt Lecture, delivered at Union

Among Catholic environmentalists we find a shift in the opposite direction, with similar results. Confronted with the environmental crisis, many Catholics find themselves searching the Bible rather than their natural-law tradition for answers. The Bible, in other words, is becoming *more* central in these circles.[6] Yet it is not, nor has it ever been, treated as an exclusive authority. Overall, then, mainline Catholic and Protestant environmentalists are converging in their interpretations of the authority of Scripture. Yet the point of convergence, the nonexclusive centrality of the Bible, differs significantly from the position of those who criticize any bibliocentrism.

How does this diversity of views on the centrality of the Bible impact the character of the Christian environmental movement? Must we conclude that this movement suffers from disabling fragmentation because of fundamental disagreements about the authority of Scripture? I submit that such a conclusion, while reasonable at first sight, overlooks an even more fundamental unifying factor in the debate. After all, those who criticize bibliocentrism and those who wish to see the Bible at the center agree on one thing, namely, that the place of the Bible in environmental ethics is an issue worth discussing. This shared assumption witnesses to a basic communal identity, which so far is proving stronger than the existence of disagreements.

One way to understand the dynamics involved here is to see the debate on the centrality of the Bible as a ritual. For some participants, the ritual is mainly an obligation. They would like to get on with exploring less biblical waters. Yet it is their sense of obligation that places even these critics of bibliocentrism in the same community as more traditional Christian environmentalists. By feeling an obligation to discuss the role of the Bible, even though this role may be minimal in their own minds, they acknowledge the concerns and beliefs of a biblically traditioned audience with whom they choose to associate. Thus the ritual of debating the place of the

---

Theological Seminary, further developed in *Unleashing the Scripture: Freeing the Bible from Captivity to America* (Nashville: Abingdon Press, 1993).

6. These shifts in Protestant and Roman Catholic circles were especially evident during the 1991 Casassa Conference on the topic "Ecological Prospects: Theory and Practice," held at Loyola Marymount University. Protestant theologian Mark Ellingson, in his paper "Toward an Ecumenical Theology: Rediscovering Creation — Reviving the Nicene Vision," argued that Protestants should become more open to the kind of natural theology underlying the doctrine of creation. Roman Catholic theologian Bernard F. Evans, in his paper "Catholic Social Thought and the Environment," argued for the importance of returning to the Bible.

It should be noted that the Roman Catholic turn to the Bible received much of its impetus from the Vatican II decree *Optatam Totius* ("On the Formation of Priests"), which states that moral theology "should be more thoroughly nourished by scriptural teaching" (par. 16).

Bible both expresses and strengthens the bonds of community, despite the variety of positions occupied in the debate.

Just as debating the centrality of the Bible has become a ritual among environmentalists, so has the practice of debating where the burden of the guilt associated with the environmental crisis should be located when it comes to the Bible. Again, two basic positions have emerged. By far the most common way of criticizing the biblical heritage involves pointing out how traditional interpretive frameworks have historically led to distorted understandings of biblical texts. These distortions would subsequently be responsible for environmentally harmful Christian beliefs, attitudes, and practices. Some environmentalists put the full burden of guilt on misguided interpretive frameworks in an attempt to salvage the entire biblical text from criticism. In the words of John Cobb, "Our task is simply to extricate ourselves from the influence of certain philosophical traditions and from a general narrowness of focus in historical Protestantism."[7]

A smaller group of Christian environmentalists argues that interpretive grids cannot carry all the blame. They point to biblical texts that, in our best judgment regarding their meanings for their first audiences, indicate a heritage of environmentally harmful beliefs, attitudes, and practices. If this is the case, problematic texts should not be explained away by means of crafty interpretations. As Jay McDaniel puts it, the attitudes evidenced in such texts should be "remembered, but not repeated."[8]

The differences between these two positions can be illustrated by tracing the debate on dominion theology. A central question in this debate is whether the Bible contains models and justifications for human exploitative domination of nonhuman creation. Most controversial are the biblical references to human dominion over nature (e.g., Gen. 1:26-28; Psalm 8). A good number of environmentalists now argue that the biblical concept

---

7. John B. Cobb, Jr., *Sustainability: Economics, Ecology, and Justice* (Maryknoll, N.Y.: Orbis Books, 1992), p. 83, also pp. 92–94. See also Charles M. Murphy, *At Home on Earth: Foundations for a Catholic Ethic of the Environment* (New York: Crossroad Publishing, 1989). Central in Murphy's ethic is a reinterpretation of the Book of Genesis, inspired by Pope John Paul II's pastoral letters. Murphy's method is summarized in the following passage: "An ethic that employs the Bible as our most available story would of necessity have to heighten elements of the story that perhaps have not been so emphasized before, the 'picking and choosing' that are always part of prophecy. But this is not to falsify the biblical message, to make it say something other than what it means to say. It is rather to do what every prophet must do when, in looking at the sins of the age, he/she points to 'the one thing necessary.' Such an ethic, though biblically inspired, would have to draw upon as well all that philosophy and science have to offer in applying its wisdom to concrete decisions and actions" (p. 58).

8. McDaniel, "Christianity and the Need for New Vision," p. 204.

of dominion must be understood in light of another biblical concept, namely, stewardship. As stewardship, dominion implies responsibility and accountability, an attitude of service rather than authoritarianism. Such an attitude is evident, for example, in Israel's covenantal legislation, which provided animals with Sabbaths and the land with Sabbath years (Exod. 23:10-12; Lev. 25:1-7). In this view, the traditional interpretation of dominion as domination is at fault for encouraging inappropriate relationships with nature, not the "truly biblical" understanding of the relationship between humans and nonhuman creation.[9] Thus, the text is exonerated.

Other Christian environmentalists do not believe that biblical references to human dominion over creation can be salvaged by interpreting them in light of the concept of stewardship. Some argue that such an interpretation runs into the face of historical evidence showing rising patterns of domination in the ancient Near East. According to Walter Wink in his article "Ecobible: The Bible and Ecojustice":

> Neither Judaism nor Christianity avoided this ethos of domination. The early Hebrews all too often behaved in a manner indistinguishable from the predators of an earlier time. I have already referred to the word "dominion" in Genesis 1:26. It means "to tread, trample, subdue, rule over, dominate." Try as exegetes may to clean it up, it is an unfortunate choice of words that did, however, express the current attitude toward nature.[10]

In addition, especially ecofeminists argue that the stewardship concept implies the same kind of hierarchical relationships as are implied in the dominion concept. Even if interpreted as "servant lordship,"[11] stewardship still implies unequal relations. If hierarchical thinking lies at the root of the current environmental crisis, then stewardship would not be a desirable substitute for dominion.[12]

9. See, for example, Douglas John Hall, *Imaging God: Dominion as Stewardship* (Grand Rapids: Eerdmans, 1986); and Murphy, *At Home on Earth,* pp. 92–98.

10. Walter Wink, "Ecobible: The Bible and Ecojustice," *Theology Today* 49, no. 4 (1993): 472. This article is adapted from Walter Wink, *Engaging the Powers: Discernment and Resistance in a World of Domination* (Minneapolis: Augsburg, 1992).

11. Presbyterian Eco-Justice Task Force, *Keeping and Healing the Creation* (Louisville: Presbyterian Church [U.S.A.], 1989), pp. 51–60.

12. Cf. Elizabeth Dodson Gray, "A Critique of Dominion Theology," in *For Creation's Sake: Preaching, Ecology, and Justice,* ed. Dieter T. Hessel (Philadelphia: Geneva Press, 1985), pp. 79–80. Dodson Gray also argues that we are neither wise enough nor good enough to be responsible stewards of creation. See also Mark I. Wallace, "The Wild Bird Who Heals: Recovering the Spirit in Nature," *Theology Today* 50, no. 1 (1993): 27–28. Others warn that

Environmentalists who take this position prefer to read the Bible against itself, lifting up its more egalitarian passages and construing those as an internal critique of biblical dominion theology. Some even go beyond the level of contrasting texts with texts, referring to a more general biblical ethos marked by love, egalitarianism, and a commitment to justice and liberation. Walter Wink, for example, claims that "the whole tenor of the gospel is the end of domination," implying that one need not find explicit texts denouncing environmental exploitation to show that the gospel condemns it.[13] In either case, the process of reading the Bible against itself essentially removes biblical references to dominion from the canon (or if they are left in, their authority derives from our need to be reminded of past mistakes, lest we repeat them through forgetfulness).

As a result of this and similar debates, there is no general agreement among Christian environmentalists on which biblical texts, if any, warrant critique. Yet again, differences are outweighed by a more significant unifying factor, so that the debate on the question of guilt must be understood as internal to a community, rather than indicative of a scattered movement.

The unifying factor in this case is the shared assumption that some parts of the Christian heritage will have to give way if we are going to deal constructively with the environmental crisis. In other words, all agree that the burden of guilt must (at least partially) be located within Christianity. The fact that some single out parts of the biblical canon, whereas others single out certain interpretive frameworks, is less significant than the fact that all agree that the tradition as a whole needs to change.

This point becomes clearer when we focus on the parallel between this debate and the ritual confession of sin. During a ritual confession of sin, different individuals will gravitate toward different parts of the confession. At the same time, communal identity is strengthened through general agreement about the need for confession. Similarly, the Christian environmental movement's general admission of guilt is creating communal identity, despite different ways of locating this guilt.[14] It is this general

---

the stewardship notion too easily removes God from the world. See, for example, Michael J. Himes, "The Sacrament of Creation," *Commonweal* 117 (January 26, 1990): 42–49.

13. Walter Wink, "Ecobible," p. 476. Wink makes a parallel argument regarding the issue of slavery: "That is why the early Quakers and abolitionists, and even Southerners today, can see that the gospel condemns slavery, even though the Bible nowhere denounces it" (ibid.).

14. This agreement can partially be traced to a commonly held environmental worldview, which favors interconnectedness over domination, holism over dualism, and creational inclusiveness over anthropocentrism. Disagreements on the redeemability of the Bible are thus not fundamental normative disagreements but rather matters of judgment

admission of the need for confession and transformation that sets Christian environmentalists apart from other Christians as a distinct community of faith, just as the Confessing Church distinguished itself during the Nazi period in Germany.

In sum, then, we have seen that the debates around the questions of biblical authority and guilt are strengthening the communal character of the Christian environmental movement by providing occasions for affirming commitment to biblical tradition and confessing sin in the face of the environmental crisis. This is not to say that the communal character of the Christian environmental movement entirely derives from the process of interpreting the Bible. For example, the parallel processes of reassessing the models provided by the saints, the liturgical and spiritual traditions of the church, and the legacy of theology and ethics also play a major role in shaping and strengthening communal bonds. Moreover, shared practices such as social activism and experimentation with sustainable lifestyles contribute in a basic way, having been the cradle of Christian environmentalism, a cradle shared with the larger environmental movement. Yet the emergence of Christian environmentalism as a *Christian* community would have been unthinkable without the unifying effects of the debates on biblical authority and guilt.

To conclude the section, I would like to highlight two striking characteristics of the emerging Christian environmental community: its ecumenicity, and its praxis orientation. Christians from the diaspora find themselves uniting for the common task of healing God's creation, shaping a deeply ecumenical church community in the process. Especially the rapprochement between mainline Roman Catholics and Protestants is noteworthy. It is as though this community, in its very constitution, tries to illustrate that the more pressing question for Christians today is not to which church one belongs but whether one cares for God's creation.

Second, this community is oriented to praxis. The fact that there is so much theoretical debate among Christian environmentalists does not indicate a hedging of practical commitment; rather, it expresses the widely shared belief that desirable and lasting social change will not take place without change at the level of consciousness.[15] For Christian environmentalists, therefore, the debate about the role of the Bible in environmental

---

regarding the detailed process of understanding the links between values and biblical traditions.

15. See, for example, Douglas C. Bowman, *Beyond the Modern Mind: The Spiritual and Ethical Challenge of the Environmental Crisis* (New York: Pilgrim Press, 1990), p. x.

ethics is not an academic exercise but rather an attempt at *metanoia*, from which communal action will spring.

Retrieving Biblical Texts: The Creation of a Story

While shared interest in the question of biblical authority and shared confession of sin is strengthening the communal identity of the Christian environmental movement, the process of retrieving biblical texts for an ecological age is shaping this community's understanding of the Christian story. Christian environmentalists are actively searching the Bible for illumination and spiritual empowerment. One finds a refreshing openness to the text throughout the literature, evidenced by an abundance of positive Scripture references. In fact, my own informal survey of Scripture indexes shows that positive references to individual texts outweigh negative references by a ratio of 15:1.[16] This observation again indicates that on the whole, Christian environmentalists prefer to target their critique at frameworks of interpretation, saving the Bible itself for the positive task of constructing an ecological theology.

A pattern is emerging in the retrieval of biblical texts for environmental ethics. Certain verses have become favorites among environmentalists. They can be organized according to central themes in Christian environmental thought, such as:

- the intrinsic (noninstrumental) goodness of creation (e.g., Gen. 1:31; Psalm 104)
- natural theology (e.g., Rom. 1:20)
- God's care for creation (e.g., Gen. 9:8-17; Psalm 104)
- the link between humans and the earth (e.g., Gen. 2:7)
- appropriate human care for nonhuman creation (e.g., Gen. 2:15; Exod. 23:10-12; Lev. 25:1-7; Prov. 12:10; Luke 14:5)
- the link between justice and the environment (e.g., Deut. 29:22-25)
- the salvation and renewal of the entire creation (e.g., Ps. 36:6; Isa. 11:1-9; Rom. 8:22; Rev. 21:1)[17]

16. Few works on environmental ethics provide Scripture indexes. I am indebted to my research assistants, Julie Morris and Kevin Williams, for compiling annotated indexes of key works in this area.

17. This list is not meant to be exhaustive of themes and texts occurring in Christian environmental literature. I mainly want to sketch the core of a pattern of interpretation that

These and similar favored texts are repeated in the literature in almost mantric fashion. They form a pattern of environmental biblical interpretation, held together by the internal consistency of the values and beliefs that characterize environmental literature.[18] (In a sense, then, environmentalists are finding in the Bible what they want to see there.)

It would neither be accurate nor desirable, however, to brand this pattern as a new "canon within the canon." The retrieval of texts is still too much in process to speak of any authoritative subcanon. Besides the cited clusters of favored texts there are many other texts that are occasionally retrieved, but not frequently enough to discern a pattern. Moreover, certain texts have received rather contradictory treatment in the literature. John 3:16 ("For God so loved the world . . .") is a good example. In *Beyond the Modern Mind*, Douglas C. Bowman retrieves this text and warns against interpreting it anthropocentrically as "God so loved humans . . .": "Given the dangers in the world today, we must begin training ourselves to read the text as it is written: 'God so loved the *world*.' We must begin to ponder implications beyond the human sphere."[19]

In H. Paul Santmire's *Travail of Nature*, however, we find a rather different interpretation. Santmire has reservations about retrieving John 3:16, and the Gospel of John in general. Citing the work of biblical scholar Ernst Kasemann, he writes: "Notwithstanding the oft-quoted words of John 3:16, about God loving the world . . . , the disciples in John's view go out into a world which 'at its core is an alien realm . . . just as according to John, Jesus himself has been an alien sojourner in this world below.' "[20] For Santmire the Gospel of John represents a clear limit to any ecological reading of the Bible. In light of such differing interpretations, then, it would be premature to speak of a "canon within a canon" emerging in environmental literature.

Nor is the establishment of a subcanon necessarily a desirable goal. With canonization also comes the suppression of diversity within a community of interpreters. Since inclusiveness is a central value in the environmental movement, speaking of an emerging canon would hardly seem appropriate.[21]

---

is continually expanding and being refined. The list is limited to themes and texts that directly deal with creation or nonhuman nature, yet the literature also provides abundant examples of other texts that are creatively reinterpreted in an environmental context.

18. For these values, see n. 14.

19. Bowman, *Beyond the Modern Mind*, p. 19.

20. H. Paul Santmire, *The Travail of Nature: The Ambiguous Ecological Promise of Christian Theology* (Philadelphia: Fortress Press, 1985), p. 213.

21. For a parallel argument on the inappropriateness of establishing a feminist biblical canon, see Elisabeth Schüssler Fiorenza, "The Will to Choose or to Reject: Continuing Our

It is possible, however, to claim that the patterned repetition of certain biblical texts, in conjunction with general environmental values and beliefs, is giving rise to a new articulation of the Christian story. This story is the saga of a wondrously created web of connections, threatened by human pretensions and yet still carrying the promise of universal well-being. Some environmentalists explicitly recite this story;[22] others imply it in their work. Clearly, no one tells or implies exactly the same version, yet the story is always recognizable for its connectionalism, its message of divine grace in the midst of environmental disaster, and, above all, its "earthiness." Overall, the distinguishing mark of this new articulation of the Christian story is that it is clearly "good news" for all creation.

Based on selected clusters of biblical texts, this gospel for an ecological age in turn leads to further exploration of the Bible. It throws new light on many texts that do not immediately seem relevant to an environmental ethic. For example, the story's universal connectionalism has inspired the extension of "love of neighbor" to "love of nature."[23] This rereading of the Bible, based on a renewed awareness of God's good news, is generally experienced as leading to an increased sense of biblical relevance and coherence. In the words of Wesley Granberg-Michaelson, "The Bible simply makes more sense when we recognize that it is the story of how God, humanity, and the creation relate to each other."[24]

In sum, then, one could say that the communal process of retrieving biblical texts, a process marked by open-endedness and contradictions as well as by patterns, is giving rise to a new articulation of the Christian story, which in turn inspires refreshed respect for the Bible. Morever, this process is itself community-forming, for nothing is more powerful in shaping communal identity than a shared story.

Critical Work," in *Feminist Interpretation of the Bible,* ed. Letty M. Russell (Philadelphia: Westminster Press, 1985), p. 131.

22. See, for example, Matthew Fox, *Creation Spirituality: Liberating Gifts for the Peoples of the Earth* (San Francisco: HarperSanFrancisco, 1991), pp. 1–4; and Jay McDaniel, "Emerging Options in Ecological Christianity: The New Story, the Biblical Story, and Panentheism," in *Ecological Prospects: Scientific, Religious, and Aesthetic Perspectives,* ed. Christopher Chapple and Mary Evelyn Tucker (Albany: State University of New York Press, 1994).

23. See, for example, James A. Nash, *Loving Nature: Ecological Integrity and Christian Responsibility* (Nashville: Abingdon Press, 1991), p. 143.

24. Wesley Granberg-Michaelson, ed., *Tending the Garden: Essays on the Gospel and the Earth* (Grand Rapids: Eerdmans, 1987), p. 3.

Fruit of a Storied Community:
The Creation of a Virtue Ethic

The full significance of the emergence of the Christian environmental movement as a storied community strengthened by the practice of interpreting the Bible becomes clear when we consider that the presence of a community with a shared narrative is crucial for maintaining and cultivating the life of virtue.[25] In other words, it seems that two necessary conditions are in place for the cultivation of attitudes, habits, and dispositions suitable to Christian living in an ecological age. This is a seminal development indeed, for many environmentalists see a change of attitude as being at the heart of what is needed in response to the current crisis.

In fact, trends in the literature already indicate the emergence of a Christian ecological virtue ethic. This ethic is still inchoate in shape, yet distinctive both in relation to developments within the larger environmental movement and in relation to Christian virtue tradition.[26] For example, one finds calls for a new form of humility in response to human arrogance vis-à-vis nonhuman creation; for simplicity, frugality, and temperance in response to consumerism; for earthiness in response to otherworldliness; for respect and care in response to cruelty and manipulation; for hope in response to despair in the face of environmental degradation; and for the right balance between romanticism and realism, between passivity and control, between spontaneity and prudence, and between passion and patience. This ethic is not presented in an abstract, moralistic manner; rather, it emerges as a witness to an ongoing and widening Christian practice of ecologically responsive being-in-the-world.

The Bible plays an indirect, but noticeable role in the creation of this

---

25. See, for example, Stanley Hauerwas, *A Community of Character: Toward a Constructive Christian Social Ethic* (Notre Dame, Ind.: University of Notre Dame Press, 1981); and Alasdair MacIntyre, *After Virtue: A Study in Moral Theory,* 2d ed. (Notre Dame, Ind.: University of Notre Dame Press, 1984).

26. See, for example, Jay B. McDaniel, *Of God and Pelicans: A Theology of Reverence for Life* (Louisville: Westminster/John Knox Press, 1989), pp. 73–74; Nash, *Loving Nature,* pp. 63–67; and Louke van Wensveen Siker, "Review and Prospects: The Emergence of a Grounded Virtue Ethic," in *Ecological Prospects: Scientific, Religious, and Aesthetic Perspectives,* ed. Christopher Chapple and Mary Evelyn Tucker (Albany: State University of New York Press, 1994). The distinctiveness of this ethic largely lies in the fact that in light of the newly emerging Christian story, individual virtues and vices take on unique meaning. This does not imply, however, that the catalog of Christian ecological virtues and vices differs significantly from a more general environmental catalog. Also, despite many reinterpretations, there is still a remarkable degree of continuity with Christian virtue tradition.

ethic. This becomes most clear when one compares the ecological virtue ethic that is emerging in Christian circles with the ethic emerging in other environmental circles (e.g., deep ecology, post-Christian ecofeminism, social ecology, environmental philosophy, bioregionalism). While there is a good degree of overlap between "catalogs"[27] of virtues and vices, Christian environmentalists will regularly interpret the new ethic in light of biblical understandings of these virtues and vices, or more generally, in light of the emerging version of the Christian story. Thus respect and reverence for nature are seen as expressions of *agapē,* trust and faith are based on belief in a God who is on the side of life, patience and hope are distinctively eschatological, and pride and greed signify overstepping limits in a divinely ordered universe. Clearly, the Bible and the emerging Christian story are giving a unique twist to this emerging virtue ethic.[28]

In sum, then, we see that the process of interpreting the Bible in the face of the environmental crisis has created the communal and narrative conditions necessary for the flourishing of a Christian ecological virtue ethic, and that the ethic that is in fact emerging is itself distinctively marked by the Bible and the new articulation of the Christian story.

Conclusion

In the course of Christian history the Bible has occasioned schisms and closed-mindedness as well as unification and renewal. Christian en-

27. The literature contains very few formalized catalogs of virtues and vices, yet the repetition of certain virtues and vices indicates that authors regularly work with implicit catalogs. My current research involves the compilation of these catalogs.

28. This is true, even though the Bible and the new Christian story are not always the original or main source in the articulation of this Christian ecological virtue ethic. I see the main source in the praxis of the general environmental movement (developing alternative lifestyles, social activism) and in its science-inspired cosmological story. Here too one can speak of a community and a narrative providing the conditions for a flourishing virtue ethic. Most Christian environmentalists identify themselves with this larger community and story and will freely "borrow" its virtue-and-vice language. The process of interpreting these virtues and vices in light of the Bible and the new Christian story is thus often a secondary process. Of course this does diminish the uniqueness of the resulting ethic.

Interestingly, this process is partially analogous to the development of the early Christian virtue ethics. There is much overlap between pagan virtue-and-vice lists and those recorded in the Bible. Biblical authors would often borrow popular pagan lists. Yet the theological context in which they placed these lists and their selective alterations tended to give them a unique twist (as when Paul interprets the life of virtue as the fruit of the Spirit [Gal. 5:22–23]).

vironmentalists, despite their disagreements on biblical authority and on the critique and retrieval of biblical texts, appear to be witnessing a new experience of the transformative power of the Bible. In the process of their interaction with the Bible, we can perceive the co-creation of a new Christian community, story, and virtue ethic. Like the promise of life contained in the combination of fertile soil, seeds, and water, this community with its story and virtue ethic contains the promise of Christian empowerment for environmental action.

Toward an Ethic of Feminist Liberation and Empowerment: A Case Study of Prostitution in Thailand

NANTAWAN BOONPRASAT LEWIS

Prostitution in Thailand:
A 1984 Phuket Brothel Revisited

It was a chilly morning in early February of 1984 in Chiang Mai when I picked up a morning newspaper from the front step of my house. There it was on the front page of both the English and the Thai newspapers, a photograph showing the bodies of five young girls huddled in the charred ruins of what was once a brothel in the town of Phuket, a city located in the beautiful southern part of the country. What was left in the ashes suggested that the young girls were chained to the ground at the time of their death. The front page story shocked the nation and the world and focused the attention of the society to an extraordinary extent on the plight of young girls who were persuaded or forced into prostitution. The police, government officials, and city administrators in Phuket, as well as those in the Bangkok government, acknowledged that the tragedy in Phuket was caused by forced prostitution due to a rapid growth of the sex industry. This industry preyed on the mostly poor girls and women from the impoverished part of the nation (i.e., the north and northeast regions). Responding to a flood of criticism, responsible officials and governmental offices promised to stop forced prostitution and to attempt to deal with the contributing factors of the sex industry.

It was recognized that what happened in Phuket to five victims was just a small fraction of a much bigger and more complex picture of prostitution in the country and in the region.

A decade has passed, and many questions were proven to be and remain unanswered — particular questions as to what and how much has changed in the sex industry, as well as what has been done to prevent child prostitution in Thailand.

Sex Tourism and AIDS:
Thai Prostitution and Life in the 1990s

The 1990s have revealed yet another critical stage in the life of Thailand. A booming sex entertainment industry, which the society has grown to depend on as a major source of income contributing to the economic life of the nation, has made Thailand "the brothel of the world." But the large amount of foreign currency that this industry brings into the country also has its cost.[1] By the mid-1980s, full-blown cases of AIDS hit Thailand. In spite of its relatively small population, the country currently ranks third in the world (trailing only Nigeria and India) in the number of its population being affected by HIV and the AIDS epidemic. *Business Week* recently reported that as many as 600,000 Thais have been infected with HIV (human immunodeficiency virus — the virus that causes AIDS) in a country of 57 million, and up to 1,200 new cases are expected daily.[2]

Many Thais and expatriates are concerned that this epidemic could wipe out an entire generation of Thais. A Thai religious scholar, with whom I recently visited, was among the first within the Church of Christ in Thailand (an interdenominational institution of the Protestant church) to initiate an AIDS project as a means by which the Thai church may respond and minister more effectively to this situation. He shared with me the devastating information that it is estimated that by the year 2000, one out of three funerals in Thailand will be for a victim of AIDS.[3] The World Health Organization estimates that by the turn of the century, between two and four million Thais will be infected with the virus that causes AIDS. My Thai colleague's comment is certainly not unrealistic. Moreover, it is ac-

1. From data supplied by the Thai government, *Business Week* estimated that the tourist industry brought in at least $4 billion annually. *Business Week,* 22 February 1993.

2. *Business Week,* 22 February 1993, p. 52.

3. This was also the figure given out by a national AIDS activist, Miechai Viraraidge, as quoted in *Newsweek,* 20 July 1992.

knowledged that by the year 2000, among those infected by this deadly virus, the vast majority will be women.[4] It is frightening also to learn that Thailand may only be a harbinger of that which is coming to all of Asia.

Many scholars and sociologists agree that a major factor contributing to this epidemic ripping across Thailand and Asia is prostitution. It was not until the mid-1980s, after AIDS had gained a strong foothold in the country, that it became known that prostitution was a major source for spreading the disease so rapidly. The rampant use of intravenous drugs only worsened an already horrible situation. This disease, once believed to be a "foreigner's disease," has found a new home in Asia. It is at home here because it is sanctioned by a culture in which "safe sex" practices are not the norm; a culture in which visiting a brothel is understood as a right of passage into manhood; a culture in which visiting a brothel is a major part of doing business locally, nationally, and internationally; a culture in which visiting a brothel is merely likened to going to the barber.[5] In this culture, AIDS is no longer a "gay disease" or a "foreigner disease" but increasingly a heterosexual and family disease affecting all the people of Thailand.

The Intellectual Response: Toward Analyses of Prostitution

The severity and extremity of sex tourism and AIDS have prompted responses from all concerned, including government officials, business and community leaders, scholars, social activists, and religious heads, as the epidemic poses a serious threat to the well-being of the country. Several attempts have been made to understand and solve this situation, which many view as nothing short of sexual genocide. Many studies indicate that special attention must be given to the structural dimensions — political, social, and economic — as well as the national policy on Third World development in a globalized context. Some studies indicate that the religious and cultural value system and the treatment of women are important dimensions of this situation. Some have begun to understand power relations in the domain of sexual labor, based on a belief in male dominance, as another factor. A journalist working on the issues of AIDS and prostitution in Thailand points out that a real challenge lies in the Thai and foreign tourists' attitudes about sex. As Ron Moreau states, "before Thai

4. See in particular Ron Moreau, "Sex and Death in Thailand," *Newsweek,* 20 July 1992.
5. See Steven Enlanger, "A Plague Awaits," *New York Times Magazine,* 14 July 1991.

men can really change their attitudes about sex, they need first to change their attitude about women. Most men consider women to be either sexual objects or obedient homemakers."[6]

While numerous studies exist on sex tourism and the traffic of women and their connection to AIDS, they have mostly concentrated on the socio-economic and political relations of the situation. Little has been done in the areas of cultural and religious values or belief systems. This study is an attempt to focus primarily on this aspect of the issue. More specifically, it is articulated from a Christian feminist perspective with particular attention on the sociopolitical and moral location of the women involved in the sexual labor industry. It is my hope that this approach will allow the voices of those women to be heard, and that articulating the ethics of feminist liberation will aid the effort of all concerned in providing a clearer under-standing of and seeking a desirable solution to this dreadful situation.

A Vision of Liberation — in a Reality of Survival

Sometimes the suffering
has no voice, it is silent.
It is a question of survival,
and the poor have no choice.

Sister Naoko Iyari, MMB[7]

It has been several years since this poem appeared on the front cover of *In God's Image*. It has been more than a decade since I began my research on the issue of prostitution in Thailand and throughout southeast Asia. My involvement in this issue began on an occasion when I walked, along with two friends, from one bar to another along the infamous Bangkok road. My friends and I observed firsthand the way many Thai women earn their livelihood (and by which many poor rural families are supported). I had the opportunity to sit down with several of these "bar girls" and listen to their stories. I watched painfully through a gigantic mirrored door of a massage parlor, as male customers eyed and picked out their "girl" for an evening's pleasure. As the men made their selections, I saw the hapless girl,

6. Moreau, "Sex and Death in Thailand."
7. *In God's Image*, June 1990.

whose number (no name) was announced over the loudspeaker, come and meet her customer. This experience compelled me to ask a question of myself and the Christian community in Thailand and around the world, concerning our responsibility and accountability as believers in and responders to the message of Jesus Christ.

The words of the poem by Sister Iyari captured my understanding of the struggle of women involved in prostitution in Asia. My interviews with the bar girls indicated that they did not find pleasure in their line of work. They would very likely share the feelings of their fellow worker who said

> "My life was like an animal's. I was sold three times. I begged (my boss) to let me go home, but she said I owed much money and must pay it back. Everyday I had to sleep with men. I was not allowed to leave even during menstruation. I was told if I escaped, they would track me, kill me and my parents too."[8]

The passivity of masseuses and bar girls in Bangkok, their unmade-up faces that one encounters in the mornings as they gather around food vendors on the street corners are witnesses to the story of their lives — a struggle for survival.

To speak of and to realize a vision of liberation in this situation, it seems to me, is to recognize these women's reality primarily as a struggle for survival. It also means to reflect on the rhetoric of liberation in the light of their paradigm of struggle with serious consideration of their societal and cultural structure of oppression and marginalization. To do otherwise is to obscure the power of the message of liberation in a community where an appropriation of the message is urgently needed. In other words, an ethic that embodies the message of liberation to Thai women in sexual labor must strive to comprehend more fully the social, political, economic, cultural, and religious factors impacting their lived experience. It must, in addressing their reality of survival, recognize that women have a pivotal role to play in solving the AIDS epidemic in Thailand. This ethics of feminist liberation seeks to provide a framework in which to articulate a moral/religious vision that empowers women as they struggle to be economically independent while confronting the patriarchal ideology and ethos.

Furthermore, in developing resources for this ethics of feminist liberation, I suggest that categories such as women's historical agency, women's

---

8. *Times*, 21 June 1993.

experience, self-redefinition, self-acceptance, self-affirmation, and global-ized solidarity are crucial in articulating "theological strategies."[9]

Women as Historical Agents: Victors/Survivors

Often prostitutes and/or women who earn their livelihood in the sexual entertainment business are viewed as victims. They are also stigmatized by cultural and moral attitudes embedded in the societal system that look down upon their professions as social ills. They are excluded from deci-sion-making processes that directly affect their lives and their professions. Women in prostitution are systematically marginalized. All of this has historically contributed to a widely spread social perception of women as passive agents of history. Emerging views and studies of women in the sex industry challenge this understanding. For example, in her study entitled "Nuns, Mediums and Prostitutes in Chiang Mai: A Study of Some Marginal Categories of Women,"[10] Khin Thitsa argues that three groups of women, namely nuns (mae chii), mediums (maa khii), and prostitutes (so pae nee), have demonstrated the use of three different strategies to overcome modern and traditional forces that condition and control their lives — both in private and public spheres. She concludes,

> Renunciation, possession and prostitution all constitute roles in which women exercise a comparatively high degree of determinacy once they have assumed their roles, whatever material forces of poverty and deg-radation have driven them to employ their sexuality towards each other.[11]

Thitsa's argument in this study is helpful for us to see that in claiming their rights to live and to have control over conditions that affect their lives, women who are nuns, mediums, and prostitutes exercise their choice on options available to them. This is to the extent that they assume marginal roles in society. For prostitutes, it means to go to extremes of risking their health and ruining their lives and destroying their family's reputation, an act that is

9. In the words of Elisabeth Schüssler Fiorenza in "The Ethics and Politics of Libera-tion: Theorizing the Ekklesia of Women," Discipleship of Equals (New York: Crossroad, 1993).

10. Khin Thitsa, "Nuns, Mediums and Prostitutes in Chiang Mai: A Study of Some Marginal Categories of Women," Center for SE Asian Studies, University of Kent, Canterbury, 1983.

11. Ibid., p. 13.

224

comparable to losing face — a value that is highly revered in Asian culture. However, it is important to recognize that in exercising their choice these women demonstrate responsibility to define themselves in the existing framework of social relationships. More significantly, in choosing this profession they refuse to be victims of their living conditions and have taken a more active role in determining their lives and destiny. Such an act, much as it is condemned by the society that actually benefits from their labor, enables them to be survivors of oppressive and exploitative structural systems. Women in this profession, in essence, have taken a role of historical agency in determining their lives and destiny. This is indeed a challenging view in interpreting the struggle for survival of the majority of prostitutes in Thailand.

Women's Experience:
From the Periphery to the Center

It is imperative that an ethics of feminist liberation addresses the necessity of viewing women's experience as integral to the societal experience. In particular, this means an acceptance of the presence of women in prostitution and their role in solving societal problems, including the AIDS epidemic. It is an act of embracing the marginalized, who can become responsible victors in the struggle for their well-being. In fact, this is already happening. In her critical work on prostitution and tourism in Southeast Asia, Thanh-Dam Truong discusses at length how prostitutes' labor has benefited many societies. She then ethically challenges the public, saying,

> If the rehabilitation of individuals is necessary, the target group should include not only prostitutes, but also those who have found it legitimate to use prostitutes' labor for their own profit and pleasure while condemning them to moral, social and legal isolation.

Truong believes that

> Prostitutes' demand for recognition and emancipation must be seriously considered. Recognition of their work would enable the provision of a certain political space for organization to articulate the needs, their perception of themselves and their relationship with society as a whole.

If one concurs with her viewpoint, this is perhaps what is yet to be fully implemented in a societal attempt to address the situation of prostitutes and AIDS in Thailand. Discussions of solutions to the AIDS epidemic often occur among scholars, health providers, social workers, and government officials, but such discussions rarely if ever include participation from women in the sex industry. It is apparent that these women's experiences are not considered of much importance in this critical process. Empowering women in this profession begins with creating political space for them in the decision-making structure, so that they are no longer at the periphery or viewed as problems to be solved but recognized as contributive members of society and agents for societal improvement. This is of course far from simple. It requires women's personal transformation in terms of self-acceptance, self-definition, and personal strategies for survival. At the same time, the societal, cultural, and belief systems that have been oppressive to women must be re-examined and challenged. In the case of the women in sexual labor, a situation not limited to Thailand but present throughout the world, solidarity among concerned groups and individuals must also be recognized in these terms.

Self-Redefinition:
Self-Rehabilitation and Self-Acceptance

Bein alive & bein a woman & bein colored is a metaphysical dilemma/i havent conquered yet.

Ntosake Shange[12]

Although Shange's statement expresses the lived experience of a woman of color in the United States, it rings true to the experiences of the majority of women in Thailand. Critical analyses of the situation of women in sexual labor, which show the interconnection of capitalism, classism, racism, and patriarchal domination, indicate the webs of oppression and degradation these women encounter. This is compounded by popular and powerful religious and cultural teachings and practices that view women as inferior to men. As Hantrakul, a foremost Thai feminist journalist who has done extensive research on Thai prostitutes, describes,

In everyday life, there are customs which attribute defilement to the female sex. A woman's clothes should not be washed together with those

12. Ntosake Shange, *For colored girls who have considered suicide when the rainbow is enuf* (New York: Bantam Books, 1980), p. 48.

of a man; neither should they be hung in areas where a man might pass below. In either case, the man will lose his power, or spiritual superiority. A truck that lets a woman climb up on the top is believed to be doomed. She is of course generally not allowed to touch sacred Buddha images.[13]

In terms of social relationships and relationships with men, Hantrakul rightly points to a familiar Thai popular cultural belief, in which

> Having a daughter born in the family is even compared to having a toilet room built in the front of the house. This means that great caution is needed to keep it clean and odorless. . . . Marriage often means a woman is transformed from her father's custody to her husband's.[14]

This perception and treatment of women as possessions and sources of defilement is further enforced by the "Law of the Three Seals," which has become the traditional Thai code of conduct. As again pointed out by Hantrakul, it was mentioned in the law that "a good woman should not let more than one man gain access to her body."[15] This instruction has become a cultural expectation of the Thai woman's sexual behavior.

As far as the popular Buddhist belief is concerned, it is generally understood that one is born a woman because of bad *karma* or lack of adequate merit being stored in previous lives. A woman must strive to perform "merit activities" in this life so that she might be reborn as a man in her next life. Being born a man is to be born into a condition elevated toward enlightenment as well as into a higher status in society.

In light of the discussed Thai popular cultural and religious beliefs, it is no surprise that some scholars would suggest that with the low value attached to the female body and the female spirit by Buddhism, she has been sufficiently degraded to enter prostitution.[16]

As one who was brought up in this tradition, I recognize that such popular beliefs have had great influence in the socialization of Thai girls and continue to affect our self-definition and code of conduct as we enter our womanhood.

To develop an ethics of feminist liberation in this particular context

13. Sukanya Hantrakul, "Prostitution in Thailand," paper presented at the Women in Asia Workshop, Monash University, Melbourne, Australia, July 22-24, 1983, p. 2.

14. Ibid., p. 3.

15. Ibid.

16. Khin Thitsa, "Providence and Prostitution: Image and Reality for Women in Buddhist Thailand" (mimeograph, 1980), p. 23.

requires that one explore the power of self-redefinition and self-rehabilitation that may lead to a sense of self-acceptance and empowerment. Black feminist Pauli Murray correctly cautions that a system of oppression "draws much of its strength from the acquiescence of its victims, who have accepted the dominant image of themselves and are paralyzed by a sense of helpfulness."[17]

This of course can lead women to a state of being a "willing victim," especially in the case of Thai prostitutes. The testimony of a Thai feminist journalist working on the issue of prostitution, however, affords us a glimpse of the power of self-redefinition. In her contact with prostitutes with whom she established a relationship, Hantrakul powerfully testifies to this self-transformation process:

> Personally, I very much valued the spirit and struggle and the relatively independent and defying attitudes of the prostitutes I know which I rarely found in women who are not of this kind. They are women who have the spirit of a fighter — in sexual relations and others. While their middle-class sisters are being repressed by conservative values and the sexual double standards, they seem to have more autonomy in their personal and sexual lives. Their frank familiarity with the crudest facts of life and male natures is much more enlightening to themselves and others than the pretentious atmosphere of artificial and conservative thoughts in which most "good" women are confined . . . having marked themselves as whores, they have come out of their place — having broken so many repressive rules of good women, and developed the spirit of a "fighter for survival" and better living. Most of all, they have outgrown the social conditions they were born into.[18]

This testimony provides us with a new and provocative insight into what women in prostitution have been able to acquire as their "strategies of survival." Most of all it is a testimony that challenges our assessment of the courage, wisdom, and strength of those who are treated as the outcasts and powerless. Women who emerge as survivors of oppressive situations have demonstrated to us a powerful meaning of self-redefinition and self-acceptance. This is a life-giving quality that allows them to move on and live on, and most importantly, serves as a moral agent of change. It is a powerful spiritual element that must be brought to awareness and recog-

17. Pauli Murray, *Songs in a Weary Throat: An American Pilgrimage* (New York: Harper and Row, 1987), p. 106.
18. Hantrakul, "Prostitution in Thailand," p. 26.

nition within the community of faith as it strives to make visible the women's stories and struggles. In the process of striving to take control of their lives, the Thai prostitutes whom Hantrakul encountered transformed her understanding of their struggle and their survival. These are indeed powerful lessons of empowerment.

The Politics of Global Feminist Solidarity

Thus far I have discussed certain elements that must be explored more fully in the development of an ethics of feminist liberation that could speak meaningfully to a particular area of women's struggle, namely the Thai women in sexual labor and their pivotal role in the AIDS epidemic. Their struggle, I maintain, is simply a struggle for survival within a complicated political, economic, social, cultural, and religious structure of patriarchal domination. To strive to be with them and allow their voices to be heard and give them an opportunity to interpret their reality and gain control of their situation is a moral obligation that the ethics of feminist liberation demands. It is obvious that this struggle requires more than personal transformation and personal strategies of survival. The complexity of the cause and effect of prostitution and AIDS goes beyond national and regional boundaries and accountability. The sophisticated and highly technologicalized travel industry and globalized political economy have broadened the issue to a global scale. Recognizing this inherent feature, a moral response to the situation must also be conceived in global terms. One must take into consideration the politics of global feminist solidarity and all that this entails.

Elisabeth Schüssler Fiorenza,[19] in discussing the key aspects of the ethics and politics of liberation, correctly points out a number of factors to be considered, including recognition of historical multiplicity; inclusivity of feminist framework and strategic practices in terms of race, sexual orientation, gender, class, and colonialism; the particularistic nature of the patriarchal power relations in a specific context; and the right of women to self-determination. All of these deserve deliberate consideration. However, in the case of prostitution in Thailand, to which all of these certainly apply, the situation begs further consideration and urgency. This particular situation demands a closer and more critical exploration and examination into what has been an assumption, interpretation, and practice of global feminist

19. See Schüssler Fiorenza, *Discipleship of Equals*, pp. 332–52.

solidarity regarding the struggle of women in the Third World. Most critically, this includes a recognition of existing power inequalities among groups in determining responses. For those who have been victimized by race, sexual orientation, gender, class, and colonialistic oppression, this appears to be a missing element in feminist liberation and empowerment.

• 13 •

Challenge and Renewal in Protestant Ecclesiology

OSCAR S. SUAREZ

THESE REFLECTIONS are meant to offer some insights regarding our search for a new ecclesiology in contemporary Philippine Protestantism.[1] Although the present task points to various issues arising from the whole business of restructuring the constitution of the United Church of Christ in the Philippines (UCCP), our greater aim is to seek better opportunities and strategies vis-à-vis the transformation of the Protestant faith as a whole within the context of Philippine society. After all, as Professor Sitoy has put it, the UCCP history reveals the riches of its "many springs," even as they flow into only "one stream."[2]

To put it another way, the task of restructuring the church may yet be perceived by our constituents merely as an organizational problem and therefore a problem only in procedures. If that is so, then we are no better than our political institutions, whose moral sensibilities and perception of public office hardly meet even the minimum requirements of procedural

1. This is the revised text of a lecture originally delivered at the Annual Workers' Convocation sponsored by the Divinity School of Silliman University in Dumaguete City, Philippines, on August 27, 1993. The theme of the convocation, "Restructuring the Church for Vitality and Mission," was meant to address the theological and political issues surrounding the rewriting of the constitution of the United Church of Christ in the Philippines (UCCP).

2. Filipino scholar Dr. Valentino Sitoy entitles one of his recent works *Many Springs, One Stream* (Manila: New Day Publishers, 1990) to illustrate the variety of Protestant traditions that make up the UCCP.

justice. As a church called to be stewards and servants, our ultimate aim is the administration of substantive justice — that which the prophet Micah points to when he says, "What does the LORD require of you but to do justice, and to love kindness, and to walk humbly with your God?" (6:8).

The Church Always Transforming

Let me begin with the assertion that the problem of restructuring in church for vitality and mission is not only a matter of rearranging the same old furniture in our household of faith.[3] Perhaps some of them need only some kind of recycling, but I am sure we do not simply want a rearrangement of old procedures, a reshuffling of tasks, or an improvement in the observance of rituals. This, I believe, is a radical venture in transforming our ways of thinking and acting — indeed, our ways of practicing the faith. We, in other words, are in search of a fundamentally new and better way of being a church in the world. Transformation, after all, is characteristic of a church that claims to be truly and fully alive. Any person or institution that loses what Leonardo Boff calls "the beat of continuous renewal" loses its own fundamental value and thus becomes an unnecessary baggage in history. As a church, therefore, our only choice is the way of transformation, because this is the only way that points to life.

I speak here of transformation as a way of looking beyond what could be a common perception that changes in the structures of the church require only the rearrangement of the same old patterns of thinking and organizing the Christian ministry. I say this because churches seem to live their lives as if they were living in boxes. Since, in the passing of time, the church has come to be one of the world's best-known institutions, we have always confined our theological consciousness within the purview of officially established dogmas — those tenets of faith that contain what we assume to be "fixed" truths.[4] These fixated dogmas express our ways of looking at the church, and at the same time we employ them as mechanisms by which we defend and protect its institutional interests. In more conservative circles around the church, dogma defines everything, and hence, as

3. This is a borrowed insight from Professor Manfred Halpern. See his draft for a forthcoming book "Transformation: Its Theory and Practice in Personal, Political, Historical, and Sacred Being," available at the Firestone Library, Princeton University.

4. Among the fine resources on this issue is Leonardo Boff, *Church: Charism and Power* (New York: Crossroad Publishing, 1985).

Halpern remarks, the only thing demanded of the faithful is one of "unquestioning obedience."[5]

Indeed, in many areas of our church life, obedience without question is a tremendous fact, which explains why church life in our time is like living in officially prescribed boxes. In those boxes are a complete set of dogmatics that define with finality the way we should behave, the way we should speak and act as a church and as individuals. It is also because we have lived in those boxes too long that in the face of so much injustice around us, we hardly welcome relevant perspectives that are broad enough to be the basis of our speech and action.

Certainly, when people choose to live in a box, their horizon reveals only a piece of the sky — too enclosed and too narrow. But the worst thing is that one always looks up to the sky as the sole source of wisdom and inspiration, precisely because the walls of our boxes do not allow us to see, much less articulate, what we need to see and understand as vital issues for the entire society. In fact, the only way we define the things spiritual is by way of looking up or by way of scanning the heavens. Theology is thus dehistoricized, that is, unplugged from the currents of historical life.

If indeed this analogy of "churches living in boxes" captures what may be said of church life today, then our task is not confined to a mere rearrangement of the same old things within the living rooms of our faith. It becomes one of reexamining our roots, the very foundations of our faith. As I reflected on Jesus' parable of the house built on the sand as against the house built on a rock, it dawned on me that perhaps this is the first question we need to ask: On what foundation do we ground our belief and practice? After all, it was Jesus who said before his disciples: "On this rock, I will build my church." This, in other words, is a question of foundational values. When we speak of foundations, we do not simply mean officially established dogmas that, more often than not, are mere stereotypes coated with certain spiritualized language.[6]

---

5. Decades ago, no less a figure than Paul Tillich gave a serious warning regarding the place of dogma in Christian life. It would be helpful to read him again in this light. See his *History of Christian Thought* (New York: Simon & Schuster, 1967).

6. In his critique of the method of the religious Right in Brazil, Rubem Alves underscores this issue regarding language as a crucial agenda in Protestant theology. See his *Protestantism and Repression: A Brazilian Case Study* (Maryknoll, N.Y.: Orbis Books, 1985).

OSCAR S. SUAREZ

The Church's One Foundation

My proposal is that we begin with a review of our Christological affirmations. After all, Christian theology begins and ends with Jesus Christ. Hence, the Gospel of John has for its opening statement, "In the beginning was the Word. . . ." This means, at the very foundations of history was the Word, "and the Word was with God, and the Word was God." Only after we have understood what it means to affirm Jesus Christ as Lord can we begin thinking about the foundational values on which the church is built.

For this same reason, we need a critique of the conventional thinking regarding the place of Jesus Christ in our moral and religious life. We need this critique as a way of reflecting more deeply about the ultimate ground on which our faith stands, which, in the course of time, has been loosely understood. This need is quite apparent in the language and theology of contemporary fundamentalist sects, such as when they arbitrarily employ such notions as "the acceptance of Jesus Christ as personal Savior and Lord" in relation to the whole project of individual transformation. More often than not, such notions serve merely as magic words for a largely emotional recognition and acceptance of their personal guilt, yet leave unexamined the greater guilt of society and its structures. In short, we may open the possibilities of transformation in the life of the church by welcoming critical inquiry and thinking in the conduct of faith.

Indeed, the church's one foundation is Jesus Christ her Lord. But if Jesus Christ is reduced to a mere mouthful of dogmatic statements, a kind of stereotypical language, or simply an object of devotion, then he is no more than a big icon that commands us to do certain things and has thus been transformed into the image of an authoritarian God.

Yes, Jesus is Lord, but his lordship takes many dimensions and an infinite variety of expressions. This fact is captured by Karl Barth in his phrase "the freedom of God." God is free from the doctrinal structures of thoughts in which we often confine God. One cannot put God within the confines of a box, no matter how big that box, just as one cannot put God in one's pocket as a mere personal savior. While God in Jesus Christ is Lord of history, he does not simply command it from afar — he participates in it as a lowly servant, as a victim, as one of the oppressed, and therefore also as its prophet, judge, and redeemer. This whole dialectic of Christological images is very important for us to understand, because the moment we spiritualize our notions of Christ, he will remain a sacred icon that lives simply in one small corner of our personal lives — someone who cares only about the rituals and routines of our religious life and less as someone who

234

leads us in the deconstruction of oppressive and despotic structures of history.

As I say this, I do not intend to propose the issue of a legislative provision in the constitution. Nobody legislates on theology, just as nobody legislates on issues like love, justice, and peace. But somehow we must find a way by which these foundational issues are seriously brought to bear in the process of revising or reworking the church constitution.

Ecclesial Identity and Historical Vocation

I begin with issues relative to Christological affirmations, since we need to lay down the necessary framework for a transformed ecclesiology. Here I wish to pay some attention to questions and issues that I trust will shed light on our search for a new way of being a church.

The first major area that needs further study is the question of ecclesial identity. By this I refer not only to the name by which we are called in the public realm but to the historical vocation for which we stand as a confessing community. I say "historical vocation" because, theologically speaking, no church worth its salt can exist apart from a clearly defined historical project. To me this is a crucial issue, considering the fact that Philippine Protestantism in general is a by-product of a colonial history that had once defined and therefore dictated our self-understanding, our purpose, even our historical task as a people.

The history of Protestantism in the Philippines, for example, demonstrates this point. In retrospect, the thought of doing mission work in the Philippines inspired the American Board of Missions in the United States at the turn of the century only after receiving the news of Commodore Dewey's so-called victory over Spain in the battle of Manila Bay. Thus when in the United States the debate regarding American occupation of the Philippines ensued, among the first to give a strong favorable endorsement were the mainline Protestant churches. Despite the protest of the Anti-Imperialist League, led by such celebrated personalities as Mark Twain, former presidents Cleveland and Harrison, and many others, the Protestants in the United States believed without doubt that God had thrown the Philippine Islands into American hands — a tribute to the quickly shaping partnership between the Protestant missionary enterprise and the American colonial government.[7] As the rest of the story goes, such partnership led to the

7. See Kenton Clymer, *Protestant Missionaries in the Philippines, 1898–1916* (Urbana:

partitioning of the entire colonial project between those who represented the realm of political governance and the spiritual formation of the colonized. I say "partitioning" because while the missionaries supported the aims of the colonial government, their work was confined to evangelizing and introducing Protestant faith to the natives and had very little voice in criticizing the political policies of the latter, much less in their formulation. In fact, despite the war that eventually raged between the nationalist Filipinos and the American government, the Board of Missions in the United States had often warned their missionaries against any involvement in the political and social issues obtaining in the country.

This history partially also explains why missionary theology gives little attention to injecting a kind of Christian political ethics that took seriously the nationalist aspirations of the Filipino Protestants and the greater public. And so, after many long years, Philippine Protestant theology remains repressed and reactionary — always unmindful of the everyday history that is occurring right under its nose. As I stated in an unpublished paper, "Protestant Absence" in the realm of politics merely reflected the continuing hold of a historically disinterested theology — a tradition too deeply ingrained today in the minds of Filipino Protestants.[8]

In this light we thus need to reexamine who we are as a church. To do that, we must acknowledge our task as one of clarifying our historical calling in the face of so much misery and injustice in society. The failures and shortcomings of our past must not condemn us to a marginal participation in national life, lest we end up capitulating to the dominant and dominative interests of treacherous institutions and powers.

Months ago, I was on my way home and happened to pass by a church that is apparently one of the home bases of the El Shaddai ministries.[9] In front of the church was a huge billboard with this message: "You don't need to know where you are going, as long as you know that God is leading." In other words, it doesn't matter if we are historically innocent or blind, as

University of Illinois Press, 1986). See also Gerald Anderson, "Providence and Politics behind Protestant Missionary Beginnings in the Philippines," in *Studies in Philippine Church History*, ed. Gerald Anderson (Ithaca, N.Y.: Cornell University Press, 1969). See also Roger Bresnahan, *In Time of Hesitation: Anti-imperialist League and the Philippine-American War* (Manila: New Day Publishers, 1981); and Stuart Creighton Miller, *Benevolent Assimilation: The American Conquest of the Philippines, 1899–1903* (New Haven: Yale University Press, 1982).

8. See my dissertation, "The Self-Understanding of the Church and the Quest for Transformation" (Princeton Theological Seminary, 1992), p. 44.

9. This is one of the fastest-growing Catholic charismatic movements in the Philippines. It is led by Bro. Mike Velarde, a former businessman.

long as God leads the way. That statement upset me because deep within me was a strong objection to any assumptions that we can reduce God into a seeing-eye dog. No matter how we read it, such a statement reflects only the way a church evades the need for a clearly defined historical agenda. They care not where they are going, much less what they want to achieve for a historical project. Yet, even in the Bible it is clear that God raises servants in order to lead people out of their miserable histories into a new and better promise. In the Old Testament God always reminded the people that they were called for a certain vocation in history and that the covenant between them and God would be rendered meaningless without a real awareness that they were indeed chosen to shape and fulfill their calling. In that sense we cannot afford to be blind followers, obeying God under the dark shadows of ignorance. God has no need for disciples and servants who are incapable of seeing the hard facts of life and the visions of a new story as a people.

The need to define the historical vocation of the church becomes a much more urgent problem when we consider the sweeping national and global changes taking place today. When I returned home a few months ago from graduate work in the United States, my friends in Manila gave me an update on the situation in the country and the church, including President Ramos's plan that he proudly calls "Philippines 2000." I was told that it projects a highly industrialized and modernized civilization, very much like the process that swept much of the Western world in the last few decades. It is not that I want to stand in the way of progress (after all, transformation has everything to do with questions involving human progress). My concern is with the logic of relationships that accompanies the very process of modernization.

Modernization is not entirely new to us. In fact, the so-called Social Gospel brought to us by the missionaries reflects the very idea of progress they wanted us to absorb. Thus, at the turn of the century, aside from putting up churches, they also put up hospitals, orphanages, and, most important, schools. These institutions were meant to be the first and basic instruments of modernization and progress. Through the schools they built they were hoping to lead us out of the world of primitive life and superstitions to a world of modernity. They taught us to speak their language so we can better appreciate the culture of the West and in so doing made it easier for us to put it into practice. After many years, they were extremely successful, and we hardly expressed any remorse about the American colonial history in the Philippines. Today, our ways of thinking and acting, whether in the realm of religion or of politics, reflect no more than what

I call the ideological captivity of the Filipino. As a theorist has said, "Those of us who have been dominated for so long no longer know how to tell our tales except in the visions and language of the dominant."[10]

Now almost a hundred years after the American occupation, all we get is what Gustavo Gutiérrez calls "the underside of modernity," a people that is well educated but yet remains dominated. The situation points clearly to the underside of modernity if only for the fact that instead of being on top, we have been relegated to the very bottom and margins of social and economic life. I mean to say, in other words, that President Ramos's modernization project is no different from our previous experiences. When that time comes, we would surely be bombarded with many promises and propaganda and would be swayed easily by their grand plans, for which we would be asked to give our support. And yet as far as our experience goes, this is a venture always dominated and played only by the technocrats, the hardcore capitalists and the politicians. The way things are going now, this is likely to be another conspiracy against those of us who are not in the power blocs of Philippine society. And so the question remains: What price do we have to pay for this? Who pays for, and who benefits from, this idea of progress?

It is precisely for this reason that the church must be firm enough in clarifying its historical task. In this process of clarification we need to ask, In whose defense do we exist as a church? By "historical task," then, I mean not simply being prophetic or giving rise to more and more activists in church. Rather, I mean the church's participation in the creation of a fundamentally new and better story as a people. We cannot remain simply telling sad stories of our past. We should look back at them, but they cannot remain the only contents of our memories. Somehow we must learn to take charge of what we want to be as a nation, for our church will be judged in the final reckoning not by the number of congregations we have organized throughout the land, nor by the number of souls we have brought to the fellowship of the church, but ultimately by the kind of stories and tales that come out of the lips of our people. Whether they are sad stories or victorious ones will be the bone of contention in the future.

We thus are after some kind of a shareable story — one in which everyone, regardless of color, gender, or station in life, has a unique contribution. Should not the women, for example, start creating a fundamentally new and better story for themselves? Should not our peasants, our teachers, our urban dwellers, our factory workers, our entire country create for themselves a shareable story? Why so? Because we cannot talk about God as Savior and

10. Halpern, "Transformation."

Lord while dodging the core dramas of our life — those conflictual moments of our narratives. It is for the same reason that in the Old Testament we have a story of a people summarized in one single confession of faith:

> My ancestor was a wandering Aramean, who took his family to Egypt to live. They were few in number when they left there, but they became a large and powerful nation. The Egyptians treated us harshly and forced us to work as slaves. Then we cried out for help to the LORD, the God of our ancestors. He heard us and saw our suffering, hardship, and misery. By his great power and strength he rescued us from Egypt. He worked miracles and wonders, and caused terrifying things to happen. He brought us here and gave us this rich and fertile land. (Deut. 26:5-9, TEV)

Because of our quest for a shared and fundamentally new story, the church must define its historical vocation in society. In the absence of a meaningful participation in a shared historical project, our ministry has no substantive content and our churches will remain mere repositories of arbitrary dogmas and beliefs.

Quest for a Christian Political Ethics

Complementary to a shared historical vocation is a search for a relevant Christian social and political ethics. I am aware of the negative connotation the word "politics" has acquired in our recent history, whether in the ecumenical circle or within the life of individual denominations. The Protestant evasion of politics is a phenomenon that runs throughout most of our history and thus has become a widely accepted ethos in church life. Politics, as the conventional thinking puts it, is not compatible with ecclesial business and, hence, must be kept outside the church door. This assumes that to be a church is to be competent only in things spiritual, or that to be a church is to maintain political innocence.

Such stereotypes reveal to us our inclination to look at the reality of human life in its fragmented forms — fragmented precisely because we cannot see how the varied faces of human life hang together. That which we call a human being constitutes one with a multitude of faces — personal, historical, political, and sacred. Therefore, to deal with persons as if they were mere fragments is to reduce them into partial beings.[11] No wonder

---

11. This contribution of Halpern is more profoundly explained in his work "Transformation."

there are church people today who confess only their personal sins on Sunday morning yet leave intact the ugly realities of structural guilt. There are those who accept Jesus as their personal Savior and Lord and leave their history and destiny in the hands of worldly powers. There are those who anxiously ask God for salvation yet refuse to understand the true nature of hell on earth. These people are nothing but partial beings who embrace nothing more than a partial agenda of life. That perhaps explains why the gospel speaks of the broken body of Christ. Our calling thus becomes one of mending all the fragments of this sacred body that finally we may experience genuine wholeness.

This experience of wholeness makes us free to embrace all aspects of human participation, including politics. Without the experience of wholeness, we would remain captives of dualist and exclusivist theologies, always unable to bridge the gap between the world of faith and the world of politics. Our experience of wholeness, however, brings us to a realization that politics is not a monopoly of the public bureaucrat or any institutions of power. Rather, as Halpern puts it, "politics is participation in a shared enterprise," and therefore no one, no institution, should be outside of political responsibility, not even the strongest defenders of religious orthodoxy. The moment we refuse to deal with things political, we would leave them to the hands of the politicians, the ideologues, and, perhaps worst, the state.

In line with my proposal to launch the quest for a relevant social and political ethics, I wish to point out a few areas of concern that warrant an urgent and serious ethical reflection.

At the top of my agenda in this section are questions involving church and state relations, ideology, power and the administration of justice — those that pertain to the parameters of church participation in political life and the nature of such participation. These are crucial components of ecclesial agenda, at least in our own milieu, considering the vast areas of conflict and the extent to which these conflicts rage in contemporary national life.

The failure of much ethical reflection in the past is its inclination to relegate ethical decisions and choices to individual and personal prerogatives (after all, in a liberal society individual autonomy is a central organizing principle of social justice). While the individual is certainly important, we cannot be blind to the fact that the miseries of society are traceable to their structural roots and therefore are shared by the entire community. Seen in this light, ethics thus must address those issues and must find a way to be operative in the public realm.

Second, it is my conviction that in the face of changing times, our church must be sensitive to a world characterized by cultural pluralism. We must open our ears to a variety of voices that seek to be counted in the search for transformed relationships in church and social life as well as a transforming outlook for ministry. Any church with fixed dogmas is vulnerable to an exclusivist posture. Our experience in the recent past was one of conflict between those who are deemed to be "outsiders" by virtue of their "unfamiliar" political, ideological, and theological positions, and those "insiders" who look at themselves as defenders of tradition. Earlier I spoke of churches living in boxes, meaning that their well-established walls always restrain them from welcoming other ways of being religious or other ways of interpreting Christianity. In those boxes are established tenets of faith, which to many of our church people represent the fixed truths about our faith. Thus any perspective that sounds unfamiliar could be taken as a departure from, if not a negation of, the accepted beliefs. Some people in church feel they are the vanguards of their doctrinal boxes, and so for them, theological dissenters are always suspect.

Here is where we might look at the phenomenon of pluralism as a major item in the agenda of church life. This is no easy venture, especially when we deal with people from the Left and from the Right, women who have been assigned to the margins of participation for so long, struggling professionals who have been fighting on the side of the oppressed sectors of society and for that are themselves oppressed, church workers who have not been given their fair share of opportunities in service, or persons who have become objects of ridicule for their disclosure of sexual preference. I do not have answers to many of these issues, but I am sure that our openness may someday lead to some form of a democratic ecclesiology where we no longer make distinctions between the insiders and the outsiders, between the included and the excluded.

I believe it is a legitimate church business to engage in a quest for a relevant Christian social and political ethics in view of the foregoing arguments. Our failure in this area not only would mean stripping the church of its prophetic task; it also would make the church an anachronism — disappearing into irrelevance at a time when its presence must be visible and its voice clearly heard.

PART THREE

RELIGION, CULTURE, AND POLITICS

• 14 •

Struggles for Peace:
Transformative Cultural Practices
and the Discourses of Dissent

LESTER EDWIN J. RUIZ

Try to love the questions themselves like locked rooms and like
books that are written in a very foreign tongue . . . and the point
is, to live everything. Live the questions now. Perhaps you will
then . . . live . . . into the answer.

Rainer Maria Rilke, *Letters to a Young Poet*

Contestation has become the defining practice of the historical
moment. How we deal with it, how we seek to resolve it, how we
respond to its dangers and possibilities, will determine whether
we are worthy to be called radicals, revolutionaries, democrats, or
whether we are nothing more than the children of modernity's
underside — that self-same practice that has kept the world en-
thralled by its promises, while leaving us in chains.

Lester Edwin J. Ruiz, *A Letter to Colleagues
in the Struggle,* January 6, 1992

An earlier version of this chapter was published under the title "Toward a New Radical
Imaginary: Constructing Transformative Cultural Practices," *Alternatives: Social Transformation and Humane Governance* 19, no. 2 (Spring 1994): 247–61.

Introduction: Peace, Politics, Transformation

With the end of the so-called Cold War, the hope for peace burst onto the world's stage, offering most of the world's peoples the real opportunity to create a more just and humane future. This hope was all but extinguished in the aftermath of the Gulf War and the post post–Cold War era that it ushered in. Mikhail Gorbachev's imaginative vision gave way to George Bush's apocalyptic fantasy of a "new world order." Haiti, Rwanda, and Yugoslavia remind us of the realities of this so-called new world order.[1]

This new world order is believed to be an "international community of states." Even in the post post–Cold War era, the states system has remained as resilient as ever. Many still believe that the territorially bounded state is still the primary political reality of our time. Wars continue to be fought in the name of nation-states, or, at least, the desire for one's own nation-state. The state has successfully claimed the monopoly not only of the legitimate use of violence or coercion but also of how and where political activity legitimately occurs. In this context, politics continues to be defined largely within a statist framework and cannot be understood apart from it.

At the same time, even if one is to assert that the state is the dominant political reality of our time, it is no longer possible to deny that it is a historically constructed "imagined community." Despite the cliché that the state is the primary locus of political activity, all states are now caught up in processes of economic, technological, social, cultural, and political transformations that may be *local* in origin but that are clearly *global* in their trajectories. More

1. Bill Clinton's own international vision, unfortunately, has hewed toward the Reagan-Bush legacy. Indeed, the world's self-appointed leaders today, exemplified by the G-7 countries, have displayed a remarkable lack of imaginative vision as well; they seem prepared to accept, in Jacques Atalli's phrase, the "millennial losers."

In this context, as I complete this article, a U.S.-led military invasion of Haiti is more than likely; over one million Rwandans, tens of thousands of whom are expected to die from cholera, have crossed over into neighboring states as refugees; and the former Yugoslavia remains locked in the conflict in Bosnia and Herzegovina. It is deeply disturbing that all this is happening at a time when the United States, Germany, and Japan are experiencing unparalleled prosperity.

The point is starkly simple: any discussion of Christian ethics needs to face the nihilism that the present global system oriented around multinational capitalism generates. For a fuller discussion of this argument, see Lester Edwin J. Ruiz, "Pastoral Care and Counselling in Twenty-first Century Asia: Meditations on a World Made New," in *Pastoral Care and Counselling in a Pluralistic Society,* ed. Mesach Krisetya (Salatiga, Indonesia: Satya Wacana University, 1994).

important, the plurality of subjects and subject positions that accompany these transformations guarantees that politics, including revolutionary and progressive politics, can no longer be construed as mere contests for power and legitimacy; also, and perhaps more accurately, they are struggles for identity and/or the creation of new and/or alternative forms of community.

Beginning at the End

There are a number of ways to approach politics in this period of profound global transformation. Following Ernesto Laclau's suggestion that "politics is an ontological category; there is politics because there is subversion and dislocation of the social,"[2] I explore in this article the possibility of politics being articulated as *discourses of dissent*. In this context, it is important to identify current sites of struggle or contestation in politics throughout the world as an appropriate context for the articulation of what I shall call in this article "transformative cultural practices." Here there are two somewhat divergent, though not unrelated, conventional logics or trajectories: (1) how the aspirations and approaches of so-called globalists should be developed and recast in the light of recent local historical, political, and intellectual transformations; and (2) how the aspirations and approaches of so-called localists should be developed and recast in the light of recent global historical, political, and intellectual transformations.

Unfortunately, the formulation of these logics is somewhat perplexing, particularly since they seem to presuppose that each one is — or can be — constituted apart from the other. I do not think that this is politically possible or philosophically desirable. At the same time, it is important to emphasize that these logics not only point to some of the current sites of struggle or contestation in politics throughout the world, but they also suggest that the received traditions of politics, whether mainstream, progressive, or leftist, have lost their power to shape human identities and destinies. After all, many will argue, we have reached the "end of history"; in particular, some might even add, the end of *leftist* politics. This seems to be the tired, if unconvincing, conclusion some Western analysts have drawn since Francis Fukuyama deployed Hegel to explain the so-called triumph of the capitalist West and the demise of actually existing socialism, if not socialism itself.[3]

2. Ernesto Laclau, *New Reflections on the Revolution of Our Time* (New York: Verso, 1990), p. 61.
3. Francis Fukuyama, *The End of History and the Last Man* (New York: Free Press, 1992).

The idea of "the end of history" certainly did not begin with Fukuyama. Nor did he exhaust its meaning or significance. Philosophically, many of the works of, say, Martin Heidegger and Jacques Derrida may be interpreted as posing the question of how one does philosophy once philosophy (as a grand narrative) has come to an end. Methodologically, scholars like Hans-Georg Gadamer or Jürgen Habermas may be read as addressing the question of how we do history once history (yet another grand narrative) has come to an end, or what is involved in the study of human practices after positivism has been displaced. From Michel Foucault to Cornel West and Gayatri Spivak, the question "Who comes after the subject?"[4] has hovered behind many of the most profound interrogations of the possibilities of contemporary politics. As Laclau has put it:

> The intellectual climate of recent decades . . . has been dominated by a new, growing and generalized awareness of limits. Firstly, limits of reason . . . from epistemology and the philosophy of science to post-analytical philosophy, pragmatism, phenomenology and post-structuralism. Secondly, limits, or rather slow erosion of the values and ideals of radical transformation, which had given meaning to the political experience of successive generations. And finally, limits arising from the crisis of the very notion of "cultural vanguard" which marked the different moments of modernity.[5]

This awareness of "limits" has generated a number of responses: on the one hand, a sustained defense of modernity, as in the work of Jürgen Habermas, particularly as an epistemological, moral, and political justification of the project of Enlightenment freedom; on the other hand, an equally passionate affirmation of "postmodernity," as in the work of Jean François Lyotard, especially as a philosophical, methodological, and political antidote to the effective historical consciousness of modernity. In fact, the question of limits is one form of the question of "end," which can be interpreted as having a double signification. First, we are today faced with a profound skepticism about modernity as the commanding practice of our age, due in part to the failures of modern institutions to deliver what they promised; second, we are experiencing the limits of human understanding, what some unrepentant moderns call "the crisis of reason," precisely because of the contingent and precarious nature of the historicity of being, or what I prefer to call human practices.

---

4. Eduardo Cadava, Peter Connor, and Jean-Luc Nancy, eds., *Who Comes after the Subject?* (New York: Routledge, 1991).

5. Laclau, *New Reflections on the Revolution of Our Time*, p. 3 n. 1.

Yet, this coming to an "end," far from leading to the surrender of emancipatory projects, actually opens up to extraordinary opportunities for dissent and transgression, for a radical critique of the different forms of domination in our time; they can lead to the formulation of liberation projects until now restrained, if not curtailed altogether, by what Laclau called, rather tongue-in-cheek, the "rationalist dictatorship of the Enlightenment." Indeed, as I will try to argue in this article, following Laclau (though at some distance), the recognition of contingency and of the historicity of being are preconditions for the construction of transformative cultural practices: concrete, empirical realities embodied in rhetorical forms, gestures, procedures, modes, shapes, genres of everyday life — discursive formations and/or strategies, if you will, which Michael Ryan understood as a "radically contingent arena of imagination, strategy, and creative manoeuvre."[6] It may lead to the articulation, not only of a new progressive politics, but of transformative cultural practices that are discourses of dissent.

On the Role and Meaning of Dissent

Julia Kristeva, French feminist philosopher, writes in her essay "A New Type of Intellectual: The Dissident" that "Our present age is one of exile. How can we avoid sinking into the mire of common sense, if not by becoming a stranger to one's own country, language, sex, and identity? Writing is impossible without some kind of exile . . . [which is] already itself a form of dissidence, since it involves uprooting oneself from family, a country or a language. . . . For true dissidence today is perhaps simply what it has always been: thought."[7]

In a different, though not unrelated, vein, Michel Foucault writes in *The Order of Things*, "It is no longer possible to think in our day other than in the void left by man's disappearance. For this void does not create a deficiency; it does not constitute a lacuna that must be filled. It is nothing more, and nothing less, than the unfolding of a space in which it is once more possible to think."[8]

6. Michael Ryan, *Politics and Culture: Working Hypotheses for a Post-Revolutionary Society* (Baltimore: Johns Hopkins University Press, 1989), p. 97.
7. Julia Kristeva, "A New Type of Intellectual: The Dissident," in *The Kristeva Reader*, ed. Toril Moi (New York: Columbia University Press, 1986), pp. 292–99.
8. Michel Foucault, *The Order of Things: An Archaeology of the Human Sciences* (New York: Random House, 1973), p. 32.

At the heart of dissent — as exile and sites of contestation — is both the recognition of limits and the transgression of those limits. It is, to borrow from R. B. J. Walker and Richard K. Ashley, "a readiness to question how meaning and order are imposed, not the search for a source of meaning and order already in place; the unrelenting and meticulous analysis of the workings of power in modern global life, not the longing for a sovereign figure (be it man, God, nation, state, paradigm, or research program) that promises deliverance from power; the struggle for freedom, not a religious desire to produce some territorial domicile of self-evident being that men of innocent faith can call home."[9]

This transgression of limits is more than refusal. Unlike conventional criticism, it always and already includes a recognition of possibilities — the opening of new spaces for thinking, feeling, and acting — and the articulation of strategies of questioning, analyzing, and resisting. But why dissent *as transgression?* First, my own reading of the struggles for peace and justice that I mention in this article is that they are discourses of dissent precisely because they articulate alternatives to the dominant forms of thinking, feeling, and acting. Second, and this is the central argument of this article, discourses of dissent, often misunderstood as simply the regulative dimension of an otherwise totalized, if not hegemonic, political reality, in fact are not only constitutive of political discourse but are the condition of possibility for any kind of progressive, transformative politics.

By "discourse" I mean something more than speech — indeed, more than what Habermas calls "performative speech," or even "communicative action." Speech, to be sure, is socially structured discourse. The latter, following Foucault, comprises plays of power that mobilize rules, codes, and procedures to assert particular meanings through the construction of knowledges within these rules, codes, and procedures. Often, these rules govern human practices that are implicit and not clearly defined, but since they are socially constructed in specific contexts, they have institutional origins and commitments. To put it another way, discourses are systematically organized sets of statements that express the meanings and values of an institution. Beyond their role in defining, describing, and delimiting what is possible to say and not to say, they circumscribe what can and cannot be done.

9. Richard K. Ashley and R. B. J. Walker, "Speaking the Language of Exile: Dissident Thought in International Studies," *International Studies Quarterly* 34 (September 1990): 265.

A New Progressive Left Politics
in a Post Post–Cold War Era?

Understanding these transformative cultural practices can be achieved only by traveling through concrete, historical movements. Thus, it is necessary to ask whether progressive and leftist discourses are still a reality, not to mention whether they are desirable or achievable, in the post post–Cold War era. I believe with some confidence that we can answer in the affirmative. But why "progressive and leftist" movements? Only because they are articulations of what I have called sites of dissent, contestation, and difference. As I will argue in this article, these sites are critical to the articulation of transformative cultural practices; they are constitutive of these struggles.

In July 1990, at the invitation of the Workers Party of Brazil, some forty-eight leftist parties, organizations, and fronts — including the Sandinista National Liberation Front (FSLN), the Farabundo Marti National Liberation Front (FMLN), the Democratic Party of the Revolution of Mexico (PDR), the Broad Front of Uruguay (FA), the Free Bolivar Movement of Bolivia (MBL), the United Left of Peru (IU), and the Lavalas Movement of Haiti — met in São Paulo for what was perhaps one of the major gatherings of progressives and leftists after the so-called end of the Cold War. The final resolution of this historic gathering expressed the "joint determination to renew leftist thought, to correct erroneous conceptions, to overcome all bureaucratism and all obstacles to an authentically social and mass democracy."[10]

Sixty popular, democratic political formations from Latin America and the Caribbean, three major conferences and statements (São Paulo in 1990, Mexico City in 1991, and Managua in 1992), and now, five years after the first of those conferences, the Movimiento y Partidos Políticos del Foro de São Paulo has developed into a major leftist political formation that underscores the profound transformations that are occurring in leftist theory and practice in the South. In the June 1991 meeting, hosted by the Mexican Democratic Revolutionary Party, the forum described itself as "frank, open, democratic, pluralist, and unitary, involving a broad spectrum of forces . . . [and declared that] some of us identify ourselves as nationalist, democratic, and popular, and others are decidedly socialist. We are all committed to the structural transformations of our societies necessary to fulfill the aspirations of our peoples for social justice, democracy, and national liberation."[11]

10. "Declaración de São Paulo," São Paulo, July 4, 1990, in *Boletín Sur-Sur* 1 (1991): 6.
11. "Declaración de México," Mexico City, June 15, 1991, in *Boletín Sur-Sur* 1 (1991): 8.

In a different, though not unrelated, event, the III Encuentro Continental de Resistencia Indigena, Negra y Popular, representing twenty-six countries without distinction of race, language, or culture, met October 7–12, 1992, in Managua, reaffirming both their campaign, begun in 1989, against the Five Hundredth Centennial (1492–1992) and their goal to "generate a broad, pluralistic, multi-ethnic and democratic movement" to work for a new international economic, social, political, and environmental order.[12] The "Declaración de Managua" was passionate even as it was incisive, uncompromising even as it was compassionate. In part it read:

> At five hundred years — here we are! In a world in which the plundering and the secular exploitation of our resources and our labor changed us into an inexhaustible power of capitalist accumulation and of the industrial development and technology of our new masters; prisoners of the profiteering and the merchandising of an unending chain of consumption for some and scarcity for others; victims again of a new conquest whose religion is money and individualism; with the people of our land divided between those who have concentrated power, technology, and well-being and those who are marginalized and excluded. . . .
>
> . . . The new crusaders of neoliberal civilization speak to us now about democracy, about development, about modernization and productivity, when in our countries democracy turns out to be unattainable in the face of the increasing polarization between rich and poor and the rise in unemployment, malnutrition, and illiteracy; in the face of the increasing erosion of social gains and collective rights, the accelerated privatization of state enterprises and of social services, the crisis of values and the deepening of racism and discrimination. In their arrogance, these new preachers pretend to hide a reality that we can see clearly: capitalism does not have the solutions needed to guarantee a world of peace and social justice. . . .
>
> . . . At 500 years — here we are! We are rediscovering our roots, men and women, without differences based on skin color, language, culture, or territorial boundary; we are recovering what is ours and constructing an alternative framework to that which threatens and attacks us. In this new framework misery and suffering are excluded; our cultures, languages, and beliefs flourish without fears or prohibitions; we recover our autonomy and the forms of self-government that made us great in the past; we find the enablement of our native aptitudes for art and beauty; we destroy the chains of oppression shackling our women and provide

12. "Declaración de Managua," October 12, 1992, in *Boletín Sur-Sur* 3 (1993): 4ff.

a future for our children and young people; Mother Nature is reconciled with her human children in her lap; war exists only in the memory of evil times; we can look at ourselves face to face, the one to the other, without feeling the embarrassment of hate or contempt; and we are united in love, solidarity, and hope.[13]

William I. Robinson observes that as a progressive and leftist framework, the formations noted above have articulated a theory and practice that challenge not only the sectarianism and vanguardism of the more conventional, if not traditionalist, leftist perspectives but the very paradigms on which these practices rest. Robinson summarizes his observations thus: revolution and democracy are indivisible; revolutionary projects may unfold in the context of political and social pluralism, civic and electoral competition; military fetishism is out of date; revolutionary movements must move from ideology to a politics rooted in the specific realities of the nation; progressive change and revolutionary transformation of society are not one-class projects; the relations among the state, civil society, and power must be restructured; the days of vanguardism and verticalism are over; the autonomy of the new social movements must be respected and encouraged.[14]

A number of themes that have a direct bearing on the central argument of this article stand out in Robinson's description. Unfortunately, he fails to mention the feminist, ecological, and nonstatist dimensions of these new movements, thereby overlooking the critical transformations that are occurring in these movements, which make them significantly different from their predecessors. First, there is a clear, even fierce, affirmation of the peoples of the South as the subjects of their own history. Second, there is an unequivocal emphasis on the plurality of struggles not only at the level of strategy and tactics but especially at the ideological, political, and organizational levels. Third, there is an uncompromising commitment to a nationalist, popular, and socialist vision of the future of the peoples of the South, and, in contrast, a clear repudiation of the present global system oriented around the logic (and practices) of multinational capitalism. I interpret these themes to be pointing to the three questions I focus on in this article: (1) the question of the Subject — not only *who* the subject is but *what* being a subject entails; (2) the question of the social totality, that is, its historicity, contingency, and plurality; and (3) the question of the construction of a new radical imaginary, not just theoretically, but practically. Taken together, these three questions

13. Ibid.
14. William I. Robinson, "The São Paulo Forum: Is There a New Latin American Left?" *Monthly Review* 44 (December 1992): 1–11.

may be read as suggesting what elements are needed for the articulation of a politics demanded by the needs of a post post–Cold War era.

Transformative Cultural Practices:
The Question of the Social Totality, the Myth of the Subject, and the Importance of a New Radical Imaginary

The work of the World Order Models Project (WOMP) has received considerable attention from peace activists, public policy experts, and academics, particularly in its earlier formulations. WOMP is a transnational association of scholar-activists who, through interdisciplinary, multicultural research, education, and advocacy, are committed to peace, economic well-being, social justice, ecological balance, and positive identity. The various responses to WOMP have been interesting, instructive, sometimes even inspiring. Unfortunately, many critics have failed to see its significance as a site of struggle or contestation, a metaphoric disclosure, if you will, of larger social and political questions. As a consequence, the debate has concealed some of the fundamental philosophical, methodological, and political questions, three of which I have already noted. It is these questions that I want to explore in this article not simply as a review of WOMP but, more important, as an articulation of questions and issues that confront scholar-activists in the peace and world order studies field, in particular, and of politics under the sign of modernity, in general.

The Question of the Social Totality

First, I want to suggest that one of the important contributions of WOMP, in particular, and peace and world order studies, in general, to the construction of transformative cultural practices is its insistence on posing the question of the social totality. Challenging the statist, technostrategic, and decontextualized rationality of what Richard Falk calls the realist consensus, a number of scholar-activists associated with WOMP have asserted that the social totality cannot be reduced to statist, empiricist, and positivist construals of political identity and practice.[15] This is the meaning of that

---

15. See, for example, R. B. J. Walker, *One World, Many Worlds: Struggles for a Just World Peace* (Boulder, Colo.: Lynne Rienner Publishers, 1988); Saul H. Mendlovitz and R. B. J. Walker, eds., *Contending Sovereignties: Redefining Political Community* (Boulder, Colo.: Lynne Rienner Publishers, 1990).

254

intensely problematic, but nevertheless significant, phrase "peace and world order perspective." But what is included in this perspective?

First, a struggle theory of history, which recognizes the poor and the oppressed, the marginalized and the dispensable, as critical fountainheads for transformation, but which does not reduce struggle to the Marxist-oriented idea of class struggle. Second, a pluralistic notion of political agency, best exemplified by critical social movements and of global civil society, but also of statist-oriented actors involved in some aspects of political and social change (e.g., progressive political leaders, progressive state-oriented blocs, international organizations). Third, a value-explicit understanding of political practice and identity. In fact, these scholar-activists have recognized the intensely contested character of planetary life, as well as its unevenness and asymmetry. As well, they have defended the necessity, if not desirability, of incorporating a multiplicity of subjects both in its analysis of "what is" and "what ought to be."[16]

What is interesting, however, is not the established consensus around a struggle theory of history, or even the affirmation of a plurality of subjects and transition strategies to arrive at what in WOMP discourse is called a preferred world. Rather, what is critical is the *significance* of this struggle theory, or, put more precisely, the significance of struggles in the constitution of a peace and world order studies perspective or framework. I take this to be Laclau's argument, in his work cited earlier in this article, on the constitutive character of antagonism and dislocation for a new and radical politics for our time. But what is this peace and world order studies framework? What is its "end"? It may be argued that there are a number of competing ends within the field of peace and world order studies. I want to suggest that there is an implicit, if not tacit, acceptance of a global polity as the end that ought to, if not actually, organize the social totality. In fact, there appears to be agreement that there is indeed some ultimate coherence and rationality in history — that is, that a fixed positivity or objectivity is both possible and desirable.[17]

16. Publications of scholar-activists involved with the World Order Models Project (WOMP) include Saul H. Mendlovitz, ed., *On the Creation of a Just World Order* (New York: Free Press, 1975); Richard Falk, Samuel Kim, and Saul Mendlovitz, eds., *Towards a Just World Order* (Boulder, Colo.: Westview Press, 1982); Richard Falk, Robert Johansen, and Samuel Kim, eds., *The Constitutional Foundations of World Peace* (Albany: State University of New York Press, 1992). See also WOMP's quarterly journal *Alternatives: Social Transformation and Humane Governance.* For a complete bibliography of works published under the auspices of WOMP, write World Order Models Project, 475 Riverside Drive, #460, New York, New York 10115, USA.

17. See Mendlovitz, *On the Creation of a Just World Order,* as well as Richard Falk's

But this is precisely what is in question. To put the matter in its most blunt form, I want to suggest that a peace and world order studies perspective is today impossible — at least as it has emerged within the project of modernity, which assumes an ultimate coherence and rationality in history. For the idea of a global polity, apart from what appears today as the existence of such a global polity, particularly under the sign of modernity, requires not only an understanding of what constitutes that polity; it also must posit its constitution or institutionalization. To be sure, there are competing visions of a global polity — Leninist, Wilsonian, Gandhian, to name only a few. But the conditions of their being constituted are, at best, contested. And as long as they are contested, their constitution as an objectivity is put in question. They are contested by the antagonisms and dislocations inherent in the multiplicity of subjects and subject positions that today characterize the social totality.

In brief, following Laclau, I want to argue that for as long as antagonisms (and not simply contradiction) exist, global polity or even peace, but especially politics, cannot constitute itself into a fixed positivity. For antagonism is the limit of all objectivity; that is, it prevents the constitution of objectivity itself. I suspect that the idea of global polity (and other similar notions) tends to function as a Hegelian house of identity. It provides political and methodological distanciation that allows for critique, it creates a space in which differences may be recognized, and it supplies a *telos* (a rationality, if you will) so history can have meaning. But again, it is this meaning, this end, that is problematic, since it subsumes, and thus overcomes, differences even as it classifies the world. It is somewhat ironic, then, that even as WOMP, for example, opens up to a fundamental and radical critique of the social totality by insisting on the importance of struggles in the construction of transformative cultural practices, it tends to step back and attempt to integrate this understanding into a rather traditional kind of grand theory of history or politics. It continues to dwell in Hegel's house of Reason, which in our time could very well be a house of cards.

This is not to reject the idea of a peace and world order studies perspective or even a political project to constitute a global polity. In fact, I will suggest later in this article that the latter may very well be necessary to the construction of a radical imaginary. But let me dwell on this matter of antagonism for a moment longer. It is critical to emphasize that antag-

---

report to the Global Civilization Project, entitled "Challenges for Sovereignty, Democracy, and Security," published as *From Geopolitics to Humane Governance: Toward a New Global Politics* (Cambridge: Polity Press, 1994).

onism is not just a theoretical construct. Antagonisms are practices articulated by a multiplicity of subjects and subject positions. Scholar-activists in WOMP, for example, have recognized these antagonisms inherent in the multiplicity of subjects and subject positions in their continuing quest for appropriate forms not only of resistance and solidarity but also of polity and governance. It has quite successfully, in my view, made the case for the normative and analytic importance, even decisiveness, of practices that have come under the names "movement for a just world peace," "critical social movements," and "global civil society."[18]

What is interesting, from the perspective of this article, is less the achievement of incorporating, if not taking seriously, these subjects in political theorizing and practice, and more their importance in the very transformation not only of our frameworks but of our constructions of transformative cultural practices. The affirmation of plurality, or difference, or the multiplicity of subjects and subject positions implies a fundamental challenge to some of the preferred trajectories or favorite strategies of peace and world order practices. In fact, this affirmation has a twofold significance. On the one hand, plurality presupposes the recognition of different centers of power, thereby challenging those centralizing logics implicit in many of modernity's projects. Such centers function as dislocatory practices, putting in question institutional logics that are hegemonic and underscoring the historical and contingent character of these logics and practices. On the other hand, plurality points to different constructions of community and identity, alternative forms of knowledge and being, and diverse political strategies — all of which underscore the impossibility not only of a fixed positivity but of genuinely *other* spaces for the construction of transformative cultural practices. Precisely because of this multiplicity of subjects and subject positions that function as dislocatory practices, we understand that our frameworks and perspectives — indeed, our preferred worlds and transition strategies — are radically contingent, precarious, and historical. We are brought face to face with our end, with our limits.

The importance of acknowledging our limits or the radical historicity of our being and of our projects through a recognition of the plurality of subjects and their dislocatory effects cannot be underestimated. The very construction of transformative cultural practices, including the determination of the subjects of transformation, rests on this. More important, the

18. See especially Walker, *One World, Many Worlds;* see also Falk, *From Geopolitics to Humane Governance;* and Saul H. Mendlovitz and R. B. J. Walker, eds., *Towards a Just World Peace: Perspectives from Social Movements* (London: Butterworth, 1987).

fact of our limits puts us in proximity with what might be called the constitutive outside of the limit itself, which is an absence. But this absence is not a lack. In fact, it is the dimension of mystery, of the nonconceptualizable, of the unimaginable — which is the condition of possibility for articulating transformative cultural practices that are fundamentally new and better. This is how I read Laclau's suggestion, noted in this article, that any radical imaginary "bears no relation of continuity with the dominant 'structural objectivity.'" In sum, as Laclau notes: "The plurality of dislocations generates a plurality of centres of relative power, and the expansion of all social logic thus takes place on a terrain that is increasingly dominated by elements external to it. Accordingly, articulation is constitutive of all social practice. But if that is the case, to the very extent that dislocations increasingly dominate the terrain of an absent structural determination, the problem of who articulates comes to occupy a more central position."[19]

The Myth of the Subject

A second important contribution of peace and world order studies, in general, and WOMP, in particular, to the construction of transformative cultural practices in our time is its insistence on the need for the creation of a new myth of the Subject: the global citizen. Indeed, it is possible to argue that the work of some peace scholar-activists is a sustained exercise in articulating not only *who* is the subject of transformation but also *what* being a subject entails. In the World Order Models Project, for example, this question of the Subject finds its most recent formulation in the work of Saul Mendlovitz, though in its various forms it has been articulated as Richard Falk's idea of the citizen-pilgrim, or the Global Civilization Project's notion of the politics of conviction, or R. B. J. Walker's idea of critical social movements. On their own terms these notions of the subject are a powerful and intriguing invitation to consider not only a new myth of the Subject but new forms of identities and/or cultural practices. At the same time, not only do they underscore a plurality of perspectives on this question among peace scholar-activists, but they also reveal in a poignant way the difficult problems of identity and agency posed by the question of the Subject.

In an essay coauthored by Saul Mendlovitz and Lester J. Ruiz entitled "Algunas notas sobre mitos, política e identidad: El sujeto, el constitucionalismo global y la identidad basada en la especie," Saul Mendlovitz reaffirms

19. Laclau, *New Reflections on the Revolution of Our Time*, p. 59.

his long-held basic assumption that human history is at an axial moment in which the effective historical consciousness of a territorially fixed identity that has been wedded to the nation-state is breaking down in the face of an emerging global civilization or polity and its accompanying myth of species identity, that is, the global citizen.[20]

This argument is not new, especially within WOMP. What is interesting, however, is its articulation as a cultural practice within the framework of a global civil society, democratic constitutionalism, and a global human interest. By human interest I mean those broad sets of normative practices, articulated in people's struggles and their histories, and often expressed as concerns for the possibility of justice. To be sure, myths and mythmaking are critical to the construction of transformative cultural practices. Mendlovitz recognizes this factor but diverges from Ruiz in arguing that the importance of the myth of the global citizen lies in its being *already* historically constituted, that it is an *objective* identity. Indeed, his argument is that not only is it desirable to construct a new myth of the Subject, but that this subject has already come into being — and therefore one need only recognize this historical emergence and increase its number throughout the planet. This is an almost irresistible argument. For it is, indeed, a desirable political project; at the same time, I fear it continues to be entangled with a metaphysics of presence that seems to have accompanied WOMP in its many political and epistemological travels. Additionally, it undermines the metaphoric character of myth, thereby working against its transformative potentials.

In his article cited earlier, Laclau has argued (persuasively, in my opinion) that any subject is a mythical subject. By "myth" he meant "a space of representation which bears no relation of continuity with the dominant 'structural objectivity.'" They often emerge in those times when there are structural dislocations in the social totality. But because of the very structure of myths (i.e., what Paul Ricoeur called their tensive character) and their emergence in times of structural dislocations, they function as a constitutive outside to the existing identities that have been constructed and have crystallized into fixed positivities. This is part of the argument that is being made for the emergence of a new myth of the Subject in the work of Mendlovitz and Ruiz noted previously.

The historical effects of myths on objectivity are similar to the effects

20. Saul H. Mendlovitz and Lester Edwin J. Ruiz, "Algunas notas sobre mitos, política e identidad: El sujeto, el constitucionalismo global y la identidad basada en la especie," in *Paz y prospectiva: Problemas globales y futuro de la humanidad,* ed. F. Munoz, J. Sanchez Cazorla, et al. (Granada, Spain: Servicio de Publicaciones de la Universidad, 1994).

of contingent, dislocatory practices on fixed positivities. They place in question existing structures, decenter centralizing logics, and hasten the destructuration of structural determinations. Laclau's notion of the political as an ontological category, Victor Turner's liminality, and Gadamer's "transformation of play into structure" may be read as parallel, if not similar, notions of dislocatory practices.[21] This is where WOMP's myth of the Subject needs to be located, both functionally and structurally. It is noteworthy that the essay alluded to above seeks to shift the focus of the question of the Subject from *who* the subject is to *what* being a subject entails, as well as underscores that mythmaking involves historical and contingent constructions of human identity, interest, and practice. At the same time, it is not altogether clear, particularly in the other works of Mendlovitz, whether this myth of the Subject is construed as a fixed positivity or whether it is a dislocatory practice. Whichever function it plays or is made to play in our discourses will have significant bearing on our capacity to enhance or extend the possibilities of radical transformation in our time.

The Importance of a New Radical Imaginary

The myth of the Subject, at least in WOMP, is closely tied to the notion of an emerging global polity or civilization. As noted above, the emergence of a global civilization and the construction of practices and identities that are appropriate and adequate to this historical emergent require accompanying historical agents. At the same time, however, these historical agents are always in the process of being constituted; human agency is an incomplete (contingent, historical, precarious) project of articulation. But precisely because the myths of the Subject are metaphoric in character, which means it has both literal and figurative dimensions, surface and depth structures, they are essentially unstable. Moreover, this instability reinforces a profound semantic ambiguity in the structure of myths that, in turn, creates a radical undecidability, even as it creates an epistemological (and political) realm of freedom. Put differently, the meaning of a myth is external to its structure. That is, it requires a horizon that both limits and expands its structure and character.

21. See Hans-Georg Gadamer, *Truth and Method* (London: Sheed & Ward, 1975); Victor Turner, *Dramas, Fields, and Metaphors* (Ithaca, N.Y.: Cornell University Press, 1974). The comparison is meant to suggest the widespread recognition of the significance of antagonism and dislocation (Laclau), play, ritual, and art (Gadamer), and liminality (Turner) for politics and transformation.

An imaginary, Laclau points out, is a horizon. It is, he notes, "not one among other objects but an absolute limit which structures a field of intelligibility and is thus the condition of possibility for the emergence of any object."[22] The construction of these imaginaries, it has been pointed out, occurs as stable structures of meaning break down. In short, the existence of antagonisms and dislocations are necessary to the emergence of new imaginaries. The opposite of this is also true, namely, when antagonisms are disciplined and therefore devolve into mere contradiction, the possibility of a new imaginary is seriously compromised. More important, the historical — indeed, dynamic — conjuncture of instability, freedom, and the emergence of new social imaginaries is the context for the articulation of normative frameworks, the "ground," if you will, for ethics. Similarly, the loss of this dynamic conjuncture heralds the eclipse, if not the death, of ethics. Thus, this is where the importance of a new radical imaginary may be situated.

Of a number of ideas that have functioned over the past twenty years as quasi-imaginaries in the field of peace and world order studies, but especially in WOMP, one might suggest that it is the idea of an emerging global civilization or global polity that has gained some prominence. This functional equivalent is not unrelated to the idea of a peace and world order studies perspective. Thus, it has historical, structural, conceptual/philosophical, normative, and analytic dimensions. But precisely because it tends to be construed as a historical "fact" and not as a dynamic horizon, it has tended to conceal, if not altogether obliterate, the conditions of possibility for the constitution of a radical imaginary, not to mention new subjects and subject positions. In fact, the ideas of world order, or global civilization or global polity, have tended to lose their metaphoric character as their literal content overcomes the mythical space to which the imaginary points. The disjuncture of "is" and "is not" succumbs to the literalization of the horizon. This loss of the metaphoric character of both myth and horizon is most probably related to the failure to problematize the language itself, but it also may be due to a lack of appreciation for the significance of antagonism and dislocation for the very constitution of the myth and of the horizon (or the imaginary).

In fact, it is important to acknowledge that the idea of global polity or global citizen has emerged in the context of the particular experiences of WOMP scholar-activists throughout the world. It may be argued that the idea of peace and/or world order (as with the ideas "the state," "the

22. Laclau, *New Reflections on the Revolution of Our Time*, p. 40.

Communist society," or "modern civilization" that arose in the context of particular historical needs) emerged as a result of particular demands in particular social groups and has functioned as a wide-ranging set of dislocations: the struggles against statist, positivist, empiricist theories and practices of the 1960s and 1970s, and supplemented by increasing social demands from other contexts that, in turn, increased the number of dislocations within specific disciplinary methodological and substantive horizons. In this sense, "peace and world order studies" was genuinely and closely tied to the individual and collective identities of the participants themselves and thus was truly mythical and imaginary. Unfortunately, the metaphorization of literal social demands appears to have gradually been literalized in the field, or at least is in danger of being literalized. And the idea of global polity or global citizen, because of the insistence on fixed interpretations of these myths, has made it increasingly difficult for the imaginary to absorb or integrate new antagonisms and dislocations. Thus, its being a horizon or an imaginary is lost.

Therefore, the idea of a horizon or of a radical imaginary is inextricably tied to the personal, political, and historical dimensions of community and identity. It is the dislocations experienced by particular social groups that are the conditions of possibility for the articulation of new imaginaries. And it is these social groups, as subjects and subject positions, that articulate these new imaginaries. At the same time, these imaginaries, once articulated as metaphoric disclosures of "what is" and "what is not," horizon the possibilities of constructing transformative cultural practices. Without a radical imaginary, the transformation of the subjects and of subject positions within the social totality is questionable; but without these subjects and subject positions that articulate dislocatory practices, the radical imaginary devolves into a literal construction without meaning.

Thus, as we look beyond the context of WOMP's Cold War era and toward the articulation of new and/or alternative progressive politics for a post post–Cold War period, it may be necessary to reexamine our imaginaries and to ask, once again, whether the horizon of global polity or global civilization or peace and world order studies, especially under the sign of modernity, do in fact function as genuine radical imaginaries; or whether, in our carelessness, we have allowed them to devolve into mere literality. To say that our imaginary has been literalized is not to suggest that it belongs in the "dustbins of history," as some critics have suggested. In fact, imaginaries do get constituted and dissolved, metaphorized and literalized. What is critical is the dislocation of a literalized imaginary, to open it once more to the possibility of metaphorization. As I argue in this article, this dislo-

262

cation is achieved as the antagonisms of the social totality are recognized and taken with utmost seriousness. What kinds of dislocatory practices might be identified to open to the conditions of possibility will be taken up in the next section.

Dissent as Affirmation and Transgression of Limits: Transformative Cultural Practices and the Politics of the Political

I want to suggest that the future of the peace and world order studies field, in particular, and of any progressive politics, in general, lies in taking seriously what Laclau, noted earlier, called the subversion and dislocation of the social. One of the critical roles scholar-activists can play is to participate in communities of dissent. In order to do this we will need to find the grace and the courage to affirm and transgress our limits, dissenting against established orthodoxies — whether they be personal, historical, or religious. When put in this way, a number of pathways present themselves to us.

1. joining or constructing communities of resistance and solidarity, not just in order to create or re-create the world, but to construct social agents who transform their worlds and themselves while forging new identities;
2. celebrating the refusal to constitute theoretical and practical fixed positivities or objectivities, guarding against the temptation to suture what appear to be structural dislocations within social totalities;
3. welcoming antagonism and dislocations, seeking to expand their range and depth as conditions of possibility for the construction of transformative cultural practices;
4. engaging in democratic struggles that decenter logics of domination and exclusion, not simply working toward structures without a center, but engaging in the practices of decentering through antagonisms or dislocatory practices.

Can these pathways be further delineated? Indeed, what might communities of dissent look like?

In the first place, communities of dissent, which are at the same time communities of resistance and solidarity, are political communities that are committed to deliberation as constitutive of their existence. Deliberation

263

cannot be reduced to mere speech. It encompasses the whole range of participative practices that Habermas, when disciplined of his flirtations with "ideal speech situations," is pointing to in his theory of communicative action; it is illustrated by Paulo Friere's dialogics of liberation; it is exemplified by Manfred Halpern's politics of transformation.[23] These communities presuppose a recognition and affirmation not only of the plurality of human life, celebrating difference as constitutive of human life, but also of meaningful and direct participation in the governance of the community — whatever level is called for. As Charles Taylor puts it, though in a different context: "It is not enough that a given regime take account of my values, which it might do without thought or action on my part . . . what is important is that I play a part in a common deliberation."[24]

This practical activity of participation and solidarity challenges the statist, bureaucratic, and hierarchical structures of domination. This is the significance, for example, of the Base Ecclesial Communities in Central and South America, the Philippines, and elsewhere. These communities of resistance and solidarity are models of radically democratic, participatory political communities that not only are reversing hierarchical and bureaucratic structures of religious and political institutions, shifting the locus of power from these dominative centers and restoring it to those who are struggling for liberation and transformation, but are retrieving the meaning and significance of popular participation, which has largely been eclipsed by formal representation in liberal democratic regimes. In short, they are political events that mark not only the rediscovery of democracy but also its deepening.

Deliberation, when located within the historical framework of domination, becomes deliberation about and toward liberation. Here liberation may be interpreted as a radical imaginary. It thus shapes the struggles for liberation even as it seeks to deny the closure of liberation while refusing to be reduced only to a tool for attaining the goals of revolution. Using the analogy of speech, it may be argued that part of the problem of the practices of domination is the refusal to allow the voices of the people to be heard. Deliberation is the restoration of speaking to the speechless, of granting

---

23. Cf. Jürgen Habermas, *The Theory of Communicative Action* (Boston: Beacon Press, 1984–87); Paulo Friere, *The Pedagogy of the Oppressed* (New York: Herder & Herder, 1970); and Manfred Halpern, "Transformation: Essays for a Work-in-Progress," unpublished manuscript, Princeton University, 1993.

24. Charles Taylor, "The Philosophy of the Social Sciences," in *Political Theory and Political Education,* ed. Melvin Richter (Princeton: Princeton University Press, 1980), p. 79.

power to the powerless, and of protecting and nurturing these voices from those who would silence them. Politics turns out to be a politics of struggle.

In the second place, as deliberating communities, communities of dissent point to the creation and preservation of what Hannah Arendt called the common, that is, the public realm.[25] Contrary to those dominative practices that reduce the common to a pre-given structure of reality through discursive strategies that naturalize and universalize particular ethnocentric projects, the common is the space for difference constructed by deliberating communities as they seek meaningful consensus. Political communities committed to the critical retrieval and preservation of the common, particularly a global common, cast suspicion on the logocentric and totalizing dispositions of the dominant narrative of modernity and undermine its hegemony. It also redefines the common beyond the boundaries of the present states system, recognizing not only our shared global context or our profoundly pluralistic existence but our identity as human subjects and as subject positions.

In the third place, communities of dissent articulate human identities that are historical, contingent, and precarious. They are points of entry and departure, beginnings but not final solutions. This is not a deficiency, however. Such a construal of community not only celebrates the fact of its historicality, that is, its always being in the process of being created and re-created toward, in this instance, shared goals of justice and freedom. More important, it affirms their given limits, rooted in their own space and time and culture and society. This necessary limitation, which reveals the realm of mystery, of the nonconceptualizable — of transcendence, if you will (what Derrida may be alluding to in his notions of the undecidable, the incommensurable, the incalculable) — is transformed into a practical critique that makes transgressions possible, thereby undermining, subverting, and putting into question those dominative practices that shape present-day political experience. Equally important, this limitation guarantees the possibility that "the executioner does not have the last say," or, in theological language, that justice and not law is the last horizon for human life.[26]

Moreover, such communities cannot be limited to one historical expression, such as an encompassing political subject, a universal class, or the rational state. This is not a refusal to identify which historical communities are the bearers of the possibilities of transformation. Rather, it is a recog-

25. Hannah Arendt, *The Human Condition* (Chicago: University of Chicago Press, 1958).

26. See, e.g., Jacques Derrida, "Force of Law: The Mystical Foundation of Authority," in Drucilla Cornell, et al., eds., *Deconstruction and the Possibility of Justice* (New York: Routledge, 1992), pp. 3–67.

nition that struggles for peace may require different understandings and practices that acknowledge but do not totalize racial, sexual (gender), and class categories. These communities of dissent throughout the world are linked by their proximity as well as through comportment. They may be identified by their unwavering dreams for a truly just and humane global polity and by their unequivocal commitment to the struggles of the poor and the oppressed, the marginalized, the dispensable, who are the "bearers of the battle between freedom and order, justice and law, humanization and dehumanization, true and false piety, in the world."[27]

Finally, communities of dissent are concerned with truth. But truth is always *located* truth. Perspective, as well as context, is critical. Since these communities engage in a politics of struggle that is situated within a context of domination, their struggles become practices of clearing. Even as they seek to open intellectual, moral, and political space so that the "fundamentally new and better" can emerge, they also seek to deliberate on that character of that space — what it means, for whom is it space, which spaces are important. Indeed, communities of dissent, engaged in a politics of struggle, may very well be, borrowing M. Richard Shaull's phrase, the heralds of a new reformation — witnesses, if not bearers, of the possibilities of peace in the world of the twenty-first century.

A 500 años, !aquí estamos!. En un mundo, en el que el saquéo y la explotación secular de nuestras riquezas y de nuestro trabajo, nos convirtió en fuerza inagotable de acumulación capitalista y del desarrollo industrial y tecnológico de los nuevos dominadores; prisioneros de la ganancia y la mercancía de una interminable cadena de consumo para unos y escasez para otros; víctimas renovadas de una nueva conquista en la que religión es el lucro y el individualismo; que divide a los pueblos de la tierra entre los que concentran el poder, la tecnología y el bienestar y los que son marginados y excluídos. . . .

Los nuevos cruzados de la civilización neoliberal nos hablan ahora de democracia, de desarrollo, de modernización y productividad, cuando en nuestros países la democracia se torna irrealizable ante la polarización cada vez mayor entre ricos y pobres, el aumento del desempleo, la desnutrición, el analfabestismo; ante la pérdida creciente de conquistas sociales y derechos colectivos, la privatización acelerada de las empresas estatales y de propiedad social, la crisis de valores y la profundización del racismo y la discriminación. Los nuevos pregoneros en su arrogancia,

27. Paul Lehmann, *The Transfiguration of Politics* (New York: Harper & Row, 1975), p. 258.

pretenden ocultar una realidad evidente ante nuestros ojos: el capitalismo no tiene soluciones para garantizar un mundo de paz y de justicia social. . . .

A 500 años !aquí estamos!, reencontrándonos desde nuestras raíces, hombres y mujeres, sin diferencias por el color de la piel, lenguas, culturas, demarcaciones territoriales y fronteras; recuperando lo que es nuestro y construyendo un proyecto alternativo al que nos amenaza y nos agrede; un proyecto en el que se excluye a la miseria y el sufrimiento; en el que nuestras culturas, lenguas y creencias florezcan sin miedos ni prohibiciones; en el que retomemos nuestra autonomía y las formas de autogobierno que nos hicieron grandes en el pasado; en el que se potencie nuestras aptitudes para el arte y la belleza; en el que destruyamos las cadenas de opresión sobre las mujeres y en el que los niños y las jóvenes generaciones tengan futuro; en el que la madre naturaleza se reconcilie con sus hijos humanizados en su regazo; en el que la guerra quede en el recuerdo de los tiempos malos; en el que podamos mirarnos cara a cara los unos a los otros sin sentir la vergüenza del odio o del desprecio; unidos, pues, en el amor, la solidaridad y la esperanza.[28]

28. "Declaración de Managua"; see pp. 240–41 above for English translation.

· 15 ·

The Religious Dimension
of Social Change

CHARLES W. AMJAD-ALI

THIS TITLE brings together two elements that are generally perceived to have a problematic relationship, and are even considered to be irreconcilable trajectories in human affairs. We therefore first need to lay out some parameters of definition and the implication of each component of this theme.

Social Change, Politics, and Religion

When looking at "social change," one is immediately struck by the fact that it has deep political significance. I view social change as *a public, self-conscious, and deliberate activity and/or mechanism that, to a large measure, deals with the issues of distribution of power and scarce resources in any given human community.* This is what gives social change political significance, and this is at least its institutional definition. Later we shall attempt to define it more foundationally. Since the activities and/or mechanisms for social change are largely dependent on the structure and role of authority in the public arena (which is a perennial issue), religion and politics play important roles in determining the nature of social change.

Any discussion of social change is therefore also fundamentally a matter of politics, and both political and social dimensions in human affairs are dependent on intersubjective activity and therefore fundamentally related to religion. By "intersubjective activity" I mean any human interaction of which we are a part and which we need to do, and can do, together. Intersubjective activity therefore entails all acts that bring people together for participatory activity in the public arena.

Most theories of social change can be lumped together into two broad frameworks. The first, generated largely by Max Weber's thesis in his famous work *The Protestant Ethic and the Spirit of Capitalism*,[1] I shall call a religio-cultural reading of social change. The other is the common theme that runs through the works of writers like Herbert Spencer, Emile Durkheim, and Talcott Parsons, which combines social differentiation (defining explicit social roles) and social integration for their reading of social change on a unilinear scale (i.e., on an evolutionary developmental line) and is "progress" oriented. Briefly, the theory states that a society and culture evolve or progress from superstitious religious irrationality to a rational scientific basis for organizing social relations.

It is apparent, both through the appropriation of these two social theories by political thinkers and through the very political nature of these theories, that the issues of social change and politics are interrelated and are interchangeable when one is involved in analyzing and theorizing about "values" that are constitutive of human affairs. It is also exactly at the point of values that religion becomes a very important key for understanding and evaluating the whole process.

Religion, broadly speaking, constitutes structures that promote belief in a "mystery" that decisively moves our lives. We can give this mystery the generic term "the sacred." Every organized religion claims the deepest human loyalty on the ground that it truly represents the sacred and the symbols surrounding it. The belief behind such a position is that if there is no sacred reality, then human beings would lack any shared ultimate grounds both for their very existence and also for justifying the meaning and purpose of anything they do together.

Among its other facets, organized religion, through its claim of access to the sacred, represents largely the networks of powers designed to defend established ideas, values, and norms, as well as power itself. Therefore, the basis on which we define and choose the arenas and space of organized religion and organized polity become very fuzzy in terms of our allegiances. Since we are connected to both the political and religious arenas (i.e., we are simultaneously *Homo religiosus* and *Zōon politikon*) through a whole web of relationships in the community, politics, sociality, culture, econom-

---

1. Max Weber, *The Protestant Ethic and the Spirit of Capitalism*, trans. Talcott Parsons (New York: Scribner, 1975).

ics, and so forth, the problem is how to define our own roles in this nexus on a personal level. This is the axiomatic question that both the religious realm and the political realm pose for us; this question defines the nature and character of change in those patterns of relationships and interaction in which we find ourselves. Put another way, how we understand others and their underlying nature (e.g., as having the *imago Dei*) shapes our attitude and our interaction with them. Reciprocally our attitude and interaction with others and their underlying nature shape and reshape how we understand them.

Looking at social change phenomenologically in the context of societies that are undergoing the maximum social change — that is, those of the Third World — it is apparent that for a vast majority of men and women in the world today, religion still constitutes the core value for integrating society, providing coherence to their intersubjective activity, and therefore for creating an understanding of, and participation in, a polity. The inner linkage between religion and politics in the Third World is both fundamental and complex. However, since most of the fundamental problems of social change in the world today continue to be issues concerning religion and politics, having life-and-death consequences, one cannot avoid a careful discussion of the subject.

The Separation between Religion and Politics in the West

We will look briefly at the history of the inner link between religion and politics, especially in the context of the Third World,[2] in order to grapple with the issue of social change. In the precolonial era a wide range of kingdoms and principalities shared some basic notions regarding the sacred nature of the state and government. The extent of this belief varied, but there always was some sacred justification for the political order. In this form of religio-political systems, the ideological foundations for the state were firmly established on some form of religious ideals. In different places and at different times, the laws generated from these religious ideals were not followed to the letter, but such religious ideals invariably provided the underpinning for the state.

2. The term "Third World" is being employed in a political way as defined in the Bandung Conference of 1956 (i.e., those countries that were nonaligned). It is not used to define the status on an economic and developmental scale. The Third World also represents two-thirds of the world in numbers.

This integrationalist perspective of the state, however, was disrupted in a very fundamental way with the intrusion of Western ideas, education, and politico-economic power, especially as all these factors fundamentally demanded the separation of religion and politics. This was the origin of the long, uneven, and complex process that has come to be called the modernization and secularization in the Third World.

The West, however, has suffered a confusion, of which the Third World has become an unnecessary victim. This confusion emerges with the mixing of two seemingly interchangeable bipolarities. These are the bipolarities of religion and politics, and church and state. The religion and politics bipolarity deals with foundational issues of human participatory life and generates values that claim to have at least similar goals or ends *(telos)*, even though they may be from different sources and principles *(archē)*. The church and state bipolarity deals with institutional issues and the distinct spheres of their respective influence. While the polarities of church and state are separated and should be separated (especially where such distinct institutions do exist), the former (religion and politics) cannot and should not be separated.

With the confusion of these bipolarities, the West has not only claimed the separation of church and state but also an (unreal) separation of religion and politics that I shall now attempt to demonstrate. This confusion of categories does not allow for a proper analysis of social change.

The breakup of the medieval Catholic synthesis of church and state and of religion and politics was generated much before the Reformation by the work of such people as Marsilius of Padua, author of *Defensor pacis* (Defender of peace) in 1324. In *Defensor,* Marsilius uncompromisingly resolved the perennial conflict of jurisdiction between ecclesiastical and temporal order in favor of the temporal (i.e., the state). He then went on to argue that the church should be stripped of its power in the temporal arena and that the state should have sole authority over all its subjects, including the clerics. *Defensor pacis* is considered to be the most influential contribution to the development of later political theory and is considered to have laid a firm foundation for all future attacks on the notion of a united Christendom ruled over by a central authority in Rome. *Defensor* influenced the work of such people as John Wycliffe (1330–84) and the Reformers of the sixteenth century, especially John Calvin's notion of the removal of the king by a lesser magistrate in the fourth book of the *Institutes.*

Lorenzo Valla (1407–57), whom many regard as the father of historical criticism, challenged the authenticity of a number of accepted documents by carefully scrutinizing their literary style. His most significant contribution was to expose the late date of the famous "Donation of Constantine," challenging thus the primary basis for the claim to highest power in the spiritual and temporal areas that the document granted to the pope, supposedly through the hands of Constantine. Valla's critical method later stimulated a much broader attack by the northern humanists on the theology, doctrine, and political practices of the church.

Following Marsilius and Valla, the person best known in this process is Niccolò Machiavelli (1469–1527), whose main historical work, *The Prince* (1512–13), searched for an amoral reading of the political life (notice it is not "immoral" but "amoral"). He provided a critique of the Florentine republic, rigidly rejecting all theological interpretations of the state, and sought to discover the natural laws that should govern the life of people in the state.

Then there is Martin Luther's *On Civil Government* (1523), written before the peasants' revolt of 1525. In this work Luther largely reacted to his being condemned as an outlaw by the Holy Roman Emperor Charles V, but he also negated the Roman Catholic idea of the supremacy of the church over the state (echoes of Marsilius). After the peasants' revolt, Luther wrote a very different treatise, entitled *Against the Thievish, Murderous Hordes of Peasants*. Here he defends order and promotes the exercise of force by the *polis* only, by what he termed, lawful authority. Whereas earlier Luther had challenged the existing lawful authority of the pope and the Holy Roman Emperor, he now asks the newly created order of independent nobility to kill the rebellious peasants and Anabaptists.

We then have the *Institutes of the Christian Religion,* written by John Calvin around 1559, in which, especially in book 4, he deals with the issues of religion and politics, church and state. He says that if the king does not fulfill his covenant or his duties, then the lesser magistrates may throw him out; this is clearly a reiteration of Marsilius of Padua's position in *Defensor pacis.*

In the West the theme of the religious dimension of social change has therefore had a particularly problematic history and has been normally cast in the separation, or even divorce, of church and state, even though each of the writers cited was clearly operating from a religio-political motive.

The most debilitating effect has emerged, especially since the religious wars of the sixteenth and seventeenth centuries, especially in the bloody Thirty Years' War. The document of concord, which was mainly drafted by Hugo Grotius (1583–1645), and the Peace of Westphalia in 1648 concluded these wars. Political institutions as we know them, including the modern nation-state, are all post-Westphalian developments.

The history of this debate is different in England and emerges mostly in an attempt to define the role of the Church of England vis-à-vis the Holy Roman Emperor. The debate in England, however, underwent a major shift in character with the Cromwellian, or Puritan, revolt, which took place between 1624 and 1660. Michael Walzer calls this the revolution of the saints and sees in it the breakdown of the old political order of monarchy and nobility and the emergence of a bourgeois polity, which, however, in 1660 ends up with the restoration of monarchy. Puritan revolt does later lead to the so-called Glorious Revolution of 1668–89, which destroyed once and for all the divine right of kings (and through achieving this also contributed to the American and French revolutions at the end of the eighteenth century) and led to the triumph of parliament over the king.

It is very interesting that the Puritans had to go across to America in order to change the very central Christian symbol of polity of "kingdom of God" to the "commonwealth of God," reflecting their antipathy toward the notion of kingdom and opening the door for what came to be called, and is, the American experiment. Here we have a clear case of politics even determining shifts in fundamental religious symbols.

To read this largely European history, however, as a valid development for the total *oikoumene* is inappropriate. It advances a Eurocentric pseudo-universal that is seen as a genuine universal applicable and valid for all everywhere. This is not only bad historiography, it is also a blindness to other realities that exist. It is, in fact, an eclipsing of these realities as they impinge on history everywhere. But the European history is important, since the modern state is a product of this history and determines the history of all those who seek to be a modern nation, with all its dimensions of social change.

The Close Linkage between Religion and Politics in Islam

Throughout the millennia of world history and the countless peoples, it has been normal for religion to be closely linked with politics. The prejudice of the West of separating church and state has made Western scholars also very suspicious of the relation between religion and politics. As we have said earlier, however, while church and state is an institutional issue, religion and politics is a more fundamental issue of life and the meaningfulness of human existence. It concerns human beings' intersubjective activity as they live together. Because there has been an inability to make, or even see, the distinction between the foundational bipolarity of religion and politics and the institutional bipolarity of church and state, there are some serious difficulties in understanding or even appreciating those societies and cultures where such distinctions have not existed and where this sort of bifurcation between religion and politics is almost considered a moral death. In the study of such societies and cultures, there has been an imposition of unquestioned epistemological and metaphysical prejudices. This has led to an inability to see fundamental values in societies where religion and politics are very closely linked or are seen as intercritiquing axiomatic structures.

Such a close linkage of religion and politics is central to Islam. For the Muslim the idea of Islamic nationhood is part and parcel of any discourse on politics. Islam contains both an ethical ideal and guidelines for a polity; furthermore, it regards the whole Muslim world as being fundamentally one in its concept of *ummah* (community), which should be constituted structurally as one state. At the same time, since (unlike Christianity) it has no clear ecclesiastical structure or clerics, Islam considers meaningless the notion of the separation of church and state.

In the Muslim view, a common acceptance of the laws of Islam, and not the division between church and state or a division based on ethnic or linguistic distinctions, is the proper basis for organizing a polity. While the ethnic and linguistic distinctions may continue to remain in Islamic polity, they are seen as "signs" of Allah's mastery and creativity.[3] Allah made humanity into tribes and nations so that individuals and groups have location and bonds with one another. But these distinctions and identifications are not pertinent for the Islamic polity and state as such. All Muslims, regardless of their distinctions, have the same rights and obligations, even though Islamic polity may remain diverse on other grounds.[4]

In ideal form, then, an Islamic polity calls for a single Muslim state that should encompass the entire *ummah* and negate separate Muslim states. Islamic law deals with individuals on the basis of their being Muslims; the territory or the state to which they belong becomes an issue only when such a territory is or is not governed by Islamic law.

Islamic theorizing on the state contains two central elements. First, since there is a radical emphasis on monotheism, sovereignty in all areas belongs exclusively to Allah and his law; it therefore applies equally to all

3. Quran 30:22, "And among his signs is the creation of the heavens and the earth, and the variation in your language and your colors."
4. Quran 49:13, "O mankind! We created you from a single (pair) of a male and a female, and made you into nations and tribes, that ye may know each other (not that ye may despise each other)."

believers. The logic pushes, thus, for a single authority figure who should express and implement this law. This authority figure will also be there by the unified will, and thus express the consensus, of the whole *ummah,* in which he shall be the enforcer of the law.

Historically this was the situation in the Islamic community until the assassination of Caliph Uthman (the case of *fitnah,* or "trial") in 656. Since then there have been various political fragmentations, as is clear in the simultaneous caliphate of the Abbasids in Baghdad, Fatimids in Egypt and Syria, and Umayyads in Spain. At times, as was the case with later Abbasids, the centralized caliphate did not have power in the provinces. The provinces were governed by provincial governors and generals who through revolts had established themselves as independent emirs and sultans, acknowledging the caliphate only as a spiritual head of the Muslim *ummah.* Thus, in practice, there has been a separation of temporal and spiritual realms.

The second important element in Islamic theory of the state is the search for a Muslim state that will fully follow Islamic law. Islamic scholars agree that since 661 and the beginning of the Umayyad rule, no Muslim state has truly qualified to be called an Islamic state.

Islamic polity, as providing a cohesive bond for community, encountered further practical challenges when culturally diverse groups (e.g., Persians and other non-Arabs) became part of the *ummah.* In the context of a society, which though it shared a common faith also had cultural plurality, it was important to search for integration and for the implementation of the Islamic vision of good society. Here the egalitarian principle was not purely a matter of spiritual concern but had to deal with the crucial issues of sharing political power and economic resources.

Muslim scholars, from very early in Islam's history, have thus had to deal with the problems of multiple political authorities, the legitimacy of a ruler and his authority, and the presence of culturally diverse groups under a single Muslim state. The basic approach to these problems was primarily pragmatic, applying, according to Gibb, the principle that "necessity dispenses with stipulations which are impossible to fulfill," and that the possibility of injury to the public interest "justifies a relaxation of conditions."[5] This can be seen especially in the works of Al-Baillani (d. 1012), Al-Mawardi (974–1058), Nizam-i-Arudi (twelfth century), Al-Baghdadi (d. 1037), Al-Isfarayini (d. 1027), Juwayni (1028–85), Al-Ghazali (1058–1111), and Ibn Jama (1241–1333).

5. H. A. R. Gibb, *Studies on the Civilization of Islam,* ed. S. J. Shaw and W. R. Polk (Boston: Beacon Press, 1962), p. 164.

Religion and Social Change in the Third World

After this brief historical survey, we can return to the issue of the religious dimension of social change, especially in the Third World. Under the influence of Western education in the Third World, there developed among those who came under its influence a certain comprehension and with it a commitment to secular political values and political theory. The masses who never experienced this kind of direct influence, however, remained steeped in the religious mode of thought on social and political questions. In any case they did not play any central part in the newly created political process.

The emergence of new nation-states in the 1940s and 1950s, which came to constitute the Third World, reflected the chasm between the Western-educated elite and the considerably secularized masses, who were led in the struggle for independence from Western colonial powers.

The elites were confronted with dual complex dilemmas. They struggled against the very structures of which they had become a part. Their momentum came from a desire to be independent from the colonial power, but their notion of independence was itself generated largely from within the structure that they wanted to be independent from. They also wanted to create modern states that were to be structured largely on the basis of states that they wanted to get rid of.

The other dilemma they had was largely postcolonial in nature. Significant socioeconomic change, which they felt was necessary to achieve a modern nation-state, depended in a large measure on their achieving a secularization of society and culture. That is, there was to be a millionfold repetition of their own experience of secularization in order to achieve a modern society with commitment to Western secular polity with its social contract among a differentiated society, representative governments, tricameral democratic structure (executive, legislative, and judiciary), and so forth. This aim, however, assumed an increasing participation of the masses in society. The question, however, was how an elite could maintain its political leadership on the basis of this ideal, which was largely alien to the masses, who were now essential to achieve these very ideals. Religion, the traditional glue for social, economic, and political structures, once again presented itself as the most qualified candidate to achieve this new job. So in order to achieve a modern secular state, religion was employed. Given the choice between a secular modern society and religious legitimation of politics to achieve such a society, a compromise was struck that produced a strange hybrid called a *religious republic*. This for the elite was a matter

276

of strategy and timing and not conviction. A modern secular society continued to be the long-term goal, but political legitimation for the authority of the elites in this new society was an immediate necessity for achieving this goal. So while remaining within the sphere of religious society, there was much broader participation of the masses in the sociopolitical sphere, and the government had to take responsibility for the social, educational, and economic welfare of the masses.

This process of secularization of society over the last fifty years or so is unquestionably the most fundamental process in changing the inner link between religion and politics in the Third World. However, paradoxically, as the society became more and more secular, new religio-political phenomena have arisen. It is almost ironic to see that religious interest groups, religious political parties, and religious communal groups have now become much more prominent actors than ever before in the new mass society generated by and through the quest for a secular society. Individual religious leaders and groups utilize sacred symbols of faith to mobilize the masses for nationalist struggle, liberation, internal revolt, election campaigns, justification for authority which is abused, and even for riots that are aimed against religious communities other than their own.

It can be argued on the basis of our political experience that the very participation in the modern political process from a religious stance has somewhat of a secularizing effect on the masses. In societies with broad religious and ideological pluralism, the obvious necessity of compromise will clearly water down any hard religious stance. But even in a society with a large following of a singular religious ideal, the fact of the existence of multiple hermeneutics of given religious symbols, and the attraction of affiliation with varying ideologies that emerge in the international context, produces a give-and-take that reflects a certain acceptance of pluralism of perception and a giving up of rigidity based on a singular religious premise.

This, however, does not mean that the new political manifestations of religious consciousness are therefore not significant. For we see that religion played a very crucial role in the anticolonial nationalist movements, and we find these patterns reappearing, certainly modified, after independence in the constructing of the new nations. Religion and nationalism coalesced very early in the course of the freedom struggle, and the enormous power of religious symbols to move the masses to dangerous self-sacrificial action has been conclusively demonstrated. These facts cannot and should not be denied in any proper appraisal of the issues at stake, especially since nationality itself acquires precisely the same kind of quality for many of the secular nationalists.

On the flip side of the coin, the politics of religious pluralism itself has been another form of religious influence on the political process. The competition and conflict among different religious communities have invariably erupted into communal violence. Separatist movements have developed out of such communal conflict. Both political parties and political movements based on religious ideologies that, while exalting their own religious and cultural qualities, denigrate and suppress the religion of minorities have emerged out of this conflict.

In the new states of Asia, Africa, and Latin America there is a much broader expectation of social, political, and economic changes from the governments. The legitimacy of government is now largely measured on the basis of this index. Thus the religious reinterpretation of society has had to deal with material well-being as a central component, and in this it has had to borrow from the more progressive elements of social criticism from the West itself. Religion has therefore become an important factor in bringing about political change; governments have been overthrown and even elections have been won by religious groups and parties through evoking the power of religious symbols. Before the last twenty or so years, this political change was seen to have as its effective goal the acquisition of power. The change that has come about in recent years is in looking at society from a religious perspective to ask for social change as well.

In my view, religion and politics not only *are* closely linked, they *ought to be* so connected, and we must take this fact seriously as we try to understand the present situation in Pakistan. This is not to say that I am therefore asking for a theocratic polity. My argument is rather that whenever politics becomes serious enough, whenever there are men and women willing to die for the causes they support or at least bear some form of serious hardship, there has to be some deep driving force in their lives that makes them take such a committed stance. Usually such a force can be supplied only by a religion or an ideology that is acquiring some of the functions of religion, such as making people aware of their own power or struggle for justice. This constitutes the religious dimension in the struggle for social change.

· 16 ·

Christian Ethics in the Muslim Context: The Doctrine of the Trinity and the Ethics of Transcendence in the Theological *Summa* of Abu Is'haq Ibn Al-'Assal

PETER B. DOGHRAMJI

> Now the LORD said to Abram, "Go from your country and your kindred and your father's house to the land that I will show you. I will make of you a great nation, and I will bless you, and make your name great, so that you will be a blessing. I will bless those who bless you, and the one who curses you I will curse; and in you all the families of the earth shall be blessed."
>
> Gen. 12:1-3

Beginning the Journey:
From Idolatry to Monotheism

When Abraham decided to move out from Ur in the land of Chaldea to the land of promise, he also bequeathed to his posterity the legacy of a journey. Those of us who claim his parenthood, whether planned, illegitimate, or adoptive, are the heirs of that legacy engaged in a restless pursuit of the promised land of rest. We Jews, Christians, and Muslims are in search of a settlement, both as a location and as a solution to conflict. The sojourn of our wandering Aramaean father continues in our own journeys. In turn, they lead us at times to spiritual crossroads and, at many other times, to battlegrounds. We claim a common origin, yet we end up with conflicting destinies.

One of the hottest battlegrounds today is former Yugoslavia, where Abraham's heirs, who for centuries have lived together as neighbors, are engaged in a genocidal conflict over their separate destinies. Ironically, they lived in relative peace under an ideology foreign to both. But with its demise, Christian Serbs and Muslim Bosnians resumed the path of massacre and bloodshed. In the Sudan, the death of multitudes and the widespread famine are the result of ongoing battles between the Muslim North and the Christian South. Christian Armenians and Muslim Azeris continue to fight over Ngorno-Karabakh. Only a tenuous truce separates the Christian and Muslim factions from the resumption of their decades-old warfare in Lebanon. Fighting erupts from time to time between Muslim guerrillas and Christian government forces on the volcanic islands of the Philippines. Most dramatic and pernicious is the incessant conflict in the "land of promise" itself. Gone are the ancient foes, whether the resident Canaanites or the invading Assyrians, Babylonians, and Egyptians. The feuding parties in the land of promise are Abraham's family.

In the "old" days (and some of us still live in those days), theology was fought, not discussed. Gods and their royal counterparts were often at war with one another. The social, political, and military conflicts of the family of Israel with the local tribes were also theological. These tribes worshiped numerous centers of power or idols, whether natural or man-made. Abraham's journey started in obedience to the One who claimed to be the only true center of power. Israel's spiritual pilgrimage thus had as its origin the worship of the God of Abraham, Isaac, and Jacob. This was a movement from the general to the particular, from the common practice of worshiping the Baals, or lords of power, to the exclusive worship of this one God, who in turn set aside this particular piece of real estate for this particular people to worship in this particular temple. It proved to be a perilous journey because the possession of the land and the building of the temple did not end it but became the beginning of yet another journey involving internal division, loss of sovereignty, and eventual exile and dispersion throughout the world.

The Journey at a Crossroads:
New Partners in Monotheism

In the fullness of time Abraham became the spiritual father of another "family." The original members of this family were themselves the children of Abraham, Isaac, and Jacob. They too hoped for the fulfillment of the promise and the return of the power and glory to Israel, the people of God, through God's Messiah. Their point of departure, however, was the fulfillment of the promise through Jesus as the Christ of God. At first this sounded like good news. It looked like the resumption of the original journey to the land of promise. But when the movement picked up momentum, and multitudes of Greeks, Romans, and other aliens were incorporated as partners in the journey, it became evident that the direction of the journey had changed — in fact, reversed. This was not a movement from the general to the particular, from the many to the one, but from the particular to the universal. The claim to Abraham's ancestry was adoptive through the same faith that Abraham had in God. Conflict was inevitable. Followers of Jesus the Christ were dispersed throughout the Roman Empire primarily because of persecution by fellow Jews as well as Gentiles. At first, for almost three hundred years, Christians were a powerless minority within the empire. But soon the church became the ruling power in Europe, North Africa, and the Middle East, and the persecuted of yesterday turned into the persecutors of tomorrow. Now it was the turn of Christian Europe to persecute the powerless Jewish minorities for more than fifteen centuries, culminating in the Holocaust. The children of Abraham, promised and adoptive, were in conflict, despite their partnership in the journey.

The third "family" of Abraham started its pilgrimage in seventh-century Arabia. The Prophet Muhammad's flight *(hijra)* from Mecca in 622 A.D. was similar to Abraham's leaving his home town, albeit under different circumstances. The Prophet's life was in danger because his was primarily a protest movement against false centers of power, as well as their worshipers. More positively, his message was a testimony *(shahadah)* to the one great God, Allah, the God of Abraham, whose power is unsurpassed. All other powers are, and must be, in submission to this one true center of power, hence *Islam,* meaning "submission." Despite their common heritage, however, the children of Jacob and of Ishmael became confrontational in Arabia. The creation of the modern State of Israel and the wars that have followed it constitute the latest chapter in a long history of conflict and violence.

Bloodier still have been the conflicts and struggles between the other two families: Christianity and Islam. Soon after the Prophet's victory over polytheists in his native Arabia, the Muslim journey in monotheism covered the entire Middle East, North Africa, and parts of Europe and Asia. Despite internal struggles for power for the caliphate, Islam's proclamation of the oneness of God was, at the same time, an effort to unite and unify the world in the name of Allah. Very often the sword provided credibility to the power of proclamation and persuasion. The response of Christian Europe was the Crusades. For three centuries, from the First Crusade in 1095 A.D. to the Ninth Crusade, terminating with the fall of Acre in 1291, Western Christianity attempted to recapture the "holy lands" and establish a Christian kingdom in Jerusalem. The Crusades had also another objective: to win back the "unorthodox" churches of the East, such as the Monophysites and the Nestorians, for Rome. It is not at all surprising, therefore, that these fiercely independent ethnic churches welcomed the rule of their Muslim cousins and resisted the West, even to the extent of fighting with Muslims against the invading Crusades. Consequently, Christians were often tolerated by the caliphs when times were good. At other times, they were regarded with suspicion because of their common links with their spiritual brothers and sisters in Europe.

Islam regrouped under the Ottoman banner, and the battles continued. Christians under the Ottoman rule were officially recognized as *millets,* autocephalous ethnic communities of faith subject to the rule of the Sublime Porte. Christians were deprived of political (and military) power, because the European powers regarded them as their "protectorate." The Greek millet was claimed by Russia, the Catholic millet by France, the Protestants by England and Germany. Russia would also claim the Armenian millet, although there were others, depending on the political climate. In this context Christians grew weaker through deprivation of their basic rights and persecution. The Armenian genocide during the First World War was a last-ditch effort of Ottoman Islam to execute a systematic ethnic cleansing. More than a million Armenians perished, and the remnant were driven out of their homes as refugees all over the world. In all fairness, it should be pointed out that this was not the unanimous Muslim strategy. Muslim Arabs, following the termination of the caliphate, regarded the Ottoman Turks as an alien occupying power. However, much as they resented the Ottoman rule, they were adamant against European colonialism, which carved out new countries, set new borders, and divided what was once a mighty empire in the Middle East and North Africa into smaller, weaker, and less-threatening states. Once again, Islam regrouped in the Middle East under the banner of Arab nationalism. Still, political divisions, the creation of the State of Israel, and the politics of oil have progressively weakened it. The rise of Muslim fundamentalism, despite its terrorist manifestations, is an attempt to restart the journey in its original form. The same is true about Jewish Zionism. The children of Abraham are still on a perilous journey in search of a destiny.

Ethos of the Journey:
Voice of the Powerless

Islam is a powerless minority in the Christian West. The same is true about Christian minorities in the context of Islam. They are the Greek Orthodox (the *Rum,* or Romans, in Arabic), the Armenians, the Suryanis (or Jacobites, the original inhabitants of Syria or ancient Aram, whose language is Syriac or Aramaic, the language of Jesus), the Copts (inhabitants of Aegyptus, modern Egypt), the Nestorians (Church of the East) in Mesopotamia, and all their Uniate (Catholic) counterparts, as well as a variety of their Protestant or evangelical descendants. Unlike the roar of the minaret, the individual and collective ringing of the church bells of these minorities is seldom heard in their native land, much less abroad. Caught in the crossfire between East and West, Islam and Judaism, Christians voice a moral dilemma: "How can we live as Christians, as believers in Jesus Christ and members of his church, in the context of Islam?" To put it in the first person singular: "How can I practice and live out my Christian faith, or even preserve my Christian ethnic identity, within an environment that curtails my rights, limits my freedom, deprives me of my power, and ultimately threatens my very existence? Believing in the one and the same God, what are the fundamentals of my own faith that characterize my behavior as Christian in contradistinction to that of my Muslim neighbor? Can I and my neighbor walk together in our journey to a common destiny, to a land of promise?"

My dual heritage, Armenian and Suryani, is the existential base for my academic research for answers under the guidance of Professor Charles West of Princeton Theological Seminary. My parents and grandparents, themselves refugees from Urfa, the ancient Crusader fortress town of Edessa, and remnants of the genocide in 1915, personified the question of Christian ethics in the Muslim context. Eyewitness accounts of atrocities by a remnant people sharpen the question. They also exemplify the struggles and the pain through which answers are born. Some are traditional but not authentic to the Christian faith; they do not flow out of the fundamentals or origins of our journey of faith. Thus, violence, retaliation, and the use of force are not consonant with faith in the God of Abraham and the Father of the Lord Jesus Christ. The brief account here of the ongoing conflicts should also serve as a commentary on the futility of answers whose exponent is power. There is no solution in violence. Its perpetrators are also its victims. Moreover, as children of Abraham, we have already rejected all centers of power as unauthentic to our faith journey, although at times we ourselves have become those centers of power in conflict and confrontation.

At the opposite extreme is the answer of withdrawal and resignation. This seems to be authentic, emanating from the acknowledgment that power belongs to God. In the Muslim context, the island or fish-bowl existence of Christian minorities is partly enforced upon them, and partly chosen by them. Its counterpart, in terms of piety, is otherworldliness. Almost all the hymns we sang in church ended with some allusion to our "eternal home," "Jerusalem," "Zion," the crossing of the "Jordan," and heaven. This too is not a genuine answer if it is the only one. The hope in the world to come is indeed in the very nature of our journey. But an ethic that is solely based on the not-yet tends to escape from the reality of the already, contemplating the rewards of heaven "for us" and the punishment of hellfire "for them." For thirty-eight long years Saint Simeon sat on a pillar not far from my home town, Aleppo, in northern Syria. The ruins of a church nearby and the remaining base of that pillar are silent reminders of the futility of such passive otherworldliness.

To look for authentic answers, to do Christian ethics in the Muslim context, we must first examine the principles or theological presuppositions that distinguish them from those of the other partners in the journey. The Christian faith has much in common with Judaism and Islam. All three are children of the original Abrahamic faith in the one God who is powerful, wise, and just. But within this one great family there are three major paths with distinctive theological markers. Our task is to unearth and dust them off to discover their ethical direction. In other words, if monotheism is the exit from polytheism, the negation of idols of power together with the liturgy of their ideologies, we must ask ourselves how we Christians, a powerless minority in the Muslim context, may interpret the direction of our theological markers so that we do not return to Ur or Egypt or Mecca but press on our journey to an ethic of power that transcends it.

The Journey Described:
The *Summa* of Abu Is'haq

We turn to a man who attempted to answer the question of Christian ethics in his native Egypt in the thirteenth century A.D. By that time the Coptic Christian community had adopted Arabic as their vernacular, although like other Christian communities such as the Greeks, the Armenians, and the Suryan, they retained their native languages for their liturgies. Therefore this learned Copt's name was also in Arabic: Abu Is'haq Ibn al-'Assal (literally, the father of Isaac, the son of the honey merchant). The al-'Assal family was well known in Cairo for many generations. Two of Abu Is'haq's brothers, al-Safi Abu al-Fada'il and al-Asad Abu al-Faraj Hibatallah, were scholars in their own right; the former was a philosopher and an expert in canon law, and the latter, a biblical exegete and a philologist. Abu Is'haq was all these and more. He was a systematic theologian. He was an enlightened priest in the Church of St. Mary in Mulallaqah in old Cairo, deeply involved in the reform of the hierarchy and the renaissance of the Coptic Church. At the same time, he held high office as a civil servant in the Arab Muslim government. Thus, one of his honorific titles was *Mu'taman,* "trustee," of the church (*al-din,* religion, implying the Christian faith) and the state.

A contemporary of Saint Thomas Aquinas, Abu Is'haq completed his *Majmu' usul al-din* (Summary of the principles of religion) shortly before his death in A.D. 1260, only a few years before Thomas embarked on his *Summa Theologica.* Thomas wrote in Latin, and his work is published. Abu Is'haq wrote in Arabic, and except for minor excerpts, most of his works, including the *Summa* (henceforth our term for the *Majmu'*), are unpublished. Both of them were Schoolmen, fully conversant with the philosophical works of Plato and Aristotle and their interpretation by Arab and Jewish scholars and translators. Both lived in the final days of the religious Crusades. They must have been fully aware of the failure of armed confrontation as the commonly employed method for resolving differences. For these men of learning, Greek philosophy provided the power of reason, and Christian theology the truth of revelation: A synthesis was necessary whenever differences arose. This was based on their faith in the one God who is both the author of reason and the source of revelation.

The thirteenth century was an opportune time for such a synthesis. It was one of those pregnant moments in the history of thought that gave birth to many giants of knowledge and learning in philosophy, theology, philology, and the sciences. The dramatic changes in the political scene were highlighted by such epochal events as the destruction of Baghdad by the Mongols in 1258 and the end of the Abbasid Caliphate, and the tragic end of the Crusade of Louis IX in Egypt in 1250, followed by the fall of Acre (Akko in modern Israel) in 1291 as the last Christian stronghold in the "holy lands." These were important factors in shifting the focus from the sword to reason. If the sword was ineffective in achieving the objectives of Christian Europe (i.e., control over Islam and ultimately its conversion to Christianity), other methods that were more in line with the nonviolent spirit of the gospel were employed. It was in this century, then, that the Children's Crusade took place in 1212. A few years later, in 1219, Saint Francis of Assisi visited the court of Kamil and preached before him. Francis was treated with respect, yet neither he nor the "children" were able to win any converts. Unlike Abu Is'haq, they were outsiders, distant partners in the journey.

We meet many other illustrious figures at the end of the twelfth century and the beginning of the thirteenth. Moses Maimonides (1135–1204) was a student of Aristotelian philosophy and a physician in the court of Saladdin. Averroës (Ibn Rushd) (1126–98), a contemporary of his practicing medicine and law in Cordoba, was translating and interpreting Aristotle. In England Roger Bacon, a towering man of encyclopedic knowledge, drew his philosophical and scientific inspiration from Arabian Aristotelianism and his theological insights from Augustine as well as the Bible. Yet unbridled knowledge was a threat to the church. He was imprisoned because of his views until shortly before his death in 1294, which illustrates the struggle of the church for the supremacy of revealed truth. It is not surprising, therefore, that the papal Inquisition was established in 1233 by Pope Gregory IX to extend his power and control on behalf of the church. In the same century, while intellectual freedom was being checked, the Magna Carta was being signed in England (1215), emancipating the subjects and checking the power of the king. Despite the Inquisition and religious intolerance, universities began to flourish. These include Cambridge (1209), Rome (1242), Oxford (1249), and the Sorbonne (1253). There was a movement from the monastery to these centers of learning. The great Averroist and French theologian Siger of Brabant (d. 1277) and saints and doctors of the church such as Albert the Great (d. 1218) and Bonaventura (d. 1274) are prime examples of this movement. The overall concern of these Schoolmen was the synthesis of seemingly irreconcilable theses based on scientific observation, religious faith, and philosophical insight. We should note in passing that the origins of the two great orders of the church, the Franciscan (1209) and the Dominican (1215), also belong to this century.

In this notable century of transition and change there were attempts toward political and social accommodation and compromises. As mentioned above, the Christian communities in the Muslim context adopted the Arabic language as their vernacular. The accompanying danger was loss of their faith in favor of adopting the religion of Islam. But this never happened. Although their original languages were not understandable to most of them, Christians kept the faith and their identity through their liturgies, traditions, mores, and customs. There was virtually no intermarriage between Muslim and Christian communities, and very rarely among the various Christian communities themselves. Each ethnic group tried to preserve its identity, and Islam tolerated it, and even made it official. Each millet was governed by its own internal rules. As long as Christian minorities kept the status quo, they posed no threat to the ruling power of Islam. They were, and still are, not allowed to evangelize the Muslim. Conversion of the Christian to Islam is legal, but the reverse is not. The church in the West created its own Christian context, molding the social and political life of the people on the principles of the Christian faith. It was therefore possible to do Christian ethics in a context conducive to itself. In the Middle East, the context was and still is predominantly Muslim. How could Christians, in their powerlessness, influence the context and even change and transform it? It is in this context of powerlessness, of the constant struggle for self-preservation against the threat of annihilation through violence or containment, that Abu Is'haq's Scholasticism exhibits a new dimension in doing ethics. This is much more than an academic effort for synthesis. If Christ has indeed pulled down the dividing wall of hostility, how can his followers simply maintain a truce between children of Abraham turned into enemies? The *Summa* of Abu Is'haq is a deliberate attempt to provide a rational account of Christian (Trinitarian) theology as the basis for Christian ethics in the Muslim (unitarian) context.

Spiritual Markers of the Journey: The Principles of Religion

It is clear that Islam, like Judaism and Christianity, affirms the monotheistic starting point of Abraham's journey. Belief in one God in Islam takes the form of a testimony *(shahadah):* "I testify that there is no god but God." In Judaism, it is the hearing *(shema)* of the Decalogue: "I am the Lord your God; thou shalt have no other gods before me!" The Roman West codified *belief* through credal formulations (the *Credo*); the Semitic East codified *morality* through tradition *(hadith* and *halaga).* As a member of the Abrahamic family, Abu Is'haq fully understands the *shahadah* and the *shema;* like other scholars of his time, however, he translates them into philosophical language. Arabic, the language of the *Qur'an* (literally, "recitation" or "reading" — the holy book of Islam), was enriched by the introduction of Greek ideas by the Scholastics. What the power of the sword could not achieve for the West, Greek philosophy did by invitation, entering into the world of Islam through its own language. Abu Is'haq could have written his *Summa* in his liturgical Coptic language, had his purpose been solely an internal dialogue among the learned men of the church. But his choice of Arabic, as the common language of Christians and Muslims alike, was itself an invitation to the Muslim to enter into the life and thinking of a Christian community contained and confined by Islam. It was an invitation to a neighbor who was a potential enemy, an invitation that could change potential enemies into neighbors.

Abu Is'haq not only adopted philosophical terminology but also utilized concepts that were, and still are, exclusively used by Islam. Instead of calling the head of the church the patriarch, a Western concept that is commonly used in its Arabicized form *batreek* by Christians in the Middle East, he calls him by the proper Arabic name, *imam,* ("leader," one who is in the front), which Islam commonly uses. Similarly, Islam adds the ascription *'alayhi al-salam* (peace be upon him) every time a prophet's name is mentioned. Abu Is'haq uses the same terminology when he mentions Moses or any of the other prophets. In describing the choosing of the apostles, he uses the word *istafa,* from which the Arabic proper noun *Mustafa* comes, meaning "chosen" (i.e., the Prophet Muhammad). Arab Christians today, however, hardly ever use this term. For Abu Is'haq, such terminology in the language of the Muslim is an invitation for a dialogue during a friendly visit. His own style of writing is also invitational and irenic rather than confrontational.

Therefore he calls his *Summa* the "Principles of Religion." Like the term "religion" in his honorific title describing him as a "trustee" *(mu'taman),* the use of the same term "religion" also here may imply the Christian faith. But the fact that he does not use another term, *madh'hab* (a path or a course), which is still used to describe the Christian, Jewish, and other faiths (religious affiliation as noted on identity cards and passports), indicates his understanding of religion in universal terms. Monotheistic religion is common to Judaism, Islam, and Christianity. In fact, it is the one, true, and universal religion adhered to by Semites, Romans, and Greeks alike. The principles (origins, fundamentals: *usul)* of this religion are rational and therefore universally valid. The various faiths, or "paths" *(madh'hab)*, within this one religion are different journeys; nevertheless, their origin is one and the same. There is no need for polemics, apologetics, or controversy at the level of origins or principles of religion.

Each faith, in turn, can and does provide illustrations about the truth of monotheistic religion from its own particular "tradition" *(masmu')*. Thus the second part of the full title of the *Summa,* which rhymes with the first, is: *Masmu' mahsul al-yagin,* "the gathering of the harvest of certainties." Such "gathering" is that which is orally transmitted and *heard* (*masmu'* from *sama'a,* "to hear"). Each faith claims certainties in revealed truth and transmits them (*tawattur,* literally the "chanting" of legends) from one generation to the other. The very title of the *Summa* is more than a rhythmic consonance; it is also a synthesis of universal (rational) religion and revealed (traditional) faith. True to his Scholastic methodology, Abu Is'haq moves from the universal to the particular, from that which can be demonstrated as rational and therefore universally valid, to stories that exemplify its truth.

The first part of the *Summa* is the first principle of religion: the doctrine of God. This also includes the doctrine of creation and anthropology. The proofs or demonstrations *(bayan)* are summarized as follows. The reality of God (the Creator, *al-Bari*) is incomprehensible because it is different from other realities such as creation. God's being is not contingent *(mutahayyaz)* and has no temporal beginning, nor is God confined in a location or direction. God's existence is necessary because variety in design presupposes the existence of a Designer to hold them together and overcome chaos. In Abu Is'haq's words: "The exalted Creator is one, and none shares his unicity [*wahdaniyyah*]. If he were many, there would be of necessity in this multiplicity an association and an opposition. Where there is association and opposition, there is composition; and where there is composition, there is that which is composited. Then there must be another preceding the Creator and composing him. But God is exalted beyond that." Then follow the arguments for the temporal origination of the world and the tripartite anthropology of mind, soul, and body, supportive of the Mu'tazilah (a heretical Muslim sect, whose name literally means "excommunicated" [by orthodox Islam]) doctrine of the freedom of the will, a point of departure from determinism or predestination *(gada'* and *gadar).*

Historical Dynamism of the Journey:
From Unity to Trinity

With the establishment of monotheism as the first principle of religion, the Muslim charge of polytheism (*shirk*, or association) leveled against Christianity is implicitly disproved. Abu Is'haq then continues the journey at the point where the other partners in monotheism stop. The oneness of God is the truth, but not the whole truth. There is a movement, a process, in the unfolding of the richness of divine truth. The methodology of moving from the universal and abstract to the particular and concrete holds true here as well. The general truth about God's oneness is imperfect. Quoting extensively from the Hebrew and Christian Scriptures, as well as theologians, Abu Is'haq tries to demonstrate the historical dynamism of the truth of Christian monotheism, which establishes both the oneness of God and the multiplicity of the divine attributes (*sifat*), without falling back into polytheism. Revealed truth unfolds in a historical process, abrogating (*naskh*) the old and ushering in the new. Thus the imperfect law of Moses is abrogated or transcended by the perfect law of Jesus the Christ. The imperfect law achieved its limited objective and came to an end (*zawal*). "The Law of Moses called a nation overcome by the law of idolatry from the worship of touchable idols to the worship of the God who is revealed and heard, from the law of nature to the law of justice ['*adl*] and prohibitions [*tawqif*]. Yet he could not lead them to the divine law that is more perfect than the law of reason or intellect." In other words, there is movement from the "natural" law or rule of the gods, the law of idolatry, to the rule or law of reason, to the perfect divine law that abrogates or transcends all precedents when their objectives are attained.

At this point Abu Is'haq introduces the doctrine of the Trinity. His theological methodology derives Christology from the doctrine of God and not the other way around. Christology may be the historical basis for the doctrine of the Trinity, but the latter is the philosophical basis of the former. Here he is more at home with Plato than Aristotle. The idea, or the form or the universal, "creates" the world of particulars. "In the beginning was the Logos," according to the Gospel of John. Therefore, the "humanization" (*nasut*) of God, God's becoming human in Christ, the incarnation (*tajassud*), is logically necessary. It is derived from the being of God, who is one in essence (*jawhar*) and three in characteristics or attributes (*sifat*), also described as hypostases (*aqnum*). The perfect knowledge of God necessitates a movement from unicity to triunity. Here is an intellectual, rational, and therefore universal invitation to Muslim, Jew, and Greek alike to continue the Abrahamic journey and experience the richness of the unfolding of God's truth in human history. The fact that God is one in substance or essence is universally established and accepted.

Abu Is'haq adds a bold corollary: "And we, the Muslims, the Jews, and the philosophers are in agreement and accord in describing God with these three attributes." Another *principle* is thus established, and it paves the way to the third, namely, the "union" of God with man, or the "humanization" of God. Before getting into that discussion, it is helpful to note that the speculative or philosophical attributes of the Trinity are explicated in terms of psychological analogy, namely, intellect, intellecter (knower), and intellected (known); the canonical or traditional are derived from biblical terminology, specifically, Father, Son, and Holy Spirit; and the theological are expressed in ethical terms, namely, power, goodness, and wisdom. Implicitly or explicitly, the second "principle" (or person, *forsof* in broken Arabic, rarely used by Abu Is'haq) is present in each case. Partners in monotheism, therefore, should take no offense when Christians describe this principle as the Son. They should remain partners in their ongoing journey.

Divine Partnership in the Journey: Our *Deus Homo*

What Abu Is'haq calls "union" is the completion of the doctrine of God. The oneness of God is imperfect and incomplete unless the union of God with man is understood to be both necessary (rational) and actual (historical). Abu Is'haq draws heavily from Yahya Ibn 'Adi (893–947), a Suryani (Jacobite) theologian surnamed al-Mantigi ("the dialectician"). Ibn 'Adi provides the philosophical framework for the necessity of the union. The argument runs as follows.

> If the Creator, glorified be his name, is the cause of the existence of his creatures, his purpose cannot be their corruption. Therefore, he must not be in opposition to them; and if not, it is impossible for him not to exist with them in one entity. One of the attributes of the Creator is pure goodness. It is obvious that the attainment of excellence (or transcendent goodness) is more excellent, for God is the supreme good, and pure goodness. Humanization is not other than the association of the Creator, glorified be his name, with human nature and his being together with it in one entity (substance). Therefore, humanization is necessary.

Polytheism or idolatry is also "association," namely, the human attempt to associate oneself with God. But the humanization of God is the "association" of the Creator with man. The initiative is God's. God is not a lesser God in "being together" with man. This is the natural unfolding of God's triune nature.

The theological delineation of the necessity of God's humanization is taken from the Nicene-Constantinopolitan Creed. A literal rendition of the Christological part has interesting nuances.

> . . . a true God from a true God, born not created, equal [*musawin*] with the Father in substance [*jawhar,* or "essence"], who for our sake we humans [*bashar,* literally "good news"; evangelism comes from the same root word] and for the sake of our salvation [*khalas*] descended from heaven, assumed a body [*tajassada,* or "became a body" — from the root word *jasad,* "body"] from the Holy Spirit and from Mary the Virgin, and assumed humanity [*ta'annasa,* literally "was humanized"]. . . .

The "incarnation," from the Holy Spirit and Mary (conception), is distinguished from "humanization," albeit both are parts of the same process of God uniting with man, or becoming man. Leaving aside these technicalities, we see the main point in this discussion is the purpose of God's union with man. God became man because God is transcendent in goodness. Thus humanization (i.e., Christology) paves the way for, and serves as the theological presupposition of, an ethic of excellence or transcendence.

The third *aqnum* (hypostasis) does not play a prominent role in the *Summa* of Abu Is'haq. There must be eternal procession *(inbithaq)* within the Trinity if the Creator is ever flowing in transcendent goodness and wisdom. Abu Is'haq discredits the *filioque* clause as inauthentic and untenable because procession cannot be from several sources. Unlike Christology, pneumatology has never been a major issue among the three faiths. Nevertheless, the rejection of the *filioque* (the procession of the Holy Spirit from the Father *and the Son*) has important consequences for Christian ethics, especially in the Muslim context. We consider this matter later.

The Road Map of the Journey: The Christological Model

Instead of the traditional strategies based on power, Abu Is'haq's theological methodology may serve as an implicit invitation for dialogue on the basis of universal principles of truth. Like the principle of the oneness of God, the principle of God's uniting with man should also be universally accepted. Karl Barth's "humanity of God" echoes this Christological truth. The ethical implications of the doctrine of God, including the Trinity and Christology in particular, are thus far reaching. In the Muslim (and Jewish) context, it makes sense to say that the one God who unites himself with the wholly other also calls us to unite ourselves with each other. In this "union" we are no longer strangers to one another. The model of God's "humanization" ("for our sake and the sake of our salvation") can and should also serve as the moral imperative for human behavior. For God united with man, albeit with a particular Jew at a particular time in a particular place; but the man Jesus is the representative (in Arabic the word is *mumath'thil,* closely related to the Hebrew *mashal,* which means rule by representation, thus meaning also "parable" or "symbol") of the entire humanity, including those who are already in the Abrahamic family (Jews, Christians, and Muslims), as well as those who are not yet (Gentiles, pagans, worshipers of other centers of power, and all other potential partners in the one authentic journey of faith). What separates us humans from each other, that "dividing wall of hostility" as Paul calls it, is not, according to Abu Is'haq, a matter of essence or substance. Our differences are due to our traditions, customs, and languages and not to the principles of religious truth. Quoting Ephesians 2:15, Abu Is'haq lays down this universal truth as the basis for a more excellent or transcendent imperative for human behavior (i.e., God's humanization in Christ abolished this wall of hostility and united us with each other).

Similarly, the almighty Creator united himself with the powerless creature, because God is more excellent in goodness than in sheer power; God is also more excellent in wisdom. God's transcendent goodness and wisdom necessitate the union of power with powerlessness, the almighty with the weak. The humanization of power is not only the ethical standard for moral behavior but also a universal judgment upon all centers of power that are ends in themselves, devoid of goodness and wisdom. This is the crux of evil: power pretending to be good and wise. All those who have had power are agents or representatives of the one and only center of power, God the almighty Creator. Those who deviate from the true path of religion and use power for other unauthorized objectives that divide and separate people from each other are under the judgment of God. This includes the crusading powers of the West as well as the ruling powers in the East.

Another important ethical ingredient in the Christological model of Abu Is'haq is the emphasis on God's humanization as a *voluntary* act. In chapter 35 of the *Summa* he describes Christ's setting an "example" *(mathal)* by his suffering and crucifixion "as a voluntary act so that believers who are hated (persecuted) for the sake of religion may follow his example." The necessity of God's union with man is, paradoxically, a "free necessity," an inner necessity of divine goodness and wisdom, rather than an externally coerced one. As the Gospel of John testifies, there is no greater love than that a man should (feel compelled to) lay down his life for the sake of his friends (who turned out to be his enemies). In Abu Is'haq's words, "His divine wisdom made it necessary" (*qtada*, literally "decreed"). God was not forced to suffer by uniting with man. His power was not diminished but transcended. Therefore, voluntary suffering is not weakness, as Islam sees it, but the best example of transcendent goodness, or pure love. (Islam denies the crucifixion of Jesus, maintaining instead that another, who was like him [*shubbiha lahu*], was actually crucified and put to death.) No one forces God into this union; neither does God coerce man into it. Truth cannot be coercive but invitational. Similarly, logical necessity does not abrogate freedom of the will because it is intrinsic and common to man. Unlike the imposition of false powers to weaken the powerless, the voluntary union of God empowers them.

In an unrelated context in which Abu Is'haq discusses the truth of the gospel, we have a rare glimpse of this truth about the empowerment of man. He argues that the gospel writers were not ignorant people and their story not a legendary fabrication. Otherwise, they would not have recorded "that the man became God [*al-insanu sara ilahan*], that he suffered, was crucified, buried, rose. . . ." Humanization, God's becoming man in this union, is also *man's divinization,* "man's becoming God, his glorification and empowerment." This is indeed an extremely bold statement to make in the Muslim context, but Abu Is'haq would rather speak the truth that shocks than perpetuate a falsehood in silence. He would not "defend" God's divinity when God has let down his defenses in uniting with man. God has empowered man to be like God. In the words of the Gospel of John, "He gave them the power to become children of God." This is man's origin in creation, and his destiny at the journey's end.

Yet another important ethical consequence of Christology emanates from the explication of the manner in which the two are united into one. This follows "logically" from the Trinitarian model of monotheism in which the three hypostases (*aqanim*) of God are distinct and different. In the first chapter of part 3 of the *Summa,* Abu Is'haq writes: "The union of divinity with the humanity of the Christ is of the *qunum* of the Word and the *qunum* of man. He was formed from both and became one substance from their two substances, with the substance of each remaining as it was. They were not mixed or confused . . . , nor transformed . . . , nor changed . . . , nor separated after the union."

In other words, the union does not annihilate differences but preserves them. There is multiplicity in the one God; there is also otherness in God's union with man. Therefore, in this journey, uniformity or conformity are unnecessary, and even destructive. This is also a judgment: a negation of the island existence of the Christian communities in the sea of Islam, and the rejection of the Muslim attempt to melt down ethnic communities of faith for eventual assimilation or reduce them to political impotence. Although Abu Is'haq does not discuss the consequences of the distinctness (otherness) of the *aqanim* for social ethics, he does lay down the principles *(usul)* for it. The implication is that without the loss of their identity, the partners in the journey can and should unite in attaining their common destiny. Abu Is'haq calls this "the politics [*siyasah*] of God." It is God's foresight and plan for humanity, the divine *oikonomia (tadbir)* and providence *('inayah)* or care that establish justice and mercy in the world. Difference and otherness in the *aqanim* of the Trinity do not threaten God's essential oneness but enhance and enrich the transcendent glory of God. Difference and otherness of the *aqanim* in God's voluntary union with man do not annihilate the weak but preserve and empower it within the union. Again, this reveals the transcendent goodness of God, whose politics is the preservation of human life in the multiplicity of its manifestations. Actually this is the first part of the politics of God, which involves God's going a second mile "for the sake of us humans" and for our salvation. The second part of the politics of God involves nature, or the entire creation. This is consonant with what Paul describes as the plan *(oikonomia)* of God in Christ, namely, to *unite* (literally, to bring or summarize under one head, to gather up) all things in him, things in heaven and things on earth (Eph. 1:10).

The Christological model provides the road map, or example, for Christian ethics. This is where Abu Is'haq stops. Although he takes the doctrine of the Trinity seriously, he does not give the attention that the third *aqnum,* the Holy Spirit, deserves. Here he misses a golden opportunity in making the transition from theology to ethics, from theory to practice. Christology adds the divine partner to the Abrahamic journey. It is not only Abraham who leaves his native Ur, but also God who descends from the throne of power and glory to befriend him. In this journey of faith, "Abraham was called the friend of God" (James 2:23). In Christ, God became more than a friend. God united with man and became an inseparable partner in the journey.

Abu Is'haq stops at the conclusion of the Gospel story about Christ; he does not move on into the Acts of the Apostles, which portrays the activity of the Holy Spirit in this journey. Pneumatology, especially with the *filioque* clause, makes the journey an existential, as well as a philosophical or rational, necessity. The eternal procession of the Holy Spirit is not only from the Creator but also from the Savior; because it is eternal, it is also historical and *present.* The God-Man journey, continuing the Abrahamic, has not run its course but is, in this present time, an open invitation to all religious traditions — Christian, Muslim, Jewish, and all others alike — to participate in the search for an authentic human destiny with the full participation of God. The *shahadah* and the *shema* about the oneness of God, and the *Credo* about the history of God's union with man, set the stage for the ongoing activity of the Holy Spirit of this one God to unite the brokenness of the universe with the full partnership of man. In the absence of a fully developed doctrine of the Holy Spirit, social ethics, as is the case in the *Summa,* is confined to almsgiving and other acts of charity within the Christian community. This is also true of all other theologians in the Muslim context of the Middle East; we might say they are still in the Upper Room or within Jerusalem. The road map is carefully preserved in the museums of ethnic custom and liturgical tradition. Despite his insight into abrogation of the old and its transcendence by the coming of the new, Abu Is'haq, together with the entire Christian community in the Middle East, awaits the "baptism of the Holy Spirit."

The Journey's End:
Toward an Ethic of Transcendence

Abu Is'haq does not give a complete answer to the question of Christian ethics in the Muslim context; he merely points in that direction by laying down the philosophical and theological foundations or principles for it. The one God is also triune, overflowing and transcendent in goodness, which is also understood in the Christian West as love. Therefore, Christian ethics is first a reminder to the Christian partners in the Abrahamic journey that they are called (invited) to be more than the children of Abraham, more than those who return the greetings of those who greet them or the love of those who love them. They are called to be the children of God in excellence and transcendent goodness, for he "makes his sun rise on the evil and on the good, and sends rain on the righteous and on the unrighteous" (Matt. 5:45). It is an imperative to go out of confinement and seclusion and discover the potential neighbor in the foe; to excel in goodness not only toward the "righteous" next of kin but also toward the "unrighteous" alien; to go a second mile voluntarily after going the first mile forcibly;

and to bear the cross and even die voluntarily, not for the sake of preserving one's ethnic identity on the island, but for the sake of the other. Such excellence transcends the law that aims at the minimum of goodness that guarantees the mere preservation or maintenance of life. As Abraham is invited to be a blessing for all nations, Christian ethics is, in the second place, a living demonstration of the implementation of the "politics of God," to bless the Muslim and the Jew, the Roman and the Greek.

Transcendent goodness is also transcendent wisdom and power. Islam testifies to the transcendent power of God; there is none greater than Allah. An ethic that is built on the foundations (principles) of God's oneness, triunity, and union should heed "the call of the minaret" (in the words of a book by Kenneth Cragg) in terms of the *shahadah,* and should hear the "ten words" of the *shema.* The journey in transcendence is still engaged in deposing the idols and struggling against the "principalities and powers" that continue to dominate and overpower the children of God in one form of enslavement or another. Otherwise newer idols are created daily and legitimized by centers of power that are in warfare against the one center of power. In their experimentation with power, Christians in the West have learned the subtle art of creating "golden calves" by collecting the wealth of the people and throwing it in the refining fire of science and technology. Aaron, in the absence of the *shema,* may still pretend to be the priest of God while engaged in the manufacture of idols. Ideology then becomes the liturgy of the gods. Paradoxically, the beginning of the journey is also its end, and vice versa. We begin this journey by the worship of the one God, besides whom there is no other god or power. As we continue the journey, we realize that this power has a mind and a heart. We encounter a God "humanized" for our sake, and therefore not a stranger to us. We develop an ethic in which we too are humanized. Power is no longer an idol we force each other to worship, but the manifestation of the transcendent goodness and wisdom of God for the empowerment of the powerless, the "divinization" of man, toward a genuine partnership in sharing power wisely for the good of all. Like the beginning, the end of our journey is the worship of God, our Creator, our Savior, and our Redeemer.

We close with Abu Is'haq's doxology in the introduction to the *Summa:*

Glory be to God who speaks [or reasons, *nataqa*] in the unity of the language of universals and particulars; who describes himself by the three eternal [or ancient, *qadim*] and revealed [*shar'iy*] attributes [*sifat*], which are those of transcendent [*'azza wa jalla*] perfection [or completeness, *kamal*] without diminution of the perfect. Praise be to him . . . who is worshiped as being worthy of worship and submission [*islam*] . . . and steadfast in his rule . . . raising the dead, healing the paralytic and the possessed [*makhlu'*], cleansing the leper . . . and restoring the mind of the deranged [*matbu'*]. . . . There is absolutely no associate to his lordship. . . . He shows his goodness to us by his union with the humanity of the Master the Christ [*al-sayyid al-Masih*]. . . . He renders the essence of man as the best of essences by his uniting with him. . . . By him all are led to the faith, the wise and the ignorant, the perfect and the imperfect, intellectuals and common laborers . . . worshipers of idols and graven images . . . masters of the sciences and wisdom, all peoples and nations.

Glory indeed be to God, who is our common origin and our eternal destiny!

Bibliography

For a complete annotated bibliography on primary and secondary sources about Abu Is'haq Ibn al-'Assal, see my 1969 Princeton dissertation, "Christian Ethics in the Muslim Context."

The following are the unpublished primary sources that I have consulted, parts of which I have translated in my dissertation.

Majmu' usul al-din wa masmu' mahsul al-yagin (The *Summa*). Paris: Bibliothèque Nationale, Archive no. 200; Beirut: Oriental Library of St. Joseph University, Archive no. 583.
Al-tabsira al-mukhtasara (The demonstration). Vatican, Archive no. 103.
Ablagh al-wasa'il ila 'ilm al-rasa'il (Commentary on Pauline epistles). Vatican, Archive no. 46.
Khutab (Homilies). Vatican, Archive no. 91.
Adab al-kanisah (Church polity). Vatican, Archive no. 123.

· 17 ·

Toward a Religiously
Informed Environmental Ethic:
A Pragmatist's Account

THOMAS D. PARKER

IN AN UNPUBLISHED PAPER prepared for the 1993 Parliament of the World's Religions in Chicago, Professor Hans Küng proposed that agreements on a global ethic should be concerned with "binding values, nonnegotiable standards and interior fundamental attitudes." He believes that the religions of the world have a responsibility to lead in securing a fundamental consensus on these three levels that will contribute to a better global order for the sake of "human rights, freedom, justice, peace and the preservation of the earth."

Küng believes the religions have a contribution to make to securing a better global order because religion converts the heart to a new orientation to life from false paths that breed destructive behavior. They provide people with a horizon of meaning for their lives and standards by which to live. A religiously inspired ethic nourishes a universal obligation to acknowledge the intrinsic dignity of all human persons, their inalienable freedom, their equality in principle, and their necessary solidarity with each other. Such an ethic is foundational for a global order that is "nature friendly" as well as economically and socially viable.

Küng's proposal raises the question of how an appropriate ethic can affect global discussions and decisions about environmental problems. On the one hand, there is the question of the standards (read: values) by which human beings live and interact with the world. An appropriate environmental ethic will propound alternative values to the consumptive and destructive values of technological society. These values can provide legitimation for shaping social policy on technology, economic patterns, and political organization that bear on the environment.

On the other hand, there is the question of the horizon of meaning, the grand narratives by which human beings come to envision a better global order because it more realistically portrays the career of humanity in a cosmic context. Values do not stand alone; they are expressions of the interpretations of how things are in the world, who human beings are among the inhabitants of the planet, and what the conditions are within which human beings have come to be and continue to be. Historically the religions have been the carriers of these narratives. In the present time a story of origins and a picture of the world rooted in the commonplaces of modern science are widely persuasive. An appropriate environmental ethic will "follow nature," as it were, by authorizing decisions and actions with respect to the environment that fit into the larger story of which our time is but one — not the last — chapter.[1]

Professor Küng's proposal has a religious focus as well: the creation of conditions for more holistic "fundamental attitudes" that nurture caring about the environment and struggling for more sustainable and just policies

---

1. Ian Barbour's second course of Gifford Lectures, *Ethics in an Age of Technology* (San Francisco: HarperCollins, 1993), takes the first option. In the face of the almost insuperable problems for human well-being and the environment created by technological developments, there is a growing consensus that human action with respect to the environment should be governed by the values of justice as fair and equitable distribution of resources and products, by citizen participation in decisions affecting the "commons," by sustainable development, and by efficiency in production (a low environmental cost to a high benefit ratio). These values are derived from an analysis of human and environmental values that are relevant to the appraisal of technologies (chaps. 2–3, summary on pp. 80–82).

Holmes Ralston III, in *Environmental Ethics: Duties to and Values in the Natural World* (Philadelphia: Temple University Press, 1988), takes the second option. He proposes a theory of natural value based on a grand narrative as a basis for environmental ethics (chap. 6). This theory takes as its foundation the now canonical narrative of the emergence of life on earth, a natural history culminating (so far) in *Homo sapiens*. Beginning with the precise balances in the original conditions of the universe, and the arising of the solar system from materials produced in stellar furnaces, this grand narrative of how-it-all-came-to-be underwrites a vision of an "inventive universe" that is value creating and poised toward increasing complexity and richness. The nature system, far from being a stasis, is constantly giving birth *(natura)* to the myriad creatures that inhabit it. All value is rooted in the positive creativity of the evolutionary-historical ecosystem that is our universe. Whatever makes a favorable difference to an ecosystem has value; it contributes to the richness and diversity of the whole. Whenever each entity exists for the whole as well as for itself, there exists value in the most fundamental sense. Everything has a systemic value as well as intrinsic and instrumental values (pp. 225–31).

governing human relations to it. He believes that without a conversion of the heart to less destructive and more life-affirming interior attitudes, an effective global ethic will not be realized.

This aspect of ethics directly engages what pragmatists assume to be the basis of ethics: the moral life of persons and communities who make ethical decisions regarding values that shape action according to some horizon of meaning. Values are not just out there in the world, although the goods valued are; values have a life history in the transactions of human beings in community and with nature. The conditions of existence within which persons flourish or dwindle affect what they value and hence what the environment can mean or not mean for them. The personal histories of human beings also affect the commitments they make to values they prize; not all things in the environment are held equally dear. Nor are habits of thought or action always consistent with values professed or "nonnegotiable standards."

It is a virtue of the American pragmatist ethic that it takes the concrete situation in which persons value, inquire, and act as the starting point for the interpretation of ethics. This situational (contextual or field) starting point gives the pragmatist ethic an affinity for the special challenges and opportunities of environmental ethics. This essay examines the contributions such a perspective might make to the current discussions of environmental ethics. It focuses on the work of John Dewey as an ethicist because, among the pragmatists, Dewey offered the most sustained attention to the problems of ethics and public issues. The insights shared by the pragmatists are elaborated in Dewey's work with particular sharpness in his interpretation of the moral life, the problem of valuation, and critical practice.

A Naturalistic Ethic

The task of ethics, according to Dewey, is to discover the laws and principles of the moral life and, by so doing, to contribute to its power and effectiveness by making ethical reflection more intelligent.[2] The key to a more intelligent ethics is to understand the moral life as a living adjustment to changing conditions and to use the best available knowledge of those con-

---

2. John Dewey and James Hayden Tufts, *Ethics,* 2d ed. (1932), in John Dewey, *Later Works, 1925–1953,* ed. Jo Ann Boydston and Barbara Levine (Carbondale: Southern Illinois University Press, 1989), 7:462.

ditions to form purposes and instrumentalities that will secure the largest possible good. Ethics that merely applies preexisting principles or abstract ends to ever-changing circumstances in order to direct action cannot construct the values required for effective action, nor can it gain the social cooperation necessary to realize them.

Underlying this vision of ethics is a thoroughgoing contextualism[3] that Dewey called naturalism. Along with other radical empiricists (e.g., William James), he rejected the ontological division of reality into opposing principles such as nature and culture, matter and mind, or society and individual. Such terms refer to foci of attention within experienced reality rather than separate spheres of reality apart from or behind it. Human beings do not cease to be biological or physical when they behave personally in a social context. Rather, human social relations are as much a product of natural and organic factors as they are of culture and social relations. We may focus on one or another aspect of experienced reality for good reasons, and deal with it as an object of some interest, but that does not make it something that exists independently of everything else.

Like many other twentieth-century intellectual currents of thought, pragmatism was influenced by evolutionary biology. The model of live organisms interacting within an environment of living and nonliving creatures shaped Dewey's thinking about everything.[4] In this context, naturalism means that nothing is to be understood in isolation from its concrete conditions. The causes that operate to effect human life are causes within a natural web of events. Within this matrix, new and unprecedented realities emerge that have their own patterns and significance. They cannot be reduced to the conditions from which they emerged, although they are dependent on those conditions, just as subsequent events are dependent on them. By the same token, they cannot be abstracted into logical types derivative from some overarching principle. In its concreteness, everything that is, is the culmination of a series of natural events as a particular location in space-time and itself contributes to the continuation of the series. Nature is historical. In human beings, nature is social, cultural, intellectual, and spiritual in an indissoluble unity.

The interpretation of naturalism is heuristic rather than ontological.

---

3. This is Stephen Pepper's characterization in his *World Hypotheses* (Berkeley: University of California Press, 1970), chap. 10. For the following, see John Dewey, *Logic: The Theory of Inquiry* (New York: Holt, Rinehart & Winston, 1938), chap. 2.

4. John Dewey, *Experience and Nature*, 2d rev. ed. (New York: Dover Publications, 1958), chap. 1.

The problems people face cannot be solved by appeals to metaphysical concepts as in idealism or materialism. The problem with appeals to nonnatural events or entities to explain anything is that such explanations actually block inquiry rather than advancing it. They introduce indeterminate notions to resolve determinate problems. Nature is the sum total of all that is, in an interconnected whole. It offers sufficient reasons for anything being what it is or can be in its concrete history. This is not to reduce *ought* to *is,* as a kind of "naturalistic fallacy" (G. E. Moore). *Is* and *ought* are distinct aspects of a problematic situation, namely, the initial conditions and the ends-in-view. Neither needs a sufficient reason for itself in nonnature.

The human world, the world of human experience, is a world that conduces to active struggle to exist. It is stable enough to be reliable in the general but precarious enough to instigate intelligent action concretely.[5] The practical need to achieve a harmonious relation to the environment and to flourish in the face of ever-changing circumstances drives both the knowing intellect and the moral will. The objects of knowledge are not the factors with which cognition begins (e.g., a threatening situation) but the interpretation of the situation achieved at the end of an inquiry (a knowledge of the source of the threat and of ways to deal with it). The values prized are not given ready-made at the beginning (e.g., personal worth) but are constructed in the course of taking action to further life (safety or protection). The moral value of preserving life arises in the struggle to survive (as a good to be sought), just as knowledge of actual threats to life arises in connection with the need to neutralize or convert them to something useful.

In this account of knowing, doing, and prizing, there is no need to transpose what is into what ought to be. Both are ingredients in any human experience whatever, without being reduced to the other. Nor are human knowing, doing, and prizing subjective additions to an indifferent material-mechanical world. They are qualities of situations as a whole in which human beings transact their lives within the natural-social-cultural environment. To know or to prize, to suffer or to act is to participate in lived experience in a foresightful, reflective, and intentional way, rather than to stand outside nature as a spectator whose mind mirrors nature.[6]

---

5. Ibid., chap. 2.
6. John Dewey, "The Need for the Recovery of Philosophy," reprinted in *The Philosophy of John Dewey,* ed. John J. McDermott (New York: G. P. Putnam's Sons, 1973), pp. 88–97.

A Pragmatist Account of the Moral Life

"Moral conceptions and processes grow naturally out of the very conditions of human life."[7] Since ethical reflection is a central feature of moral life, it too arises directly from the career of human beings who live in an environment of nature, society, and culture as well as having their own biography and psychic interiority. As long as custom and habit are sufficient guides to maintain and further human existence in a precarious world, there is no need for ethical reflection. But when the fragile balances upon which human life depends are threatened, ethical questions emerge. What is good for human communities to seek in the changed conditions? What is right intention and action when the social rules themselves are called into question by new circumstances? What is of highest value to realize when traditional values are no longer certain? Ethical reflection is based on the need to make intelligent moral decisions about human conduct in situations where there is doubt and disagreement about these questions.

Dewey's strategy for developing an ethical position on particular ethical questions is to frame a theory of the moral life in the light of which such questions can be more intelligently discussed. Theory indicates the complexities that need to be dealt with by any proposal for resolving them. It furthers deliberation about courses of action by pointing out the ethical complexities involved in choices, the knowledge needed to understand them, and courses of action that take into account the widest dimensions of the problem. Ethical discourse is an inquiry into actual human problems and ways they can be resolved with moral integrity.

The optimal moral situation would be one in which the demands arising from participation in society would be in accord with natural needs and express the widest range of values. It would satisfy the conditions of human being in the world. In traditional societies that assume such a harmonious state of affairs, the only ethical questions are those of individuals who need to adjust to "reality" that envelopes individuals. But in the modern age characterized by previously unimagined powers of technology and communication (this in 1932!) and rapid social change, the socioethical dimension of moral life leaps into prominence. The meanings of traditional ethical terms are reframed; "justice," for example, is more than personal right-doing, giving to each their due, for the agencies by which this is decided are social and institutional for the most part. But ethics retains its

7. Dewey and Tufts, *Ethics,* p. 308.

basis in the moral life of persons, however institutionalized its agency becomes in new circumstances.[8]

The Moral Unity of the Person

Four aspects of moral life receive particular attention in Dewey's exposition. First, there is the moral unity of the person, existing by transactions within a significant environment. Dewey's preferred term for the moral life is "conduct." Human beings conduct their lives. The career of a person is not constituted by disjointed and isolated acts so much as by a continuity of growth that creates a "serial whole."[9] Conduct mediates initial conditions and consequences in an "enduring unity of attitudes and habits." In the course of conducting one's life, habits are formed that give each person a distinctive character. Thus conduct is more than an instrument for achieving certain ends; it is the means by which the dispositions of character are formed. Even if an act has a merely instinctive beginning (e.g., hunger), its course is shaped by previous experience and present circumstances, and it has consequences that qualify future conduct.

Human conduct is always more than an individual matter. It takes place at the intersection of nature, society, and culture within an environment that supports it and limits its possibilities. Not all things are possible for any particular person or community of persons. Geographic and social location, historical moments and cultural forms, and physiological and psychological factors lend concreteness to conduct. Even if there were agreement on an abstract idea of justice (e.g., "to each their own"), the meaning of justice for conduct in different circumstances would still have to be worked out by specific persons, and their different claims adjudicated in the light of environmental factors, social-systemic constraints, and cultural values. Since others are affected by the environment, have a stake in the society, and share in the culture, human conduct is a fundamentally moral matter.

The moral question of conduct is accordingly much more than a question of duty, a previously settled ideal of what is good, or the expression of well-formed values. It is a question of how an entire situation can be transformed into a better condition. There are natural, social, and cultural

8. This accounts for the prevalence of individual rather than social ethics in the history of moral reflection, that is, what the individual should do in particular cases rather than how the situation should be modified to achieve a better condition (ibid., pp. 314–20).

9. Ibid., pp. 163–73.

givens to be taken account of. There are the habits of character and conduct to be honored (or qualified). There are the historical moments that offer particular ways but close off others. There are scientific understandings and technological possibilities. And always there is the serendipity of working collaboratively with others to achieve common goals ("ends in view"). The moral dimension of conduct is also political.

Ethical inquiry joins what we know on the basis of previous inquiry with what we hope for as a transformation of a problematic situation. But it is not disembodied. It is inquiry done by persons who have established habits of conduct and the resources of historical memory. Hence, the question can never simply be about what is to be done in general but is always concrete: What can we do here and now to achieve a more satisfactory and worthy state of affairs? General perspectives play a critical role in specific inquiries; they indicate possibilities for human action as such, and they may be decisive under certain conditions. Their power depends on how they are engaged in the specific inquiry, however, and not on justification either by convention or by theory outside the framework of inquiry.

In Dewey's view, the character of the persons who must decide moral issues is an essential part of the problematic situation and hence of any ethical resolution proposed to ameliorate it. Persons are not just actors playing out rational social roles; they are embedded in contexts and possessed of definite character and interests.[10] Persons are always agents, not simply means to other ends. The actions they take either singly or in concert are actions that affect them as well as have consequences in the larger world. The unity of self and action in agency is the basis of motivation. The personal career of any agent is on the line in any ethical decision about ends to be sought and conduct to realize them. Hence motivated behavior joins needs and objectives in the lives of persons. Ethical inquiry is always reflexive as well as oriented to worthy ends.[11]

The Idea of the "Good"

Pragmatists argue that ideas of the "good" are constructed by persons and communities engaged in an effort to transform their actual conditions of

---

10. Ibid., pp. 285–92.
11. Responsibility and freedom are the culminating ideas arising from the facts of moral personhood. Both are connected to the possibility of growth, of the modification of persons and social communities that ethical inquiry presupposes (see ibid., pp. 303–9).

life. In their view, what is good to believe as knowledge, or good to become as virtue, or good to do as action is decided in view of the consequences of particular practices. Things that are known or valuable or effective are shown to be so through a process of trial and error they called inquiry. This is what is usually taken to be the heart of pragmatism, that the meaning of anything is found in the consequences to which it leads. Means and ends are tightly bound together.[12] It will not go unobserved that this makes both science and technology species of moral life.

Dewey often criticized traditional notions of the "good" (or the "true") as an enduring repository of value given antecedently by appeals to nature, to society, or to culture. In his view, it was the cardinal intellectual sin, for it removed all ideals from the actual history in which they are generated to a metahistorical realm of unchanging forms. The irony of calling such a realm "reality" and calling actual history "appearance" runs through his writings. By contrast, the method he called "experimentalism" was urged as being the method not only of the sciences and of common sense but also of ethical reflection. Even the term "reflection" is chosen to indicate a process of deliberation by which persons decide what is good to do (or to believe).

So described, ethical inquiry follows the same lines of problem solving as common sense (trial and error) and science (theoretical-experimental). The difference is that the focus of the moral life is on the maximum human good achieved through action informed by ethical inquiry rather than certified knowledge or merely personal problem solving. Even common sense and science have moral dimensions, however, and rest on the foundation of the human person embedded in nature, society, and culture as an intelligent, free, and responsible organism. Likewise, no ethical deliberation that ignores either science or the social habits of common sense can be moral.

"Growth" as the Largest Good

For pragmatism, the largest good is to foster the conditions for human flourishing in transaction with the environment. Dewey's favored word for this is "growth."[13] A healthy human person or society is one that is alive

---

12. See Dewey, *Logic,* pp. 104–5, for an outline of the method.

13. Dewey and Tufts, *Ethics,* pp. 12–14. Cf. John Dewey, *Reconstruction in Philosophy,* enlarged ed. (Boston: Beacon Press, 1957), p. 177.

and growing, realizing the capacities for development that are inherent in the biological, social, cultural, and moral aspects of human existence in the world. Just as the cardinal sin in intellectual life is to block inquiry, so the cardinal sin in moral life is to inhibit growth. Because the social and ecological dimensions of human existence have become so decisive for the future of humankind, to say nothing of the planet, no ideal of growth that does not include them is acceptable. The largest good is concern for the whole; the more connections, the greater richness, the greater good. Ethics thus culminates in the achievement of a larger community and not merely in individual virtue or duty.[14]

The notion of growth as an end serves two important functions. It binds ends to means in such a way that the means used determine the ends achieved. No means that reduces the potential for growth can produce the end of growth. When the ends sought determine the means used in this large sense, not any means will do. The larger good to be achieved through thought and action qualifies both immediate ends and the ways to achieve them. One of the reasons "instrumentalism" is not a happy term for Dewey's ethics is found here: the means used also have intrinsic worth as consummations, and the ends sought become means to further growth. Moral life is not a treadmill to nowhere.

It also conceives of human struggle and consummation as an unending process. There is no conceivable point at which one could determine that either ethical or scientific inquiry was finished and optimal humanity achieved. The best achievements are fallible and give rise to further inquiries. This point is important, for it suggests inherent limits to growth; the largest good is a harmony with the conditions of human flourishing in a sustaining and supportive world. Human societies that do not adjust to the limits of their environment do not survive.

Moral Judgments

Moral judgments are judgments of value.[15] What is good is concretely good for someone or something; it is prized for its worth as discerned by those

---

14. John Dewey, *Human Nature and Conduct: An Introduction in Social Psychology,* in *The Philosophy of John Dewey,* ed. John J. McDermott (New York: G. P. Putnam's Sons, 1973), pp. 712–23.

15. Dewey, *Reconstruction in Philosophy,* pp. 185–86, 209. Cf. John Dewey, *Theory of Valuation* (Chicago: University of Chicago Press, 1939).

who appreciate it. Some things are prized for their intrinsic worth because, like a beautiful landscape, they are immediately enjoyed without reference to what other good they serve. Others are prized for the good ends to which they lead, such as a serviceable tool. Some, like a satisfying meal, are immediately enjoyed and also serve a further good, sustaining the body. Values are inherent in the human situation; we live by them.

Moral judgments are called forth in situations where values come into conflict, where the process of recognizing and bestowing value becomes a matter for ethical reflection. Since not all goods can be had at once, which are the most valuable ones to pursue in a concrete situation? Moral persons must appraise things, events, and situations and make choices in an intelligent way, rather than depending on intuition or convention, which may mislead by wrongly appraising things. Intuition and convention remain as sources for moral deliberation, however, since they are powerful factors in any problematic situation. Moral communities provide the conditions for ethical inquiry that takes account of the widest environment in which they exist. This process of deliberation is called valuation; it yields leading principles that direct action so as to realize the value sought in the transformation of existing situations.

Dewey hoped his interpretation of valuation would overcome the dualism of fact and value and would promote the use of scientific information in ethical discourse. The decisions as to what to value connect with the knowledge of how things are related. The decisions as to what to investigate connect with the values placed on things that need to be known. When values are found in concrete particulars connected to human interests and needs, they are subject to empirical inquiry. Ethical principles become leads to worthy ends, while theories propose methods to realize them in fact. The moral life embraces inquiry both into how things are and into how they might be transformed for the better — that is, inquiry into both science and technology.

Ethics for a Democratic World

The ethics of pragmatism is a theory emerging from the active participation of pragmatists in the intellectual and social life of the American republic, particularly in the first half of the twentieth century. This context is especially prominent in the work of Dewey. He wrote articles and books on the interconnection of democracy, science, education, art, and religion and on the increasingly complex economy of industrial capitalism. His view of ethical issues arising from concrete situations demanded detailed attention to the ethical problems of the society in which he lived. Dewey was a public philosopher and a liberal democrat.

Since the test of any moral theory is found in the consequences that ensue upon its enactment in policies and programs, the idea of democracy is the centerpiece of Dewey's ethics. The account of the moral life undergirds his democratic commitments, while the democratic society provides the conditions for the full flourishing of the moral life among its citizens.[16] Every society has its notion of what is "right," that is, a collection of concrete demands imposed on its members as a condition for their participation in its life. But such demands can be destructive of persons, of associations, or of the environment if not constantly subject to criticism. The "right" can become the "good" only if there is a feedback system in which its effects are constantly monitored and reconstructed. This is the moral meaning of democracy; it is the form of society that enables the fullest flourishing of all its members through their participation in its constant criticism and reconstruction.

The participation of all persons in organizing and governing the structures of their association is also a condition of their freedom, and the emancipation of culture, including science, the arts, and religion, from blind adherence to social habits that have outlived their usefulness. Such participation implies a class-blind political organization, since class barriers impede rather than further participation. It also implies a justice in which the larger goods of the society are equitably distributed rather than assigned differentially to groups according to their social power. Most important, it implies the control of future possibilities through shared social power. And this in turn presumes a universal system of education for social participation and cooperation.

This concept of democracy is an ideal type indicating its largest good; it is not an empirical description of any existing democratic system. The theory of the democratic society offers a standpoint for criticism of the social and political democracy in the United States.[17] In principle, democracy unites the largest common good with liberation of persons for their maximal development. It does this through the active participation

16. Dewey and Tufts, *Ethics*, pp. 348–50. For the following, see pp. 351–71. William Andrew Paringer (*John Dewey and the Paradox of Liberal Reform* [Albany: State University of New York Press, 1990]) faults Dewey's pragmatic meliorism and progressivism in the name of what he believes is a more thoroughgoing ideological critique.

17. Dewey and Tufts, *Ethics*, pp. 356–58, 406–11.

of persons in the institutions of society. A weakness of the tradition of democracy is that it has heretofore been framed without regard for the impact of the economic system on the politics of a society. But the industrial, and now the technological-informational, organization of society makes this no longer possible. Human beings are abstractly equal but concretely unequal in the productive relations of society. Full participation must be economic as well as political, and concern for just distribution of resources must accompany concern for the franchise.

The impulse of pragmatism is reformist rather than revolutionist. The account of the moral life as seeking maximal adjustment to new conditions in order to realize the widest and richest good in concrete conditions implies this quality. Moral deliberation takes account of the existing social and personal habits as well as new theoretical and practical possibilities for reconstructing actual conditions. Over time, the accumulation of particular changes has led to structural change and will continue to do so. The role of democracy is central to this strategy, since the socialization of the economic system depends on the widest participation of persons in decisions that affect the common destiny.

Dewey cites the continuing political tradition of control of economic life in the United States as both fact and example. The capitalist economy has been modified by legislation concerning the safety of the workplace, the public interest in maintaining and extending competition in opposition to monopoly practices, fair-trade laws, the direct income tax, and control of immigration for economic reasons, among other things. For the future, he envisioned the continued shaping of the economic institutions of the society by democratic practices to ensure the common good[18] through such improvements as the increase of efficiency in production and decrease in waste, a social safety net, standards of health and safety, improvements in products, and a more just distribution of gain based on what is necessary to ensure a good society. Such a society secures justice, fosters the choice of worthy values, takes account of the ensemble of human relations, including the family,[19] and increases democratic transformation of the institutions of society.

18. Ibid., pp. 428–37. Dewey assumed the economic system will continue as a mixture of benefit and liability. Hence efforts should go toward reforming it by concrete improvements. If, as Parringer believes, it is hopelessly faulted, such improvement will only delay the coming of a better system.

19. Ibid., pp. 450–62.

THOMAS D. PARKER

The Role of Religion

The widest environment within which the moral life takes place is the larger universe, of which human life is but one part. None of the pragmatists was unaware of this wider dimension, though each one thematized it quite differently.[20] Dewey was concerned with what he understood to be the "religious phase of experience" rather than with particular religious experiences or religious ideas.[21] All agreed that the meaning of religion is found in its leading to increased value in human life.

Dewey's work on religion was occasioned by a conviction that religion was too important to be left to the religious institutions, which tended to block rather than enhance religion. As a quality of any moral experience, religion is at once much more and much less than a religious institution. It is much more because it belongs to the consummatory phase of any struggle to realize worthy ideals. It is much less because it is not concerned with beliefs, rites, or commands. Religious institutions may contribute toward the enhancement and expression of the religious quality of life as persons involved in them may experience a genuinely religious transformation. But he was pessimistic about how seldom that happened and optimistic about how often true religion took place in ordinary experience without being recognized as such. Any activity pursued in relation to an ideal end, in spite of impediments and with a conviction of its enduring value, may have a religious quality.[22]

The heart of religion is a "natural piety" toward worthy ends in a supportive environment. This piety involves a transformation of the person in relation to the whole within which we are situated, a change that Dewey calls adjustment.[23] A deep adjustment embraces not only the self but also the conditions of life and brings a sense of peace and well-being. It reaches out to the enveloping whole that contains the conditions for realizing value and also the ideal elements that lay hold on human imagination. Taken as an individual in separation from culture, nature, or society, no human being can be either moral or religious; such isolates are irreligious.[24]

20. William James spoke of the "more" that environs human experience and comes to expression in religious experiences but remains beyond our grasp, adumbrated rather than clearly known. Charles Peirce considered ways the idea of God might be justified in relation to a pragmatic understanding of meaning, given an epistemological realism.

21. John Dewey, *A Common Faith* (New Haven: Yale University Press, 1934), p. 2.

22. Ibid., p. 27.

23. Ibid., p. 16.

24. Ibid., p. 25.

The religious quality of life is felt when there is a unification of the self through allegiance to inclusive ideal ends (e.g., growth) that imagination presents and to which human will responds. Such ideals have roots in natural conditions; they are valuable and therefore are appropriately valued. They are not fantasies. They exist in human character and action in actual conditions. The active interplay of ideals and existent conditions is the basis for creative advance in human life.[25] Dewey's sharp opposition to traditional religious institutions or their "atheistic" opponents lies in his conviction that they distract from giving attention to genuinely religious qualities of ordinary experience. The same is true for a human-centered religion that forgets the environing world that supports and limits all human moral and intellectual striving.

Dewey believed that the future of religious institutions lay in their recognition of the religious element in ordinary human association and struggle, and also in their celebration of the realization of value in the active union of worthy ideals and actual conditions in the enveloping world.[26] Both the secular and the religious aspects of life are saved (as it were) by the cultivation of this natural piety. It imbues human association with religious devotion, and it identifies religious values with natural human ideals and the connection to a larger world. In a democratic society, such religious institutions can play a vital moral and spiritual role by supporting faith in the capacities of persons freely cooperating to guide human action in ways that realize the fullest development of society and the persons who compose it.

Although Dewey's focus was on social reconstruction and the growth of persons toward fuller life, the undergirding assumption is that the "totality of being" we call the universe is the source of support and limitation for social and personal goods. Its continued flourishing is the condition of our continued flourishing, for there is a community of causes and consequences in which human beings are embedded that binds them to the larger world as well as to the specifically human world. The office of religion

25. Ibid., pp. 48–50. The idea of God represents the working unification of the ideal and the actual as it brings forth increased value. This unification expresses the connection of human striving to the enveloping world. The use of the word "God" for this connection gives it supreme significance and protects from despair. Dewey's sharp opposition to traditional religious institutions and their "atheistic" opponents lies in his conviction that they distract from giving attention to genuinely religious qualities of ordinary experience. The same is true for a human-centered religion that forgets the environing world that supports and limits all human moral and intellectual striving.

26. Ibid., pp. 80–84.

is to draw attention to this environmental dimension of life. Society and the self can be made whole only by being creatively interconnected with the environing world. No moral life that fails to idealize the largest good can be fully mature.

Although the precise interpretation of many of Dewey's ideas about religion has been the subject of intense debate ever since they were first published in 1934, the purpose of religion and its effectiveness in democratic processes of moral deliberation are clear enough and fit in with the account he gives of human knowing, doing, and appreciating. It is a strong statement of the significance of the religious quality of life for the moral life, with particular relevance for the transformation of human relations to nonhuman reality.

Toward a Pragmatic Environmental Ethic

The environmental problems facing every human society at the end of the twentieth century are forced upon us by the pace, extent, and quality of social and technological changes. These changes have been accompanied by a rapid growth in population and rising disparities of productivity and income.[27] It is clear that an ethics of the environment is connected with a much wider range of ethical issues than merely technical or economic ones. If, as pragmatists contend, the natural, social, and cultural conditions are a seamless whole, issues concerning the natural environment are also social and cultural issues. The important role of social policy for governing relations to the environment is attested by legislation across the globe on such matters as biodiversity, fossil-fuel burning, and the pollution of the air, water, and soil.

There is agreement in the literature that social policies should be regulated by values commanding wide consent and sifted by critical discussion. Ethicists commonly combine environmental values with personal and social values in order to show that environmental questions are always implicated with other ethical questions.[28] But it remains unclear how to

---

27. Paul Kennedy, *Preparing for the Twenty-first Century* (New York: Random House, 1993). In the first chapter of his *Ethics in an Age of Technology,* Barbour also analyzes the complex challenge.

28. Barbour summarizes personal, social, and environmental values relevant to the appraisal of technologies (*Ethics in an Age of Technology,* p. 81). Ralston argues for placing the ecosystem on a par with social and personal values. The values of the ecosystem such as beauty, stability, and integrity may on occasion be privileged (Ralston, *Environmental Ethics,* pp. 230–32).

move from values to policies, and from policies to programs and personal decisions. Between decisions about values and decisions about what is to be done in particular cases there is a social process of moral decision making with political and economic aspects.

Dewey's ethics critically interprets this more pragmatic and personal process. The values generated by critical inquiry are one of the most important ingredients in responsible and free moral decision making; along with scientific knowledge they can inform ethical reflection on purposes to be served by human action. Values are selectors among options; the best action is that which serves the most well-founded values. They represent the wisdom of a social community as it sorts through its problems.

Prior agreement on general values does not translate into policy or action for change. Yet, from the pragmatist point of view, the transformation of a situation is the purpose of ethics. The contribution of pragmatism is to focus on the act of valuing rather than the values prized, and thus to redescribe ethical reflection as a socially transforming process. Participation in this process *is* ethical reflection by engaged moral persons and communities. It is inseparable from the ethically informed action of critical practice.

In summary, several aspects of Dewey's pragmatist ethics have particular relevance for environmental ethics and recommend pragmatist ethics as a significant theoretical contribution to contemporary discussion and action respecting the environmental problems of the late twentieth century.

The first of these is its naturalism. As described above, this is not an ontological theory so much as an interpretive description of human life in the world. The social process of ethical reflection is a natural fact, a form of human transaction within the environing world. It is part of an intelligent way of adjusting to changes in habitat, in social organization, in means of production, and in culture. A society is moral when its structures, processes, ideals, and ends correspond with the widest values, including biophysical conditions of life. Its system of wants represent real needs, and its imagination of fulfillment builds on real possibilities. The reverse is equally the case; the "natural" world is socialized through the agency of human action.

Dewey's concept of transaction names this intimate reciprocity. An environmental ethics that "follows nature" and thinks to find the measure for human action by looking at the nonhuman forgets that even the notion of nature itself is a historical construct and reflects the interests dominant in a particular culture (as in "social Darwinism"). By the same token a utilitarian ethic that makes the wants of a particular society dominant over nonhuman natural processes forgets that the infrastructure of any society is the environment it exploits and enriches. While values of the ecosystem are different from values of political economy or personal relations, they are equally important. And under certain conditions they may be privileged.

The emphasis in pragmatism on the moral person widens the scope of environmental ethics. Human beings transact their lives in an environment of culture, within traditioned communities and social arrangements that depend for their existence on language and communication. There are habits of thought, of purposes, and of action that form the initial conditions of any ethical reflection. There are institutions and economies by which they get on in the world. And each person has his or her own biography and family history. Present circumstances and hoped-for outcomes are always laden with the consequences of previous thought and action. Dewey interprets this as wisdom, the fund of experience by which action in the world is guided if it is deliberate and responsible. It is a necessary, if not sufficient, condition of environmental ethical inquiry.

The term "conduct" carries the meaning of moral persons as a historical project. These moral agents are the carriers of the culture and social patterns. Since ethical reflection is carried on by such agents, their interests and commitments shape its outcome. Hence family patterns, personal experiences, community culture, and so forth contribute to the valorizing of certain ends and the construction of specific means that impact the environment.

The pragmatists remind us that value is always value for some persons or communities who recognize and seek to realize it. The decisions required by environmental problems are not just "out there"; they are always decisions and actions required of some persons affecting other persons, and hence of some cultural and social worlds in encounter with others. Since the environment is the widest horizon encompassing many persons and their conduct, the duty to recognize a common context is laid equally on all persons and communities.

Pragmatist ethics emphasizes that the idea of the environmental good is socially constructed. This is not to deny that there are natural goods that are required by living organisms, including the social and cultural life of human beings. Food is a good required to nourish the body, whether or not a particular ascetic community might value it appropriately. While not denying the obvious "goods" of nature, culture, or society, the search for what is morally good in human transactions with the environment arises where there is a conflict between such goods and hard decisions must be made.

Ethical inquiry is always a search among genuine goods for those that will transform the situation into a better condition. Among the ends that might be desired, and those among them that are most worthy, the deliberation as to which ends should be sought in a particular circumstance is always a social process. The interests of competing communities play an indispensable role because the negotiation of interests is a necessary condition of an outcome that will be valuable as well as workable. This means that no adequate environmental ethics can overlook the claims on any community in the formation of policy or instigation of action.

While the term "growth" has become incorrect in recent discussion because of its identification with the emerging world of late capitalism and its narrow interpretation of economic development, it is a term pragmatists have historically used to signal human flourishing in transaction with the enveloping world. Living organisms seek to enhance and fulfill their lives, realizing the possibilities of their genetic heritage, their environment, their species relations, and so forth. Human beings are no exception; their moral and scientific striving exemplifies natural growth. The strongest disvalue is to block growth and cut off the possibilities for expressing a wider range of value. Such action diminishes human beings and, indirectly, nature itself.

The ideal value of growth encompasses both means and ends, since the ends achieved are the outgrowth of the means used, and the means used are guided by purposes envisaged in ends sought. It encompasses the range of contexts from the ecosystem through sociocultural, political, economic, to the personal and spiritual. Sustainable development, the integrity of organisms and systems, and similar factors are not different in kind from personal moral and intellectual flourishing or social well-being. Instead of thinking of trade-offs, this overarching norm suggests symbiosis and confluence of interests. Instead of setting short-term interests against long-term interests, the ideal of growth directs attention to the continuity of interest over time. It joins systemic, intrinsic, and instrumental aspects of value.

For a pragmatist ethic, the transformation of human relations to the environment is connected with the spread of the democratic process in moral decision making. As Dewey often noted, individuals alone would not need ethics, but only techniques of problem solving. It is human sociality and coexistence with other life-forms that raises questions of value and of moral ends. Deliberations about paramount values and means of realizing them involve other interested persons. In the sense that all ethics is social ethics, the most approved form of ethics is a democratically deliberated one, for it takes into account the widest set of interested parties.

The mediating communities in which most decisions are made are communities where personal interest and participation embrace those affected by the decisions. Social units such as the family, neighborhood, religious organizations, and economic and vocational groups are settings of face-to-face relations and communications. Countless decisions affecting the environment are taken in farming, manufacturing, and service-based communities across the globe. Their cumulative effect is enormous. Larger social institutions involve groups of persons in more formal and representative relations. A formal process of extending the discussion to include (in principle) all who are affected by an environmental action is required because the scale of the impact affects so many.

The problem of democratic participation in the global economic and political system is vexing partly because the institutions with global competence are so weak and partly because the sense of human relatedness to the environing world is attenuated through destructive social practices. Creating a constituency for a global environmental ethic is a paramount task. Recall Professor Küng's claim that "interior fundamental attitudes" are crucial for the realization of global values and standards with respect to emerging global issues and his conviction that the religions of humankind have a responsibility to lead in securing a public consensus for a better global order. Why should concern for the environment be a part of everyone's moral conduct? Whence the habits of respect, reserve, carefulness, or right thinking that such an ethic requires? Pragmatists believe such attitudes are qualities of an environed moral person. Dewey was explicit in connecting religion positively with consummatory experience in the struggle for social reconstruction, and therefore with nurturing such moral character.

Pragmatists agree that the meaning of religion is to be found in its leading to increased value in human life, as noted above. The distinct province of religion lies in the unification of the self through its allegiance to inclusive ideals and action taken on their behalf. Persons are transformed in the struggle for a better condition when it is coupled with the transformation of the whole in which they are situated. "Goods are ours through a grace not ourselves," yet such grace is directly had in connection with the "doings and sufferings of the human community of which we are but a link."[29] It is in the network of causes and consequences in which we are enmeshed that we are aware of the mysterious totality of being we call the universe. The emphasis is not on the idealized past or primordial reality

29. Dewey, *Experience and Nature*, p. 42; Dewey, *A Common Faith*, p. 87.

318

but on the idealized future, and the consummations of realized value through action in a supportive and challenging environment.

The emphasis on the wider environment as the horizon of meaning for religious experience is a "natural piety." It can be had in any struggle for worthy ideals that results in significant transformation of a situation. It results in an interior transformation as well as in changing the world, furthering and qualifying human moral life with a deeper peace and more creative faith in the most inclusive ideal ends. "The religious attitude needs a sense of the connection of man . . . with the enveloping world."[30] Religion as natural piety has the virtue of ennobling and correcting every worthy human action. In its reference to the wider environment, religion reminds human beings that they are not all there is, and their significance as agents of transformation is drawn from and refers back to the mysterious whole of which they are but parts.

A paradox suggests itself. Only insofar as human beings sense their own relativity in relation to the environment can they act to transform their relations to it. Anthropocentrism destroys the natural fabric that is the basis of human life; it is irreligious. But a passive relation to the environment can never rise to the heights of religious awareness of the whole, for it can never experience the harmony of worthy ideals to the world of nature, culture, and society that gave it birth. This is a twentieth-century version of the dialectic of dependence and freedom. Dewey's term "adjustment" says far less than he intends; the adjustment in human life within the nonhuman world is a mutual transformation, not an accommodation to or modification of its natural conditions.

---

30. Dewey, *A Common Faith*, p. 53.

· 18 ·

The "Holy Materialism": The Question of Bread in Christian and Marxist Perspectives

JAN MILIČ LOCHMAN

THE SLOGAN "holy materialism" was coined by Leonhard Ragaz and was in frequent use among Swiss and Czech religious socialists. This watchword has its polemical dimension. Its users protested against the "idealistic bias" of the main streams of traditional theologies, that is, against the notorious tendency to interpret the themes of biblical faith under spiritualistic presuppositions as themes from the realm of "metaphysics and inwardness." In its positive sense, the slogan tried to remind Christians of the holistic nature of biblical thought, which encompasses "heaven and earth." As Ragaz said: "Matter, too, is God's creation. It is sanctified by him. It belongs to him. It must serve and glorify him."[1]

Such emphases express a clear socioethical concern. They strengthen the longing for just social conditions, for such a solution of the bread question that would be more faithful to the biblical imperative of righteousness. In this essay, special attention will be devoted to the fourth petition of the Lord's Prayer as a key expression of the biblical "holy materialism."[2] How should we understand the bread petition of Jesus? How does it contribute to our understanding of our human condition? In three steps I shall try to deal with these issues.

---

1. Leonhard Ragaz, *Von der Revolution der Bibel,* vol. 1, *Das Unservater* (Zurich, 1942), p. 17.
2. In the broader setting, I dealt with the fourth petition in my recent book *The Lord's Prayer,* trans. Geoffrey W. Bromiley (Grand Rapids: Eerdmans, 1990).

320

Hungering Human Being

Give us this day our daily bread. In the light of this petition, humanity is seen basically to be hungry, to be dependent constantly on bread, to be needy. The biblical view of humanity takes this elemental human condition very seriously. There is a holy materialism of the prophetic and apostolic message. Humanity's material needs must never be underestimated. They have their rights and dignity on the basis of God's good creation. Taken from the earth, we are earthly creatures. God has given us the earth and its material powers and resources. We depend on them. We need not be ashamed of this dependence. We need not keep quiet about it or repress it. We are body as well as soul, with all that this implies. We have impulses, needs, and material interests. To have no material needs is not in itself an ideal. In this regard the Bible parts company with many religions and philosophical trends in which asceticism plays a decisive role. Diogenes with his program of setting aside every need is no "saint," no model of Christian piety, even though he might have found many admirers and disciples in church history, especially in monastic circles. Asceticism as an end in itself is not a biblical way.

In the context of human life before God, however, the fourth petition of the Lord's Prayer defines not only the worth of material needs but also their comparative worth. At this point we must allow for the opposing emphasis. More common perhaps than the first case is a second misunderstanding of material interests in human life: an overvaluing of them rather than an undervaluing. As things are — or, to put it theologically, under the *signs* of the Fall — human needs have a notorious tendency to grow, and to grow to excess. There is also a perverted hunger that is oriented to accumulation and growth and that knows no bounds. There is hunger for power. Human drives, including the sex drive in distinction from this drive in other creatures, often go beyond what is in keeping with creation. In principle at least they become insatiable. Material interests take over the heart and become idols.

The petition "Give us this day our daily bread" sets clear limits to this temptation that bedazzles us by its mention of the expressions "daily" and "this day." They limit the question of bread even as they take it seriously both quantitatively and qualitatively. They put what is essential to life in the center: our daily bread today. They set the corresponding priorities. Those who pray this prayer must also set them. This means that we may not put anything we please under the protection and promise of the Lord's Prayer. In the history of exposition and in many sermons on the fourth petition, one may detect a tendency in this direction, even in the best commentators. I recall the fine saying in Luther's Small Catechism in which he lists under "daily bread" not merely nourishment but houses, farms, fields, wives, families, health, and honor. I think that this is basically right, yet it opens the door to misunderstanding. It is as though we could set an extensive list of needs under the petition for bread and in this way justify them. The brief and sober wording of the petition — especially the "daily" and "this day" — counsels restraint as regards this tendency toward free expansion.

Thus in praying the prayer, we must show not only our freedom as regards material needs but also our readiness to test them critically, not to let them grow excessively, not to fall victim to them. Jesus was well aware of the latter temptation. We need only think of the parable of the rich farmer (Luke 12:16-21). This man died because of his obsession with the question of bread. He died both in time and eternity. For, as Jesus said pointedly, "One does not live by bread alone" (Matt. 4:4). Criticism of needs and interests is required.

This criticism was always required, but it is urgently required today. For in distinction from past epochs in world history, we industrialized countries have reached a stage when elemental needs are for the first time met, or, as we might say more cautiously, can be met. We live in a society of superfluity. An unchecked thirst for ever more striking luxuries and their shameless display has recently put forth its artificially cultivated blossoms.

Has it brought with it a leap from the realm of necessity to that of freedom? At first sight it might seem so to an observer from past centuries. Much has been achieved compared with the elementary conditions of life that obtained for our ancestors. Yet most of us know better. In relation to our society we cannot speak of the realm of freedom in the full sense. Our realm of freedom is at the same time a realm of new compulsions. Many of these are linked to the excessive, artificially provoked and manipulated needs of our consumer society. They do not make us freer or richer. At the cost of our true human and cohuman needs, they make us poorer and more dependent.

The prayer for bread in the Lord's Prayer ought to make us rethink the situation. It should do so in the personal sphere by encouraging us freely to restrict our needs. In this sense, we must positively accept ascetic impulses. Let us not forget that in the Sermon on the Mount something is said about fasting (Matt. 6:16-18). Naturally, asceticism will not be an end in itself; it will be a tool in the urgent clarifying of priorities. It will accomplish this in the area of thought by encouraging the church's theology to submit the ideologies and strategies of need in our consumer society to a critical test. It will accomplish it also in social ethics by working out the social dimension of the bread and emphasizing it. This brings us to our second heading in the present discussion.

Bread and Justice

In our commentary thus far on the fourth petition we have not mentioned one little word that appears in two forms. It is the pronoun "us" and "our." We must not overlook it, for it draws our attention to a central point. We do not ask for ourselves alone but in a human community. The bread that we pray for is concretely and expressly our bread, but it is not ours alone. It is our common bread that we share with others. From the standpoint of God's kingdom, the question of justice — along with that of bread — is at the heart of the Lord's Prayer. The bread of the fourth petition is bread that must be shared.

It is noteworthy how often and emphatically in the Old Testament the motif of bread is linked to the command to share. Thus we read in Isaiah 58:7, "Share your bread with the hungry." The psalmist, too, praises God as the one "who executes justice for the oppressed, who gives food to the hungry" (Ps. 146:7). The impressive references to the hungry and oppressed, and the emphatic word "justice," cannot be excluded from any theologically responsible discussion of the petition for bread, and certainly not in any circumstances today. For the nub of the problem is that there are hungry people in our world, masses of them. This is true at a time when, as noted, in vast areas of the world the question of bread is to a large extent detached from the context of physical hunger. In this situation of sharp contrast the words "right" and "justice" have a special force that must very deeply affect Christians who pray the Lord's Prayer. There is something very wrong about our handling of bread if, near and far, millions of hungry people are watching our mountains of bread and butter constantly growing.

Today, especially in so-called better circles, a new use has been found for the word "sin," which otherwise occurs only infrequently. After lavish meals people may say, "I have sinned today." What they mean is that they have sinned against their waistlines. Against their better judgment they have put on too many pounds. But this word, which in these instances is uttered complacently, jokingly, and with the patting of a well-filled stomach, might well take a serious and ominous turn. Extravagant consumption, not only of food but also of other basic raw materials, might become a real sin against

323

our needy fellows and against God, and hence it might also become a judgment. Conversion is needed.

In these circumstances the prayer for bread becomes a word of conversion. "Bread for Brothers" is fittingly the title of an annual ecumenical Swiss collection on behalf of the Third World. Here in fact, face to face with the need of bread in our modern world, Christian philanthropy, the demonstration of practical love of neighbor, is demanded. At the heart of our praying, and also of our readiness to give practical help, the work of relief must be taken up and supported. Even small steps count.

But the scope of the petition is broader. The issue is not just one of private renunciation and benevolence, though these are not to be disparaged as obligatory marks of conversion. Under the conditions of our one world, which is increasingly brought closer together in mutual involvement and dependence, we also must question the systemic conditions under which hunger arises and the gap between rich and poor countries grows. The religious socialists already saw clearly that the Lord's Prayer must be applied in this area that seems to be dominated by forces that are hard to change. Leonhard Ragaz pointed out that in asking for daily bread, "we ask for change in the modern social order, which rests on exploitation and profit. We ask for the overcoming of greed and fear, for fair pay for fair work, for the ending of unemployment, for the disappearance of alcoholism and prostitution, for the saving of nature from destruction by a technology that works in the service of false gods."[3]

For decades ecumenical thinking has been moving in this direction, first (in the 1940s and 1950s) under the slogan "responsible society" (with a predominantly Western orientation), then, after 1966, as Christians from the Third World became increasingly involved, under the slogan "responsible world society." Today we discuss models of a new society, and ways to it, under the slogan "just, sustainable, and participatory society." Note the predicates. The economic order must be just but also sustainable (embracing the environment that is threatened with destruction). Above all, it must be oriented to participation and sharing. Is the ecumenical movement becoming involved in side issues in this regard? I think not, so long as it maintains a theological perspective, reflects and acts in a differentiated way, and avoids ideological shortcuts. The fourth petition encourages us to take steps in this direction. As a Latin American prayer puts it, "O God, to those who have hunger give bread; and to those who have bread the hunger for justice."[4]

3. Ragaz, *Das Unservater,* p. 19.
4. Quoted by Krister Stendahl, "Your Kingdom Come," *Cross Currents* 32, no. 2 (1982): 263.

God and Bread

To pray "Give us this day our daily bread" is to confess that God and bread belong inseparably together, whether the movement be from God to bread or from bread to God. Thus far we have been looking in the first direction. God comes into the question of bread, and God's justice applies there. Let us now stress the other aspect. When we receive, we eat our bread before God. The fourth petition of the Lord's Prayer and the whole Bible, especially the Old Testament, teach us to value bread as a good gift of God. True, bread is also a product of human hands, the result of economic activity. For biblical faith, however, it is at the same time infinitely more; it is a proof of the goodness of the Creator.

From the standpoint of the Lord's Prayer, then, the question of bread is not just an economic matter. It is also a theological matter and primarily a doxological matter. In the Bible praise and thanksgiving constantly ring out for daily bread, for ours and for the food given to our fellows and to fellow creatures. The words of the psalmist are unforgettable: "The eyes of all look to you, and you give them their food in due season. You open your hand, satisfying the desire of every living thing" (Ps. 145:15-16). A Jewish grace from the time of Jesus is to the same effect: "Praised be you, O Lord our God, king of the world, who feeds the whole world by your goodness. In grace, love, and mercy he gives bread to all flesh. . . . For he feeds and provides for all and shows his kindness to all and assigns food to all his creatures which he has made. Praised be you, Lord, who feeds all."[5]

In such texts, for which the New Testament has parallels in various contexts, two emphases stand out. First, they portray God as a generous Creator and extol God as a giver of bread. God grants food not just to those who have merited it but to all. We recall the saying of Jesus in Matthew 5:45 that the sun shines on the evil as well as the good and that the rain refreshes all. Fundamentally, God's righteousness is not oriented to work or merit; it is rich in grace. This is worth noting, with all its ramifications. In a humanitarian society the question of bread cannot take the rigid form of a question of mere achievement. It is true that in everyday life in society we can hardly avoid evaluating achievement. We need the carrot and the stick if we are to focus our gifts and forces, to mobilize them and put them to use. But before God the mentality and society of achievement find their limits. They do so concretely in the

---

5. See P. Billerbeck, *Kommentar zum NT aus Talmud und Midrasch* (Munich: Beck'sche, 1928), pp. 6, 531.

matter of bread. Bread — that is, the elemental conditions of life — must be made available, as far as possible, to all. Various measures that are being taken in East and West to achieve this goal are steps in the right direction.

The second emphasis is that if bread and God belong together, then for us bread and thanksgiving belong together. The texts already quoted are thanksgivings, graces. The people of the Bible, and devout people in all ages, realize that we cannot take bread for granted. This fact bitterly confronts them in experiences of want and hunger. From a vertical standpoint (i.e., in relation to God), bread ultimately comes from God. It is a sign and gift of God's grace. Recollection of the story of the manna offers an illustration. The first thing we ought to do when we take bread, even before eating, is to give thanks, to say grace.

We are probably tempted to dismiss this matter as nostalgic. But more is at stake than the fine habit of saying grace or table manners in general. (It should be noted that in our lands of overabundance, there is vacillation between the two extremes of fast food, hasty eating with no social contact, and lavish display, meaningless and unworthy excess. Both fall short not merely in terms of human culture but also of the dignity of bread as the good gift of God.) From the standpoint of the spirit of prayer, we must handle bread differently, namely with glad thankfulness and respect.

The Czech language has a fine term for bread that was earlier used as an equivalent for grace in popular speech: boží dar, "God's gift," often in the diminutive with a suggestion of tenderness, boží dárek (which is very hard to translate). Thus if a piece of bread fell from the table in peasants' houses, the custom was to lift it up very carefully and to kiss it reverently.

Now in saying this, I am not calling for compulsory grace or for training in the kissing of bread. What I am asking for is reflection on the essential point that the inseparable relation between God and bread brings before us, namely, that we cannot take bread for granted, or, to put it positively, that we must learn to eat bread thankfully. We do not live by bread alone. This statement also means that the mere eating of bread alone, without gratitude and in detachment from God and neighbor, cannot be a means of blessing to us. We die by bread alone. This is a danger that threatens to destroy us both morally and socially in our society of overabundance, whether before God or our hungry fellows. To take things for granted in our dealings with bread, to have the lack of gratitude and respect that may be seen in our madness of consumption and waste — these things attack at the roots of a "just, sustainable, and participatory society." Here again we must say that conversion is needed. To pray "Give us this day our daily bread" is for us the beginning of revolt against this disorder in the world.

In Dialogue with the Marxists

The subtitle of this essay speaks of "The Question of Bread in Christian and Marxist Perspectives." Until now I have not referred to the latter problematic. Still, it was present. Biblical interpretation was carried out in the presence of the Marxist challenge. Granted, biblical interpretation must primarily respect the biblical text and context; it occurs in connection with the church's history of interpretation. But beyond that, it stands in direct or indirect dialogue with the thought of the time.

The thought of the time — for me that was and is especially, though not exclusively, the thought of the Marxist. Now, Marxist ideology has suffered a crushing defeat in Eastern and Central Europe in the last few months. Above all, the foolish elevation of Marxist theory to the only permissible worldview of "real socialism" was revenged, in that the breakdown of the totalitarian system was felt by most citizens to be a breakdown of Marxism itself. I palpably experienced this on the occasion of a recent engagement at the universities of Brno and Bratislava. I spoke in the auditoriums of both universities, which once displayed the proud inscription "Marxism-Leninism — the science of all sciences and the art of all arts." This totalitarian claim has utterly foundered.

Has, thereby, for us theologians, the Marxist challenge been laid to rest? I would like to warn against such a conclusion. To answer totalitarian pseudoclaims with such a blanket statement would be a short-circuit hardly worthy of a free — above all, theological — way of thinking. It is imperative to combine criticism with self-criticism. In this context — that of the question of bread — I would like to close this article with three short points that follow the three trains of thought developed above.

First, Marxism to me is important as a historical-material theory. In every age theology lives in dialogue with philosophy. For centuries theology had its choice, but mostly in the direction of idealistic ways of thinking, such as Plato, Aristotle, or German idealism. These are all respectable names and movements. Nevertheless, the successors of these traditions often underestimated the material world and the concerns of the flesh. Marxism, as historical materialism, forces us to take seriously the material, above all economic questions, and thereby to rediscover something of biblical realism. The concrete *need of the hungry* should not be spiritually transfigured or softened. Thus, "holy materialism." It is no accident that this slogan has been preferred by religious socialists, that is, those theologians who have engaged themselves with Marx. Leonhard Ragaz rightly formulated: "From Christ to Marx — from Marx to Christ."[6] He was correct in both parts of this book title.

Second, Marxism reminds us of the prophetic truth that the question of bread as a material question is at the same time a social question, and therefore a question of *social justice.* In that regard the Marxist challenge enjoins us especially strongly to pay attention to the structural aspects of the problematic. "The human being — that is the world of human beings." "Human nature is the ensemble of social relationships." These classic formulations of the young Marx are one-sided. The human being is not *merely* that. Nevertheless, they address important aspects of the question of bread, that is, the problematic of justice. This viewpoint concerns not only personal behavior, as important as it is in the life of faith, but also order, circumstances, and conditions. These aspects have seldom received their due in the history of theology. Meaningful initiatives in the area of philanthropy, the alleviation of need, were often encouraged, but an analysis of the conditions and engagement to change them followed only seldom. Here Christians must make up for much neglect and could learn from Marxists.

Three, there are certain cases, however, in which — from the Christian viewpoint — Marxist ideology and strategy come up short on the question of bread and are in need of supplementation. I am thinking especially of the question-complex "God and bread." Marxism tried to eliminate God and, wherever possible, to shut faith out of public life in Marxist-dominated societies. Thereby, however, the essential *condition humaine* was distorted, the knowledge of the earthly accountability of the human being diminished. The question of justice was dogmatically reserved to a particular ideology and party, with alienating consequences in the interpersonal and also the economic areas. The question of bread cannot be solved if one understands the human being only as the "world of human beings" and the "ensemble of social relationships" and undervalues the personal worth of the individual, with his or her creative and destructive possibilities; or concretely, if one forgets that "one does not live by bread alone." It appears that today, in this age of perestroika and of drawing from the experience gained from the Christian-Marxist dialogue, critical Marxists are becoming open to this insight.

6. Leonhard Ragaz, *Von Christus zu Marx — von Marx zu Christus* (Wernigerode, 1929).

Here the meaning and contribution of the churches in Marxist society have become visible. The churches were for decades unwelcome. Yet, they remained and created in time, in spite of all enforced restrictions of their possibilities, a modest, though highly significant, *free space*. That free space was above all present where they tried without bitterness to render their special service out of the spirit of the gospel in the middle of the totalitarian temptations of their societies. They did this — with regard to the question of bread — through the steadfast prayer "Give us this day our daily bread," through practical engagement for a just solution to the question of bread, and through persistent witness that "one does not live by bread alone, but by every word that comes from the mouth of God" (Matt. 4:4). It is imperative to pay attention to all these three accents — in the East and in the West.

19

The Voluntary Principle and the Search for Racial Justice

PETER J. PARIS

V OLUNTARY ASSOCIATIONS are essential marks of a democracy. Unlike
the two natural associations of family and state, voluntary associations
imply the experience of public freedom and individual choice.[1] The striking
novelty associated with the so-called democratic experiment in the nascent
United States was the ubiquitous function of the voluntary principle
throughout the society. In describing this phenomenon, Alexis de Tocqueville wrote in the 1830s,

> In no other country in the world has the principle of association been
> more successfully used or applied to a greater multitude of objects than
> in America. . . .
>
> The citizen of the United States is taught from infancy to rely upon
> his own exertions in order to resist the evils and the difficulties of life;
> he looks upon the social authorities with an eye of mistrust and anxiety,
> and he claims its assistance only when he is unable to do without it. This
> habit may be traced even in the schools, where the children in their games
> are wont to submit to rules which they have themselves established, and

1. Most of the salient characteristics of voluntary associations are set forth in an essay
entitled "The Nature of Voluntary Associations" by Karl Hertz, in *Voluntary Associations: A
Study of Groups in Free Societies: Essays in Honor of James Luther Adams*, ed. D. B. Robinson
(Richmond, Va.: John Knox Press, 1966), pp. 17ff. This author is also indebted to several
other essayists in the above volume as well as the works of James Luther Adams, who is often
called "the father of voluntary associations."

to punish misdemeanors which they have themselves defined. . . . In the United States associations are established to promote the public safety, commerce, industry, morality and religion. There is no end which the human will despair of attaining through the combined power of individuals united into a society.[2]

Tocqueville concluded that everything in America was republican, including its religion, which was a most surprising discovery for him, since the spirit of freedom that expressed itself in the French Revolution had not extended to religion. Rather, the church in France had continued to enjoy its place of transcendence over the state in contrast to the separation of church and state that had developed in the United States. Hence, Tocqueville admitted surprise in his discovery that one meets a politician every time one meets a priest in the United States because the latter had to rely on the art of persuasion rather than the command of authority as the first principle of effective leadership. More important, the voluntary principle implied an egalitarian society that permitted no entitlements of governance to political, social, or religious elites. Rather, individual choice was to govern all associational relations. In other words, the freedom of individuals to choose both their political and religious associations relativized the traditional authority of each and, hence, grounded both in an understanding of humanity that was heavily indebted to the political philosophy that stemmed from the Enlightenment.

The Voluntary Principle and Freedom

The primacy of the voluntary principle in associational life subjects all authority to the will of the people. When institutionalized, this principle presupposes the conditions of freedom of speech and association, including that of religious liberty and political dissent. Under such conditions, all agree that freedom of the press, freedom to vote on all public matters, freedom to function on juries, and freedom of worship are the essential rights of all citizens. Inevitably, such an understanding of freedom has shaped an ethos in American society wherein most are suspicious of all authority and strongly opposed to any authority that is not subject to the will of the people. The rise of political parties and religious denominations

2. Alexis de Tocqueville, *Democracy in America*, vol. 1 (New York: Vintage Books, 1945), pp. 198–99.

in the United States is expressive of this voluntary principle.[3] Certain economic philosophies, bureaucratic and military procedures, as well as some ecclesial traditions find themselves in tension with the implications of voluntarism whenever they are pressed to justify their heteronomy. Interestingly, many ecclesiastical hierarchies in the United States receive their legitimation directly from the people whom they lead.

Clearly, every form of heteronomous rule abhors dissent and, consequently, must rely on some form of effective coercion in order to maintain itself. In the interest of order, heteronomy views dissent as illegitimate. Under such conditions, all social reform must be initiated by those who rule. Such leadership from the top down kills imagination and creativity and takes responsibility away from the ruled, who are inevitably viewed either as innocents or rebels. Hence, the rate of social change is necessarily slow. Democratic governance, in contrast, encourages its people to be continuously vigilant concerning public affairs and to exercise their freedom of speech and of association in initiating social criticism and, through the art of persuasion, to generate public support and action. That is to say, in a democracy, the starting point for social change is the perceived discontent of some people relative to a *felt* issue, which in turn leads to the expenditure of energy aimed at bringing this felt issue to public visibility and thereby creating a public issue, that is, one supported by a plurality of people acting together for its effective resolution. Such cooperative activity constitutes the purpose of voluntary associations, even though it must be noted that social change is not always the aim of all voluntary associations.

On the contrary, voluntary associations may have innumerable purposes, ranging from those that are strictly private and professional (i.e., bent on supporting and promoting some form of the status quo, to say nothing about those that seek to prevent others from sharing some particular benefit or right) to those that expressly aim at social transformation. In short, voluntary associations do not exhibit a shared moral ethos. The common characteristic among all of them is people organizing their own groups for their own purposes. In this respect, voluntary associations represent manifest freedom. Most important, they evidence the rights of all to dissent and to mobilize public support for social change. Respect for pluralistic perspectives on public issues inheres in the voluntary principle. It

---

3. See James Luther Adams, "The Voluntary Principle in the Forming of American Religion" in *The Religion of the Republic*, ed. Edwin A. Smith (Philadelphia: Fortress Press, 1971), pp. 217ff. See also Sidney E. Mead, *The Lively Experiment: The Shaping of Christianity in America* (New York: Harper & Row, 1963), chaps. 7 and 8.

is evident, however, that leadership from the bottom up constantly threatens social coherence and social order. Thus, their strong affirmation of pluralism implies strong support for social conflict with respect to public issues.[4]

The African-American Struggle for Racial Justice

Unfortunately, the experience of freedom has not always been available to all persons and groups in the United States.[5] For nearly a century following the period of Reconstruction, the majority of African-Americans living in the former states of the old Confederacy were systematically disfranchised and socially oppressed both by law and by social custom. These and similar conditions prohibited viable public associational life among African-Americans. The latter were permitted, however, to organize churches and selected other associations as long as they posed no threat to the social order and its customs. It was not uncommon for the legal and judicial authorities to ban certain groups when they failed to live up to the expectations of the white majority. Legal controls were aided and abetted by the vigilante activity of the Ku Klux Klan, a constant source of terrorist threat.

In spite of these many strictures, however, the Montgomery Improvement Association in close alliance with the black churches emerged in 1956 in the heart of the old Alabama Confederacy for the purpose of challenging the laws and customs of racial segregation and discrimination. As the precursor to the Southern Christian Leadership Conference, formed in 1957 by Martin Luther King, Jr., the association was dedicated to the purpose of extending the Montgomery struggle for racial justice throughout the South.[6]

Interestingly, King's work was supported morally and financially by many religious and civic associations outside the environs of the southern states. In fact, King and his followers relied heavily on the U.S. Supreme Court and the attorney general's office for supportive leadership and

4. See George H. Williams, "The Religious Background of the Idea of a Loyal Opposition," in *Voluntary Associations: A Study of Groups in Free Societies,* ed. D. B. Robertson (Richmond, Va.: John Knox Press, 1966), pp. 55ff.

5. Charles H. Long, "Civil Rights — Civil Religion: Visible People and Visible Religions," in *American Civil Religion,* ed. Russell E. Richey and Donald G. James (New York: Harper & Row, 1974), pp. 211ff.

6. This story is told best by Martin Luther King, Jr., in his *Stride toward Freedom: The Montgomery Story* (New York: Harper & Row, 1958).

worked diligently to persuade Presidents Eisenhower and Kennedy to act decisively in support of the goals of racial justice. Eventually, the long-awaited presidential leadership (from Presidents Kennedy and Johnson) followed by the Civil Rights Bills of 1964 and 1965, provided the long-desired legitimation from both the executive and the congressional branches of government.[7] But one should not suppose that such came either easily or early in their struggle. Clearly, the moral legitimation of both the churches (white and black) and the state were important sources of encouragement for both King and his nonviolent resistance movement, whose goal was the eradication of the sociopolitical system euphemistically called "Jim Crow."

Contrary to popular opinion in the South, many in the North and around the world viewed King and his followers as courageous social-change agents worthy of emulation. In spite of their destiny of having to suffer immensely at the hands of Bull Connor's dogs and water hoses, Sheriff Pritchard's whips and jailings, bombings of homes and churches, brutal beatings and many killings, the movement itself eventually assumed the character of a nonviolent holy crusade. Before long, it became a matter of moral virtue for many whites throughout the nation to express their solidarity with this nonviolent resistance movement by marching in support of civil rights for black Americans. Not surprisingly, blacks who advocated the use of violence as a measure of self-defense (i.e., some SNCC leaders and Malcolm X) received no legitimation whatsoever from the white society. In fact, such advocates were invariably condemned forthrightly. Clearly, whites were not disposed to fight another civil war in order to ensure the civil rights of black Americans, and the latter generally knew that they were too small a minority to wage an effective battle independently. Hence, the civil rights movement and its leader, Martin Luther King, Jr., conjoined the African-American tradition of moral suasion with the novel and creative activity of nonviolent direct resistance in a most successful way — methods, incidentally, that are essential marks of voluntary associations, namely, freedom to dissent and to protest.

Yet in the South, a generalized social consensus characterized the vast majority of whites relative to the quest for racial justice. In fact, the majority

---

7. This is a recurrent theme in the masterful study of Taylor Branch, *Parting the Waters: America in the King Years, 1954–63* (New York: Simon & Schuster, 1988), see pp. 181–83, 219–22, 399–400. See also King's agreement with this judgment, which he expressed in "A Testament of Hope," in *A Testament of Hope: The Essential Writings of Martin Luther King, Jr.,* ed. James M. Washington (New York: Harper & Row, 1986), p. 320.

of southern whites seemed to oppose virtually everything that characterized the thought and action of Martin Luther King, Jr. They rightly saw that the so-called civil rights movement posed a major threat to the social order. Like King and his followers, these often appealed to both biblical and ecclesial traditions as religious and moral grounds for justifying their opposing position. These conflicting traditions necessitated adjudication by the superior legal authorities of the nation, namely, the U.S. Congress and Supreme Court.

The most obvious contemporary example of a similar struggle in the quest for racial justice was the antiapartheid movement in South Africa. Unlike the American struggle, the opponents of constitutional apartheid could appeal to no legitimate authority within the Republic of South Africa for either moral or legal support. As with every state, legitimation was derived from the law. Hence, antiapartheid activities were long rendered unlawful by the constitution of the Republic of South Africa. Consequently, many nonviolent protesters in that land were tried for treason (punishable by the death penalty) because their objections did not aim at legal reform but, rather, the need for a new constitution. Lest there be doubt about this matter, the Government of South Africa frequently declared national states of emergency in order to give law enforcement officials unlimited powers in terminating civil protests.

Following his first visit to South Africa in 1985, James Cone, the progenitor of the black theology movement, said that being in South Africa made him imagine what it would have been like for a black American to be in the South during the 1940s and 1950s with no North.[8] That is a graphic description of one of the major differences between the two struggles. All moral and religious support for the antiapartheid movement from outside the country was devoid of legitimacy by the ruling elites. Hence, the latter considered all such persons as enemies of the state, that is, revolutionaries in both the form and aim of their protests. In South Africa no appeal to either rational or religious sources could be effective in changing the moral and religious perspectives of the proponents of apartheid. As with similar struggles elsewhere, few converts were made from either side by persuasion alone. Even appeals to majority rule (i.e., one person, one vote) as a self-evident democratic principle could have no credibility in a society that excluded the majority of the population from citizenship. Had the southern states been successful in seceding from the

8. James H. Cone, *Speaking the Truth: Ecumenism, Liberation, and Black Theology* (Grand Rapids: Eerdmans, 1986), p. 164.

union in the 1860s and had they constituted themselves into a sovereign nation with a constitution legitimating racial segregation and discrimination, the result would have been strikingly similar to what obtained in the Republic of South Africa until very recently.

The moral and religious problem evident in the above comparison is that of conflict between moral and religious traditions. When religious and moral understandings between plural communities are diametrically opposed to one another, how can such be effectively resolved? More specifically, in both South Africa and the United States, opposing racial groups regularly appealed to common source materials (i.e., the Bible and ecclesial tradition) to justify contradictory societal practices and perspectives. No attempt will be made in this essay to determine the original causation of either. Suffice it to say that rigorous consistency of argument attends both sides of the conflict, and both positions can be argued either deductively (i.e., from theological position to social practice) or inductively (i.e., from social practice to theological position). Clearly, neither side can gain the loyalty of the other by moral and religious suasion alone. Other relevant resources must be employed.

Voluntary Associations as Agents of Social Change

If the practical problem of racial justice cannot be solved by theological and ethical appeals alone, then on what additional agency should one rely for effective social change? I contend that parapolitical agency is the key to the answer. In other words, the issue of racial justice must become a public issue with sufficient breadth of perspective, depth of analysis, and popular appeal in order to attain the desired goal. What, then, are the basic conditions and capacities for such activity? Freedom of speech and of association are necessary conditions for the type of public debate and deliberation that is required. When these are denied, social-change agents are forced to rely on illegal, clandestine activities as means to their desired goal. By definition, both their means and purposes are judged as radical by the established authorities. More often than not, these conditions lead social-change agents to consider seriously the use of violence in pursuit of their goals. More moderate means of nonviolent resistance, however, may often be effective in achieving moderate goals of social reform, as evidenced in Martin Luther King's southern strategies. Curiously, similar moderate means of nonviolent resistance may be effective in bringing about radical social change as revealed in the success of Mahatma Gandhi's movement in overthrowing

British colonialism. The desire for broad-base association comprising a rich diversity of peoples and perspectives in search for a common life is a primary indicator of the human capacity to construct a viable deliberate process for the continuous pursuit of that goal.

Whenever a moral, religious, and/or political conflict emerges between human communities, no lasting effective resolution can be had apart from the willingness of all relevant parties to negotiate a just outcome. Even if the groups should war violently against each other, the final, lasting goal can only be an agreed-upon, just peace. Conquest alone can never lead to a just peace; rather, it leads only to two perpetually alienated groups: the conquerors and the conquered. The alienation is not overcome either by conquest or the threat thereof. There thus can never be any peace under the conditions of tyranny, in spite of certain social indicators implying the contrary.

Why is the political quest for a community of diverse peoples morally, religiously, and politically good? More important, why should such a quest be preferred to that of maintaining and promoting a more homogeneous society? Our answer to that query is built, first of all, on the fact of human nature. Humans have the capacity to transcend their natural communities of family and tribal belonging by forging wider communities of belonging not by the brute force of conquest but by the persuasive art of design. In exercising that capacity, humans reveal their unique nature, namely, their capacity for establishing, nurturing, enhancing, and expanding moral communities. By so doing, humans overcome certain inclinations toward contentment with limited tribal and parochial experience.

Resources abound in the Judeo-Christian tradition supportive of narrow tribal religion, on the one hand (e.g., the election of Israel as God's chosen people and the various forms of Christian sectarianism), and a more universal community, on the other (e.g., the Judeo-Christian God portrayed as Creator of all that is and, hence, divine parent of all peoples, implying kinship relations among them all).[9] Every form of racism, tribalism, sexism, nationalism, and classism among Christians has appealed selectively to biblical and ecclesial traditions. That is to say, they wrench the specificity of Jewish or Christian tribal relations from the universal divine relation and its implica-

9. In my explication of the moral and religious tradition of the black churches, I have described the black Christian tradition as expressive of a nonracist biblical principle, "the parenthood of God and the kinship of all peoples," which has been institutionalized in the black churches, making them the only institutions in America rightly claiming a nonracist history. See my *Social Teaching of the Black Churches* (Philadelphia: Fortress Press, 1986).

tions for worldwide community among all peoples. In doing so, they distort the Judeo-Christian tradition and advocate morally perverse social and political relations accordingly. Those who oppose the oppressive results of such narrow parochialism by pressing for a broader community of belonging are more faithful to the holism implicitly and explicitly evident in the Judeo-Christian tradition. But the opposition to all forms of external control and the thrust for the reform of social systems are set in motion by persons and groups voluntarily acting in association with one another. Whenever reform comes from the top down, it necessarily reflects more the values and interests of the top than those at the bottom. This may not be totally bad by any means. In fact it may well be a good beginning. But change from the top down is almost never sufficient because the values and interest of those at the top and those at the bottom never coincide completely.

Now, the key element in understanding the nature of social change at any time is the purposive activity of those voluntary associations whose primary aim is that of correcting some moral problem(s) in the social order. Such associations are the source of creative initiative and patient persistence in defining public issues, mobilizing support for those issues, advocating necessary correctives, and designing instrumentalities for effecting the desired changes. Their power lies in their capacity to energize their constituencies to coalesce around a common cause and participate in activities that disturb the regular patterns of thought and practices held by the relevant centers of power. By fomenting social conflict, they seek legitimation for and redress of their moral claims. The more proximate goal of legitimation is sometimes realized when the relevant centers of power agree to negotiate and when the final objective is evidenced in a mutually satisfactory redress of the problem(s) through policy agreement. This process may be a relatively simple one, most often demonstrated in the arbitration process for resolving management-labor disputes, or as complex as the quest for civil rights for blacks in the United States, which necessitated the involvement of various levels of interconnected governmental and judicial processes all the way from local municipalities to the U.S. Congress, the office of the president, and the Supreme Court. It is our hypothesis that both the form and the rate of social change depend on the availability of viable voluntary associations, the validity of which requires the following conditions: (1) their legitimation and protection by law, (2) the absence of terrorist threats relative to the public expression of grievance, and (3) the availability of an adequate number of courageous, self-conscious, discontented people desirous of improving the quality of the social order and morally disposed to act in pursuit of it.

With respect to racial justice, the form of its pursuit and the rate of progress in its attainment are directly proportionate to how free and courageous its advocates are, since the formation of voluntary associations with public purposes for effecting social change requires both freedom and courage. Let us hasten to say, however, that we assume that those on whom injustice is inflicted must always be the primary agents both in resisting the injustice and in advocating a just corrective.[10] Others who might join in solidarity with that quest can serve only auxiliary functions. They rarely initiate the quest for systematic change on behalf of others. Their acts of compassion and support are always welcomed but should not be confused with the essential activity of the primary actors.

The primacy I give to voluntary associations as agents of social change implies an associational theory of society, which I contend is the essence of any democratic community. Hence, the full realization of democracy in America for all its citizens represented the raison d'être of the African-American struggle for liberation and justice, a struggle that both then and now was institutionalized in the black churches and their allied organizations.

Ironically, whenever legalized racial segregation of large concentrations occurred, there inevitably developed a parallel social system of segregated schools, colleges, trade schools, businesses, churches, and the press, to mention only a few. E. Franklin Frazier and others concluded that there virtually developed within the United States "a nation within a nation," differentiated by the principle of race. South Africa's apartheid state exhibited the most blatant form of this pattern in our day. In each case, the constellation of segregated institutions unwittingly provided relatively independent spaces that nurtured an ethos of suspicion vis-à-vis the external racist world, which in turn encouraged the spirit of criticism, humor, knowledge, and moral discernment concerning their respective social situations. Thus, some degree of critical social analysis and advocacy for social change appeared in some form or other throughout that segregated space. That ethos of criticism constituted the first principle for constructive thought and practice relative to the desired change.

10. Here the author reveals the influence of Reinhold Niebuhr's view of the morally deceptive and hypocritical nature of the privileged class, which inevitably protects its own moral virtue through varying forms of rationalization. See his *Moral Man and Immoral Society* (New York: Charles Scribner's Sons, 1960), chap. 5.

Racial Justice and the Realm of Politics

Assuming the laudable history of the black churches as institutional agents in the enduring struggle for racial justice and assuming their continuing primacy[11] as voluntary associations concerned with enhancing the quality of social justice in our black communities, let us turn to the contemporary moral and religious demand that the black churches need to accept if our blighted communities are to be restored to viable health. Clearly, the black churches have an enviable history as prophetic organizations demanding social justice via the art of moral suasion and varied forms of nonviolent resistance. The lawful demise of racial discrimination and segregation in the public domain marks a turning point in the public mission of the churches. The latter must now become more self-consciously political in the broad sense of the word — that is, directly aiding a people's deliberate efforts to build structures for enhancing the quality of human association that, in turn, will provide the necessary conditions for the lives of all citizens to flourish.

This political function is not alien to the black tradition. In fact, W. E. B. DuBois argued that the church represented all that was left of African tribal life on these shores. Accordingly, he wrote:

> As a social group the Negro church may be said to have antedated the Negro family functions. Its tribal functions are shown in its religious activity, its social authority and general guiding and coordinating work; its family functions are shown by the fact that the church is the center of social life and intercourse, acts as a newspaper and intelligence bureau, is the centre of amusements — indeed, is the world in which the Negro moves and acts. So far reaching are these functions that its organization is almost political.[12]

Although the black churches have traditionally addressed all sorts of public issues and although they have spearheaded numerous voter registration drives and voter education projects, including endorsements of candidates, campaigning, poll watching, and fund-raising, we propose that

11. This assumption is strongly confirmed by the conclusions drawn by C. Eric Lincoln and Lawrence Mamiya in their massive empirical study of the black churches, *The Black Churches in the African American Experience* (Durham, N.C.: Duke University Press, 1990).

12. This quotation is from an essay by Kelly Miller Smith, "Religion as a Force in Black America," in *The State of Black America, 1982,* ed. James D. Williams (New York: National Urban League, 1982), p. 215.

they must now intensify all of these latter efforts, including the increased fielding of candidates for public office. This must now be done for theological, moral, and political reasons.

Theological Rationale

The gospel of liberation and justice, long proclaimed by the black churches, implies institutionalization, lest it be cast aside as an abstract, formal platitude devoid of historical appearance. As the black churches constituted the original institutional locus for a nonracist Christianity,[13] in sharp contrast to their white counterparts, and as they expressed their devotion to such a viewpoint in their moral support and engagement in a myriad of organizations and associations dedicated to the pursuit of social justice, so now they must continue that tradition of enriching the public realm with their self-conscious involvement in all aspects of electoral politics. Undoubtedly, their experience in parapolitical activities can be immeasurably helpful in defining public issues and mobilizing support in their behalf. Even more important, these churches are peculiarly capable of making good moral judgments about human character and, accordingly, can exercise leadership by giving their blessings to men and women of integrity who view public service as an expression of their Christian devotion.

Such a venture implies many difficulties, none of which are insurmountable. In fact, the political experience and wisdom of many who are both church leaders and politically experienced, such as Shirley Chisholm, Walter Fountroy, William Gray, John Lewis, Floyd Flake, Patten Mitchell, Andrew Young, and Jesse Jackson (to mention only a few), constitute a reservoir for critical thought and guidance. (Note that all of these stand in the tradition of such notable Reconstruction trailblazers as the Reverend Hiram Revels, first black U.S. Senator; the Reverend Richard Cain, who served both as state senator and U.S. Congressman; and the Reverend Adam Clayton Powell, Jr., who, from 1944 to 1970, served with distinction in the U.S. Congress.) The same black church that produced numerous prophets, educational and civic leaders, men and women of unusual practical wisdom, courage, and devotion, as well as countless numbers of enthusiastic supporters from all walks of life must now enhance its rhythm of social protest with the activity of political consolidation and expansion. In brief,

13. See the author's *Social Teaching of the Black Churches* for a full description of this viewpoint.

the fathers and mothers of the liberation struggle must now pass the mantle to their successors, who will be the "nation builders." These must occupy the seats of power in order to contribute to the task of constructing a good and just society wherein the sociopolitical structures will facilitate the well-being of all citizens and hinder none from actualizing their potentiality.

Moral Rationale

The purpose of the good state should be that of enabling the good of all its citizens, that is, the promotion of justice for all. Thus the purpose of good politics is ethical in nature, namely, to help citizens internalize the purpose of the state by becoming just persons themselves. The black churches and their allied associations have had excellent preparation for such a moral task, the most recent evidence of which being the process by which the civil rights movement under the leadership of the Reverend Martin Luther King, Jr., effected a moral revolution in the nation's legal framework. For more than a decade, black church leaders rendered public service by giving persuasive moral fiber to the pressing issues of racial justice in the body politic. Their accomplishments marked the end of an era in American history and the beginning of a new epoch filled with potentiality. They must now become the torchbearers of a more substantive political agenda and exercise leadership for its actualization.

The aspect of their prophetic tradition that should serve black church leaders well in this new mission is the public-regarding spirit that disposes them to seek justice for all citizens rather than the few alone. In fact, Martin Luther King, Jr., predicted the need for this present moment and saw political organization as the logical step following the legal guarantee of basic civil rights. Consequently, he called for such nonviolent expressions of resistance to evil as boycotts, peaceful demonstrations, individual and collective sacrifice, education, and political organizations.

> To produce change, people must be organized to work together in units of power. These units might be political, as in the case of voters' leagues and political parties; they may be economic units such as groups of tenants who join forces to form a tenant union or to organize a rent strike; or they may be laboring units of persons who are seeking employment and wage increases.
>
> More and more the civil rights movement will be engaged in the task of organizing people into permanent groups to protect their own inter-

ests and to produce change in their behalf. This is a tedious task which may take years, but the results are more permanent and meaningful.[14]

And in his last SCLC presidential address, King addressed the need for power.

> Another basic challenge is to discover how to organize our strength in terms of economic and political power. No one can deny that the Negro is in dire need of this kind of legitimate power. Indeed, one of the great problems that the Negro confronts is his lack of power. From old plantations of the South to newer ghettos of the North, the Negro has been confined to a life of voicelessness and powerlessness. Stripped of the right to make decisions concerning his life and destiny, he has been subject to the authoritarian and sometimes whimsical decisions of this white power structure. . . . The problem of transforming the ghetto, therefore, is a problem of power.[15]

King then continues his discussion of power by offering a corrective to those clergy and others who view power as devoid of love and justice. Clearly influenced by Paul Tillich, King argues, "Now we've got to get this thing right. What is needed is a realization that power without love is reckless and abusive, and love without power is sentimental and anemic. Power at its best is love implementing the demands of justice, and justice at its best is power correcting everything that stands against love."[16]

Political Rationale

Several years ago Professor Charles V. Hamilton drew an important correlation between American political leadership and that of the black churches by arguing that both were rooted in local organizational structures primarily concerned with the well-being of their constituents. Both political and religious leaders must maintain the trust of their people and be sensitive

14. Martin Luther King, Jr., "Non-Violence: The Only Way to Freedom," in *A Testament of Hope: The Essential Writings of Martin Luther King, Jr.,* ed. James M. Washington (New York: Harper & Row, 1986), pp. 60–61.

15. Martin Luther King, Jr., "Where Do We Go from Here?" in *A Testament of Hope: The Essential Writings of Martin Luther King, Jr.,* ed. James M. Washington (New York: Harper & Row, 1986), p. 246.

16. Ibid., p. 247.

to their needs and be willing to be public advocates for their relief. In other words, he argued that black clergy possess all the elements for good, effective political leadership — namely, high social respect, excellent rhetorical skills, knowledge of local issues and their relatedness to larger social problems, and good moral character. Furthermore, black clergy have the ear of the community, which helps immeasurably in mobilizing volunteers for electioneering purposes.

An important constraint on clergy moving quickly into the arena of electoral politics is the negative moral image that has come to be associated with professional politicians. To date this has not tarnished the character of those black clergy already in public office, and that fact in itself should demonstrate that political office does not necessarily lead to moral decline.

Accepting such a charge could lead to improved public debate on matters relative to the common good. Not since the civil rights movement has the public realm been dominated by a substantive debate about societal structures and their impact on the quality of human life. Black church leaders alone have the capacity to initiate and to mobilize widespread public debate on the devastating social problems presently threatening the lives of one-third of its citizens. This debate must be waged by public policy makers, which implies the necessity of putting in office sufficient numbers of morally qualified people to make the difference.

Thus, an associational theory of society helps to explain in every period the form and rate of social change in America relative to racial liberation and justice. The black church independence movement institutionalized black America's prophetic tradition and provided basic leadership in each period for the long, arduous struggle that reached a watershed in the Civil War and finally culminated in the civil rights legislation of 1964 and 1965. Similarly, the black churches must now become the locus for intensive political activity by deploying their institutional resources to the task of electing church leaders to public office, since the primary need in our day is the consolidation of the civil rights gains into substantive public policy. The black churches have been America's embodiment of the voluntary principle in the search for racial justice. They alone represent the leadership potential that must now actualize itself in the domain of public offices.

20

An Ethical Reflection on the Political Process in a Multireligious Context

K. C. ABRAHAM

THE FOCUS of our reflection in this chapter is the political process necessary for the building of a community based on justice, peace, and human values, with the cooperation of all religions. In a situation where politics is increasingly becoming amoral and seems to have no ethical moorings and the essence of all religions is being undermined and their appeal subverted by fundamentalist upsurge, it is by no means easy to delineate such a process.

I speak primarily from my own Indian experience. India has been a multireligious society for many centuries and continues to be so. In India, Muslims and Christians form two important minority groups. Sociopolitical pluralism that prevailed in the premodern stage in India was based on a culture drawn mainly from the Hindu tradition, whose framework was extremely pluralistic. India never had a political center; the basic identity was cultural.[1] But all religions somehow or other felt at home in that situation.

The emergence of the modern state, thanks to the British rule and the impact of the West on the elite, has changed the political scenario. A secular framework largely based on the liberal humanist traditions of the West was adopted by the elite as a common, centralized political authority. Recent developments have shown that this framework has failed to unite the different religious communities. On the contrary, it has divided them,

---

1. Rajni Kothari, "Cultural Context of Communalism in India," *Economic and Political Weekly* (Bombay) 24, no. 2 (January 14, 1989).

generating antagonistic feelings, violent conflicts, even bloodshed. The very basis of a common political framework in a multireligious context is raised with urgency. The issue discussed and debated in India about the relationship between sociopolitical pluralism and religious pluralism is important to all who strive for a political process necessary to safeguard peace and justice.

My thesis can be simply stated. The search for a common political framework based on human and secular values should be rooted in the religions and cultures of people. The liberational strands within the various religions have the potential for creating a new culture through the "humanizing of myths." Such a culture is necessary for providing a new orientation to the political process. The thesis assumes that the peaceful coexistence of different religious communities is possible only if religions and politics will make a "preferential option for the suffering victims of this suffering earth."[2] This choice will help usher in a new kind of global solidarity that is significantly different from the grand alliance of the politics of domination and religious fundamentalism.

Indian Context: Some Pressures

In India there is a universal acceptance of the concept of pluralism. It is rightly affirmed that plurality belongs to the very structure of reality.[3]

Religious pluralism is a fact of life. It needs to be affirmed and celebrated. Only by doing so can we achieve and practice coexistence in our multireligious context. Our everyday life and relationships in the rural areas are plural. The reality of pluralism comes under severe test in the political realm, however, which is governed by a monolithic state structure and rigid ideologies. Our political process includes various pressures.

2. Paul Knitter, "Cosmic Confidence or Preferential Option?" *Bangalore Theological Forum,* December 1991.

3. S. J. Samartha, *One Christ — Many Religions* (Maryknoll, N.Y.: Orbis Books, 1991; Bangalore: Sathri, 1992), p. 4. Samartha observes, "Religious pluralism is part of the larger plurality of races, peoples, and cultures, of social structures, economic systems and political patterns, of languages and symbols which are part of the total human reality." He considers religious pluralism important, as "it touches ultimate questions about human life and destiny." But perception of such pluralism is influenced by the changes in sociopolitical and cultural realms of life. Perhaps one may agree on a model of mutual interpenetration of these varieties of experience of pluralism, although one may also make a distinction between plural and pluralism. (The latter is perhaps necessary for theoretical discussion, but a plural form of life is integral to the survival of life.)

The Pressure of Group Identities and the Impact of Fundamentalism on the Political Process

A new national consciousness emerged during the struggle for independence. Nationalism was a powerful ideology that brought people from different backgrounds against a common enemy, the colonial power. It was able to hold people together as long as they were fighting the common enemy. After the enemy was driven out, however, it ceased to be an integrating force. A national consciousness with positive content did not emerge. In contrast, the self-consciousness of separate groups and communities emerged with greater force than during the colonial era.

When hitherto subjugated peoples are awakened to their political rights and become conscious of the power they wield by their number and influence, there comes a resurgence of their separate religious and cultural heritages. Values enshrined in old traditions and customs are subjected to critical scrutiny. Some are rejected, some are reinterpreted, and others are reaffirmed with renewed vigor. This process of going back to the origins is important. It can be a source of genuine movement for selfhood and necessary for a mature growth of persons in a community. In fact, Paul Tillich points out that the traditional religions and cultures confront the meaning of transcendence when they raise the question of whence (i.e., the question of their origins). For this reason, land, language, and other fundamental factors assume a spiritual significance. It is therefore important that we realize the spiritual-ideological dimensions of the groups' identities and their potentialities for building a healthy nation.

However, group identities can be a source of endless conflict when each group tries to absolutize its past identity. To a large extent, this has happened in India. In that process, the memories of the past domination or exploitation of one group by another and the conflicts between them come alive with a new force and become the source of group tension and disharmony.

There is today an upsurge of fundamentalism in the name of self-identity, in all religions. This has vitiated the essence of the religions. A fundamentalist ideology in any religion generates hatred, suspicion, and fears in the minds of its votaries toward other religions. At the slightest provocation or supposed slight to the religious sentiments of a given group, violent conflicts arise, causing untold destruction of lives and property. The wild frenzy of a religious group resulting in a total destruction of a 400-year-old place of worship was recently witnessed in Ayodhya.[4] The resulting

4. Ayodhya is a place in the state of Uttar Pradesh in India, considered the birthplace

communal disturbances and bloodshed have inflicted a deep wound in our national psyche that will take a long time to heal.

Organized in a militant way, the fundamentalist groups are determined to capture political power. This drive has vitiated and distorted our political process. When blind, religious passion rules the people, they cast aside all norms of justice and rule of law. Politicians of all parties who dabble with communal forces and succumb to their pressures deviate from the path of secular politics. The virtual collapse of the very foundation of our political life caused by fundamentalist forces and the politics of opportunism creates a serious situation. When communities are reduced to mountebanks, both people and politics suffer in the long run.

The Pressure of Modernity on Religions

It is widely recognized that the traditional societies have now come under the impact of modernity. This development involves the emergence of the nation-state, with secularization brought about by Western technology and science. Western in origin, the process of modernization spreads so rapidly, challenging the traditional culture and religion.

Traditional cultures in Asia have been religious cultures, in which there was an unbroken unity between society, politics, and religion. India, in particular, has been a communitarian society, with a decentralized sociopolitical existence.[5] Religion provided the integrating principle, and both social structure and political authority were legitimized by it. The breakup of this traditional integration has been a conspicuous aspect of the modern awakening of people to the ideas of justice and freedom and technological rationality, the foundations of a secular framework.

The reactions of religion to these changes are complex. An extreme one is the so-called traditionalist approach. It is characterized by a refusal to accept the breakup of traditional integration and the relative autonomy of society and politics, along with a desperate effort to bring them again under the tutelage of religion. The RSS and other communal ideologies in

---

of Rama. The reference here is to the sad incident on December 6, 1992, of the demolition of a structure that was once used by Muslims for their worship. Some of the Hindu groups believed that Baber, a Muslim ruler, had forcefully built it on the place where a Hindu temple existed. Controversy is now taking a serious turn, with far-reaching repercussions.

5. Kothari, "Cultural Context of Communalism in India."

India are following this line.[6] This kind of revivalism fails to see the personalistic and dynamic elements of the emerging situation and very often ends up as a struggle to preserve the interest of the elite that had traditionally enjoyed all the privileges. This attitude can easily lead to communal frenzy. What is more disturbing is that the so-called secular politicians are exploiting the situation. By whipping up communal and religious sentiments, they ensure the total support of particular groups. Democratic institutions come under serious assault through such manipulations of state power for narrow ends. The political process now obtaining in ethnically divided Third World countries is a task of reordering political equations among the ethnic groups. "The state rather than addressing itself to the creation of civil society, becomes largely a mediator of ethnic political equations."[7]

The other extreme mode of approach is that of the so-called modernists. They find the emerging "secular" state as absolute and antireligious. Often, it stands for an uncritical acceptance of Western technology, Western politics, and a Western style of life. Its antireligious stance is the legacy of the so-called modern scientific culture, in which all experiences of reality are reduced to definable and quantifiable commodities. What is "usable" and "marketable" is valuable. Reason is reduced to technical reason, and all levels of human experience are ruthlessly manipulated. We (as urban intellectuals) have been too long under the tutelage of Western rationality and have remained insensitive to the religious sensibilities of the majority of our people. This has failed, as has been proved not only through the experiences of Third World countries but also through those of Europe.

What we need is a dynamic reinterpretation of the past, taking seriously into consideration the new elements of change. The religions should see the relevance of the new secular framework that is emerging. It is based on certain values that they can affirm — such as the values of justice, equality, and participation. What is dangerous is a kind of secular attitude that is closed to religion. Any absolutizing elements in politics can turn inhuman and oppressive. A pluralistic outlook is necessary as a viable form of relating one religion to another on the basis of shared values and goals.

6. The Rashtriya Swayamsevak Sangh (RSS) is a fundamentalist group within Hinduism that was mainly responsible for demolishing the mosque in Ayodhya in December 1992.

7. D. L. Sheth, "Nation-Building in Multi-Ethnic Societies: The Experience of South Asia," *Alternatives* 14, no. 4 (October 1989): 19.

The Pressure Brought by the Struggle of the Marginalized and the Resistance to Them by Dominant Groups

Hitherto submerged groups, the marginalized everywhere, are organizing to fight for their rights, which brings tremendous pressure on the existing system. Their legitimate demands are met with staunch resistance from the wielders of power. A class solidarity of the poor in pure form has not been sustained in traditional Asian societies for various reasons. In a situation where resources are scarce, people use religion or communal grouping as the focal point and as a means to obtain their share. Secular ideologies and parties, however militant they might be, have not succeeded in proving effective rallying points for the people's fight. Still, the dominant "identity source" for the majority has been religion or communal grouping. The fight becomes intense when the resources become scarce or when one group finds itself alienated from the mainstream or losing in the game. What we see in India today is a kind of political process in which regional and other groups are struggling for their share of the pie. No one seems to be succeeding, and there is constant rivalry and clashes born out of disappointment.

In the present conflicts triggered by fundamentalist groups, the poor are used as pawns, with the benefit going to the powerful in each group. They whip up caste or communal feelings in order that they may continue their dominance.

Paul Brass, in his analysis of politics and ethnicity in South Asia, mentions two possible approaches to the question of ethnicity, what he calls primordial and instrumental. Both views have some relevance, but he argues in favor of the latter after having closely observed the dynamics of religious and ethnic conflict in South Asian countries. He observes, "The cultural forms, values and practices of ethnic groups have become political resources of elites in competition for political power and economic advantages."[8]

Andre Beteille, in his study *Caste, Class, and Power,*[9] analyzes the change that is taking place in the group relationship in our society. The power has shifted from the rich landlords and other traditional rich groups — not to the poor, but to a middle group, mostly politicians who, with the support of the rich, continue to use the system to further their interests.

8. Paul Brass, *Ethnicity and Nationalism* (New Delhi: Sage Publications, 1991), p. 15.
9. Andre Beteille, *Caste, Class, and Power* (Berkeley: University of California Press, 1965). Although this study was conducted three decades ago, its thesis stands valid today. The power nexus has not changed significantly since then.

The landless, the laborers, and other lower strata of society do not share political power. They are onlookers at a game played by the new elite. Caste allegiance still plays a prominent role, and it is easy to exploit it for one's own ulterior motives.

Class solidarity that cuts across the boundaries of religion and caste has not emerged in any significant degree among the weaker sections in India. Even in areas where Communist parties have been powerful, the habit of thinking along caste lines has not disappeared. The poor Brahmin still thinks that the untouchable is his greatest enemy. Little does he realize that the rich landlord of his own community can be the oppressor in the changed system of economic relationships. It is also understandable that two backward communities would fight as they both strive to get their share of economic benefits; competition and mutual suspicion are bound to arise. The oppressed everywhere should realize that their best interests are served if they come together and put their collective pressure on the system for its transformation.

In the process, the primordial elements that form ethnic identities should find a significant place in the strategizing. In finding this combination, we seek the liberative traditions of the religions and culture of the poor.

The Pressure of the Global Economic System on National Politics and Culture

With the disappearance of the socialist world, the Third World countries have entered a new phase in the saga of their development. They are now totally and completely dominated by the financial institutions and global market engineering of the First World. The gap between the rich and the poor countries has become greater, and this gap is no longer a relative, surmountable gap, but absolute in terms of access to key factors of production such as capital (including technology).[10]

> Third World Debt is now around $1.3 trillion, which accounts for 44 per cent of its GNP. The net flow annually from developing countries to developed countries, from South to North, is $50 billion. The money lent by the World Bank in 1989 as concessional aid was only $28 billion. In effect, the South has been subsidizing the high consumption growth

10. Lawrence Surendra, "Global Solidarity for the Future: Where Do We Go from Here in South-North Relations?" unpublished paper presented to a YMCA Consultation in 1993, Bangalore, India.

of the North, as a result of the debt crises of the South. According to Susan George, OECD figures show that the debtors are reimbursing their loans at a rate of over $3 billion a week. Even more astounding, they have sustained this rate of repayment over a decade.[11]

Globalization and modernization through technological growth have brought other serious problems. Increasing marginalization is the inevitable consequence of a capital-intensive, urban-centered model of growth. The new economic policies introduced in India, allegedly at the behest of the IMF and World Bank, will not alter the basic pattern of development that has been inimical to the marginalized. There is no doubt that we need to link ourselves to the global market system and that we should clear away what is unprofitable in the public sector. But an unfettered growth of multinationals and the emphasis on foreign trade are not conducive to a pattern of development that is oriented to the needs of the poor.

A concomitant problem that this model of growth creates is the ecological crisis. Fast depletion of natural resources, pollution of air, land, and water, the global warming, and other atmospheric changes have catastrophic effects. A consultation on ecology and development has correctly observed that while all are affected by the ecological crisis, the life of the poor and marginalized is further impoverished by it. Storage of fuel and water adds peculiar burdens to the life of women. It is said that tribals are made environmental prisoners in their own land.

> The Dalits, whose life has been subjected to social and cultural oppression for generations, are facing new threats by the wanton destruction of the natural environment. As the Chernobyl and Bhopal incidents show, ecology knows no national boundaries. Climatic changes and related environmental consequences are globally experienced. What we witness today is a steady deterioration and degradation of the bio-sphere, all life and physical environment.[12]

The consultation further notes that

> the enormity of the problem is caused by the wasteful life-style of the rich and irresponsible use of the natural resources and the degradation of environment by the profit oriented industry. In this sense, the problem

11. Ibid.
12. Daniel Chetti, ed., *Ecology and Development* (Madras: UELC/Gurukul and BTESSC, 1991), p. 96.

of ecology is closely linked with the pattern of development, which continues to create imbalances between different sectors and allows massive exploitation of rural and natural environment for the benefit of dominant classes.[13]

In this connection we must be aware of a more far-reaching impact, and perhaps the most devastating, that this model of growth has on our culture. The tendency is to create a monolithic culture that encourages consumerist and profit-gaining values, destroying whatever infrastructure is indigenously available to people. Ashis Nandy's words are pungent:

As this century with its bloodstained record draws to a close, the nineteenth century dream of one world has re-emerged, this time as a nightmare. It haunts us with the prospect of a fully homogenized, technologically controlled, absolutely hierarchized world, defined by polarities like the modern and the primitive, the secular and the non-secular, the scientific and the unscientific, the expert and the layman, the normal and the abnormal, the developed and the undeveloped, the vanguard and the led, the liberated and the savable.[14]

While the elite-controlled governments in most of the Third World countries follow the logic of the technological growth model, which inevitably leads to the erosion of values germane to the indigenous culture and religion, serious questions are raised by some concerned groups about an alternate model of modernization. M. M. Thomas calls for a "philosophy of modernisation which goes beyond the materialistic world-view and respects the organic spiritual dimension of human community life."[15] Actually, all religions and cultural traditions of the Third World are quite sensitive to these dimensions through their reverence for nature and concern for the primary communities like the family; therefore, any emerging new socialism needs to assimilate some of the traditional spirit and values in their renewed form. This will also help to give modernization indigenous cultural roots, without which it often brings demoralization.

In other words, Third World development should go beyond the classical capitalist-socialist models to develop "a society appropriate for the

13. Ibid.
14. Ashis Nandy, *The Intimate Enemy: Loss and Recovery of Self under Colonialism,* quoted in Surendra, "Global Solidarity for the Future."
15. M. M. Thomas, "Current Issues in the Third World Approach to Modernisation," *Bangalore Theological Forum,* December 1991, p. 38.

multifaceted nature of human beings and their social and transcendent dimensions."[16] Thus, the pressures that impinge on us are political, cultural, and religious. They point to the urgent task of building an alternative view of society where all human beings live and experience themselves as "persons-in-community, in various forms of daily social life."[17] Diversity is the natural state of a society like ours. Plural identities should be the basis for the state. What we need are new "confederate perspectives of unity from bottom up."[18]

Toward Building a Global Solidarity

The role of religion in building a pluralistic society should be affirmed. Religion is all-pervasive in the experiences of ordinary people. It is futile to think that we can build a society that has no place for religion. An economist gives a description of religion in everyday life in India:

> In a sociological sense religion is a powerful force in India. For the vast majority of people in this country — rich and poor, learned and other-wise — religion is the foremost influence in life from birth to death, deciding what one may eat, what vocation to go into, whom one may marry (or not marry), whether one is to be buried or cremated when dead. Of course, it is not the same religion for everyone, but it is religion all the same. Whoever says that religion should be a matter of private commitment has no understanding of the Indian social reality.[19]

Perhaps we are only stating the obvious. At this point in time, however, it needs stating. The question, however, is what kind of religion? Can we be ignorant of the fact that our religions have been and continue to be a source of oppression, providing as they do a protective veneer for vested interests? Do we not know that superstition and several religious myths make the masses accept their lot passively?

With all such dangers, we cannot dismiss the fact and the reach of religious reality. Much of the distortion of religion and culture has come

---

16. Leonardo Boff, "Liberation Theology and the Collapse of Socialism," *Youth of India* (National YMCA), Summer 1991.

17. Bastian Wielenga, "The Changing Face of Socialism and Its Relevance to the Churches," *Christian Marxist Dialogue,* Spring 1991, quoted in Thomas, "Current Issues in the Third World Approach to Modernisation."

18. Kothari, "Cultural Context of Communalism in India."

19. C. T. Kurien, "The Role of Religion," unpublished paper.

about by the dominance of the elite, who use every available mechanism, religion included, to usurp and maintain power. We need to rediscover the people's tradition that preserves autonomy and dynamism.

Liberative Ecumenism

The Ecumenical Association of Third World Theologians (EATWOT), in their consultation "Religion and Liberation," states that all religions, Christianity included, "are in various ways and to various degrees both oppressive and liberative."[20] They are oppressive because they legitimize unjust social systems like apartheid and caste, and because they create their own special forms of religious bondage. But history shows us that religions can be liberative too. They have inspired powerful movements of social protest (like Hebrew prophetism in monarchical Israel or the *bhakti* movements in medieval India), which have attacked both the oppressive rigidity of the religious systems themselves as well as the unjust socioeconomic and political structures of the societies in which these religions flourished.

Religion can be corrupt, but at the same time it provides the dynamic to transcend corruption. Its identity necessarily involves intolerance and a sense of exclusivism, but within that identity there is the provision to transcend such intolerance and exclusivism. The inclusive and liberative face of religion should be consciously nurtured.[21]

In the Third World, where all religions together face the challenges from enslaving social and cultural factors and the need to struggle for justice, religions should meet each other willingly and should share their liberative elements. There should be a form of interreligious dialogue that is concerned not so much with hair-splitting doctrinal arguments and esoteric spiritual experiences as with the contribution to human liberation different religions can make.

This is the liberative ecumenism to which we should commit ourselves. This calls for a new way of approaching interfaith dialogue.

In Christian faith the approach of liberation theology has come as a

---

20. "Religion and Liberation," ed. EATWOT, *Voices from the Third World* 11, no. 1 (1988): 152.

21. Inclusive/exclusive dimensions are present in every religion, but the places and reasons for emphasizing one over the other depend on various factors — minority complex, economic scarcity, political manipulation, and so forth. A careful scrutiny of these and historical factors is necessary for a smooth relationship.

breath of fresh air and provides the way of liberative ecumenism. It is based on a "rereading" of Scripture and doctrine from the perspective of the poor, which is closer to the origin of many religions. A brief discussion of its direction and methodology is relevant at this point, as it holds the possibility of helping us evolve a common framework for religious cooperation.

Liberation Theology

Liberation theology, a new means for interfaith dialogue, was first articulated by theologians identified with the struggles of the poor in Latin America. It is a mistake to assume that Third World liberation theology is primarily a Latin American phenomenon. Neither is it a monolithic system — Africans and Asians as well as blacks in the United States and women have made important contributions to the development of liberation theology. A unique dimension of liberation theology is brought out by Asian theology, which is set within a plurality of religions. There are important differences among Third World liberation theologies, but they converge in their attempt to do theology from a particular experience of marginalization. They emerge from a concrete context, but they articulate what they believe to be the core of the Christian gospel. Their particular insights are offered to all people. In this sense they are, in effect, proposing a paradigm shift. For our purposes, we will focus on three elements.

Social Origins of the Christian Faith

There is a new awareness about the social background of Jesus and of the fact that Jesus' movement arose among the poor who were victimized by the religious authorities and political mechanisms of that day. After a meticulous study of the Jewish Scriptures and New Testament, the Indian biblical scholar George Soares-Prabhu, S.J., has come to the conclusion that:

1. The poor in the Bible are a *sociological* group whose identity is defined not by their religious attitude but by their sociological situation.
2. The poor in the Bible are also a *dialectical* group whose situation is determined by antagonistic groups standing over and against them.
3. The poor in the Bible are a *dynamic* group who are not the passive victims of history but those through whom God shapes his history.[22]

22. George M. Soares-Prabhu, "Class in the Bible: The Biblical Poor, a Social Class?"

Jesus with the harassed and victimized crowd is a picture that appeals to the Asian Christians. His table fellowship with the outcasts and the humiliated and his running controversies with the rulers of the time appeal to them. In him they see the face of the humiliated *dalits*[23] or the harassed *minjung*.[24] This has opened to them a way of affirming their solidarity with the poor everywhere, not necessarily in their own religion. It has produced a particular and relevant faith praxis.

Identification with the poor meant an overriding emphasis on justice. In this Jesus stands in the prophetic tradition of the Jewish faith. Prophets projected an appealing vision of God, who appears as the defender of the vulnerable groups from whom all rights are taken away — widows, orphans, aliens, and the poor. For them to know God is to do justice. For them it was a universal message. Their relentless struggle was against leaders and people who domesticated the faith, turning it into a closed ideology.

Among some of the Muslim thinkers I see an attempt to take a new look at the social origin of Islam. Asghar Ali Engineer, in his book *Islam and Liberative Theology*,[25] attempts to bring out the liberative elements in Islam. He points out that the Prophet as the messenger of God "threw a powerful challenge to the traders of Mecca" who had "violated the tribal norms and completely disregarded the poor and the needy." He further notes, "When the Prophet began to preach his divine message, it was the poor and oppressed of Mecca, including many slaves, who joined him."[26] For the oppressed, Mohammed was the liberator, "not only a teacher and a philosopher, but also an activist, a participant and a fighter." Furthermore, "openness, tolerance and respect for other religions is another important liberative element."[27]

Vidyajyoti 49 (1985): 320–46, quoted in Aloysius Pieris, *An Asian Theology of Liberation* (Maryknoll, N.Y.: Orbis Books, 1988), p. 122. On the basis of this analysis, Pieris affirms that "biblical liberation is *more* than class struggle. It is the God-encounter of the poor, the poor by choice (the renouncers) and the poor by circumstances" (p. 123).

23. "Dalits" literally means "oppressed." It denotes the people belonging to the former untouchables in India.

24. "Minjung" is a Korean term for people, the marginalized and exploited.

25. Asghar Ali Engineer, *Islam and Liberation Theology: Essays on Liberative Elements in Islam* (New Delhi: Sterling Publishers, 1990).

26. Ibid., p. 373.

27. Ibid., p. 30. In this connection we may mention another book by Engineer, *The Islamic State* (Delhi: Vikas Publishing House, 1980). In it he approvingly quotes W. C. Smith's observation, "The Islam enterprise has been the most serious and sustained endeavour ever put forward to implement justice among men, and until the rise of Marxism was also the largest and most ambitious" (p. 200).

Looking at the origin of these two faiths, one may conclude that identification with the poor, a critique of the wielders of power, a prophetic zeal for justice, and an openness to other traditions are the hallmarks of early beginnings of these faiths. In the course of time, powerful vested interests made use of them and turned them into an ideology of status quo and otherworldly piety and generated a feeling of suspicion and hatred for others. Sifting through the elite distortion of religions and finding our way through the grandiose edifice built by the dominant classes, we need to recover the essential dynamism of these faiths. This can be done when the poor themselves appropriate these traditions and insofar as we make a "preferential option for the poor."[28]

Interreligious Dialogue Grounded in a Preferential Option for the Poor

Interfaith dialogue is necessary to sustain a pluralist form of polity. The preferential option for the poor will provide the necessary grounding and a direction that would integrate "the mystical with the concrete prophetic concern." In his response to Pannikar's proposal for a "cosmic confidence" that sustains an interreligious response and cooperation, Paul Knitter points out that "it needs to be grounded and inspired by a preferential option for the suffering and the victims of this world." He further elaborates this point:

> But if our criterion for judging what is true or false, good or bad, is no longer "Is it in the Bible or the Upanishads or the Koran?" but rather "Does it remove suffering and promote life?" . . . then we cannot apply it without listening to the poor and the victims. The oppressed, the marginalised, those who, in the past, "didn't count" must also have a voice in a soteriocentric dialogue; they must speak with and to the so-called experts. It is their voice and their experience — much more than exegetes, theologians, popes, or even mystics — that will tell us what in our religious beliefs and practices promotes human well-being and thus what is faithful to our scriptures.[29]

28. The concept of a preferential option for the poor is central to liberation theology. It was first articulated by the bishops of Latin America in 1968 in a meeting held in Medellín, Colombia. It stands for God's compassion for the oppressed and Jesus' solidarity with the suffering. The church is called to opt for the cause of the poor as well. This emphasis has given a clear direction to theology. In this chapter I wish to affirm the same option for the poor in our interreligious dialogue and politics.

29. Knitter, "Cosmic Confidence or Preferential Option?"

Faith and Political Praxis

Liberation theology makes a significant contribution through its emphasis on praxis as the essence of faith. Praxis is "thought emerging in deed and deed evoking thought." By praxis, we do not mean rejection of theory. On the contrary, we need rigorous theoretical reflection, but it should emerge from the practice that is oriented to transformation. Otherwise, it will be an artificial construct that lends itself to domination by alien thought patterns.

Liberation praxis has already generated a political praxis different from the politics of domination in some countries in Latin America. In making this world more human and leading men and women to transcendence, which is experienced as ultimate openness to one another and creation, that essence of the faith is realized. We can affirm that "all who work for justice are God's co-workers."[30] On this basis a new political culture should be produced by the cooperation of Islamic and Christian faiths.[31]

A New Politics Directed toward a New World Solidarity

Politics always has been, right from Plato's *Republic* till now, controlled by and directed toward the interest of a powerful minority. Notable breakthroughs were made by the organized struggle of the people. Secular ideologies of liberal democracy and Marxism, reflecting the concerns of the masses, have attempted to overthrow the elite domination in politics. With a framework rooted in Enlightenment humanism, "in which the transcendent spiritual dimension of the human person was denied, it paved the way to dissolving the transcendent ground of human dignity in any ensemble

---

30. Samuel Rayan, "The Search for Asian Spirituality," in *Asian Christian Spirituality,* ed. Lee Fabello and Kwang SunSuh (Maryknoll, N.Y.: Orbis Books, 1992).

31. One may quote the stirring words of Deane William Fern at the close of his essay "Third World Liberation Theology: Challenge to World Religions," in *World Religions and Human Liberation,* ed. Dan Chohn-Sherbok (Maryknoll, N.Y.: Orbis Books, 1992): "Liberation theology issues a call not only to Christianity, but to the other religions of the world as well. Are these religions willing to show 'a preferential option for the poor'? Can the communities of the poor which are irrupting throughout the Third World be the basis for a new 'people's theology' which seeks to liberate humanity from all forms of oppression: poverty, servitude, racism, sexism, and the like? Can justice and spirituality become partners in a world-embracing enterprise? Can the struggle for justice and belief in God come to mean one and the same thing? Herein lies the stirring challenge of third-world Christian liberation theology" (p. 19).

of social function and relation."[32] In any case, the ideologies too have betrayed the people in the Third World. They have become tools in the hands of elites to further their interests. And the nexus between the elites of politics and the elites of religion continues to oppress the people. The disappearance of socialism from the Soviet Union and Eastern Europe is a turning point. All these together compel us to search for a new political culture that is rooted in the experience of the poor. Liberative sources of religion, as we have tried to show, have a significant contribution to make as they emerge from the depths of the experience of the poor.

The transition from religion (even the liberative form of it) to politics is still uncertain. But movements of indigenous and other grassroots-level people, environmentalists, and feminists are already generating a new political culture based on spiritual and social visions of their tradition. They challenge us to live by plurality of culture; they demand justice as a prerequisite for a meaningful form of human solidarity, urging us to commit to a set of communitarian and bonding values necessary for the building up of human community; they show us the need of a viable ecosystem in order to survive. How do we channel these so as to alter the present political process?

A tentative suggestion is offered as a conclusion. One of the lessons we learn from the present-day politics and the nonparty political formations of grassroots-level movements is the potential of "myths" to change the political behavior of people. Often these myths are rooted in the religion and culture of the people. They appeal to the emotions, not reason. They are used sometimes by the elite for their purpose, even deliberately fabricating further myths. They are used by fundamentalists to arouse suspicion and hatred toward other religious communities. Can we, drawing upon liberative traditions, embark on a simultaneous process of demythologization and remythologization? This will involve the deliberative exposure of oppressive myths and the creation of humanizing myths. Our religions are themselves repositories of such liberative myths. They can mobilize people for the building up of a community of communities where all live without fear or domination. Father S. Kappen, reflecting on the recent clash between religious communities in India, poses this challenge.

> What we need today is a new generation of Hindus, Muslims and Christians who will recapture the humanising universal perspective and give shape to it in basic human communities. These basic human communi-

32. Thomas, "Current Issues in the Third World Approach to Modernisation."

ties and basic peoples' cultural movements will have to come into being embodying the humanising vision of religions. So, it is time for creating cultural movements which will produce humanising myths, counter myths, counter rituals, and counter ceremonies without demonisation.[33]

33. S. Kappen, "Role of Religion in Combating Communalism," in *Ayodhya* (Bombay: BUILD, 1992), p. 73.

· 21 ·

Renascent Religions
and Secularism in India

M. M. THOMAS

I DEEM IT A PRIVILEGE to have been invited to contribute an essay to this
Festschrift for Dr. Charles West as he retires from his professorship of
Christian ethics at Princeton Theological Seminary. I have had the joy of
knowing him since 1947, the year I joined the staff of the World Student
Christian Federation with responsibility for Asia. He was then a missionary
in China. Later I had the opportunity to work with him in the World
Council of Churches studies on ecumenical theological approaches to rapid
social change in the modern world. He traveled to India, visited my home,
and helped in the work of the Christian Institute for the Study of Religion
and Society, of which I was director. After my retirement, I was invited to
join the Princeton Seminary faculty as guest professor for ecumenism and
missions. As a colleague on the seminary faculty for several years, I came
to know Charlie and his family more closely. I have treasured his lifelong
friendship. It is thus a special pleasure to make a contribution to this volume
published in his honor.

I have chosen a topic related to secularism, about which Charlie has
made an impact on my thinking through the years. I pursue the topic in
my Indian context. It draws on an unpublished paper entitled "Concept of
Secularism" presented at a multidisciplinary national Seminar on Secularism in India at the Tara Institute of Social Science, Bombay, in September
1989. My aim in this essay is to explore the idea and structure of a healthy
and viable Indian public philosophy of secularism. It should be noted that
while a distinction is made between secularization and secularism in West-

362

ern discussions, in India the word "secularism" is used for both concepts, and the distinction is made by pointing out the area of its application.

Not only in India, but the world over, there is a resurgence of religious fundamentalism and aggressive denominationalism (called "communalism" in India), which threatens the political, social, and cultural achievements of movements of secular humanism. This resurgence is in part backward-looking; in part, however, it is an attempt to go beyond a secularism that in the application of technical rationality has lost its democratic humanistic character and has become as dogmatic, closed, and authoritarian as religions in the past; it has also produced a spiritual vacuum by ignoring the transcendent dimension of community identity that traditional religion expressed. This article argues for what may be called a concept of open secularism, which can strengthen democratic secularism in India by its openness to reforming and renascent religion as opposed to revivalist religion. In my assessment, religious reform and renaissance are the result of religions absorbing within their concepts of transcendent spirituality a limited but real process of secularization. Since atheistic secular ideologies have also begun to recognize some limits to the secularization process and have become more sensitive to the need to protect the dignity of human life as well as the natural environment, a dialogue between these ideologies and reforming religion on the idea of secularism is possible today. It is also necessary if we are to save democratic secularism from being subverted by religious revivalism on the one hand and closed secular ideologies on the other.

Secularism in the West

Secularism is related to the process of secularization of corporate structures of life and thought, which has been an essential aspect of modern history. Since that history had its dynamic in the West, it may be relevant to start with the evolution of the concept of secularism in the West.

The structural aspect of secularization is the breakup of the traditional institutional integration of culture, society, and state with one established religion. In the West this came about as the result of the breakup of Christendom and its linkages between church, community, and state. This process was accompanied by two affirmations of human freedom. The first was the affirmation of the autonomy of various areas of corporate life — science, philosophy, politics, economics, and culture — from the dictates of religious authority to follow ends and laws naturally inherent in each of them. The second was the establishment of the sovereign nation-state within geographic boundaries, with increasing recognition of legal toleration and protection of the plurality of thought, belief, and expression in society by the state.

The anthropological concepts behind these structural changes have been changing throughout the history of the modern West, beginning with the cultural Renaissance and Protestant Reformation of the sixteenth century, and the American and French revolutions of the eighteenth century. The general conceptual framework, however, may be defined as a movement from a sacred to a secular ethos in corporate life. This humanist secularism had three features.

First and foremost was the discovery of the sovereignty of the individual person and the right and obligation of each person to follow one's reason and conscience in the pursuit of truth — an idea that became embodied as fundamental law in the constitutions of nation-states. This means that cultures and societies recognize individual personality as the only ultimate center of significance and that all other aspects of corporate life are only instruments of service to the human person.

Second, and accompanying the first, was the desacralization of nature, the idea of nature devoid of spirits, so that experiments with nature by technology would be possible without fear of violating the sacred order.

Third, along with the desacralization of nature came the desacralization of social and political structures and laws. The idea of an eternally fixed sacred moral order or law to which society and state must conform gave place to the idea that social and political realms are realms of secular human creativity based on empirical scientific analysis and technical planning, with human welfare as the only moral goal.

The desacralization of nature and laws of corporate life, the recognition of religious plurality, and the large role given to scientific and technical rationality raised the question of the character of religion in relation to nature and society. The Enlightenment and later the Feuerbach-Marx tradition included the following assessments: (1) religion is an illusion characteristic of the childhood of the human race, which will outgrow it with adulthood; (2) religion as the sanction of the oppression of individuals is the main hindrance to social progress; and (3) religion is an illusion organically related to our subhuman corporate consciousness as the reflection of the unfulfilled hopes and aspirations of humanity; religion will consequently wither away as revolutionary action establishes a just humanity.

Underlying these concepts of religion was an understanding of human nature and an interpretation of history first expressed in the idea of inevitable progress, and later modified in the idea of dialectical progress.

From the beginning, however, there were movements of religious believers who took different postures in their approach to the secularization process. Some battled with it as an unmitigated evil; return to Christendom was the ideology of several Christian political parties in the European continent formed in opposition to the tide of the French Revolution. The Roman Catholic Church gave its official approval to religious pluralism based on the civil right of religious freedom only at Vatican II in the 1960s.

Other movements of religious reform accepted a good deal of the critique of religion by atheistic secularism and welcomed the separation of religion and state as good, not only for politics and society, but also for religion. They welcomed the emergence of the individual person's authority in religion as well as the desacralization of nature and law in the name of the principle that the Sabbath is made for humanity and not humanity for the Sabbath. They also understood religion to transcend the existing social and political structures and thus to be able to evaluate them critically. The Protestant spirit at work in the struggles of Free Churches in Europe and in the Pilgrim fathers in North America contributed indirectly to the creation of the idea and structure of secularism. It is significant that the constitution of the secular state of the United States has in it the clause that the inalienable rights of freedom and the equality of citizens have their sanction in the Creator God. This view was the result of a dialogue between atheistic rationalism and religious belief among the founding fathers. It affirms the conviction of religious believers that the respect for all members of society and protection of their human rights cannot be maintained without recognizing the sacredness of the human person. Along with the desacralizing of nature, politics, and society in the name of the sacredness of human beings (i.e., their freedom and creativity), the reformed religious sensibility posits that human persons have ends and loyalties beyond the state and society. Religious liberty becomes the guardian and guarantee of all human liberties.

Also in democratic secularism's concept of making political power responsible through checks and balances, there was the impact of the Calvinistic Puritan understanding of the essential corruption of human nature. This served to correct the ultraoptimism of the rationalist idea of progress. The idea that none can be entrusted with a monopoly of power but that the one holding power must be checked by law, custom, and the counterpower of the opposition is the result of the application of a religious insight to politics. Robert Bellah has pointed out that American secularism and its democratic civil loyalty in the context of religious pluralism had the support of the undercurrents of a "civil religion" that drew its tenets from the religious tradition. And in Germany under Hitler, it was the spiritual resistance of the Confessing Church that was the sustaining force for universal humanism. Albert Einstein once said that when the press, the trade unions, and the universities succumbed to Hitler, it was the religious resistance that had staying power.

In fact, in the twentieth century, the emergence of Hitlerism and Stalinism as ideological "theocracies" signaled the breakdown of democratic secularism. Today there are many who feel that the idea and structures of democratic secularism have no future. They can cite resurgence of religious fundamentalism seeking return to a religious theocracy, whether it finds expression in the Moral Majority movement in the United States, the Return to Christendom groups in Europe, the Islamic revolution of Ayatollah Khomeini, or the RSS movement for Hindu Rashtra.

Countering these movements toward a religious theocracy, creative searches have arisen for ways to redeem the structures and values of democratic secularism for the future by relating them to a realistic understanding of the rational and spiritual dimensions of the human self made evident by twentieth-century history. For instance, there is the rediscovering in our time of the need to limit technological aggression on the natural environment by a greater reverence for nature. There is also a growing awareness of the need to redefine democratic secularism so as to affirm reverence for human individuality without either making individuality a law unto itself or giving in to collectivism. Finally, there is the rediscovery of the tragic dimension of the self expressed in the self-righteousness of good people and in the difficulty of the task of building up human hope for the future without giving in to the idea either of inevitable utopia or of inevitable doom as the natural goal of history. All these redefinitions call for a new understanding of the contribution renascent religion can make to a culture that supports a public policy of open secularism.

Neoliberal social thinkers like Walter Lippmann and Robert Bellah, as well as Neo-Marxist thinkers like Jean-Richard Bloch, Vitezslav Gardavsky, and Antonio Gramsci (along with Mikhail Gorbachev's ideas of perestroika and glasnost), speak of the significance of the dialogue between religion and atheistic secularism to correct the tendencies inherent in them to create closed societies and to develop a body of insights of a secular anthropology that can sustain democratic secularism against the onslaughts of religious authoritarianism and secular totalitarianism.

The Concept of Secularism in India

Against this background of the global concept of secularism, let us look at the concept of secularism in India. Here the concept of secularism as a political philosophy emerged in the movement for national independence. The ideology of secular nationalism, which sought the inclusion of people of all religions in the struggle, had to battle against both Hindu nationalism and the Islamic theory of two nations. Though independence came with the partition of India that established Pakistan, under the leadership of Gandhi and Nehru, India was successful in overcoming the tide of Hindu communalism to establish a secular state. The concept of the secular state in India, as it has evolved through the independence movement, the Constituent Assembly, and the period after independence has two very clear tenets. First is the declaration of religious liberty as a fundamental civil right of every citizen, making possible the common effort of different religious communities in the development of Indian nationhood and its expression in a democratic nation-state, without destroying or suppressing the diversity of our religious and cultural pluralism. Second is the need for eventually transforming all traditional societies in the light of the democratic principles of freedom, equality, and justice according to the Directive Principles of State Policy that were adopted. That is, the coexistence of different religions and cultures should be interpreted, not statically, but in dynamic interaction with the modern democratic ideals of community living that we have accepted in common.

Relating to the first, namely, religious liberty, the Indian constitution has the following juridical provisions: (1) the fundamental right of all persons equally to "profess, practice, and propagate religion"; (2) the right of every religious denomination or any section thereof to "establish and maintain institutions for religious and charitable purposes and to manage its own affairs in matters of religion"; and (3) the freedom of citizens from discrimination on "grounds of religion" with respect to any employment or office under the state.

Because the British policy offering safeguards like elections by religious affiliation and special provisions for economically and socially oppressed groups was interpreted as alienating them permanently from the mainstream Hindu community by building up special interest groups, there was general opposition to it. By affirming the fundamental rights of individual persons irrespective of religion, the Constituent Assembly was able to avoid linking separate political rights with specific religious communities, while still preserving the religious rights of all.

In this connection it is interesting to recall how the right to "propagate" religion became accepted as part of religious liberty. The propagation of religion leading to conversion in the sense of change of affiliation from one religious community to another is not characteristic of "mystic" religions like Hinduism; it is integral, however, to "prophetic" religions like Islam and Christianity. Therefore debates on this topic in the Constituent Assembly were heated. Of course, propagation and conversion along with communal electorates and other political rights for religious communities can acquire a communal political color. Thus when the leaders of the Indian Christian community announced their decision to forgo communal electorate or other communal safeguards, Sardar Patel enthusiastically responded by arguing for including the right of propagation as part of religious liberty. This was a concept of religious liberty that went beyond the Hindu concept and related the idea of tolerating "real" difference in the realm of religion. And nonreligious leaders like Nehru also welcomed it because if religious propagation and conversion are banned in law, that might lead to the eventual banning of cultural and even political propaganda and conversion. Of course, the religious liberty of persons as it now stands is a democratic concept and needs defense in any secular concept of the toleration of the plurality of religious and antireligious ideologies. The debate on this question is still going on, and the matter must be looked at from the point of view of the future of democratic secularism in India.

Furthermore, the coexistence and plurality of religious communities and cultures in the Indian concept of secularism is not an acceptance of their coexistence as static communities as in the traditional view. It is conceived as active and dynamic, involving the transformation of all social structures associated with the different religions, in the context of the new national commitment to build a new society based on liberty, equality, fraternity, and justice.

The fundamental rights resolution adopted by the 1934 Karachi Congress under pressure from Nehru and the congress socialists was a milestone in this respect. It called not only for land reforms and other measures of economic justice but also for changes in the traditional social structure of extended family, caste, and village that had perpetrated injustices like untouchability and personal laws exploitive of women, with the sanction of religion. Therefore, the secular state of India never accepted the principle of a "wall of separation" between religious communities and the state that is characteristic of the U.S. concept of the secular state. It envisaged radical democratic legislative, judicial, and executive interventions into the life of religious communities to change oppressive systems and customs in positive response to the demand of the oppressed sections of these communities.

The constitution of India makes the right of state intervention in the secular aspects of religion in the name of justice a part of the clause granting religious freedom. It states clearly that the right of the religious freedom of citizens shall not prevent "the State from making any law regulating and restricting financial, political, or other secular activity which may be associated with religious practice," like restricting entry into temples and use of temple roads and facilities on any discriminative basis.

These new elements of Indian secularism that go beyond the traditional framework of toleration were a result of the impact of Western democratic and socialist secular ideologies, which envisaged the idea of a more egalitarian society. There was political intervention in relation to traditional social laws from the beginning of the national movement. Untouchability was outlawed from the start by independent India. The state recodified Hindu law against the protest of Hindu communalism as well as Hindu religious authorities. Speaking of the Indian objective of forming a society in which "the difference based on birth, income, or position are not great," Nehru said:

> In our attempt to achieve it, we want to put an end to all those infinite divisions that have arisen in our social life. I am referring to the caste system and other religious divisions, call them by whatever name you like. . . . It is thus one of our objectives to get rid of them and give every individual in India an opportunity to grow, as also to build a united nation where individuals do not think so much of their particular group or caste but of the community at large.

The changes were thus aimed at a relative detaching of the "individuals" socially from closed religious communities so as to enable them to relate to "the community at large," represented by the nation. Here the concept of Indian secularism envisages a measure of secularization of society for the sake of forming a national community on shared social ideals. Thus the concept sees the growth of "individualism," the sense of the "larger community," and the development of a "united nation" as interrelated and involving greater autonomy of society and social laws from the established authority of religions. The civil Marriage Act that the Parliament passed was in a sense the nucleus of a civil law transcending religious communities. This was the furthest India went toward evolving a common civil code.

Renascent Religions and Indian Secularism

I conclude with a few notes on the role that religions, especially the rena-scence of the religions of India, have played and can play in the Indian concept of secularism.

While toleration of religious and cultural plurality has gone beyond the traditional Hindu ideas of toleration, Hindu acceptance of a plurality of religious forms, as well as Hindu philosophy, mysticism, and spirituality with its vision of ultimate unity, have contributed greatly to the develop-ment of the new toleration of religious and cultural diversity, as all writers about Indian secularism have pointed out. In fact, Nehru was never tired of quoting the Asoka's Rock Exiot no. 12 regarding the toleration of differ-ent dharma as the basis of the coexistence of religion at home and of ideological systems internationally.

Nehru was sometimes criticized for initiating the recodification of Hindu law without touching Islamic or Christian personal laws. The answer to this criticism is that recodification of Hindu law had the sanction of Neo-Hindu movements led by reformers from Raja Mohan Roy through Vivekananda to Gandhiji, who sought to assimilate egalitarian humanism into Hinduism. Also the untouchables, women, and other weaker sections of Hindu society had been awakened by Hindu reform movements to the injustices they suffered, and anti-Brahmin movements were challenging traditional Hindu laws. This made recodification of Hindu law possible. Within the Muslim community such religious reformation did not emerge in strength, and the enhanced minority consciousness after partition and the religious riots made them view both liberal reform from within and pressure for reform from without as threats to their religious identity. The Law Commission initiated a study of the reform of Christian law but stopped the process when religious heads opposed it, even though many groups in the Christian community supported it. When the law of equality between son and daughter in the share of intestate parental property was validated by the Supreme Court, it was accepted without protest by the Syrian Christian community, which shows either that the Law Commission was too timid or that the ruling party did not want to lose the Christian votes that the church leaders could deliver to them. The point I am making is that the introduction of secular egalitarianism in Hindu law was based on the support of a Hindu religious renaissance, and a similar sanction is necessary if the changes demanded by Indian secularism are to succeed with other religious communities.

In India, too, leaders of atheistic secular humanism like Nehru have begun to see the need of some kind of spirituality to fill the vacuum created by secularization if the process is not to be reversed. Nehru's evolution in this regard is significant, as is that of Jai Prakash and several others.

In the early days, Nehru envisaged without any regret the prospect of the destruction of the religions and religious cultures of India by the impact of secular technological culture from the West. Through the course of his life, however, he searched for an ethical and spiritual force to fill the vacuum created by secularization so as to humanize the technological culture. In an interview with Karanji in 1960 he said: "Yes. I have changed. The emphasis on an ethical and spiritual solution is not unconscious. It is deliberate, quite deliberate. There are good reasons for it. First of all, apart from the material development that is imperative, I believe that the human mind is hungry for something deeper in terms of moral and spiritual development, without which all the material advance may not be worthwhile." Evidently under Gandhi's influence and in the light of the growing dehumanization and threat to all life inherent in technological culture, the secular totalitarianism of Hitler and Stalin and others, Nehru's scientific secularism was opened to spiritual realities as a means of strengthening its humanism.

Though Nehru did not go further than this, it points to the need to take seriously the renewal of the religious traditions of India to provide this spiritual humanizing force modernizing India. It is a call toward a new composite culture in which the religious cultures that contributed to the molding of a composite Indian culture in the past are redefined in their relevance to the humanization of the modern secular culture of science and technology. It is thus that the concept of open secularism can be strengthened in India. As Professor Leroy Rouner of Boston University puts it in an essay entitled "Civil Loyalty and New India":

> The political paradox concerning religion in India is that precisely because religious ideas and values have been so much a part of India's problem, they will have to be part of India's solution. There is no empirical evidence that religion is waning as an influence in Indian political life. So a realistic political strategy must incorporate religious energy in the service of national goals, or watch it continue to corrode them.

Chronological Bibliography
of the Works of Charles C. West

Chinese Period (1947–51)

"Christianity in Communist North China." *Christianity and Crisis* (New York) 7, no. 17 (October 13, 1947): 3–7.

"Redemptive Opportunities amidst Political Futility." *Christianity and Society* (New York) 13, no. 3 (Summer 1948): 8–10.

"Christianity and Communism in China." *Christianity and Crisis* 8, no. 13 (July 19, 1948): 98–101.

"Chinese Communist Ideology and the Christian Faith." *Social Action* (New York) 15, no. 6 (June 15, 1949): 16–27.

"Facts and Ideals in Communist China" (under pseudonym "Observator"). *Frontier* (London) 2, no. 5 (May 1951): 179–94.

Christian Witness in Communist China (under pseudonym "Barnabas"). London: Student Christian Movement Press, 1951. German translation, Munich: Chr. Kaiser Verlag, 1951. Danish translation, Copenhagen: Dansk Missionsselskab, 1953.

"Recent Events and the Church in China." *Background Information* (Geneva: World Council of Churches), no. 1 (March 1951): 11–16.

German Period (1952–56)

"Some Ethical Problems of Christians Living in East Germany" (anonymously published). *Background Information,* no. 4 (April 1952): 11–15.

"New Pressures on Church and Society in Eastern Germany" (anonymously published). *Background Information,* no. 7 (April 1953): 8–13.

"Challenge from the East: Josef Hromádka." *Christianity and Crisis* 13, no. 17 (October 19, 1953): 131–34.

"The Church Situation in East Germany, April–August 1953" (anonymously published). *Background Information,* no. 8 (November 1953): 1–6.

"The Faith and Life of East German Christians." *Religious Book Club Bulletin* (London: Student Christian Movement Press), no. 97 (November 1953): 1–5.

"Talk across the Iron Curtain?" *Christian Century* (Chicago) 71, no. 5 (January 27, 1954): 109–11.

"The Christian, the University, and a Communist Land." *Christian Scholar* (New York) 37, no. 2 (June 1954): 106–13.

"Christianity in Its Political Setting." *Religion in Life* (New York) 24, no. 1 (Winter 1954/55): 17–29.

"God's Gifts in a Communist Land." *Crossroads* (Philadelphia: Presbyterian Church [U.S.A.], Board of Christian Education) 5, no. 2 (January 1955): 10–13.

"East Germany, 1956: The Spirit and the Iron Curtain." *Christianity and Crisis* 16, no. 11 (June 9, 1956): 81–88.

Publications, 1956–62

"Christian Church and Communist State: How Far Can They Work Together?" *British Weekly* (London), November 15, 1956.

Communism and the Theologians. Philadelphia: Westminster Press; London: SCM Press, 1958. Paperback ed., New York: Macmillan, 1962, additional preface.

Coedited with David Paton, *The Missionary Church in East and West.* London: SCM Press, 1959. Contributed two chapters: "This Ministry: An Introduction" and "Mission in East and West."

Outside the Camp: The Christian and the World. Garden City, N.Y.: Doubleday, 1959. German translation, *Zwischen Religion und Revolution.* Gutersloh: Gerd Mohn, 1962.

"Het Communisme in Azië, zijn werfkracht en zijn gevaren." *Wending* (The Hague) 14, no. 7 (September 1959): 416–41.

"L'incontro missionario fra protestanti e cattolici." *La missione* (Milan), 1960, pp. 115–28.

"Is There Something More Than the Golden Rule?" *Discovery* (Philadelphia: United Presbyterian Church, U.S.A., Board of Christian Education) 13, no. 1 (October 1960): 2–4.

Translated with introduction, *A Christian in East Germany.* By Johammes Hamel. London: SCM Press; New York: Association Press, 1960.

"Kommunismus-Marxismus." In *Weltkirchenlexikon: Handbuch der Oekumene,* pp. 758–59. Stuttgart: Kreuz Verlag, 1960.

Religious, Revolutionary, and Secular Man (pamphlet). Colombo: Ceylon Publishing House for Christian Literature, 1961.

"On 'Christian' Service." *Religion and Society* (Bangalore, India) 8, no. 1 (April 1961): 1–4.

"Christ, the Light of the World: Some Reflections on Theology, Religion, and the World in Which They Meet." *Theology Today* (Princeton) 18, no. 3 (October 1961): 281–94.

"Josef Lukl Hromádka." In *Sons of the Prophets,* ed. Hugh T. Kerr. Princeton: Princeton University Press, 1962.

"Towards an Understanding of Secularism." *Religion and Society* 9, no. 1 (March 1962): 47–61.

Reports and Lectures from the Ecumenical Institute, Bossey, 1956–61

  "Consultation for Sociologists and Theologians." April 1957. Report.

  "Consultation on Evangelism and the Structure of the Church in City and Industry." May 1957. Report. Conference on the same subject, June 1958. Report.

  "Christian Community and Sociological Communities." August 1958. Report of a conference for theologians and sociologists.

  "The Meaning of the Secular." September 1959. Report of a conference of university teachers on secularization, academic disciplines, and Christian faith.

  "The Concept 'Responsible Society': An Analysis and Some Questions." June 1960. Prepared for a conference on the topic "Responsible Society and Christian Social Decision." Published in French as "La société responsable" in the journal *Christianisme sociale,* May 1960.

"Theological Discernment in Conditions of Social Change." August 1960. Report of a course for theological students.

"Religion and the Christian Faith." June 1961. Report with appended papers on a conference.

Publications, 1962–75

"The Post-Christian Explosion," "The Nuclear Bomb," and "Discipleship in the Atomic Age." *Theology Today* 18, no. 4 (January 1962): 493–502.

"The Ideology of Communism." In *Focus,* ed. Samuel N. Gibson, pp. 25–39. University Park: Pennsylvania State University, University Christian Association, 1962.

Coedited with Robert C. Mackie, *The Sufficiency of God: Essays on the Ecumenical Hope in Honor of Dr. W. A. Visser 't Hooft.* London: SCM Press; Philadelphia: Westminster Press, 1963. Contributed final chapter: "The Sufficiency of God," pp. 220–40.

"Church and World in the Soviet Union." *Christianity and Crisis* 22, no. 19 (November 12, 1962): 195–200. Reprinted in *Princeton Seminary Bulletin* 56, no. 2 (February 1963): 19–28.

"The Visit of the Russian Churchmen." *Christianity and Crisis* 23, no. 6 (April 15, 1963): 54–55.

"Changing Forms of the Church's Witness." *Concept* (Geneva: World Council of Churches), no. 6 (January 1964).

"Secular Man and the Resurrection." *Christianity and Crisis* 24, no. 4 (March 16, 1964): 29–31.

"The Second All-Christian Peace Assembly." *Christianity and Crisis* 24, no. 19 (November 16, 1964): 225–29.

"On Accepting but Not Glorifying History." *Theology Today* 21, no. 2 (July 1964): 223–24.

"The Missionary Context of Christian Ethics." *Princeton Seminary Bulletin* 58, no. 1 (October 1964): 20–33. German translation in *Zeitschrift für evangelische Ethik* 10, no. 4 (July 1966): 213–27.

"Other States in Eastern Europe." In *The Prospects of Christianity throughout the World,* ed. M. Searle Bates and Wilhelm Pauch, pp. 64–82. New York: Scribners, 1964.

"A Secular Relation to God." In *Education Mobilized for Mission,* pp. 1–11. New York: National Council of Churches, Division of Christian Education, 1965.

"The Obsolescence of History." *Ecumenical Review* (Geneva) 17, no. 1 (January 1965): 1–17.

"What It Means to Be Secular." *Christianity and Crisis* 25, no. 12 (July 12, 1965): 147–49. Reprinted in *The Secular City Debate*, ed. Daniel Callahan, pp. 59–63. New York: Macmillan, 1966.

"The Church's Confession." *Dimension* (Princeton Theological Seminary) 2, no. 2 (1965): 8–10.

"The New Presbyterian Confession." *Christianity and Crisis* 26, no. 11 (June 27, 1966): 25–27.

"The Church and Foreign Policy." *War/Peace Report* (New York) 6, no. 8 (August/September 1966): 25–27.

"Theological Table Talk: The Geneva Conference on Church and Society." *Theology Today* 23, no. 3 (October 1966): 417–27.

"Community — Christian and Secular." In *Man in Community*, ed. Egbert de Vries, pp. 330–58. London: SCM Press; New York: Association Press, 1966. Reprinted in *The Church amid Revolution*, ed. Harvey Cox, pp. 228–56. New York: Association Press, 1967. Also reprinted in *Secularization and the Protestant Prospect*, ed. James Childress and David Harned, pp. 117–34. Philadelphia: Westminster Press, 1970.

"Technologists and Revolutionaries." *Background Information*, no. 38 (May 1967): 2–17. An interpretation of the World Conference on Church and Society, Geneva (1966).

"Josef Hromádka." In *Modern Theologians, Christians and Jews*, ed. Thomas E. Bird, pp. 40–63. Notre Dame, Ind.: University of Notre Dame; New York: Association Press, 1967.

"Karl Barth," "Ethics of Marxist Communism," and "Ethics of the Ecumenical Movement." In *Dictionary of Christian Ethics*, ed. John Macquarrie, pp. 27, 61–63, 96–99. Philadelphia: Westminster Press, 1967.

"Technologe und Revolutionäre." In *Zur Theologie der Revolution*, pp. 1–22. Munich: Chr. Kaiser Verlag, 1967. French translation, "Technologues et revolutionnaires." In *Une Theologie de la Revolution?* pp. 76–118. Geneva: Labor et Fides, 1968.

"Christian Responsibility in Vietnam." *Worldview* (New York: Council on Religion in International Affairs) 10, no. 5 (May 1967): 4–8.

"The Two Germanys." *Christianity and Crisis* 27, no. 8 (May 15, 1967): 101–3.

"Alternative Involvement in Asia." *Christianity and Crisis* 27, no. 18 (October 30, 1967): 241–43.

"Oikoumene in Missionary Perspective." In *The World in the Third World*, ed. Joseph P. Cotter, pp. 44–111. Washington, D.C.: Corpus Books, 1968.

"Varieties of Unbelief." In *Lambeth Essays on Faith,* pp. 43–78. London: SPCK, 1968.

"Czechoslovakia." *Engage* (Washington, D.C.) 1, no. 2 (September 15, 1968): 7, 16.

"The Problem of Ethics Today." *Theology Today* 25, no. 3 (October 1968): 341–65.

"Christian-Marxist Dialogue: A Bibliographical Article." *Social Action* 35, no. 3 (November 1968): 40–48.

"Review Article: Recent Publications in Christian Ethics." *Princeton Seminary Bulletin* 62, no. 3 (Autumn 1969): 78–81.

Ethics, Violence, and Revolution. New York: Council on Religion and International Affairs, 1969.

"Act and Being in Christian and Marxist Perspective." In *Openings for Marxist-Christian Dialogue,* ed. Thomas W. Ogletree, pp. 72–97. Nashville: Abingdon Press, 1969.

"Reconciliation and World Peace." In *Reconciliation in Today's World,* ed. Allen O. Miller, pp. 105–22. Grand Rapids: Eerdmans, 1969.

"Missions and Revolution: Emerging Guidelines for the Repentant Use of Power." *Christianity and Crisis* 30, no. 1 (February 2, 1970): 6–10.

"Ein Theologe der Auferstehung" (Josef Hromádka). *Wissenschaft und Praxis in Kirche und Gesellschaft* (Göttingen: Vandenhoeck & Ruprecht) 59, no. 3 (March 1970): 81–84.

"Reconciliation and Society." *Reformed and Presbyterian World* 31, no. 2 (1970): 60–64.

"Technology and the Future of Man." *Ecumenical Courier* (New York: World Council of Churches) 29, no. 3 (July 1970): 1, 6–7.

"Hromádka: Theologian of the Resurrection" (expanded version of the March 1970 German article above). *Worldview* 13, no. 10 (October 1970): 6–9.

"Theology and Technological Change." *Theology Today* 27, no. 3 (October 1970): 277–91.

"Status Quo, Evolution or Revolution?" In *Technology and Social Justice,* ed. Ronald Preston, pp. 375–97. London: SCM Press; Valley Forge, Pa.: Judson Press, 1971.

The Power to Be Human: Toward a Secular Theology. New York: Macmillan, 1971.

"Salvation, Divine and Human." *Princeton Seminary Bulletin* 64, no. 1 (March 1971): 14–21.

"Gospel, Interest and Principle." *Theology Today* 28, no. 4 (January 1972): 494–500.

"Mission Eastern Europe: Towards a New Agenda." *Christian Century* 89, no. 1 (January 5, 1972): 13–15.

"A Theology of National Security." *Worldview* 15, no. 4 (April 1972): 38–44.

"Marxists and Christians: The Fate of the Dialogue." *Journal of Religion* 52, no. 3 (Summer 1972): 304–17.

"Interpreters of Our Faith, Walter Rauschenbusch." *A.D.*, September 1973, pp. 7–10.

"Religion, Revolution, and the Task of Ethics." Presidential address to the American Society of Christian Ethics, 1974.

"Justice within the Limits of the Created World." *Ecumenical Review* 27, no. 1 (January 1975): 57–64.

"Jesus Christ Frees and Unites: Implications for World Peace." *Princeton Seminary Bulletin* 67, no. 1 (Winter 1975): 89–102.

"Jesus Christ Unites." *Midstream* 14, no. 3 (July 1975): 357–76.

"Faith, Ethics and Politics." *Dialog* 14, no. 3 (July 1975): 169–80. Condensed version of a longer paper prepared for the Institute of Neighborhood Studies, Washington, D.C.

Publications, 1976 to the present

"The Accusation and the Promise." *Princeton Seminary Bulletin* 68, no. 3 (Winter 1976): 55–59.

"Puritans in Africa and America." *South African Outlook* 106, no. 1266 (November 1976): 167–69.

"Some Theological Reflections on China." *China Notes* 14, no. 4 (Fall 1976): 37–40.

"Theological Reflections on China II." *China Notes* 15, no. 2 (Spring 1977): 16–18.

"Christianity and China: Some Reflections" (excerpts from preceding article). *New World Outlook*, n.s., 37, no. 6 (February 1977): 14–16.

"Becoming Ecumenical: The Meaning of Bossey." *Midstream* 16, no. 2 (April 1977): 206–15.

"God's Peace and Human Parodies." *Explor* 3, no. 2 (Fall 1977): 61–68.

"Karl Barth and Radical Politics" (a review article). *Journal of Religion* 57, no. 4 (October 1977): 429–32.

"Facts, Morals, and the Bomb." In *To Avoid Catastrophe: A Study in Future Nuclear Weapons Policy*, ed. Michael Hamilton, pp. 197–220. Grand Rapids: Eerdmans, 1977.

"Reviewing and Responding to the Thought of Choan-Seng Song." *Occasional Bulletin of Missionary Research* 1, no. 3 (July 1977): 11–13.

"Education for Peace." *Peace and the Sciences* (Vienna: International Institute for Peace), no. 1 (1977): 26–37.

Foreword to *What Asian Christians Are Thinking* [1976], by Douglas J. Elwood. Manila: New Day Publishers; Philadelphia: Westminster Press, 1978.

"Theologen und Technologen." *Evangelische Kommentare* 12, no. 9 (September 1979): 517–18.

Comment on "The Contextualization Continuum" by David Hesselgrave. *Gospel in Context* 2, no. 3 (July 1979): 21–22.

Response to "Theological Education and Liberation Theology." *Theological Education* 16, no. 1 (November 1979): 64–66.

"The Theological Task in the 1980s: Some Reflections." *Viewpoint* (Princeton Theological Seminary) 18, no. 7 (February 1980): 1, 6–15.

"God, Man/woman, Creation." *Ecumenical Review* 33, no. 1 (January 1981): 13–28.

"Dehumanization and Its Curtailment." Concluding summary of an American Christian-Marxist Dialogue, Dayton, Ohio, January 1980. In *Newsletter of the Christian-Marxist Relations Task Force of Christians Associated with Eastern Europe*, no. 12 (November 1981).

"Church and State in Missionary Perspective." *Missiology* 9, no. 4 (October 1981): 423–48.

"Wealth and Power." In *Thine Is the Kingdom, the Power, and the Glory*, pp. 49–56. Study Guide for the World Alliance of Reformed Churches Conference, Ottawa, Canada, 1982.

"Comment on Reconciliation in Society." In *Reconciliation and Liberation: The Confession of 1967* (*Journal of Presbyterian History* 61, no. 1 [Spring 1983]), pp. 127–31.

"The President and the Christians." *Viewpoint*, March 24, 1983, pp. 4–6.

"Before and after Vancouver." *Theology Today* 40, no. 3 (October 1983): 336–46.

"The Churches and Refugee Policy" and "Closing Remarks." In *American Refugee Policy*, ed. Joseph M. Kitagawa, pp. 98–106, 114–15. Minneapolis: Winston Press, 1984.

"Culture, Power and Ideology in Third World Theologies." *Missiology* 12, no. 4 (October 1984): 405–20.

"Politics, Religion, and Faith." *Presbyterian Outlook* 167, no. 2 (January 21, 1985): 8–10.

"On Taxes and Cheerful Giving." *Presbyterian Outlook* 167, no. 11 (March 25, 1985): 8–10.

"Where Is Our Home, and Who Is Welcome in It?" *Presbyterian Outlook* 167, no. 22 (June 10, 1985): 14–15.

"Verantwortung für die Schöpfung." *Zeitschrift für evangelische Ethik* 29, no. 2 (1985): 147–59.

"Atheism: Is It Essential to Marxism? A Comment." *Journal of Ecumenical Studies* 22, no. 3 (Summer 1985): 506–8.

Perspective on South Africa. Princeton Pamphlets, n.s., no. 102. Princeton: Princeton Theological Seminary, 1985.

"South Africa: Reflections of a Visitor." *Princeton Seminary Bulletin*, n.s., 6, no. 3 (1985): 179–87.

"Ecumenical Fellowship and Ecumenical Realism." *Occasional Papers on Religion in Eastern Europe* 6, no. 3 (June 1986): 1–3.

"The Churches in South Africa." *Presbyterian Outlook* 168, no. 4 (February 3, 1986): 6.

"Forgiven Violence: Christian Responsibility between Pacifism and Just War." In *Peace, Politics, and the People of God,* ed. Paul Peachey, pp. 71–94. Philadelphia: Fortress Press, 1986.

"Christians and Marxists in Conversation about Peace: Realism in Politics." *Weiner Blätter zur Friedenforschung,* no. 46/47 (May 1986): 42–44.

"Ecumenical Movement: Ethics in," "Communism: Ethics of," and "Marxism: Ethics of." In *The Westminster Dictionary of Christian Ethics,* ed. James F. Childress and John Macquarrie. Philadelphia: Westminster Press, 1986.

"The Sharing of Resources: A Biblical Reflection." *Ecumenical Review* 38, no. 4 (October 1986): 357–69.

Foreword to *The Encounter between Theology and Ideology: An Exploration into the Communicative Theology of M. M. Thomas,* by T. M. Philip. Madras: Christian Literature Society, 1986.

"Ecumenical Fellowship and Ecumenical Realism." *Occasional Papers on Religion in Eastern Europe* 6, no. 3 (June 1986): 1–3.

"Marxism and Religion." In *The Encyclopedia of Religion,* Mircea Eliade, editor in chief. New York: Macmillan, 1987.

"Ground under Our Feet: A Reflection on the Worldliness of Dietrich Bonhoeffer's Life and Thought." In *New Studies in Bonhoeffer's Ethics,* pp. 235–73. Watertown, N.Y.: Edwin Mellin Press, 1987.

"Ecumenics, Church, and Society: The Tradition of Life and Work." In *The Teaching of Ecumenics,* ed. Samuel Amirtham and Cyris H. S. Moon, pp. 86–93. Geneva: World Council of Churches, 1987. Also appeared in *Ecumenical Review* 38, no. 4 (October 1987): 462–69.

"The Common Good and the Participation of the Poor." In *The Common*

Good and U.S. Capitalism, ed. Oliver F. Williams and John W. Houck, pp. 20–49. Lanham, Md.: University Press of America, 1987.

"Christians and Marxists in Dialogue: Building Confidence in a Time of Crisis." *Occasional Papers on Religion in Eastern Europe* 8, no. 1 (1988): 11–26.

"Justice and Equality in Modern American Society: A Theological View." In *Justice: Interdisciplinary and Global Perspectives,* ed. T. M. Thomas and Jesse Levitt, pp. 41–54. Lanham, Md.: University Press of America, 1988.

"Die Verantwortung des christlichen Theologen für den Frieden." In *Friedensdiskurs aus verschiedener weltanschaulicher Sicht,* ed. Rudolf Weiler, pp. 122–29. Berlin: Duncker & Humblot, 1988.

"Mission, the Christian Hope, and Secular Hopes." *Mission Studies* 5, no. 1 (1988): 98–100.

"Responding to God: Ethics and the Confession of 1967." *Princeton Seminary Bulletin,* n.s., 9, no. 2 (1988): 131–42.

"Mission to the West: A Dialogue with Stowe and Newbigin." *International Bulletin of Missionary Research* 12, no. 4 (1988): 153–56.

"Josef Hromádka and the Witness of the Church in East and West Today." *Occasional Papers on Religion and Eastern Europe* 10, no. 2 (March 1990): 366–80. Also in *Princeton Seminary Bulletin,* n.s., 11, no. 1 (1990): 32–45.

"Mission, Christian Hope, and Secular Hopes." *Midstream* 29, no. 4 (October 1990): 366–80.

"Ecumenical Social Ethics beyond Socialism and Capitalism." *Theology and Public Policy* 2, no. 2 (Fall 1990): 34–46.

"The Experience of a Confessing Church Pastor (Johannes Hamel)." In *Proceedings of the First Biannual Conference on Christianity and the Holocaust,* pp. 213–27. Rider College, 1990.

"The Future of Ideology in an Interdependent World." *Peace and the Sciences,* December 1990, pp. 18–21. Also in *Wiener Blätter zur Friedensforschung* 4 (December 1990): 6–13.

"The Future of Ideology in an Interdependent World." *Occasional Papers on Religion in Eastern Europe* 11, no. 2 (March 1991): 12–20.

"Christian Ethics and the Future of Eastern Europe." *Occasional Papers on Religion in Eastern Europe* 11, no. 6 (December 1991): 32–38.

"Ecumenical Social Ethic beyond Socialism and Capitalism" (in Japanese). *Kirisutokyo kenkyu* (Studies in the Christian religion) (Kyoto: Doshisha University, School of Theology) 52, no. 2 (March 1991): 224–34.

"Ecumenical Social Ethic beyond Socialism and Capitalism." *Ecumenical Review* 43, no. 3 (July 1991): 329–40.

"Gospel for American Culture: Variations on a Theme by Newbigin." *Missiology* 19, no. 4 (July 1991): 431–42.

"Faith, Ideology, and Power! Toward an Ecumenical, Post-Marxist Method in Christian Ethics." *Annual of the Society of Christian Ethics*, 1991, pp. 193–208.

"An Ecumenical Journey: A Conversation between Ruth and Charles West." *Princeton Seminary Bulletin*, n.s., 12, no. 2 (1991): 119–33.

"Memorial: James Hastings Nichols." *Princeton Seminary Bulletin*, n.s., 12, no. 3 (1991): 327–30.

"Baptism in the Reformed Tradition." In *Baptism, Peace, and the State of the Reformed and Mennonite Traditions*, ed. Ross T. Bender and Alan P. F. Sell, pp. 13–35. Waterloo, Ontario: Wilfred Laurier University Press, for the Calgary Institute for the Humanities, 1991.

"Ground under Our Feet." In *Bonhoeffer's Ethics: Old Europe and New Frontiers?* ed. G. Carter, R. van Eyden, H. van Hoogstraten, and J. Wiersma, pp. 40–42. Kampen, Netherlands: Kok Pharos Publishing House, 1991.

"Christianity in Eastern Europe: Traditions, Conflicts, and New Relationships." *Christianity and Crisis* 52, no. 12 (August 17, 1992): 278–80.

"Limits of Unfaithfulness." *Religious Socialism* 16, no. 4 (Winter 1992): 11, 14.

"Christian Witness and Human Power: The Dynamic of Judgment and Transformation in the Mission of the Church." *Mission Studies* 9, no. 2 (1992): 204–11.

Contributors

Charles C. West

This volume is dedicated to Professor Charles C. West in honor of his seventieth birthday and his retirement from Princeton Theological Seminary, where he gave thirty years of distinguished teaching service.

Born in Plainfield, New Jersey, Dr. West holds degrees from Columbia University, Union Theological Seminary in New York, and Yale University. An ordained minister in the Presbyterian Church (U.S.A.), he served as a missionary in China from 1947 to 1950, as a fraternal worker in Germany from 1950 to 1953, and as an assistant/associate director of the Ecumenical Institute in Bossey, Switzerland, from 1956 to 1961. In 1961 Dr. West was appointed to be the Stephen Colwell Professor of Christian Ethics at Princeton Theological Seminary. From 1979 to 1984 he served as academic dean of the seminary. He retired in 1991.

Dr. West has served as a member of numerous committees of the World Council of Churches, the National Council of Churches, and the Presbyterian Church (U.S.A.). He has served as president of both the American Society of Christian Ethics and the American Theological Society. Among the ten books he has written are *Communism and the Theologians, Outside the Camp,* and *The Power to Be Human.*

CONTRIBUTORS

K. C. ABRAHAM Director of the Ecumenical Christian Centre in Bangalore, India.

PAUL ABRECHT Associate at the World Council of Churches (WCC) in Geneva, Switzerland, from 1950 through 1983; former director of the Department of Church and Society in the WCC.

CHARLES W. AMJAD-ALI Director of the Christian Study Centre in Rawalpindi-Cantt, Pakistan.

NANTAWAN BOONPRASAT LEWIS Associate Professor of Religious Studies and Ethnic Studies, and Chair of the Ethnic Studies Department at Metropolitan State University in St. Paul, Minnesota.

SHIN CHIBA Professor of Political Thought at International Christian University in Tokyo, Japan.

PETER B. DOGHRAMJI President of Near East School of Theology in Beirut, Lebanon; Associate Professor of Theology at Aleppo College, Syria; Conference Minister in the United Church of Christ in Pennsylvania.

SANDRA ELLIS-KILLIAN Director of the Aletheia Foundation in Glenside, Pennsylvania; on the faculty of the Theological and Religious Studies Department at Villanova University, Pennsylvania.

GEORGE R. HUNSBERGER Professor of Missiology at Western Theological Seminary in Holland, Michigan; Coordinator of the Gospel and Our Culture Network.

JAN MILIČ LOCHMAN Professor of Systematic Theology at the University of Basel, Switzerland.

ANRI MORIMOTO University Minister and Lecturer in Religion and Ethics at International Christian University, Tokyo, Japan.

PETER J. PARIS Elmer G. Homrighausen Professor of Christian Social Ethics, Princeton Theological Seminary, New Jersey.

THOMAS D. PARKER Cyrus H. McCormick Professor of Systematic Theology at McCormick Theological Seminary, Chicago, Illinois.

Contributors

LESTER EDWIN J. RUIZ Associate Professor of Political Science at International Christian University in Tokyo, Japan.

RICHARD SHAULL Henry Winters Luce Professor Emeritus of Ecumenics at Princeton Theological Seminary, New Jersey.

RICHARD L. SPENCER Pastor of Saratoga Presbyterian Church in Saratoga, California; Adjunct Professor of Ethics at Fuller Theological Seminary, Pasadena, California.

OSCAR S. SUAREZ Associate Professor of Religion and Ethics, Union Theological Seminary, Manila, Philippines.

MARK K. TAYLOR Associate Professor of Theology and Culture at Princeton Theological Seminary, New Jersey.

M. M. THOMAS Ecumenical leader and author of many books; Governor of the State of Nagaland, India.

LOUKE VAN WENSVEEN SIKER Assistant Professor of Theology at Loyola Marymount University in Los Angeles, California.

RUTH C. WEST Wife of Charles C. West; Professor Emerita of Education at Monmouth College, New Jersey.

DATE DUE